Forensic Fraud

Forensic Fraud

Evaluating Law Enforcement and Forensic Science Cultures in the Context of Examiner Misconduct

Brent E. Turvey

Amsterdam ▪ Boston ▪ Heidelberg ▪ London
New York ▪ Oxford ▪ Paris ▪ San Diego
San Francisco ▪ Singapore ▪ Sydney ▪ Tokyo
Academic Press is an imprint of Elsevier

Academic Press is an imprint of Elsevier
The Boulevard, Langford Lane, Kidlington, Oxford, OX5 1GB
225 Wyman Street, Waltham, MA 02451, USA

First published 2013

British Library Cataloguing in Publication Data
A catalogue record for this book is available from the British Library

Library of Congress Cataloging-in-Publication Data
A catalog record for this book is available from the Library of Congress

ISBN: 978-0-12-408073-7

For information on all Academic Press publications
visit our website at **store.elsevier.com**

Printed and bound in China
13 14 15 16   10 9 8 7 6 5 4 3 2 1

Working together
to grow libraries in
developing countries

www.elsevier.com • www.bookaid.org

This work is dedicated to Thomas "Duke" DeLaHunt (1924–2012)—a captain of shipping vessels from Alaska to the Orient, a trusted mentor, and a friend. His vast experience and counsel regarding the politics of criminality and corruption within law enforcement during the writing of this dissertation were essential. His voice is missed.

Thomas "Duke" DeLaHunt (1924–2012)

Contents

Acknowledgments

This research would not have been possible without the support and encouragement of those in the Faculty of Humanities at Bond University. This includes those permissions given, those assurances afforded, and the helpful criticisms that kept everything on track throughout the process. Throughout the research, throughout my confirmation process, and throughout the editing process, their collective assistance was invaluable.

I would also like to thank my friends and colleagues in both law enforcement and the forensic sciences for their insights, counsel, and feedback as I progressed through the sometimes wrenching stages of examination and discovery demanded by this project's difficult subject matter: W. "Jerry" Chisum (Criminalist, California Department of Justice, ret.); Craig Cooley, JD (formerly of the Innocence Project at the Cardozo Law School in New York); Captain Thomas "Duke" DeLaHunt (Crowley Maritime, ret.); Ofc. Joe Delery (Forensic Examiner, New Orleans Police Department); Ronald Miller, MS (Forensic Investigator, Vancouver, WA); Det. Rick Ragsdale (Stockton Police Department, ret.); Det. John O. Savino (New York City Police Department, ret.); and Dr. John I. Thornton (Criminalist, University of California—Davis). Without these individuals acting as sounding boards and confidantes, the findings in this research and their informed discussion would have suffered tremendously.

It is also necessary to acknowledge the invaluable tutelage and assistance of my friend and colleague Dr. Shawn Mikulay. He taught me the value of hierarchical regression analysis, how to run said regressions, and how to faithfully interpret them with scientific caution. This was no small task, and without his assistance this part of the research would have fallen flat.

Finally, I would like to thank my family for their support and encouragement throughout my candidature. They put up with a lot given my generally intense caseload and other writing projects—and this added that much more to the burden. Mostly, however, I am grateful to my wife, Melissa—for listening, advising, and generally helping me to get there when I wasn't.

CHAPTER 1

Introduction

"Where a proffered expert knows himself or herself to be a quack or otherwise to be offering false testimony, the situation is like that of any other witness who is perpetrating a fraud on the court. Such acts are illegal as well as unethical."

Michael J. Saks (2001)
Professor of Law & Psychology
Sandra Day O'Connor College of Law

This textbook presents original research that examines and correlates the traits of fraudulent forensic examiners, their fraud-related activity, and their places of employment.[1] To ensure timeliness and provide for comparability, this research is limited in scope to those cases revealed in the United States from 2000 to 2010. It is a study that seeks to inform and add to our theoretical understanding of a specific yet influential strain of employee fraud in the criminal justice system. Based on the findings of this study, potential causal factors are identified and discussed. Subsequently, relevant fraud management strategies are proposed.

BACKGROUND

The events that have accumulated over the course of this author's career to confirm the need for this work, and to provide sufficient motivation for its completion, are numerous and ongoing. The earliest took place immediately after the completion of this author's graduate studies in forensic science in 1995: a research paper that had been placed online was taken in its entirety and presented elsewhere under the name of another. Upon discovery and further investigation, it was learned that the person responsible,

---

[1]This entire textbook, including the original research presented within, is adapted from a dissertation submitted by Brent E. Turvey in full completion of a Doctorate of Philosophy in Criminology, accepted by Bond University in October 2012.

1

Forensic Fraud. http://dx.doi.org/10.1016/B978-0-12-408073-7.00001-X

a forensic psychologist, was no stranger to fraud. Then the Chair of the Forensic Science program at National University in San Diego, California, it was learned that the plagiarist had purloined the research of others in at least one Canadian journal. He had also been accused of misrepresenting the nature of his relationship with the Orange County Coroner's Office by means of printing up misleading business cards. Further still, his professional resume was full of incomplete and misleading information and affiliations. Ultimately, and subsequent to a complaint filed by this researcher, this individual was forced to resign his membership with the American Academy of Forensic Sciences, and contemporaneously ceased to be the Chair of the Forensic Science program at National University. That someone would do these things so openly, let alone a professional of apparent high standing in the forensic science community, and that nobody had complained about it in writing save a recently graduated student of forensic science, left an impression.

Over the past 17 years of forensic practice, this author has observed or learned of countless instances of unrepentant forensic fraud by practitioners from all over the United States, and around the world. A severe outcome, with proven fraudsters stripped of their employment, penalized by their respective professional organizations, and criminally charged is not at all typical. Often fraud is minimized, ignored, or in extreme cases simply denied by those in the forensic science community. For example, Budowle (2007), speaking for the FBI crime laboratory, insists that "most people do good jobs," that forensic fraud is not a significant issue, and that any problems are "most often human error"; Collins and Jarvis (2007), speaking for an organization formed by those associated with the American Society of Crime Lab Directors Laboratory Accreditation Board (ASCLD-LAB), similarly assert that "Forensic scientists are human beings. As such they will sometimes make mistakes and, in some very rare instances, push the boundaries of ethical behavior"; and, in response to multiple and ongoing scandals involving examiner fraud since 2005 at the U.S. Army Criminal Investigation Laboratory (USACIL), the Army's Criminal Investigation Command, which oversees the lab, has conceded only that "As with all crime labs across the county, human error does occur from time to time" (Taylor and Doyle)—in essence ignoring the issue of fraud altogether.[2] Many leaders in the forensic science community, it seems, are content to explain fraudulent examiners away, or deny their existence, despite continuous and sometimes overwhelming evidence of the problem. This sets the tone for the attitudes and arguments that must necessarily follow from their subordinates, as will be discussed in later chapters.

---

[2]For further discussion, see Chapters 6 and 7 with respect to *Bad Apple Theory.*

Different from that of many forensic science stakeholders, this author's perspective has been enhanced by at least the following major events in the forensic science community over the past ten years:

1. The ongoing and in some cases repeated instances of major crime lab scandal, to include multiple instances of fraud and error, over the past 15 years (see general discussions in Cooley, 2004, 2007a, and 2007b; DiFonzo, 2005; DiFonzo and Stern, 2007; Giannelli, 2010; and Thompson, 2009).[3]
2. The publication of the National Academy of Sciences Report on forensic science (aka the NAS Report; Edwards and Gotsonis, 2009). The NAS Report was a congressionally funded system-wide investigation and review of the forensic science disciplines and related forensic laboratory practice. It was initiated by the United States Congress owing to the publication of an ongoing series of critical legal reviews regarding the evident bias and lack of science in forensic practice; the ongoing occurrence of highly publicized forensic frauds, blunders, and forensic laboratory scandals across the United States; and the ever-increasing number of DNA exonerations sourced back to flawed or misleading forensic evidence documented by groups such as the Innocence Project (see http://www.innocenceproject.org; see also Garrett, 2008; and Garrett and Neufeld, 2009). The NAS Report confirmed the lack of scientific foundation for the majority of forensic science methods, and an inappropriate alignment between forensic scientists and their law enforcement employers. It also recognized the lack of empirical research into the nature and causes of forensic fraud and error.
3. The publication of *Preventable Error: A Report on Prosecutorial Misconduct in California 1997–2009* by the Northern California Innocence Project (Ridolphi and Possley, 2010). This landmark study of the largest criminal justice system in the United States (California) found prosecutorial misconduct more common than previously thought, including that related to suppressing or misrepresenting physical evidence. It also found that when harmful misconduct does occur (p. 3) "those empowered to address the problem—California state and federal courts, prosecutors and the California State Bar—repeatedly fail to take meaningful action. Courts fail to report prosecutorial misconduct (despite having a statutory obligation to do so), prosecutors deny that it occurred, and the California State Bar almost never disciplines it." This is clearly related to, and not surprisingly similar to, the problems faced in the forensic science community regarding forensic fraud.

[3]Numerous specific crime lab scandals are adduced throughout this dissertation as necessary.

These experiences and events, augmented by ongoing myriad professional encounters with fraudulent examiners as part of regular casework, have provided a durable source of motivation for this work.

DEFINITIONS OF KEY TERMS

To contextualize this work, and facilitate continuity between this and any future or related projects, it is necessary to operationalize at least the following key terms in advance: *scientific misconduct, forensic examiner/ forensic practitioner, forensic fraud,* and *perjury*. Other pertinent terms will be defined as needed.

Scientific misconduct

According to the guidelines adopted by the United States Office of Research Integrity, *scientific misconduct* is defined by acts that include the fabrication of data, the falsification of results, and plagiarism. However, it has also been argued to include *ghost authorship* and the falsification of credentials (Krimsky, 2007). While the wrongfulness of falsifying scientific credentials and fabricating data is fairly straightforward, the longstanding practice of ghost authorship in the scientific community requires some explanation. As explained in Krimsky (2007; p. 450): "Ghost authorship occurs when the person whose name appears on the publication was not involved either in doing the research, framing the ideas behind the article, or in writing the article. Alternatively, it can occur when an individual who has made substantial contributions to the manuscript is not named as an author or whose contributions are not cited in the acknowledgments." This practice is also referred to by some as "gift authorship" (Jones, 2003; p. 245). Essentially, it involves hiding who did the work by giving credit that has not actually been earned.

Forensic examiners

The terms *forensic examiner* and *forensic practitioner* will be used throughout this text, and generally refer to any professional who examines and interprets facts, evidence, or data with the expectation of courtroom testimony. As explained in Turvey (2011; p. xxii):

> Criminal investigators are tasked with serving the criminal justice system by establishing the objective facts and evidence of a given case. Forensic examiners are tasked with analyzing the evidence and interpreting the facts objectively.

Forensic examiners are defined by the fact that they anticipate courtroom testimony. As explained in Thornton and Peterson (2007; p. 3):

The single feature that distinguishes forensic scientists from any other scientist is the certain expectation that they will appear in court and testify to their findings and offer an opinion as to the significance of those findings. The forensic scientist will testify not only to what things are, but to what things mean.

This provides that forensic scientists do not just test or examine evidence and then record the results; they are meant to explore, understand, and explain its significance to an attorney, judge, or jury. The defining quality of forensic examiners is the possibility that they will be called upon to present their findings, under penalty of perjury, in a court of law. Subsequently, they will be asked to explain to the court what those findings mean and how they came to them. This can be as straightforward as recording information about drug identifications, weights, and cash amounts; or it can be as complex as reconstructing a crime scene and determining cause and manner of death.

Forensic examiners, therefore, exist across a broad spectrum of professions. This would include criminalists and other forensic scientists such as forensic pathologists, forensic toxicologists, firearm and tool mark examiners, forensic odontologists, crime reconstructionists, criminal profilers, forensic criminologists, forensic psychologists, and even forensic victimologists. It would also include an array of law enforcement officers processing evidence or testifying as experts in a variety of specialty areas, such as gang culture, sexual assault, drug dealer profiles, drug lab profiles, and case linkage analysis. The scope of the present research is limited, however, to forensic examiners that work directly with physical evidence. The reason for this will be explained later.

Forensic fraud

Forensic fraud occurs when forensic examiners provide sworn testimony, opinions, or documents (e.g., affidavits, reports, or professional resumes) bound for court that contain deceptive or misleading information, findings, opinions, or conclusions, deliberately offered in order to secure an unfair or unlawful gain. As defined in the present research, forensic fraud is necessarily that which is committed by a forensic examiner. It is distinct from deceptive or misleading acts that may be committed by others, such as fact witnesses, patrol officers, attorneys, and judges.

Forensic fraud, while certainly a form of scientific misconduct, does not necessarily involve *perjury*. Perjury is a criminal charge. It is the act of lying or making verifiably false statements on a material matter under oath or affirmation in a court of law or in any sworn statements in writing (Black, 1990). A violation of specific criminal statutes, it is not sufficient for a statement to be false to meet the threshold of perjury; it must be an intentionally false statement regarding a material fact—a fact relevant to the case at hand. As further explained in Turvey (2003; p. 734):

> The act of lying or making verifiably false statements on a material matter under oath or affirmation in a court of law or in any sworn statements in writing. A criminal act, it is not sufficient that the statement be false to be considered perjury; it must be regarding a material fact—a fact that is relevant to the situation. Consequently, not all lies under oath are considered perjury.

For example, in Title 18 of the U.S. Code of Laws, §1621 "General Perjury" provides that perjury involves a person "having taken an oath before a competent tribunal, officer, or person, in any case in which a law of the United States authorizes an oath to be administered, that he will testify, declare, depose, or certify truly, or that any written testimony, declaration, deposition, or certificate by him subscribed, is true, willfully and contrary to such oath states or subscribes any material matter which he does not believe to be true."

As it stands, not all intentionally false statements made under oath by a forensic examiner are considered perjury—nor are all forensic examiners who give false testimony under oath charged with a crime. The decision to bring such charges is made at the discretion of the District Attorney's Office in the jurisdiction where the false testimony occurred—meaning that it is often charged inconsistently and based on political considerations rather than actual merit.

JOSEPH SEROWIK, CRIMINALIST

Cleveland Police Department Crime Laboratory

In 1988, Michael Green was convicted of rape; however, he was later exonerated by DNA evidence and released in 2001. As reported in Gillispie (2004; p. A1):

> Edward Blake, a pioneer in the use of DNA for criminal investigations who was hired by Green's attorneys, concluded that Serowik "intentionally fabricated false evidence against Green, testified at Mr. Green's trial with a reckless disregard for the truth, and committed scientific fraud."
>
> Blake wrote that Serowik turned a washcloth into incriminating evidence against Green by making assumptions that had no scientific basis. Serowik told jurors that the man who used the washcloth to wipe himself after raping a cancer patient in May 1988 at the Cleveland Clinic Hotel had the same blood type as Green's. Serowik also testified that

the semen on the washcloth could have been left by only 16 percent of the male population. Without his faulty assumptions, Blake wrote, Serowik should have concluded that no man could have been excluded as a possible source of the semen on the washcloth, rendering it meaningless in the Green prosecution.

Serowik also testified that a hair found on the washcloth shared similarities with hair taken from Green's head, and went on to say that the likelihood they came from two different people was about 1 in 40,000. But another expert hired by Green's attorneys said Serowik should not have made that assertion because hair analyses aren't precise enough to calculate probabilities.

In addition, Serowik admitted that he had no idea what part of the body the hair came

JOSEPH SEROWIK, CRIMINALIST *CONTINUED*

from, making any comparisons scientifically improper. Determining the part of the body a hair comes from is not only essential, it's easy to do, wrote Max M. Houck, director of the Forensic Science Initiative and a professor at West Virginia University. With proper training, he wrote, it's about as difficult as distinguishing a Volkswagen from a Cadillac. The fact that Serowik apparently couldn't do it, together with his misuse and misstatement of statistics, led Houck to conclude that "Joseph Serowik demonstrates a fundamental lack of knowledge about conducting forensic hair examinations."

"Mr. Serowik was allowed to conduct hair examinations without proper education, training, supervision, or protocols," Houck wrote. "He conducted these examinations in numerous cases, repeatedly made the same mistakes, and did not seek any training by qualified experts in forensic hair examinations."

Houck and Blake pointed out that Serowik was supervised by someone who knew even less about the scientific disciplines involved than he did. And yet it was [Victor] Kovacic, the lab supervisor, who oversaw and signed off on the hair analysis in the Green case. A retired police officer who has headed the Cleveland crime lab since 1985, Kovacic acknowledged in February that he had no expertise in either hair analysis or serology (the study of bodily fluids) and that his technicians could have made up their findings and he wouldn't have known the difference. It was a "gross deviation from accepted practice" to have an inexperienced serologist supervised by someone with no experience or training in the field, Blake wrote in his report.

Ultimately, Mr. Green sued the City of Cleveland and won a settlement that included 1.6 million dollars. It also included a mandatory forensic audit of the casework conducted by Mr. Serowik and the Cleveland Police Crime Laboratory in general (a random sample); this resulted in the review of approximately 100 cases (*Green v. City of Cleveland, et al.*, 2004). During his sworn deposition for that action, Mr. Serowik

agreed that his assumptions about the evidence in the Green case, and his subsequent expert testimony, were "inappropriate" (Gillispie, 2004). Despite acknowledging his false testimony, Mr. Serowik was not charged with perjury.

Initially, the Cleveland Police Crime Laboratory retained Mr. Serowik as an employee, but removed him from forensic casework. However, later in 2004, he was placed on leave and then ultimately terminated (Milicia, 2007). Mr. Serowik was never charged with any crimes, nor did he suffer any direct consequences, as the result of his conduct. Quite the opposite, in fact: in 2004, he was hired as a forensic science instructor by Youngstown State University.

As a result of the mandatory audit of Mr. Serowik's casework and testimony, two other convictions were questioned by the Innocence Project, which reported that (Salzberg, 2007):

> New DNA tests show that two men's convictions for a 1997 murder were based on fraudulent testimony from a City of Cleveland forensic analyst—whose false testimony also wrongfully convicted another man who was exonerated in 2001 and led to an audit of cases covering a 16-year period that revealed serious problems in at least a half-dozen convictions—the Innocence Project said today. In legal papers filed today, the Innocence Project and the Ohio Innocence Project asked state courts to vacate the convictions of Thomas Siller and Walter Zimmer.

In 2009, because of Mr. Serowik's testimony, Mr. Siller's conviction was vacated, and he was ordered to receive a new trial (Puente, 2009).

This case involved fraud by a law enforcement-employed forensic examiner related to both physical evidence and expert credentials. According to the record, Mr. Serowik gave intentionally false and misleading testimony about his findings, what they meant, the current state of the forensic science literature, and his expertise. As such, his acts of fraud having been uncovered during the parameters set for this study (2000–2010), data from Mr. Serowik was included in the final data set. See Chapter 8, "Forensic Fraud, 2000–2010: Data and Frequency," for details regarding specific inclusion criteria and data collected.

RATIONALE

Forensic fraud exists as a sore and often forbidden subject in the forensic science community. The frequency and conditions of its occurrence have not been studied to any significant degree, and incidents are regularly hidden from public scrutiny to maintain the reputations of those police agencies and crime laboratories that have suffered its stain. As will be discussed, this is at least in part a reflection of the reality that those who have direct knowledge of forensic fraud have a vested interest in keeping these instances from becoming public knowledge. It preserves the image of their agency or lab, and by extension their own, out of concern for present testimonial credibility and future employment prospects.

Additionally, it must be understood that forensic practitioners are by definition involved in sensitive casework. As a function of their employment contracts, they may operate under strict confidentiality agreements or non-disclosure clauses that might preclude communication of any kind about active case-work—especially that which reflects negatively on their employer. The fear of losing employment-related income (e.g., being fired), and any future employment prospects, is generally sufficient enough for most to avoid causing a breach, even when it is in the public interest.

The majority of forensic scientists are also employed directly by police agencies or by crime labs associated with law enforcement and the prosecution (Peterson and Hickman, 2005). Consequently, open discussion and study of forensic fraud have long been considered a "third rail" in the forensic community (Cooley and Turvey, 2011). A brief explanation is necessary: the third rail is the method of providing electrical power to a railway, such as a mass transit system, by means of an exposed conductor. Anyone who touches the third rail is killed instantly by a surge of electricity. So it is with the issue of fraud. Such a discussion necessarily involves critical review of the actions and motives of law enforcement, prosecutors, and their scientific agents. These are not professional communities that are generally receptive of criticism or outside review, and they are frequently hostile to external or independent efforts involving either (Capers, 2008; Chin and Wells, 1998; Cooper, 2009a; Dorfman, 1999; Mollen, 1994; and Shockley-Eckles, 2011). Consequently, any forensic practitioner who raises these or related issues risks touches the third rail—being the object of hostility and derision within the law enforcement and government lab community, and committing career suicide in the process. This means risking not only employment, but also one's friends, colleagues, and professional identity.[4]

---

[4]The issue will be discussed further in Chapter 7, "Forensic Fraud: Prior Research."

This shared cultural silence regarding the existence and persistence of forensic fraud has resulted in an absence of clear or emergent data to enable ongoing scientific study of the phenomenon. The problem faced within the forensic science community, and understood by many within the criminal justice system, is described in Castelle (1999):

> Experienced criminal defense lawyers long ago realized that police perjury haunts courthouses throughout the country. In a similar manner, lawyers with significant experience with forensic science are beginning to realize that fraudulent forensic science may be equally endemic and, with tragic results, may permeate the criminal justice system in every state.
>
> …[W]ith depressing regularity, respected forensic scientists will concede their own knowledge of instances of "dry-labbing"—faking of data by former colleagues and employees that they have encountered in their own careers. Because it is safe to assume that most of the forensic science fraud that occurs goes undetected, the amount of fraud that has been revealed bears disturbing implications for any estimate of the amount of fraud that passes without notice.

Forensic fraud, in the current setting, has remained an unexplored, undeveloped, and unresolved empirical mystery.

Anecdotal evidence is widely available, however. Individual fraudsters, such as criminalists Fred Zain of West Virginia and Joyce Gilchrist of Oklahoma, have even achieved a level of infamy. However, a larger picture of forensic fraud is lacking, as explained in Cooley (2006), where he discusses what it is fair to call "the crime lab crisis" (p. 513):

> The current state of U.S. crime labs, and their regular lack of qualified personnel, has forced Barry Scheck (2004, p. 4), defense attorney, DNA expert, and cofounder of *The Innocence Project*, to conclude, "Everyone should know our crime laboratories are in a crisis, reeling from an epidemic of scandals reflecting decades of shoddy work, usually from bad actors producing incompetent or fraudulent results, but sometimes from methodologies that have been exposed as unreliable."
>
> Although some may argue that Scheck's comments must be viewed through a cautious lens, given his allegiance to the criminal defense bar, it must be conceded that his position is actually reinforced by numerous high-ranking forensic practitioners and administrators. For instance, Milton E. Nix, director of the Georgia Bureau of Investigation's crime lab, admitted to Congress, "You may find this an unusual statement, but I am in total agreement with the National Association of Defense Attorneys when it comes to quality

and accuracy of crime lab examinations and analysis" ("Crime Lab Modernization," 2001). Similarly, Barry Fisher, director of the Los Angeles County crime lab, made the following comment regarding the lack of crime lab oversight (as quoted in Graham, 2001, p. 10): "I don't think anyone can tell you what's really going on [in the nation's crime laboratories].... The truth is, we don't know."

The criminal justice system needs a working sense of what is going on with respect to the range and frequency of forensic fraud in courtrooms, police agencies, and government-funded crime labs. Until this has been achieved, it is not possible to effectively anticipate and correct the circumstances that allow fraud to occur, let alone address fraud directly when it is revealed. That is purpose of this work: to define forensic fraud, to identify its occurrence in the justice system, to help render a sense of its nature and origins, and ultimately to help inform related legislation and agency policy. In the process, it is hoped that it will also contribute to the development policies and procedures necessary to maintain the integrity of the criminal justice system.

It is important to note that, in the current forensic science environment, empirical research on the subject of forensic fraud is necessary if only due to its utter absence (Edwards and Gotsonis, 2009). However, it is also clear that the vast majority of forensic scientists, being employed by or aligned with the prosecution, do not feel free to carry it out themselves (Inman and Rudin, 2006). It must fall to those that are generally unaffiliated to avoid political consequences or institutional sanction. It is with a keen awareness of such realities that this work has been undertaken.

SCOPE AND ORIGINALITY

A number of publications touch anecdotally, or ideographically, on the issue of fraud committed by forensic examiners (see generally Castelle, 1999; Connors et al., 1996; Cooley, 2004 and 2007b; Cooley and Oberfield, 2007; Giannelli, 1997, 2001, and 2002; Imwinkelried, 2003; Kelly and Wearne, 1998; Koehler, 1993; Midkiff, 2004; Pyrek, 2007; Raeder, 2007; Saks, 2003, Saks et al., 2007; Samuel, 1994; Scheck et al., 2000; Starrs, 1993 and 2004; Turvey, 2003 and 2011; and Wilson, 1992). All of these works reference the problem of forensic fraud while only skimming its surface, to show that it can and does happen without any sense of frequency, consequences, or community response. Additionally, these works originate almost entirely from the legal community, save Pyrek (2007), a journalist; and Starrs (1993 and 2004), Midkiff (2004), Turvey (2011), and Wilson (1992)—all forensic practitioners. Moreover, almost none of these works represent formal research on forensic fraud per se; rather they exist as technical notes, collected interviews, or discussions regarding selected case studies.

There has been only one prior study specific to cases involving forensic fraud. This was a descriptive review of limited data from 42 cases with a proposed motivational typology by the current researcher (Turvey, 2003). In this study, the scope was highly inclusive, the data was limited, the discussion was cursory, and the findings were very much preliminary in nature.

The current study not only is original, but has been conducted from a unique perspective—that of a practicing and testifying forensic scientist. It will, and for the first time, provide significant examination of the nature and breadth of forensic fraud. This is accomplished by examining the existing cases in the public domain at such a depth, and in such a manner, as never before.

As already mentioned, the nature and scope of forensic fraud have essentially been unexamined by the forensic science community, and therefore it is unknown in a formal empirical sense. This research attempts to fill that existing gap in the literature. Without it, the development and implementation of strategies to prevent such fraud, and effect forensic reform, will be under-informed and may even be misguided.

The value of this research should be self-evident: to define the nature of the problem of forensic fraud in the forensic community, to help understand the social contexts and personal motives that facilitate forensic fraud, to help develop informed strategies for mitigating forensic fraud, and to keep the criminal justice system honest regarding the types of reforms required to identify and prevent forensic fraud. It will also contribute to, and be based upon, criminological theories associated with employee fraud and general criminality.

THESIS STATEMENTS AND THE PREVAILING WISDOM

Currently, the prevailing wisdom within the forensic science community with respect to forensic fraud is that it is only a minor problem, rarely occurring— akin to a few bad apples spoiling the barrel. As explained in Thompson (2009; p. 1028): "Public discourse on this issue has construed forensic science foul-ups as the product of individual intellectual and moral failure. According to the standard account, the problem is limited to 'a few bad apples', and the solution follows from that analysis—the bad apples need to be identified and either re-trained or replaced." Similar views are expressed in Edwards and Gotsonis (2009) and Pyrek (2007), where outright fraud by forensic practitioners is presented as a "rare" event, generally contained to a single individual who has lost his or her professional compass. In contrast, this researcher's core hypotheses are as follows:

1. Forensic fraud tends to be the result of cultural, pathological, and systemic causes rather than the narrow motives of single individuals, as the circumstances surrounding it are allowed to develop and persist by those in the immediate forensic environment.
2. Though private (e.g., defense) forensic practitioners are routinely characterized as biased or mercenary, those working on behalf of the state (the police and the prosecution) are responsible for a substantial amount, if not the majority, of known cases of forensic fraud.

The current research and subsequent dissertation will seek to support, expand, or refute these statements, as well as explore the origins of forensic fraud.

APPROACH OVERVIEW

This research systemically outlines the major forms of employee-related fraud found in law enforcement and scientific cultures. As part of these initial chapters, cases excluded from the current data under examination will be discussed, and general employee fraud theories will be considered. Later chapters will deal specifically with types of fraud that exist in the forensic sciences, to include a literature review specific to this phenomenon. Theoretical causes and origins of forensic fraud will also be considered, through the related criminological lenses of Routine Activities Theory, Differential Association Theory, and Role Strain. Once the theoretical framework has been set in place, the data collection methods and results for the present study will be explained, and then research findings and conclusions will be considered. We will conclude with discussions regarding proposed strategies for enabling forensic fraud prevention and management, as suggested by a statistical analysis of the present data.

CHAPTER 2

Occupational Fraud

"False face must hide what the false heart doth know."

Macbeth: Act 1, Scene 7, Shakespeare

In the first chapter, we outlined an approach to forensic fraud as a sub-type of employee (aka occupational) fraud. The purpose of this chapter is to provide a basic discussion and literature review regarding the phenomenon of occupational fraud, and supply an understanding of how criminologists and the legal community have approached the subject in general. This is distinct from the treatment of fraud by the scientific or law enforcement communities, which will be examined in subsequent chapters.

As explained in *Black's Law Dictionary* (Black, 1990), *fraud* is an intentional distortion of facts and truth for the purposes of inducing others to give up something of value that they possess, or to relinquish a legal right that they might otherwise retain. It is additionally defined as (p. 660) "[a] false presentation of a matter of fact, whether by words or by conduct, by false or misleading allegations, or by concealment of that which should have been disclosed, which deceives and is intended to deceive another...." Further still, it is described as "[a]nything calculated to deceive, whether by a single act or combination, or by suppression of truth, or suggestion of what is false, whether it be by direct falsehood or innuendo, by speech or silence, word of mouth, or look or gesture." This exhaustive set of definitions, generally consistent with the criminological literature reviewed by this author (e.g., Albrecht and Albrecht, 2003; Albrecht et al., 2011; Bolton and Hand, 2002; Brytting, Minogue, and Morino, 2011; and Kranacher, Riley, and Wells, 2010), leaves little daylight for the willful prevaricator. *Fraud* is, ultimately, any act or omission of act purposed at gain through a misrepresentation, distortion, or concealment of the facts.

This chapter discusses the criminological literature associated with occupational fraud and begins the process of relating it to the current research effort. First, fraud is considered as a statutory violation. Second, acts of

Forensic Fraud. http://dx.doi.org/10.1016/B978-0-12-408073-7.00002-1

fraud are differentiated from acts of negligence. Third, occupational fraud is defined and discussed. Fourth, the Fraud Triangle is introduced and evaluated. Finally, the relevant traits of the occupational fraudster are discussed, based on the most current empirical research available. Each section provides an understanding for the next, dictating the order of presentation. Demonstrative case examples associated with the justice system are adduced as necessary, involving those both included and excluded from the current study.

FRAUD AS A STATUTORY VIOLATION

By itself, fraud is a general term rather than a specific one, with different implications depending on context (Albrecht and Albrecht, 2003; Ostas, 2007). Therefore, the use of the term *fraud* to describe a person or an action can imply that criminal and even civil statutes have been violated. However, this is not always going to be the case.

Historically, legal statutes have been inconsistent, failing to provide universal coverage for the many types of fraud that can occur (Branham and Kutash, 1949; Newsome, 1995). Furthermore, not every statutory violation that occurs will result in enough evidence to meet the specific legal burdens of the jurisdiction where it occurred (Albrecht and Albrecht, 2003). Each legal jurisdiction in the United States, and around the world, has its own peculiar interpretations relating to fraud as a legal concept with multiple corresponding statutes on the books (Albrecht et al., 2011). Within these jurisdictions, the general concept of fraud is the same but with varying coverage, as explained in Brown and Hepler (2005; pp. 264–265):

> The elements of fraud [require] an intentional misrepresentation of material facts; reliance by the recipient; causation, and damages. Many of these elements are omitted from consumer fraud statutes. While most statutes require some aspect of willfulness, some do not.

Brown and Hepler (2005) provide an example of this legal disparity in the United States, citing the selective use of the Uniform Deceptive Trade Practices and the Uniform Consumer Sales Practices Acts by different states when developing consumer fraud protection statutes (pp. 266–267):

> Approximately thirty states have adopted legislation based at least in part on the Uniform Deceptive Trade Practices or Uniform Consumer Sales Practices Acts. These acts are characterized by a listing of prohibited practices. Colorado, for example, lists forty-three categories of prohibited activities.... Mississippi, in contrast, lists only eleven categories of prohibited activities.

In other words, one can commit the same fraudulent act in two different legal jurisdictions (e.g., states or countries), but that fraudulent act might violate criminal and/or civil statutes in only one of them. Given the vast number of criminal and civil statutes pertaining to fraud that are in effect, and the inconsistent coverage provided by these statutes across legal jurisdictions, no single legal definition of fraud can exist that covers all possibilities (Kapardis and Krambia-Kapardis, 2004). Consequently, *fraud* is best viewed as a criminological construct with potential legal repercussions that vary depending on where and how it is committed.

Despite the lack of homogeny in criminal fraud statutes across the United States, fraud-related offenses are a required part of crime data reporting by U.S. law enforcement agencies to the Uniform Crime Report (UCR) program run by the Federal Bureau of Investigation (FBI, 2004). The FBI provides a brief discussion that both defines criminal fraud and provides examples for submitting agencies (pp. 140–141):

> The intentional perversion of the truth for the purpose of inducing another person or other entity in reliance upon it to part with something of value or to surrender a legal right. Fraudulent conversion and obtaining of money or property by false pretenses.
>
> Fraud involves either the offender receiving a benefit or the victim incurring a detriment. The benefit or detriment could be either "tangible" or "intangible." Intangibles are anything which cannot be perceived by the sense of touch. They can be benefits, e.g., a right or privilege, a promotion, enhanced reputation; or a detriment, e.g., loss of reputation, injured feelings.
>
> Examples of common fraud cases are where something of value, such as a DVD player or an automobile, is rented for a period of time but is not returned. This offense, conversion of goods lawfully possessed by bailees, is classified as fraud and not larceny. In such cases, the offenders originally had lawful possession of the property (the property was either rented, loaned, or the person was in some way entrusted with its possession) and through deceit (they promised to return it) kept the property.

Agencies must include in this classification:
- Bad checks, except forgeries and counterfeiting
- False pretenses/swindle/confidence games
- Leaving a full-service gas station without paying attendant
- Credit card/automatic teller machine fraud
- Impersonation
- Welfare fraud
- Wire fraud
- Attempts to commit any of the above

This narrow definition excludes many additional forms of criminal fraud, such as tax fraud, mortgage fraud, Medicaid/Medicare fraud, and embezzlement.[1]

The FBI's UCR program divides law enforcement crime data collection efforts into Part 1 and Part 2 offense schedules. "Part 1" offenses are the more serious violent crimes, and include criminal homicide, forcible rape, robbery, aggravated assault, burglary, larceny-theft, motor vehicle theft, and arson (FBI, 2004). The UCR program requires collecting "data on all Part I offenses that become known to law enforcement whether or not they involve arrests" (FBI, 2004; p. 139). Fraud is considered a "Part 2" offense by the UCR, meaning that law enforcement agencies need only collect and submit arrest information (FBI, 2004; p. 139). This necessarily excludes cases that involve complaints without subsequent arrest from reporting. Consequently, the fraud data collected by the FBI is limited to criminal complaints where an arrest has occurred; it does not encompass all reported instances of fraud.

According to the most recent law enforcement data published by the FBI's UCR program, the total number of estimated arrests for fraud in the United States has diminished steadily every year since 2005, from 321,521 to 187,887 in 2010 (FBI, 2006, 2007, 2008, 2009a,b, 2010, and 2011). However, the UCR data suffers from some important built-in limitations. First, and as already mentioned, the data does not include all reported instances of fraud, only those crimes within the narrow scope defined that resulted in an arrest. Also, the number of law enforcement agencies reporting crime data to the UCR program changes from year to year, as reporting to the UCR is not mandatory. This, in combination with the inconsistent fraud laws across differing legal jurisdictions, makes any subsequent UCR crime statistics a rough estimate only. In other words, what is reported to the UCR is an unknown percentage of actual cases. This renders cross-comparisons of the data collected by the UCR inappropriate from an empirical standpoint, whether city to city or year to year (FBI, 2009b), as change is expected based on the number of agencies reporting; differing interpretations and enactments of local statutes; and any alterations made to staff and budgets that might affect the ability to focus on particular kinds of crime.

Despite the steady decline in total estimated arrests for criminal fraud by the FBI's UCR, and bearing in mind the program's limitations, most researchers agree that fraud-related crime is actually on the rise (Albrecht et al., 2011; Wolfe and Hermanson, 2004). These same researchers also agree that it is not possible to know how much criminal fraud is actually occurring (as with any crime). This is due to the fact that there are many different kinds of fraud, most of which is either not uncovered or not reported to the authorities when it is

---

[1]Embezzlement has its own separate UCR listing.

(Kapardis and Krambia-Kapardis, 2004; Lord, 2010). As explained in Albrecht et al. (2011; p. 5):

> Although most people and even most researchers believe that fraud is increasing both in size and frequency, it is difficult to know for sure. First, it is impossible to know what percentage of fraud perpetrators are caught. Are there perfect frauds that are never detected, or are all frauds eventually discovered? In addition, many frauds that are detected are quietly handled by the victims and never made public. In many cases of employee fraud, for example, companies merely hide the frauds and quietly terminate or transfer perpetrators rather than make the frauds public. Companies and individuals who have been defrauded are often more concerned about the embarrassment of making frauds public, and the costs of investigating fraud, than they are about seeking justice and punishing fraud perpetrators.

Owing to its many forms, the high frequency of known cases, and high related costs (discussed shortly), it is generally agreed that criminal fraud should be a primary concern for researchers, investigators, and employers across the board—no matter the true percentage of fraudsters made public (Kapardis and Krambia-Kapardis, 2004; Karcz and Papadakos, 2011; Lord, 2010; Quail, 2010; and RTTN, 2010).

DIFFERENTIATING FRAUD AND NEGLIGENCE

Fraud is distinguished from negligence, ignorance, and error by virtue of the fact that it is intentional, involving some level of calculation (Albrecht and Albrecht, 2003). *Negligence* is "the failure to use such care as a reasonably prudent and careful person would use under similar circumstances" (Black, 1990; p. 1032). In a professional context, it is "conduct which falls below the standard established by law for the protection of others against unreasonable risk of harm … it is characterized chiefly by inadvertence, thoughtlessness, inattention, and the like" (Black, 1990; p. 1032). In contrast, fraud is not accidental in nature, nor is it unplanned (Albrecht et al., 2011; Black, 1990; and Lord, 2010). Those who commit fraud know what they are doing and are deliberate in their efforts. They are also aware that it is unethical, illegal, or otherwise improper. While this may seem an insurmountable threshold, it is relatively straightforward to investigate and establish if one knows what to look for.

In the most general terms, fraudulent intent is established by examining the documentation of decisions and behaviors associated with those under suspicion. As explained in Coenen (2008; p. 8): "Manipulation of documents and evidence is often indicative of such intent. Innocent parties don't normally alter documents and conceal or destroy evidence." Other indicators can include obstructing a fraud investigation by lying or concealing pertinent information, having a known history of fraudulent behavior, circumventing safeguards, and being the direct recipient of benefits from suspected fraudulent acts (Coenen, 2008).

EVAN THOMPSON, FORENSIC SCIENTIST

Washington State Patrol Crime Laboratory

This case was uncovered during the course of data-gathering efforts described in Chapter 8, "Forensic Fraud, 2000–2010: Data and Frequency." It involves a forensic scientist employed by the Washington State Patrol Crime Laboratory, a division of the Washington State Patrol (WSP; a statewide law enforcement agency). The head of this crime lab, which employs non-sworn scientific personnel, reports directly to the Chief of the WSP.

The facts of this case, published widely in the media at the time, are documented in the official report prepared by the Washington State Forensic Investigations Council (FIC; McEachran, 2008). The FIC was only one of the entities to investigate this matter and make recommendations (p. 2):

> During the ordinary course of peer and supervisory review of the work of Forensic Scientist Evan Thompson, deficiencies were discovered. Due to concerns he was placed on a work improvement program in April of 2006. During this review process an error was discovered on Mr. Thompson's work relating to bullet trajectory analysis. Due to concern raised about this type of work by Mr. Thompson, he was removed from bullet trajectory casework on October 2, 2006. As the review by Crime Laboratory supervisors took place, technical errors and violations of laboratory operating procedures were discovered, and Mr. Thompson was removed from all casework responsibilities on November 13, 2006. Mr. Thompson's case files were reviewed and irregularities were discovered, and then a focused casework review was undertaken of Mr. Thompson's work. During this process Mr. Thompson resigned from the State Crime Laboratory effective April 6, 2007.
>
> In order to fully examine Mr. Thompson's work, Dr. Barry Logan contracted with two independent firearms examiners, Matthew Noedel and Dwight Van Horn. They were initially directed to examine 13 cases that Mr. Thompson had completed. Other casework was also examined by the two examiners. Mr. Nodell reported that he discovered work that was poorly organized and poorly documented....

To be clear, the errors that were identified in Mr. Thompson's work were not demonstrably intended to hide or misrepresent the evidence. Rather, the errors reflected a longstanding lack of interest in following proper lab procedures and an overall carelessness with respect to documenting findings. Specific instances included releasing information to prosecutors about firearms analysis before supervisors could review the case and sign off on it, and separately the failure to identify the diameter of a bullet in a forensic report as per lab protocols (Sullivan, 2007). While Mr. Thompson evidenced ineptitude and an incapacity to learn despite repeated sanctions from supervisors, there was no manifest evidence that this conduct was intended to deceive anyone for any particular gain. Apparently, Mr. Thompson simply refused to follow the required steps when conducting his work, was unmotivated to change by being placed on a "work improvement program," and was eventually taken off casework.

It bears noting that this attitude toward casework did not distinguish Mr. Thompson, as the WSP crime lab was known for sloppiness, deficiency, and even overt fraud during the years leading up to his forced resignation (Curtis and Bowman, 2007; Johnson, 2008; McEachran, 2008; Seitz, 2008; Steiner, 2008; and Teichroeb, 2004b). However, his errors were among those discovered, investigated, and made public. He consequently chose to resign rather than face further administrative or courtroom-related consequences (e.g., suspension, loss of courtroom credibility). As of this writing, the State of Arizona's Department of Public Safety currently employs Mr. Thompson as a forensic scientist at its Northern Regional Crime Laboratory in Flagstaff.

This case involves a forensic scientist performing evidence examination and related duties within the time frame parameters set for the present research. However, given the absence of demonstrable fraud, Mr. Thompson and the errors discovered in association with 13 of his cases were necessarily excluded from the present study. This case is provided, however, to show how negligence may be distinguished from fraud in a forensic context. Specific criteria for inclusion in the present study are discussed in Chapter 8.

OCCUPATIONAL FRAUD

Occupational fraud is a sub-type of fraud associated with the workplace, referring to a range of misconduct that includes both criminal and non-criminal infractions (Coenen, 2008). It may also be referred to as internal fraud, employee fraud, embezzlement, and workplace fraud, depending on the organization or researcher (Albrecht and Albrecht, 2003; Coenen, 2008). For the purposes of this research, the descriptors *occupational fraud* and *employee fraud* will be used interchangeably.

Since 1996, the Association of Certified Fraud Examiners (ACFE) has published an annual "Report to the Nations on Occupational Fraud and Abuse," which provides a breakdown of the costs, methods, and perpetrators of fraud within the United States as compared to other major nations around the world (RTTN, 2010). The ACFE defines *occupational fraud* as (p. 6) "[t]he use of one's occupation for personal enrichment through the deliberate misuse or misapplication of the employing organization's resources or assets." This definition is intentionally broad, meant to cover the whole range of misconduct committed by employees at any level within an organization. It includes everything from stealing items out of the workplace supply cabinet for personal use to falsifying work orders or time sheets to complex forms of overcharging, debt concealment, and embezzlement (RTTN, 2010). In its ongoing effort to study this profit-motivated phenomenon, the ACFE has broken down occupational fraud into three general types: (1) *asset misappropriations,* (2) *corruption,* and (3) *fraudulent statements* (RTTN, 2010). Each has many sub-types to account for the variety of fraud that is commonly encountered in association with the workplace (see Figure 2-1).

The following definitions apply, taken from Kranacher, Riley, and Wells (2010; p. 4). *Asset misappropriations* are "the theft or misuse of an organization's assets," including skimming profits, stealing company property, and committing payroll fraud. *Corruption* is "the unlawful or wrongful misuse of influence in a business transaction to procure personal benefit, contrary to an individual's duty to his or her employer or the rights of another," including taking bribes, accepting kickbacks, and participating in business relationships with inherent conflicts of interest. *Fraudulent statements* are "the intentional misrepresentation of financial or non-financial information to mislead others who are relying on it to make economic decisions," including overstating profits, understating debts and expenses, or making false promises regarding the safety and potential of an investment.

The estimated cost of occupational fraud to U.S. businesses, in terms of loss of income to employers or clients, is approximately 5%–7% on average (Dorminey et al., 2010; Lord, 2010). Gross domestic product (GDP) is the term used to describe the value of all goods and services produced in a given country. The United States has a GDP of 14.66 trillion U.S. dollars (CIA, 2011), which translates to somewhere between $733,000,000,000 and $1,002,620,000,000 of estimated loss to fraud per year.

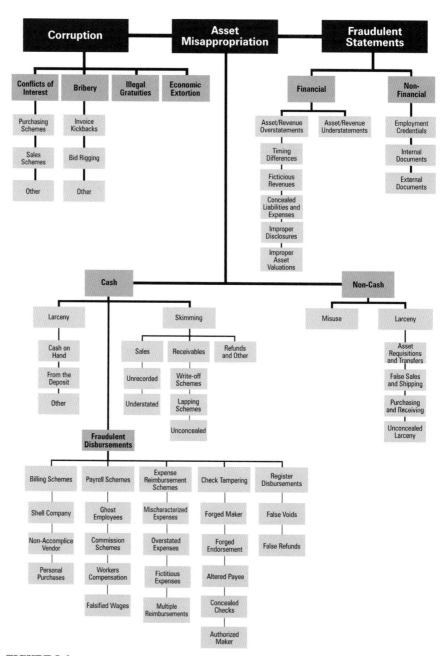

FIGURE 2-1
ACFE Occupational Fraud and Abuse Classification System (RTTN, 2010; p. 7)

24 POLICE OFFICERS

Hamilton Police Department, Hamilton, Massachusetts

This case was uncovered during the course of data-gathering efforts described in Chapter 8. It involves the unraveling of a "tradition" of fraud among multiple police officers employed by the City of Hamilton Police Department in Massachusetts. In this particular department, all police officers are required to maintain state certification as emergency medical technicians (EMTs) as stipulated in their employment contracts. It bears noting that this is not an unusual requirement for any police department. As reported in Quail (2010; p. 6):

> In 2008, a complaint was made by a police officer to the OEMS [Massachusetts Office of Emergency Medical Services] regarding the police department's (his employer) ambulance service. The complainant officer alleged that in 2006 and 2007, the police department sponsored EMT [Emergency Medical Technician] refresher and continuing education programs, but that the required number of hours to complete these programs was never met. He also reported that the primary instructor and other police officers would sign EMT attendance rosters, and then leave without attending training programs. These officers then submitted documents to the OEMS which knowingly contained false and inaccurate information in order to renew their EMT licenses (MA. DPH OEMS, 2008, August, Complaint Investigation Report # 08-0705).

> During the investigative process, the OEMS investigators acquired sufficient evidence and testimony to conclude that there was a "culture" of falsifying records and programs, which not only involved the two years cited in the complaint, but began approximately in 2000 (MA. DPH OEMS, 2008, August, Complaint Investigation Report # 08-0705).

> The OEMS conducted a trip record audit for years 2006 and 2007, to ensure patients received appropriate treatment by the police officers. The audit revealed that of the ambulance calls, 93 percent and 89 percent respectively, lacked either appropriate patient care or appropriate documentation to support the care provided to the patient. The investigation revealed that the police officers had based their treatment

decisions on outdated treatment protocols. In addition, the two ambulances licensed by the town carried expired medications and did not have a drug control license to carry such medications (MA. DPH OEMS, 2008, August, Complaint Investigation Report # 08-0705; MA DPH OEMS-Trip Record Audit #08-0705).

> The OEMS investigation concluded that 24 police officers engaged in falsifying training attendance records and were not eligible for EMT license renewal for multiple years. These police officers used the title of EMT and provided patient care as unlicensed providers, which posed a threat to the health and safety of the public. In addition, the police officers knowingly submitted false documents and fees to the state agency, stating their training records were a true and accurate reflection of their training. Furthermore, the police department ambulance service staff billed patients' insurance companies and received payment for services by unlicensed providers (MA. DPH OEMS, 2008, August, Complaint Investigation Report # 08-0705).

> The OEMS began legal action against the ambulance service by immediately revoking its ambulance license, and against the individual police officers, by scheduling multiple DALA [Division of Administrative Law Appeals] hearings. The OEMS referred their investigative findings to the OAG and OIG insurance fraud divisions for criminal action (MA. DPH OEMS, 2008, August, Complaint Investigation Report # 08-0705).

> *Discussion Case #3.* The police department and staff knowingly committed multiple acts of fraud, larceny, and health care fraud by allowing patients to be treated by unlicensed providers and submitting insurance claims for reimbursement. In addition, police officers received supplemental money and overtime pay in order to attend training classes to be licensed as EMTs. The amount of money each officer received was approximately $4,470 each year (Landwehr, 2008, 2009; Manganis, 2008).

Continued

24 POLICE OFFICERS *CONTINUED*

Originally, the whistleblower in this case was asked to keep quiet about the allegations and allow city officials to handle matters internally (Landwehr, 2008).

This case involved a network of fraud by those working within the criminal justice system on several levels, as mentioned in the discussion section provided from Quail (2010). To be more specific, it involved asset misappropriation and false statements at the very least. *Asset misappropriation* accurately describes the scheme devised to falsify training and credentials for profit. *False statements* are evident if one simply removes the unnecessary financial component of the ACFE's definition; fraud is demonstrated by the

intentional misrepresentation of information to mislead others who are relying on it to make decisions. This accurately describes the use of unearned or phony credentials, giving the supervisors and the public the false impression that they are being served by properly trained and credentialed EMTs.

However, given that these cases of fraud did not involve those designated specifically as forensic examiners in the performance of evidence-related duties, but rather non-forensic law enforcement personnel, related data was necessarily excluded from the present study. Specific criteria for inclusion in the present study are discussed in Chapter 8.

MITCHELL T. GRIFFIN AND CATHY L. DECKER, LABORATORY MANAGERS

HealthTec Labs, Merced, California

These cases were uncovered during the course of data-gathering efforts described in Chapter 8. They involve a private toxicology lab formerly operating out of Merced, California, called HealthTec Labs. The laboratory was owned and operated by a brother and sister team: Mitchell T. Griffin and Cathy L. Decker.

HealthTec Labs was one of many private labs in California contracted by state agencies and private companies to conduct employment-related or court-ordered drug testing on employees and criminal defendants (Conway, 2003a). For instance, Child Protective Services (CPS) and the courts would refer parents with drug-related convictions to Health-Tec Labs for testing in order to either regain or maintain custody of their children. The certified results of drug tests provided by HealthTec Labs would be used as administrative evidence to suspend and terminate an employee, or in a forensic (aka courtroom) context to help a judge decide custody issues. It is reported that CPS, the state agency charged with investigating cases of child abuse and neglect, accounted for approximately 20% of HealthTec Lab's business (Conway, 2003a).

According to Commander Larry Slate with the Merced/Mariposa Narcotics Task Force, complaints had been coming in for at least three years regarding HealthTec Labs; specifically, the lab was suspected of selling clean tests to parents seeking custody of their children subsequent to CPS taking

them away for drug-related offenses (De La Cruz, 2003). In December of 2002, the Narcotics Task Force laboratory tested a female suspect with positive results for drugs. Approximately two weeks later, HealthTec performed a drug test on the same female suspect with negative results, suggesting that she had been clean of any drugs for at least 90 days (Conway, 2003a). Knowing this to be false, the Narcotics Task Force began an official investigation that resulted in Grand Jury Testimony from Mr. Mitchell in late August of 2003. Subsequently, both suspects were arrested for falsifying records. Mr. Mitchell was given additional charges of perjury for lying to the Grand Jury, for possession of methamphetamine, and for being under the influence of methamphetamine (Conway, 2003b; De La Cruz, 2003).

The scheme of fraud perpetrated by Mr. Mitchell and Ms. Decker is reported in Conway (2003a):

> In CPS cases, [Commander Larry] Slate said, Griffin would ask parents for $200 for clean-test results. He allegedly asked at least one person for drugs in exchange for clean-test results....
>
> In a sting operation, the task force sent in several people who agents knew had drugs in their systems, based on separate testing. Griffin sold test results that showed the people were not using drugs, Slate said.

MITCHELL T. GRIFFIN AND CATHY L. DECKER, LABORATORY MANAGERS *CONTINUED*

A negative test for drugs does not guarantee that a parent will regain custody of his or her children, but a positive test is sufficient to postpone custody.

HealthTec did not perform laboratory work, Slate said. Instead, Griffin and Decker sent samples to Omega Lab, a legitimate company in Ohio.

Omega performs two kinds of drug tests: pre-employment screenings for $36 and forensic tests, admissible in court, for $260.

The county, for CPS cases, ordered forensic tests and paid HealthTec $100 for each one.

Authorities said HealthTec would substitute samples to guarantee clean tests.

At the same time, it would order $36 pre-employment screenings, Slate said—and collect $100 from the county.

The results for each pre-employment screening came back with a notation: "This form should not be used for forensic (courtroom) purposes." That notation would be covered with correction fluid and a photocopy of the form would be sent to CPS, Slate said.

Additionally, the Merced/Mariposa Narcotics Task Force uncovered at least one instance in which Mr. Griffin "reportedly offered to return a client's $200 back in exchange for some methamphetamine" (De La Cruz, 2003).

Of interest is the report from the Narcotics Task Force that they had warned CPS about HealthTec's suspect business practices more than once in the years leading up to the investigation (Conway, 2003b). Then Chief of CPS Kathy Hassett denied being given actionable information about HealthTec, which the Merced/Mariposa Narcotics Task Force stated was incorrect on her part (Conway, 2003a). However, Social Services Director Ana Pagan admitted that several months prior to the arrests "Superior Court Judge Frank Dougherty told a CPS court representative that the judge would no longer accept drug test results from HealthTec," which should have alerted CPS to the scandal (Conway, 2003a).

In any case, once it was confirmed that CPS continued to refer cases to HealthTec for drug testing despite these warnings, CPS Chief Kathy Hassett was temporarily reassigned, and an investigation into CPS was initiated into the matter by the state (Conway, 2003b). The results of the state investigation into CPS's handling of this matter were not made public. However, as of 2011, Kathy Hassett remained the director of the renamed Child Support Services for Merced County, under the supervision of Ana Pagan (Merced County, 2011).

The fraud in these cases can be described as including *asset misappropriation, corruption,* and *false statements.* This owing to the fact that it involved over-billing to the state for tests that were not performed as described; it involved accepting bribes for clean drug tests; and it involved false and misleading documentation relating to drug tests that were provided to the court.

Ultimately, HealthTec was shut down, the owners were convicted of criminal charges, and each of the 755 drug tests that the lab had authenticated for CPS over the previous three years had to be re-examined (Conway, 2003a). The known financial cost of this fraud would be, at the low end, an estimate of $75,500, given the $100 fee charged for each suspect drug test conducted on behalf of Merced County. This does not include the cost in person-hours for staff members assigned to review these cases, or for those involved in reviewing the custody issues that this scandal revealed. The additional cost and consequences with respect to harm caused by leaving children in the custody of drug-addicted caregivers have not been publicly investigated or addressed by Merced County.

This example involves multiple instances of fraud by those working on behalf of the justice system. Additionally, the two individuals involved lacked any formal education, were working in a forensic capacity directly with physical evidence, and were certifying the authenticity of subsequent drug tests for forensic (aka courtroom) purposes. As such, these self-proclaimed forensic laboratory technicians, having committed their offenses during the parameters set in this study (2000–2010), were both included in the final data set. Impact data was not replicated for both individuals, to prevent duplication in the data. See Chapter 8 for details regarding inclusion criteria and data collected.

THE FRAUD TRIANGLE

Donald R. Cressey, Ph.D. (1919–1987) was an American criminologist well known for his study of both theoretical and applied issues across a number of related areas. In their biography of Dr. Cressey, Akers and Matsueda (1989) explain that (p. 426)

> ...his presence in the field was felt most clearly in (1) criminological theory; (2) prisons, punishment, and corrections; (3) sociology of criminal law and justice; (4) organized crime; and (5) white-collar crime. Perhaps the most lasting influence will come from his understanding and use of criminological theory, especially his espousal, analysis, and application of differential association theory, because it pervaded virtually all that he did.

An author of multiple seminal texts and research (including *Principles of Criminology,* co-edited to the 11th edition [Cressey, Sutherland, and Luckenbill, 1992], an industry standard until just after his death), Dr. Cressey is perhaps most remembered in the current literature for his development of Fraud Triangle Theory.

Fraud Triangle Theory states that in order for an act of occupational fraud to occur, there must be a convergence of three elements: offender *motivation (aka pressure or need), opportunity,* and *rationalization* (Cressey, 1953/1973; see Figure 2-2).[2]

Motivation to commit fraud can be experienced in many forms, but often comes from a financial need to pay existing debts and maintain professional standing; a desire for increased standing, wealth, or profits; or cultural pressure to conform to pre-existing expectations within a group already engaged

FIGURE 2-2
Cressey's Fraud Triangle

---

[2]Fraud Triangle Theory is referenced throughout the literature on occupational fraud, and is essentially the same as the more broadly applied and empirically validated construct of Routine Activities Theory (see Chapter 6, "Contrasting Scientific Integrity with Law Enforcement Culture").

in fraudulent activity (Coenen, 2008; Donegan and Danon, 2008). According to Ostas (2007; p. 574): "Traditional economic analysis assumes that people, including corporate executives, are motivated by pecuniary, or material, self-interest." However, the motivation to commit fraud can also come from addiction, where fraudsters are compelled to steal money, property, or other assets in order to satisfy various forms of chronic dependence such as gambling or drug use (RTTN, 2010).

Opportunity is experienced in the form of knowledge and access to "assets, people, information, and computer systems that enables the person not only to commit the fraud but to conceal it" (Coenen, 2008; p. 12). As explained in Brytting, Minogue, and Morino (2011; p. 50):

> ...fraud also demands a possibility to cheat, combined with a low possibility of getting caught, that is, a proper "opportunity," created for instance by weak internal control systems, power to override systems, inside information, privileged access to resources, and so on. A potential fraudster will perceive an opportunity when he believes he can commit a fraud with either an acceptably small risk of getting caught, or an acceptably low risk of punishment if caught.

Donegan and Danon (2008) argue that opportunity to commit fraud is also created, or inhibited, by the cultural support that exists in a given workplace (p. 10):

> ...the nature of available social support determines whether crimes actually occur. Social support typically ameliorates the effects of strain, but can also encourage crime when provided by a deviant subgroup. Access to a deviant subgroup provides an opportunity to learn the skills needed for criminal behavior and may provide social support to the nascent criminal.

Fraud Triangle Theory suggests that when the necessary knowledge, skills, and social support are absent, the potential for committing fraud is decreased.

Rationalization involves either self-delusion regarding the acceptability of fraud-related behavior under "special circumstances," or a disregard for the law as unjust or somehow inapplicable. Coenen (2008) explains that rationalization (p. 12)

> ...is the process by which an employee determines that the fraudulent behavior is "okay" in her or his mind. For those with deficient moral codes, the process of rationalization is easy. For those with higher moral standards, it may not be quite so easy; they may have to convince themselves that a fraud is okay by creating "excuses" in their minds.

This is further developed in Dorminey et al. (2010; p. 19):

> Cressey indicated that a morally acceptable rationalization is necessary before the crime takes place. Because a fraudster does not view himself as a criminal, he must justify his misdeeds to himself before he ever commits them. For example, the perpetrator may rationalize his actions by thinking, "This is just a loan and I'll pay it back after my next paycheck." The rationalization allows the perpetrator to view illegal behavior as acceptable, thus preserving his self-image as a trustworthy person.

Brytting, Minogue, and Morino (2011) offer the following list of common rationalizations developed and held by the fraudster to allow for his or her misconduct (p. 57): "[E]veryone is doing it; it's only fair; I've (they've) no choice; it's just a loan; no one is hurt; I've (they've) earned it; they deserve it; it's not a crime; they don't mind; it's for a good cause." As a corollary, Kidder (2005) reports that (p. 390) "perceived unfairness in the workplace is a major determinant of performing 'bad' behaviors." The perception of inequity, or not getting what one perceives rightful entitlement to, is therefore a rich nesting ground for the development of these related rationalizations.

It is important to note that fraud rationalizations might also be peculiar to a deviant sub-group that tolerates or is directly involved in ongoing fraud or other criminal enterprise. Brytting, Minogue and Morino (2011) maintain (p. 50) that "[i]f an individual's identity is tied to such a sub-group of relevant others, fraud may be committed even though they have excellent knowledge about cultural norms and values on a more general level." For the purposes of the current research, this concept is particularly relevant to deviant sub-groups operating within law enforcement, and in relation to *Social Learning Theory*, as discussed in Chapter 4, "Fraud in Law Enforcement Culture."

Though Fraud Triangle Theory has been debated, adapted, expanded, and refined over the past 60 years, its core remains foundational to modern occupational fraud investigation and examination methods (Albrecht and Albrecht, 2003; Albrecht et al., 2011; Brytting, Minogue, and Morino, 2011; Coenen, 2008; and Wells, 2010). In addition, it is regularly featured as an essential starting point for new research on fraud in different contexts (Aguilera and Vadera, 2008; Dorminey et al., 2010; Kapardis and Krambia-Kapardis, 2004; Lord, 2010; Malgwi and Rakovski, 2009; Wolfe and Hermanson, 2004).

Fraud Triangle Theory is not without criticism, however (Donegan and Danon, 2008; Dorminey et al., 2010). For example, Donegan and Danon (2008) offer an overview of the major problems with Fraud Triangle Theory that can be found in the literature. This includes the fact that Dr. Cressey's theory is a generalization about all financial fraud from a sample of embezzlers involved in primarily financial statement fraud as opposed to other forms (p. 3):

> The white-collar crime literature has generally stratified offenders into higher and lower status categories, with securities law violators in the former group and embezzlers in the latter (Weisburd et al., 1991; Langton and Piquero, 2007). These studies have found significant differences between high and low status offenders; thus even if Cressey's findings for embezzlers were valid, there is little evidence to support the fraud triangle as a general theory of financial crime.

Another issue, often ignored by researchers, is that the three elements of the Fraud Triangle can be present without fraud actually occurring. This has led some to argue that the Fraud Triangle does not sufficiently acknowledge an offender's pre-existing character, or criminal predisposition, with sufficient explication. This has led to the development of the Fraud Diamond, originally presented in Wolfe and Hermanson (2004).

The *Fraud Diamond* adds a fourth element to the Fraud Triangle: *individual capability*. It includes (Dorminey et al., 2010; p. 20) "personal traits and abilities that play a major role in whether fraud will actually occur given the presence of pressure, opportunity, and rationalization." This is not conceptually dissimilar to the fraud model proposed in Krambia-Kapardis (2001), referred to as ROP (Rationalizations, Opportunity, and crime-prone Person). The occurrence of fraud is not simply a matter of creating the right circumstances; there must also be a person situated properly with the disposition to commit it. The circumstances are a door, and the propensity allows some notion of who will walk through it. Wolfe and Hermanson (2004) identify six traits of the fraudster, considered adjunct to their *individual capability* requirement, presented in Rudewicz (2011; p. 2):

1. **Positioning:** The person's position or function within the organization may provide the ability to create or exploit an opportunity for fraud. A person in a position of authority has more influence over particular situations or the environment.
2. **Intelligence and creativity:** The fraudster is smart enough to understand and exploit internal control weaknesses and to use position, function, or authorized access to the greatest advantage.
3. **Ego:** The individual must have a strong ego and great confidence he will not be detected. The common personality types include someone who is driven to succeed at all costs, self-absorbed, self-confident, and often narcissistic.…

4. **Coercion:** A fraudster can coerce others to commit or conceal fraud. An individual with a persuasive personality can more successfully convince others to go along with the fraud or look the other way.
5. **Deceit:** Successful fraud requires effective and consistent lies. In order to avoid detection, the individual must be able to lie convincingly and must keep track of the overall story.
6. **Stress:** The individual must be able to control his stress, as committing the fraudulent act and keeping it concealed can be extremely stressful.

Not all of these traits must be present to meet the threshold of individual capability suggested by Wolfe and Hermanson (2004). For example, not all fraudsters coerce others to commit or conceal fraud. Nor must they have a position of authority, operate at a supervisory level, have a big ego, or be successful and accomplished liars. The level of individual capability required is dictated by the existing level of anti-fraud safeguards in the workplace; the fewer the safeguards, the less individual capability needed by the fraudster to successfully cross the threshold.

These models, however, are steeped in *Rational Choice Theory*, which assumes that all people, including criminals, make rational choices based on a logical cost–benefit analysis of their behavior and anticipated outcomes (Scott, 2000). This is not always the case, as explained in Ostas (2007; pp. 575–577):

> A growing body of behavioral literature suggests that … rational calculations … offer only a crude approximation of reality. This literature emphasizes the limitations on the human capacity to cope with the complexities and uncertainties of life. Drawing on the field of cognitive psychology, recent research provides evidence that people routinely resort to certain heuristics and biases that prevent them from reasoning as one might presume rational people would. For example, facing a complex and uncertain computation, an executive may be overconfident in his or her ability to make accurate judgments, and if it appears that a particular act may be very lucrative, a self-serving bias may take hold and negative information may be subconsciously suppressed. Hence, behavioral insights suggest that in some situations an executive may engage in criminal activity even when a purely rational calculation would dictate restraint. Miscalculations can occur in the other direction as well. For instance, behavioral research shows that people tend to display a conformation bias, in that they seek out and process information in ways that tend to confirm preexisting beliefs. Pursuant to this bias, an executive who is generally inclined to obey financial regulations and who is predisposed to believe that insider trading is highly risky may not properly calculate the pecuniary gain available from a particular illegal trade. Here, cognitive limitations may inhibit, rather than foster, illegal behavior.

This provides that rational motives are not always relevant or applicable to criminal acts (see also Turvey, 2011). As explained in Sunstein (2005), people (and by extension criminals) are not always that logical, that deliberate, or that bright, often lacking in what may be referred to as common sense. Cognitive bias and metacognitive deficiency are only part of the problem, however (Krueger and Dunning, 1999).

In direct conflict with the assumptions *of Rational Choice Theory*,[3] certain forms of mental illness, personality disorders, criminal history, and a history of addiction can also increase individual capability to commit crime, including fraud. However, ongoing drug abuse and unchecked mental defect would necessarily reduce the fraudster's ability to successfully deceive and handle stress over time. With chronic drug use, fraud may be committed in a manner that is sloppier with respect to successful methods (aka intelligence and creativity), and the fraudster might also exhibit noticeable physical and behavioral indications of intoxication and addiction. In these kinds of cases, a capable or suitable guardian is required (Krambia-Kapardis, 2001), such as alert fellow employees who are also willing to make an official complaint. Consider the following case example.

DAVID B. PETERSON, ASSISTANT DIRECTOR

Bureau of Criminal Apprehension (BCA) Crime Lab, St. Paul, Minnesota

This case was uncovered during the course of data-gathering efforts described in Chapter 8. It involves a forensic scientist with the Minnesota Bureau of Criminal Apprehension (BCA), working as an Assistant Director at the St. Paul Crime Lab. During the same time period, he was also serving as President for the American Society of Crime Lab Directors (ASCLD). Ironically, ASCLD promotes itself as a (ASCLD, 2011) "professional society of crime laboratory directors and forensic science managers dedicated to promoting excellence in forensic science through leadership and innovation." It is also associated with the American Society of Crime Lab Directors Laboratory Accreditation Board (ASCLD-LAB), which provides voluntary certification for public and private forensic science laboratories all over the world (ASCLD-LAB, 2011).

According to the criminal complaint, David B. Peterson was arrested and charged with "wrongfully and unlawfully possess[ing] one or more mixtures of a total weight of 25 grams or more containing cocaine, a schedule II controlled substance" (McConkey, 2005). Mr. Peterson, a recovering alcoholic, came under suspicion of being under the influence of narcotics after co-workers noticed him making repeated visits to an evidence storage locker. Subsequently, they discovered unsecured drugs in the storage locker. Based on this and his erratic behavior, his co-workers filed an internal report that led to a criminal investigation.

Mr. Petersen, an alcoholic, admitted to police that in 2004 he had begun drinking again after years of maintaining his sobriety. Subsequent to his renewed drinking pattern, he began illegally accessing the BCA's walk-in evidence vault and stealing from a brick of cocaine, used by narcotics officers in covert drug operations, for personal use. As reported in Prather (2005):

> During an interview with police, Petersen told investigators he had been sober for some time but had begun drinking again. In April 2004, he took half a pen cap full of cocaine—about 1/8 ounce—from a supply of cocaine kept at the lab. Petersen said he then began coring

Continued

[3]*Rational Choice Theory* is associated with *Routine Activities Theory*, discussed in Chapter 6.

DAVID B. PETERSON, ASSISTANT DIRECTOR *CONTINUED*

out small amounts of cocaine out of a brick in storage and taking the drug home, according to the criminal complaint. Petersen estimated that he took two golf ball-sized amounts between December 2004 and March 2005.

During that time, the BCA moved its lab to a new St. Paul location. In January 2005, Petersen received a call from the new owners of the former BCA offices reporting that they had discovered a package that appeared to be criminal evidence. Petersen went to investigate and found a kilo-sized brick of cocaine that had been inadvertently left during the move.

Petersen told police this unexpected discovery was a "gift from God" and he planned to use it to replace the cocaine he had taken.

Police conducting a search of Petersen's home at 1441 N. Hamline Ave. discovered trace amounts of cocaine in a basement room hidden behind a book shelf.

On April 28, 2005, Mr. Peterson pleaded guilty to one count of possessing 25 grams of cocaine. He was later sentenced to six months in prison, terminated from his position at the crime lab, and removed as president of ASCLD. As part of his rapid removal from ASCLD, his "President's Message" for Winter 2004 was taken down from the ASCLD website leaving no reference or trace. In addition, he was stricken from the roll of past presidents (see ASCLD Presidential Page; http://www.ascld.org/about-ascld/presidential-page/), replaced by Earl Wells for the years 2004 and 2005.

This case involved an admitted 11 months of ongoing fraudulent behavior by a supervising forensic scientist at an ASCLD-LAB certified law enforcement forensic laboratory. Mr. Peterson not only engaged in repeated thefts from the evidence room that he was charged with maintaining, but also engaged in fraud by failing to document the alteration of that evidence. This type of repeated alteration of the evidence (aka skimming amounts for personal use) has an impact on any future related chain of custody logs and analytical assessments (e.g., weighing and testing). Mr. Peterson was clearly aware of this impact, as he admitted to making plans to replace the brick of cocaine he had been altering with another that had been found during inventory (this second brick was found without a chain of custody). This would have required yet more fraud, as the second brick of cocaine would have been deleted or withheld from future evidence inventory logs created by Mr. Peterson.

When this case is considered in light of the Fraud Triangle Theory and Fraud Diamond Theory, it becomes clear that all the elements are present in some form: *Motivation*, or pressure, existed in the form of an addiction to cocaine. *Opportunity* existed in the form of a supervisory position that provided knowledge, access, trust, and authority over the evidence in the vault. *Personal capability* existed in the form of a pre-existing addiction to alcohol, position, intelligence, and deceitfulness. However, this fraudster appears to have been undone by his inability to manage the fraud over time, as his skill deteriorated and his outward behavior became more suspect with prolonged drug use and increased stress from fear of discovery.

TRAITS OF OCCUPATIONAL FRAUD PERPETRATORS

Anyone can commit fraud, and those that do cannot be reliably distinguished from anyone else, making likely perpetrators difficult to predict (Albrecht and Albrecht, 2003; Kranacher, Riley, and Wells, 2010). Consequently, behavioral scientists have not been able to identify any specific set of cardinal traits to serve as a "valid and reliable marker" for the propensity of an individual to commit fraud (Rudewicz, 2011; p. 1). However, the existing empirical research does suggest some interesting descriptive information regarding known offenders convicted of fraud (Kapardis and Krambia-Kapardis, 2004; p. 197):

> ...[T]he majority of serious fraud offenders are male, aged 35–45 years, married, of high educational status, either have a serious financial problem or are greedy for money, do not have a prior criminal record, occupy positions of financial trust, rationalize their behaviour, specialize in defrauding, act alone, use false documents to perpetrate fraud, victimize two or more people they know, and are convicted of multiple charges.

Specific research findings include the following traits of occupational fraudsters:

1. Male (80% in Krambia-Kapardis, 2001; 92% in Smith, 2003; 67% in RTTN, 2010);
2. No college education (25% with an undergraduate degree and 3% with a postgraduate degree in Smith, 2003; 38% with an undergraduate degree and 14% with a postgraduate degree in RTTN, 2010);
3. No prior criminal record (56% in Smith, 2003; 70% in Krambia-Kapardis, 2001; 87% in RTTN, 2010);
4. No prior fraud (83% in Smith, 2003; 93% in RTTN, 2010);
5. No addiction problems (88% in RTTN, 2010);
6. Acted alone (70% in Krambia-Kapardis, 2001; 84% in Smith, 2003);
7. Supervisory capacity of fraudsters varies. In Smith (2003), most were found to be non-management (71%); in RTTN (2010), most were found to be owners or managers (58%).

Again, it must be noted that this is not a list of red flags, and no research efforts have been made to compare the traits of known fraudsters to non-criminal populations (Kranacher, Riley, and Wells, 2010). Therefore this information is descriptive only, and not predictive.

SUMMARY

Fraud is a criminological descriptor that can have civil and criminal implications depending on context. There are many definitions of criminal fraud, resulting in inconsistent laws and subsequent data availability for empirical research. However, fraud is distinct from error and negligence by virtue of intent.

Occupational fraud has been studied consistently since 1996, and is believed to result in a loss of income to U.S. businesses at a rate of approximately 5%–7% on average. It can usefully be viewed through the lens of Fraud Triangle Theory, and in more advanced circumstances Fraud Diamond Theory. However, these models assume an inherent rationality in perpetrator planning, foresight, and deliberation that are not necessarily warranted.

Occupational fraud can be committed by anyone. Therefore, likely perpetrators are difficult to predict. There are consequently no cardinal traits that serve as a "valid and reliable marker" for the propensity of an individual to commit fraud.

CHAPTER 3

Forensic Science: A Primer

"Forensic science is science exercised on behalf of the law in the just resolution of conflict. It is therefore expected to be the handmaiden of the law, but at the same time this expectation may very well be the marina from which is launched the tension that exists between the two disciplines."

Thornton and Peterson (2007; p. 4)

In the preceding chapter, we explored the literature related to the investigation and examination of general occupational fraud. This body of research focuses almost entirely on the study of financially motivated schemes. It also concerns itself largely with the private sector and not acts of fraud committed by those working for the government. However, many of the underlying concepts and theories are applicable to the cases associated with the research conducted for this work.

However, before we can fully apply these concepts to the types of fraud committed by forensic examiners, we must first establish an understanding of the forensic science community and its cultural context. This chapter briefly explores the nature, role, and values of forensic science. First, forensic science is defined. Then, the role of forensic science in the judicial system is discussed. This leads into a presentation of the cardinal traits of the forensic scientist. Finally, this chapter closes with a discussion regarding the occupational environment of forensic science—as born of two divergent cultures.

This chapter serves at least two vital ends: it relieves the reader of any false presumptions regarding the forensic sciences taken from film, television, or works of fiction; and it contextualizes the forensic sciences, serving as a reference point for the research that is ultimately presented.

Forensic Fraud. http://dx.doi.org/10.1016/B978-0-12-408073-7.00003-3

FORENSIC SCIENCE—DEFINED

Forensic science is the application of scientific methodology, knowledge, and principles to the resolution of legal questions, whether criminal or civil (Chisum and Turvey, 2011; Houck and Seigal, 2010; James and Nordby, 2003; Saferstein, 2010; and Thornton and Peterson, 2007). This definition, generally consistent across the forensic science literature, is intentionally broad. There are, in fact, many different forensic sub-disciplines, including (but certainly not limited to) criminalistics, crime reconstruction, forensic pathology, forensic anthropology, forensic toxicology, forensic odontology, forensic entomology, forensic mental health (psychology and psychiatry); and forensic criminology (Chisum and Turvey, 2011; Houck and Seigal, 2010; James and Nordby, 2003; Saferstein, 2010; Seigel, Saukko, and Knupfer, 2000; and Turvey and Petherick, 2010).

CRIMINALISTICS: SOME RELEVANT BACKGROUND

The most common and recognizable type of forensic scientist is the criminalist. *Criminalistics* is the division of forensic science dedicated to the recognition, examination, and interpretation of physical evidence using the natural sciences, logic, and critical thinking (CAC, 2011; Inman and Rudin, 1999; Kirk, 1974; and O'Hara and Osterburg, 1972). Criminalists are generally associated with the examination of physical evidence conducted in police or government-funded forensic laboratories. They also comprise a majority (53%) of the forensic practitioners found in the present study.

The first crime laboratory scientists were actually referred to by job title and general description as "criminologists." This is reflected in the pages of one of the first forensic science textbooks published in the United States, *Crime's Nemesis* (May, 1936; see Figures 3-1 and 3-2). The author, Luke May, offered forensic crime lab services to law enforcement and other government agencies in a time when they had yet to develop their own. In his work, May refers to the practice of crime detection and evidence examination as the field of "scientific criminology" (p. ix) and to those working in it as "scientific criminologists" (p. 2). He further refers to himself, in bold letters on the cover page, as "LUKE S. MAY, CRIMINOLOGIST, Director, The Scientific Detective Laboratories; President, The Institute of Scientific Criminology."

As explained by the late criminalist Lowell Bradford (1918–2007), in his paper regarding the origins of the California Association of Criminalists founded in 1954 (Bradford, 2007; p. 5):

> I first entered into the field of criminalistics in 1947 in the California State Crime Laboratory in Sacramento…. In those days, the terms criminalistics and criminalist were not in use. Those of us in the state

FIGURES 3-1 and 3-2

Luke May, author of *Crime's Nemesis,* published in 1936, was among the first private consulting criminalists in the world. He referred to himself as a criminologist, as did most crime lab personnel at the time. The term *criminalist* was adopted until 1949, with the publication of *An Introduction to Criminalistics* by James Osterburg.

crime laboratory had civil service position titles of criminologist. It remained for James P. Osterburg to publish "An Introduction to Criminalistics" in 1949, which marked the beginning of the usage of the terms in this country. "Crime Investigation" by Paul L. Kirk in 1953 closely followed and gave full meaning to "criminalistics."

Duayne Dillon, then Chief of the Criminalistics Laboratory for the Office of the Sheriff-Coroner in Contra Costa County, California, wrote the foreword to the second printing of Osterburg's text (mentioned above in Bradford, 2007). There he shed light on the issue of precisely how a *criminalist* is defined, while crediting the authors of *An Introduction to Criminalistics* with helping engender community acceptance for the term (Dillon, 1972):

> The authors were not only responsible for introducing many of the principles and practices of Criminalistics in an organized manner, but were a prime factor in the subsequent acceptance of the term "criminalistics" to describe the profession engaged in the examination, evaluation, and interpretation of physical evidence.

Many forensic science authors have actually credited the formulation of modern criminalistics as a discipline to the Austrian Jurist and Professor of Criminology Dr. Hans Gross. This because he coined the term *Kriminalistik,* from which the terms *criminalistics* and *criminalist* were derived (Chisum and Turvey, 2011; DeForest, Gaennslen, and Lee, 1983; Inman and Rudin, 1999; and Turner, 1995).

The term *Kriminalistic* translates literally from Austrian-German to English as *Criminology.* Moreover, a *Kriminalist* was a reference to a generalist who studied the causes of crime; the behaviors and motives of criminals; and the scientific methods of their identification, apprehension, and prosecution (Gross, 1906). The term was intended to be inclusive of police officers, investigators, crime lab personnel, forensic pathologists, and even forensic psychologists—anyone involved in the practice of applying criminology to casework.

Regardless of the original definition and intent, the term *criminalistics* was borrowed from the work of Dr. Hans Gross in the late 1940s. The reason was that the burgeoning forensic science community in the United States needed a way to conceptually separate "criminologists" working in police crime laboratories from the future police officers and social scientists studying in criminology, criminal justice, and police science programs at colleges and universities (Morn, 1995). The aim was to help professionalize the scientific examination and interpretation of physical evidence with specific principles and practice borrowed from criminology as well as the natural sciences (Morn, 1995). Forensic scientists began referring to themselves as criminalists and to their work as criminalistics (O'Hara and Osterburg, 1972). This rebranding was widely accepted within the police lab community, as evidenced by the literature and the formation of associated professional organizations, including the California Association of Criminalists (CAC, 2011).

"REAL" FORENSIC SCIENTISTS

The majority of full-time forensic science practitioners in the United States work for law enforcement agencies or in publicly funded government crime labs, providing their services exclusively to law enforcement and the prosecution

(Thornton and Peterson, 2007). As explained in the NAS Report[1] (Edwards and Gotsonis, 2009; p. 36):

> According to a 2005 census by the Bureau of Justice Statistics (BJS), 389 publicly funded forensic crime laboratories were operating in the United States in 2005: These included 210 state or regional laboratories, 84 county laboratories, 62 municipal laboratories, and 33 federal laboratories, and they received evidence from nearly 2.7 million criminal cases. These laboratories are staffed by individuals with a wide range of training and expertise, from scientists with Ph.D.s to technicians who have been trained largely on the job. No data are available on the size and depth of the private forensic laboratories, except for private DNA laboratories.

However, because of the current fractured state and the past "rebranding" of the forensic sciences, there is much confusion over who precisely the "real" forensic scientists are—and who they are not (Inman and Rudin, 1999). This confusion exists within the forensic science community, and among those operating in the criminal justice system, which has misinformed the media and the general public. An assessment of the discontinuity evident within the forensic science community is offered in Edwards and Gotsonis (2009; pp. 6–7):

> The term "forensic science" encompasses a broad range of forensic disciplines, each with its own set of technologies and practices. In other words, there is wide variability across forensic science disciplines with regard to techniques, methodologies, reliability, types and numbers of potential errors, research, general acceptability, and published material. Some of the forensic science disciplines are laboratory based (e.g., nuclear and mitochondrial DNA analysis, toxicology and drug analysis); others are based on expert interpretation of observed patterns (e.g., fingerprints, writing samples, toolmarks, bite marks, and specimens such as hair). The "forensic science community," in turn, consists of a host of practitioners, including scientists (some with advanced degrees) in the fields of chemistry, biochemistry, biology, and medicine; laboratory technicians; crime scene investigators; and law enforcement officers. There are very important differences, however, between forensic laboratory work and crime scene investigations.

---

[1]The NAS Report is mentioned in Chapter 1, "Introduction," and will be discussed more extensively in future chapters, including Chapter 10, "Conclusions and Recommendations."

Furthermore (p. 36):

> Not all forensic services are performed in traditional crime laboratories by trained forensic scientists. Some forensic tests might be conducted by a sworn law enforcement officer with no scientific training or credentials, other than experience. In smaller jurisdictions, members of the local police or sheriff's department might conduct the analyses of evidence, such as latent print examinations and footwear comparisons.

The NAS Report ultimately concludes that the forensic science community is poorly focused and badly fragmented, with no clear practice standards, consistent terminology, or standardized means of practitioner certification. That is to say, forensic science is not always practiced in a laboratory; forensic science is not always practiced by someone working for law enforcement; and forensic science is not always practiced by scientists.

At this point, it is also necessary to recognize the distinction that must be made between *scientists* and *technician practitioners* of forensic science. The NAS Report goes out of its way to explain (Edwards and Gotsonis, 2009; p. 7):

> There are also sharp distinctions between forensic practitioners who have been trained in chemistry, biochemistry, biology, and medicine (and who bring these disciplines to bear in their work) and technicians who lend support to forensic science enterprises.

The greatest distinction between the forensic scientist and the forensic technician is that of testing versus interpretation (Edwards and Gotsonis, 2009; pp. 59–60):

> Because of the distinctly different professional tracks within larger laboratories, for example, technicians perform tests with defined protocols, and credentialed scientists conduct specialized testing and interpretation. Unlike many other professions, the forensic science disciplines have no organized control over entry into the profession, such as by degree, boards or exams, or licensure.... Control mechanisms traditionally have been held through employment and job function.

The contrast between technician and scientist is at once subtle and tremendous. Adapted from Chisum and Turvey (2006, pp. xvi–xvii): A *technician* is trained in specific procedures that have been learned by routine or repetition. A forensic technician is trained in specific procedures related to collecting and even testing physical evidence found at crime scenes. This is often accomplished without any need for employing or understanding the scientific method and the limits of forensic science. This term describes police technicians documenting crime scenes and collecting evidence, and many of the forensic personnel working in government crime labs performing instrumental analysis. Conversely, a *scientist* is someone who possesses an academic and clinical understanding of the scientific method and has the analytical dexterity to construct experiments that will generate the empirical reality which science mandates. A *forensic scientist* is educated and trained to examine and determine the meaning of physical evidence in accordance with the established limits of forensic science, with the expectation of presenting his or her findings as evidence under oath.

Both forensic technicians and forensic scientists are considered forensic examiners, and as such both are included in the present study (in the present study *n* = 100; this includes 53 laboratory criminalists,[2] 15 forensic technicians,[3] 7 law enforcement technicians, 23 medicolegal examiners, and 2 digital evidence examiners; see Chapter 8, "Forensic Fraud, 2000–2010: Data and Frequency," for descriptive detail).

THE ROLE OF FORENSIC EXAMINATIONS

When there is a criminal complaint, law enforcement investigators are responsible for conducting the corresponding criminal investigation. This involves gathering evidence of all kinds, interviewing witnesses, and developing potential suspects. As explained in Savino and Turvey (2011; pp. 88–89): "[R]esponding law enforcement agencies have a duty of care—an obligation to be competent custodians of the criminal investigations they initiate and any evidence that supports or refutes allegations of criminal activity against accused suspects." This implies a duty of care that should include determining what happened, whether or not a crime has actually taken place, eliminating any suspects, and identifying and arresting any criminal perpetrators (Kappeler, 2006; SATF, 2009).

Forensic examiners, however, are responsible for corresponding scientific investigations—acting as an objective foil to any case theories that might arise from any source. The unique role of the forensic examiner is ultimately that of an educator to decision makers in the justice system, including investigators, attorneys, judges, and juries. Thornton and Peterson (2007) describe the forensic examiner as a "handmaiden of the law," while recognizing the potential for conflict between the goals of science and the criminal justice system (p. 4): "Forensic science is science exercised on behalf of the law in the just resolution

---

[2]A laboratory criminalist is a particular type of forensic scientist that is trained to examine physical evidence and interpret its meaning (see Chisum and Turvey, 2011).
[3]A forensic technician is trained to collect or test physical evidence using rote instrumentation, but generally lacks the scientific education and training to perform examinations and interpretations on his or her own (see Chisum and Turvey, 2011).

of conflict. It is therefore expected to be the handmaiden of the law, but at the same time this expectation may very well be the marina from which is launched the tension that exists between the two disciplines."

While the justice system necessarily sets two legal sides against each other, objective examiners are not meant to take up the cause of either. In fact, their only theoretical value to the legal process is with respect to their objectivity. Forensic examiners are ostensibly employed only because of their oath to advocate for the evidence and its dispassionate interpretation—nothing more. They must be capable of demonstrating that they have no emotional, professional, or financial stake in the outcome. In other words, they cannot be paid to guarantee findings or testimony favorable to their employer, nor can their advancement be connected to the success of one party over another. This is separate from being compensated for time spent performing analysis, writing reports, and giving testimony.

It should also be stressed that forensic examiners are not intended to be decision makers in the justice system—despite some misinformed fictional portrayals to the contrary. They do not decide guilt or innocence, they do not rule on the admissibility of evidence in court proceedings, and they do not typically have the power to make arrests. This is intentional, as the goals of the forensic examiner with respect to explaining the strengths and limits of the evidence must remain ideologically separate from such extraneous efforts to maintain any semblance of impartiality.

CARDINAL TRAITS OF THE FORENSIC EXAMINER

In the preceding sections of this chapter, there was some discussion regarding the cardinal traits of forensic examiners. They are in essence the traits of any scientist—those necessary for maintaining scientific integrity (Gardenier, 2011; Jette, 2005; NAS, 2002 and 2009). Forensic examiners must develop, maintain, and demonstrate *impartiality, knowledge of scientific methodology*, and the *employment of scientific methodology* in their work. Additionally, there is the corresponding need for *maintaining transparency of methods* so that others may peer review any findings that are offered. These are discussed further in Chapter 5, "Fraud and Scientific Culture."

However, forensic examiners are separated from other scientists by the likelihood that they will be called upon to present and explain their findings, under oath, in a court of law. Subsequently, they will be asked to explain how their findings were derived and what they mean. As provided in Thornton and Peterson (2007; p. 4):

> What then, of the forensic scientist? The single feature that distinguishes forensic scientists from any other scientist is the expectation that they will appear in court and testify to their findings and offer an opinion as to the significance of those findings. The

forensic scientist will, or should, testify not only to what things are, but to what things mean.

Consequently, the *anticipation of sworn expert testimony* and the *offering of sworn expert testimony* are distinctive traits possessed by the forensic examiner. The ability to provide sworn expert testimony being integral to forensic examinations, a *trustworthy character* requirement is also presumptively invoked. This is true for the majority of those working in the justice system. For example, the State Attorney General's "California Crime Laboratory Review Task Force" reports on the necessity of employment disqualifiers related to criminal history and character (CCLRTF, 2009; p. 25):

> …the Task Force recognizes that background checks are necessary because of the sensitive and critical role criminalists play in the criminal justice system. Mistakes or lack of professional standards by forensics professionals can lead, in a worst-case scenario, to wrongful convictions. The Task Force suggests that candidates, as well as those still in college who wish to become forensic scientists, be better informed that any association with criminal activity or lack of personal responsibility could preclude them from future employment in a crime lab.

Forensic examiners of every kind, like members of law enforcement, must achieve and maintain the trust of the court in order to be allowed the privilege of giving sworn testimony. This includes avoiding activities or affiliations that evidence criminality; a propensity for dishonesty; or poor character—whether past or present. If it can be shown that a forensic examiner cannot be taken at his or her word, or that he or she has a propensity for criminal activity, then the court may exclude that examiner's testimony.

A TALE OF TWO CULTURES

In this chapter, the role of forensic examiners, and their cardinal traits, have been discussed with respect to satisfying ideal requirements within the justice system. The reality, however, is much different. The occupational culture of the forensic examiner is not framed by a single cohesive group with uniform professional or scientific values. As already suggested, it is routinely suffused with conflicted goals, directives, and expectations. Specifically, the objective and impartial creed of forensic examiners is often at odds with the culture, code, and conduct engendered by the organizations that tend to employ them.

Police crime laboratories have traditionally employed the majority of forensic scientists, primarily because of law enforcement dominion over the crime scene and a subsequent responsibility for physical evidence collection and testing (DeForest, 2005; O'Hara and Osterburg, 1972; Sullivan, 1977; Thornton and Peterson, 2007; and Turner, 1995). Despite the growth of private forensic laboratories, the regular and increased outsourcing of government forensic services to the private sector (Durose, 2008; Peterson and Hickman, 2005), and some court-mandated funding for independent forensic examinations brought about by *Ake v. Oklahoma* (1985) and its progeny, this occupational dominance remains (Durose, 2008; Edwards and Gotsonis, 2009). Some explication is necessary.

In the first chapter of this work, the publication of the National Academy of Sciences Report on forensic science (aka the NAS Report; Edwards and Gotsonis, 2009) was referenced with respect to demonstrating the need for the present research. Among the findings in this watershed evaluation of the forensic sciences was the resolution that a true scientific culture cannot develop or even exist subordinate to a law enforcement agency. The NAS Report explains that the resulting conflicts are fiscal, organizational, and cultural—combining to result in the wrong kind of pressure placed on the forensic examiner (Edwards and Gotsonis, 2009; pp. 23–24):

> Scientific and medical assessment conducted in forensic investigations should be independent of law enforcement efforts either to prosecute criminal suspects or even to determine whether a criminal act has indeed been committed. Administratively, this means that forensic scientists should function independently of law enforcement administrators. The best science is conducted in a scientific setting as opposed to a law enforcement setting. Because forensic scientists often are driven in their work by a need to answer a particular question related to the issues of a particular case, they sometimes face pressure to sacrifice appropriate methodology for the sake of expediency.

Pressure to achieve results is nothing new in scientific endeavor; however, the context is quite different for forensic examiners. As already discussed, they are often working in a pro law enforcement environment that is at odds with, and even hostile toward, their scientific mandate. Moreover, strong evidence has emerged over the past two decades revealing consistent and inappropriate influence exerted by the U.S. Department of Justice, and the FBI specifically, over the forensic science community (Edwards and Gotsonis, 2009; Hsu, Jenkins, and Mellnick, 2012; and Moore, 2009).[4] In any case, when contradictory

---

[4]The FBI crime laboratory holds itself out as the premier forensic laboratory in the United States, offering services of every kind to domestic law enforcement agencies and others around the world. It is also the largest crime laboratory in the United States, "with some 500 scientific experts and special agents working in a state-of-the-art facility in rural Virginia, traveling the world over on assignment and providing forensic exams, technical support, expert witness testimony, and advanced training to Bureau personnel and partners around the globe" (FBI, 2012). Furthermore, it is responsible for maintaining a number of national forensic databases, including those related to fingerprints and DNA. As will be discussed, it also has a history of fraud and scandal stretching from the mid-1990s to the present day.

cultural directives strain the work of the forensic examiner, the dominant (and controlling) culture is best situated to prevail.

The NAS Report was not the first to raise this issue, or to recommend cultural separation. Concerns about the inappropriate influence of law enforcement culture over the forensic examiners that they employ, focusing on their contradictory values and missions, have also been outlined in works such as Chisum and Turvey (2006 and 2011); Cooley (2004); Findley (2008); Giannelli (1997); Kirk and Bradford (1965); Risinger et al. (2002 and 2003); and Starrs (1993). Until very recently, however, the precise nature and consequences of any inappropriate influences that law enforcement exerts over forensic practice have been unexamined.

SUMMARY

Forensic examiners are meant to be objective and impartial scientific instruments—for use in educating investigative and then legal proceedings. This places upon them the requirement that they conduct themselves in such a manner as to preserve scientific integrity while also maintaining stringent personal ethics. However, the majority of forensic examiners work for law enforcement or government agencies on behalf of the police and prosecution. This work arrangement, which arises from the peculiar evolution of forensic science in tandem with law enforcement, creates competing cultural pressures that have been acknowledged but remain uncritically unexamined in the professional forensic literature until recently.

CHAPTER 4

Fraud in Law Enforcement Culture

"We would like, in an ideal world, to see every applicant with a clean record, but obviously that's not reality. I don't think you'll find any departments who hire only applicants with squeaky-clean records."

Lt. Elder Dancy
City of Atlanta Police Dept.
Recruitment Unit

In Chapter 2, "Occupational Fraud," we explored the literature related to the investigation and examination of general occupational fraud. This body of research focuses almost entirely on the study of financially motivated crimes. It also concerns itself chiefly with the private sector and not acts of fraud committed by those working for the government. However, the underlying concepts and theories were applicable to the cases associated with the current research. In Chapter 3, "Forensic Science: A Primer," we learned of the role that forensic science is intended to play in the justice system, as well as the cultural challenges that practicing forensic scientists can face.

This chapter begins a more specific exploration of the literature associated with forensic fraud. Applying a sociological approach, and the theory of *Differential Association* (Sutherland and Cressey, 1966), we are admonished to accept up front that there is a "relationship between social and cultural conditions and crime" (Kennedy and Kennedy, 1972; p. 45). Specifically, we must accept that individuals develop criminal patterns in some part because they are socialized to do so by their interactions with other members of their primary group (Fitch, 2011; Matsueda, 2006; and Sutherland and Cressey, 1966). An extension of Differential Association, *Social Learning Theory* holds that "peer associations, attitudes, reinforcement, and modeling are predictors of delinquency and crime in general" (Chappell and Piquero, 2004; p. 89). These well-regarded criminological theories offer a useful perspective for understanding the context of fraud committed by forensic scientists, and are also necessary for explaining the cultural attitudes that shape them.

45

Forensic Fraud. http://dx.doi.org/10.1016/B978-0-12-408073-7.00004-5

LAW ENFORCEMENT DUTIES AND OBLIGATIONS

Law enforcement is the branch of the criminal justice system that is directly responsible for reported crime (Kappeler, 2006; Sullivan, 1977; and Turvey and Petherick, 2010). It is composed of various government agencies that are tasked with preventing crime, responding to criminal complaints, and recovering property within established jurisdictions (Bopp and Schultz, 1972). Law enforcement agents are also charged with keeping the peace, protecting the citizenry, and representing justice within a community (Kappeler, 2006; Kleinig, 1996; and Wolfe and Picquero, 2011).

Law enforcement agencies have a duty to investigate criminal complaints, establish the facts, and determine whether a crime has actually been committed (Bopp and Schultz, 1972; Kappeler, 2006; SATF, 2009; and Savino and Turvey, 2011). When their agents believe that a crime has been committed, they also have a related obligation to eliminate, identify, and apprehend any suspects (Bopp and Schultz, 1972; Kleinig, 1996). As explained in Sullivan (1977, p. 149): "It is the job of the police to enforce the law. Thus, officers must remember that they are primarily fact-finders for their department and have no authority or control over the judicial or legislative branches of government."

Specific enforcement obligations and duties are a matter of individual agency policy as well as local statute (e.g., *dereliction of duty*, *professional misconduct*, and *excessive force* regulations; *negligent failure to supervise* or *investigate* torts; and state penal codes prescribing law enforcement exemptions; see generally Bopp and Schultz, 1972; Hansen and Culley, 1973; Kappeler, 2006; Kleinig, 1996; and Vaughn, Cooper, and del Carmen, 2001). These duties, and related principles, are often a feature of the sworn oaths or pledges that officers must take when receiving their police credentials. They generally relate to maintaining professional integrity, protecting citizens and property, faithfully enforcing the laws of their state, and upholding the Constitution of the United States (Bopp and Schultz, 1972; IACP, 2011; Kleinig, 1996; Shane, 2010; and Stout, 2011). Specific values, missions, or creeds can be found on the backside of an officer's credentials, on the side of an officer's patrol car, or on the department's website.

LAW ENFORCEMENT DISCRETION AND INTEGRITY

In order to do their work, law enforcement agents, it is understood, will need to violate some of the rules and laws that the rest of us must abide, including those related to traffic ordinances, privacy, firearms possession/use, property seizure, the use of coercive force, and the use of lethal force (Bopp and Schultz, 1972; Brennan et al., 2009; Chappell and Piquero, 2004; Kleinig, 1996; Leonard, 1969; and Marche, 2009). In other words, the police must sometimes break the law in order to uphold it. They are therefore exempt from numerous legal conventions (prescribed by specific circumstances) and enjoy the privilege of exercising authority over regular citizens, under the aegis that they are engaged in an official capacity (Brennan et al., 2009; Chappell and Piquero, 2004; Kleinig, 1996; and Waddington, 1999).

This means that those employed by law enforcement agencies are required to walk a fine line while discharging their duties. On one hand, they must strive to represent law and justice to the community through honest, fair, and professional conduct. On the other hand, they are uniquely permitted to break laws that regular citizens are required to uphold. As explained in Waddington (1999; p. 287): "The notion that the police possess a distinctive occupation sub-culture … derives from the discovery that police work is rarely guided by legal precepts … police officers exercise extensive discretion in how they enforce the law." Ideally, this requires the ability to exercise discretion without a great deal of direct supervision while consistently refusing endless opportunities to engage in graft and corruption (Chappell and Piquero, 2004; Hickman et al., 2001; Kleinig, 1996; Klockars et al., 2000; Seron, Pereira, and Kovath, 2004; and Westmarland, 2005).

Exercising the proper discretion under these kinds of conditions is key to maintaining public confidence in law enforcement integrity. Law enforcement agencies are therefore best served by the selection and employment of only the highest quality applicants (Brennan et al., 2009; Vollmer, 1971). In part, this means that they are admonished to "strive to recruit, hire, and train only those who demonstrate strong moral values before they enter the academy" (Fitch, 2011; p. 1).

Unfortunately, the literature makes it clear that the selection of even the best candidates, with the least predisposition for criminality, is insufficient to prevent corruption in law enforcement. As explained in Marche (2009; p. 463): "…there is no evidence to support the traditional theory that police agency corruption is attributable to the 'individual bad-apple.' Independent of other factors, the present analysis shows that police culture fosters corruption." This is a refutation of what is referred to as *Bad Apple Theory* (BAT)—the notion that corruption is attributable to isolated individuals acting against the values and norms of a group.

Further refutation of BAT is found in a history of research demonstrating that the authority and discretion afforded to law enforcement agencies promotes and nurtures systemic corruption within the ranks, especially when relatively low levels of dishonesty are tolerated or rationalized by supervisors (Benoit and Dubra, 2004; Benson, 1988; Chappell and Piquero, 2004; Ivkovic, 2003; Johnson and Cox, 2005; Kleinig, 1996; Klockars, 1984; Klockars, Ivkovic, and Haberfeld, 2005; Klockars et al., 2000; McCormack, 1996; and Rothwell and

Baldwin, 2007). This body of research supports the view that police culture creates opportunities and provides justifications for corruption. At the same time, it also tolerates and in many instances defends it.

CARDINAL TRAITS OF LAW ENFORCEMENT CULTURE

The literature provides numerous studies on the cardinal traits of law enforcement culture. While this body of research has not identified a universal police culture, there are reoccurring themes and elements. Though often developed to protect an agency and its members, many if not most of these traits can be seen as eventual facilitators of corruption.

Waddington (1999) describes law enforcement as a canteen or clannish sub-culture, explaining (p. 287): "The core referents of 'police sub-culture' are clear enough: its sense of mission; the desire for action and excitement, especially the glorification of violence; an Us/Them division of the social world with in-group isolation and solidarity on the one hand, and racist components on the other; its authoritarian conservatism; and its suspicion and cynicism, especially towards the law and legal procedures." This is reinforced by the research presented in Terrill, Paoline, and Manning (2003), that occupational pressure, anxiety, and strain "produce two defining outcomes of police culture—isolation and group loyalty"(p. 1006). Paoline (2004) goes on to report that law enforcement (p. 207) "attitudes, values, and norms include a distrust and suspiciousness of citizens and a prescription to assess people and situations in terms of their potential threat (i.e., maintaining the edge), a lay-low or cover-your-ass orientation to police work that would discourage the initiation of contacts with citizens and supervisors, a strong emphasis on the law enforcement elements of the police role, a we-versus-they attitude toward citizens, and the norm of loyalty to the peer group." Cancino and Enriquez (2004) similarly note the following as central traits: the employment of "street justice," secrecy, solidarity, and the acceptance of peer-retaliation for violating any of these. Wolfe and Picquero (2011) agree, providing that (p. 334) "[p]olicing is characterized by a close-knit subculture because the 'unique demands that are placed on police officers, such as the threat of danger as well as scrutiny by the public, generate a tightly woven environment conducive to the development of feelings of loyalty' (Skolnick, 2005, p. 302)."

Along these same lines, Benson (2001) posits that machismo, militarism, racism, and a code of silence are primary elements of law enforcement culture, reporting (pp. 685–686): "Instead of acting upon the extensive evidence of differences between men and women police—and recruiting and promoting more women—police departments nationwide are bastions of … 'open sex discrimination and sexual harassment' and negative attitudes toward female officers." This is expounded by research presented in Garcia (2005), which explains that law enforcement culture emphasizes crime fighting, force, and masculinity while at the same time devaluing its internal social service functions that are associated with femininity. See also Benson (2001), reporting that (pp. 682–683):

> Machismo, or what some have called hypermasculinity, is the value system that celebrates male physical strength, aggression, violence, competition, and dominance. It denigrates the lack of these qualities as weak, female behavior....
>
> The practical results of this police machismo are that male officers get themselves involved in hostile confrontations with the public, use of excessive force, shootings, drug dealing, and apparently, as we see now in the Rampart scandal, framing of suspects through deceit and lies.

This issue was also explored in research presented by Harris (2000), which revealed that men in law enforcement culture experience intense pressure not to be perceived as feminine or homosexual, and that violence and aggression are the means used to assert and maintain a strong male identity.

Based on the body of literature referenced in this section, the reoccurring trait-themes in law enforcement culture identified by this researcher include

1. A "noble cause" belief system
2. Professional identity attached to authoritative/coercive control of citizens
3. Professional identity attached to masculinity and aggression, to the point of open discrimination and harassment within law enforcement ranks
4. Solidarity/loyalty to the group
5. Fierce protection of group and co-worker image of integrity
6. Deception as a viable means to an end
7. Isolation/"Us versus Them" outlook/mistrust of outsiders
8. Cynicism and mistrust toward the law
9. Secrecy/"Code of Silence"/"The Blue Wall of Silence"
10. Punishment and ostracism for those who break the code

NOBLE CAUSE AND CORRUPTION

Law enforcement culture is defined by the belief that theirs is a noble cause. A feature of this belief is that a war against crime is currently being waged against particular evils or societal ills (e.g., drugs, terrorism, gang violence), and that those working for law enforcement are on the only good or moral side of the conflict. By extension, anyone not working with or supporting law enforcement is on the wrong side of the conflict, protecting or practicing evil.

Commitment to this noble cause means an absolute commitment to preventing illegal activity and apprehending criminal offenders, also referred to as "getting bad guys off the street" (Caldero and Crank, 2004; p. 29). As described in Garcia (2005; p. 68):

> The officer is expected to seek out situations where crimes can be detected and criminals apprehended. Accordingly, the good officer holds to the noble cause of fighting crime and helping the victim … and to an image of being adventurous and brave…. The good officer must carry a gun and handcuffs and "charge the tower" at the sight of crime. However, in the process of becoming a good officer and internalizing police culture, the good officer also becomes cynical and distrusting of the citizens he or she polices….

Dedication to the noble cause both inspires the values of law enforcement culture and acts as justification for individual officer decisions (Crank, Flaherty, and Giacomazzi, 2007).

Noble cause corruption, as it is termed, refers to corrupt or illegal acts committed by law enforcement in order to secure or maintain an arrest or conviction, or some other worthy end (Caldero and Crank, 2004; Crank, Flaherty, and Giacomazzi, 2007; Martinelli, 2006; Porter and Warrender, 2009). It reflects dilemmas faced by law enforcement agents in which they must (Crank, Flaherty, and Giacomazzi, 2007; p. 105) "select between competing ethics. They either selected the legal means, playing by society's rules even if sometimes that meant letting dangerous offenders go free, or they sought a good end: they acted to prevent truly dangerous offenders from committing additional crimes, however that end was accomplished."

The justification for noble cause corruption stems from the siege mentality of law enforcement officers who believe either they are at war or that their cause is particularly righteous. This is a learned belief system, and the corresponding illegal behavior must be culturally reinforced and molded through experience within the group culture (Sunhara, 2004). When law enforcement culture reinforces a model of ends justifying the means, noble cause corruption becomes the norm that every "good" officer or agent aspires to (in comportment with Social Learning Theory). This in turn mandates acceptance of and reliance upon "The Blue Wall of Silence" for both individual and organizational survival.

THE BLUE WALL OF SILENCE

The law enforcement "Code of Silence," aka the "Blue Wall of Silence," has long been a feature of the literature related to law enforcement corruption, as an international phenomenon (Chin and Wells, 1998; Cooper, 2009a; Knapp Commission, 1972; Koepke, 2000; Mollen, 1994; Rothwell and Baldwin, 2007;

Shockley-Eckles, 2011; Skolnick, 2002 and 2005; Wolfe and Picquero, 2011). It is described as (Chin and Wells, 1998; p. 238) "an unwritten code in many departments which prohibits disclosing perjury or other misconduct by fellow officers, or even testifying truthfully if the facts would implicate the conduct of a fellow officer." As explained further in Cooper (2009a; p. 7): "what many people know as the 'Code of Silence' or 'Blue Wall of Silence' merits concern. The police subculture is dominated by the Cop Code. Its foundational norm dictates that 'cops protect cops.'"

According to Koepke (2000), the culture of secrecy is transferred between law enforcement members, in accordance with Social Learning Theory, via overt peer pressure (pp. 214–215): "The Blue Wall of Silence is legendary among law enforcement officers and is arguably the strongest form of peer pressure. Because of the Blue Wall of Silence, police brutality and police perjury have been, and continue to be, protected and facilitated by the police culture."

This is echoed in Wolfe and Picquero (2011), who explain (p. 334): "Policing is characterized by a close-knit subculture because the 'unique demands that are placed on police officers, such as the threat of danger as well as scrutiny by the public, generate a tightly woven environment conducive to the development of feelings of loyalty' (Skolnick, 2005, p. 302). The code of silence, therefore, develops into a subcultural attitude on how one must behave to be perceived as a 'good' officer by peers."

Gottschalk (2011) describes the problem as systemic, with all police officers involved in some level of corruption by virtue of engaging in either culturally approved illegal practice or its concealment (p. 170): "The role of the police culture in terms of protection of each other reduces the likelihood of being caught for corruption. This is called the code, the code of silence, or the blue curtain, or the blue wall of silence—the informal prohibition in the occupational culture of policing against reporting the misconduct of fellow police officers."

Shockley-Eckles (2011) goes further, arguing that the culture of secrecy in law enforcement protects not only those members in an immediate employment environment, but also those that have "gone rogue," been forced out of an agency, and then relocated elsewhere (p. 292):

> Now referred to as The Blue Wall or The Thin Blue Line, the solidarity that defines police work is not without its critics and its proponents. Many in mainstream society view The Blue Wall as an impenetrable fortress whereby contemporary police officers protect their own— including those who engage in misconduct—beneath a cloak of secrecy....
>
> The question of significance for the research presented here thus becomes, how far does loyalty extend itself when those in law enforcement find themselves working alongside the officer whose history is one of misconduct in another jurisdiction?

A little-known practice among most in the general public, but one that affects all in law enforcement, is the *officer shuffle* (see Goldman 2003; and Goldman and Puro, 2001, 1987). As defined by Goldman (2003) and Goldman and Puro (2001, 1987), the officer shuffle refers to the ease with which disreputable officers move across jurisdictions, thus maintaining their police certification and continuing to serve in law enforcement. These officers, referred to as gypsy cops or rogue officers, place communities at risk while often tainting the image of all police.

Aptly named, the officer shuffle (see Goldman 2003; Goldman and Puro, 2001, 1987) perpetuates the transmission of police corruption and misconduct over time and through space.

All of this conforms with Wolfe and Picquero (2011), who explain (p. 334): "Research has shown that officers who adhere to the code of silence are less likely to report fellow officer excessive use of force or corruption … and more likely to commit perjury during a trial." Wolfe and Picquero (2011) further agree that the problem is cultural, and that individual officer corruption is a reflection of their associations and group perceptions, in alignment with Social Learning Theory (p. 347):

> …officers who associate with deviant peers are more likely to subscribe to the police subcultural belief that an officer should protect his or her colleagues regardless of allegations of misconduct. Furthermore, association with deviant officer peers places officers at increased risk to believe that violating suspect constitutional rights is required if one is to achieve justice and protect the public from harm. Conversely, officers adhere to the code of silence less strictly and have fewer beliefs that justify noble-cause corruption if they view their agency to behave in organizationally just ways. That is, as officers' perceptions of organizational justice increase, their level of attitudes favorable to the code of silence and noble-cause corruption is likely to decrease.

While there are many forms of law enforcement corruption, Gottschalk (2011; p. 170) found that the "Blue Wall of Silence" provided the most protection for those officers accepting "gratuities" or using "excessive force." These are among the most tolerated forms of misconduct in law enforcement culture. This is detailed by research prepared in Chappell and Piquero (2004; p. 90):

> …acceptance of meals and gifts is the most common and most extensive form of police corruption…. Many cities actually allow officers to accept free or discount meals. It is often accepted behavior when it is an act of gratitude toward the police, but sometimes the motive is to buy protection from the police. In other words, some businesses offer free items or services in expectation for quicker response times and extra protection from the police.

Not surprisingly, free coffee, meal discounts, and other small gifts are also the gateway through which otherwise lawful officers are initiated into other corrupt group practices (see Figure 4-1). This can be witnessed on a daily basis in just about every city around the country, at any eatery where multiple police units gather for a break or a meal. For example, both the *Denny's* and *Chick-Fil-A* restaurant chains offer a 50% discount to law enforcement for all meals, as do many donut and coffee shops; Denny's actually puts "law enforcement discount" on the receipt. Officers will enter such establishments wearing their uniforms, or show their police radios or badges conspicuously when plain clothed. All of this with the hope, and often the expectation, of receiving a "law enforcement discount." Discounted meals or drinks are actually bribes, enticing officers to show favor, to give special consideration and quicker response times, or merely for the security provided by their continual presence.

Once a law enforcement officer gives up his integrity in lock step with the other members of his group, no matter how small the enticement, the potential for future and more severe forms of corruption is increased. It also provides a motive for looking the other way when something more severe is witnessed involving fellow officers. While seeming minor to some, giving in to these kinds of initial temptations teaches the new officer to become morally and ethically malleable. From a public relations standpoint, accepting gifts and gratuities also reinforces the worst view of the police held by those that are successful with enticements: that the services of law enforcement are partially or otherwise for sale.

The "Blue Wall of Silence," or "Code of Silence," is a distinct feature of the institutional corruption bred into the pedigree of law enforcement culture. It pressures new officers into conformity by exploiting their commitment to group loyalty

FIGURE 4-1
Many 24-hour coffee and donut chains offer free coffee and donuts to law enforcement. These inducements can change the pattern of assigned patrol, and also reinforce the belief that law enforcement is for sale at a very cheap price.

and the threat of peer retaliation; it protects longstanding group members from exposure by ensuring that nobody talks to outsiders, and that "cops protect cops"; and it allows for the shuffling, or continued employment, of "gypsy cops" that would otherwise have been terminated or in extreme cases indicted on criminal charges. In essence, it makes those law enforcement officers who abide into liars, by what they either report or fail to report with respect to corrupt activity.

THE USE OF DECEPTION

When agents of law enforcement lack sufficiently reliable evidence to lawfully arrest a prime suspect in a criminal investigation, they tend to focus their efforts on obtaining a confession (Magid, 2001; Thomas, 2007). One means of obtaining a confession is through the use of deception. The courts tend to have a variable yet generally permissive attitude toward the police use of deception to gain inculpatory evidence from criminal suspects—to include undercover work and ploys where false witness statements, false co-conspirator statements, and fabricated evidence are referenced or presented during interrogations (Kassin et al., 2010). Consequently, pretense, trickery, and lies are standard instruments found in many police toolkits.

There are limits set on the acceptable use of deceptive methods, generally established by state laws and departmental policy. However, some criminal justice commentators argue that deception, and outright lying, is an integral feature of law enforcement culture. One overall view is presented in Slobogin (1997), which offers a continuum of falsity that runs from justifiable to inexcusable (pp. 775–776):

> Many police, like many other people, lie occasionally, and some police, like some other people, lie routinely and pervasively. Police lie to protect innocent victims, as in hostage situations, and they tell "placebo lies" to assure or placate worried citizens. They tell lies to project nonexistent authority, and they lie to suspects in the hopes of gathering evidence of crime. They also lie under oath, to convict the guilty, protect the guilty, or frame the innocent.
>
> Some of these lies are justifiable. Some are reprehensible. Lying under oath is perjury and thus rarely permissible. On the other hand, lying that is necessary to save a life may not only be acceptable but is generally applauded (even if it constitutes perjury). Most types of police lies are of murkier morality, however.

A more chilling perspective on police deception is reported in the research compiled by Dorfman (1999; pp. 460–461):

> Police officers can be expected to omit, redact, and even lie on their police reports, sworn or unsworn; they will conceal or misrepresent

to cover up corruption and brutality; they are trained to deceive citizens during investigations as part of good police practice; they will obscure facts, and even lie, to cover up the misconduct of fellow officers. Additionally, command practice and policy gives officers every incentive to lie to cover for lack of productivity or to aggrandize themselves for recognition and promotion. And yes, police officers will commit perjury in our courts of law.

In any case, it is generally agreed that there must be clearly defined limits set against the use of deception-based police tactics, given the tremendous power that agents of the government wield (Dorfman, 1999; Kassin et al., 2010; Magid, 2001; and Thomas, 2007). However, unless there are equally clear penalties associated with violations of those limits, it seems unlikely that longstanding attitudes toward the use of deception will be changed.

Consider the following case example of police deception gone too far (repeatedly and without consequences).

MATTHEW CHRISTIAN, DETECTIVE

San Jose Police Department

This case was uncovered during the course of data-gathering efforts described in Chapter 8, "Forensic Fraud, 2000–2010: Data and Frequency." It involves the use of deception by a police detective during the course of a suspect interrogation. As reported in Griffy (2007a), Matthew Christian, a detective with the San Jose Police Department in California, fabricated a report from the district attorney's crime lab (the regional crime lab is a division of the district attorney's office: "The Santa Clara County District Attorney's Criminalistics Laboratory"). Det. Christian used the official crime lab seal to construct the fake report, and he also invented a false criminalist's name to "confirm" the presence of semen on a blanket related to an alleged sex crime. He then used this "report" as evidence during a suspect interview to gain an inculpatory statement.

Det. Christian testified later that he forgot about his deception when he put the "ruse report" into his case file alongside a real lab report that contradicted it. The district attorney proceeded to trial thinking she had hard physical evidence of the defendant's guilt—denying several defense requests inquiring after the contradictory lab results provided in pretrial discovery. When asked about it on the stand during a preliminary hearing, Det. Christian falsely testified as though the fake lab report and fake criminalist were real—as though

the laboratory findings had actually been inculpatory. The nonexistent criminalist was even placed on the district attorney's witness list.

With trial approaching, defense counsel was able to speak directly with the crime lab, and the scope of the detective's deception was revealed. This information was forwarded to the district attorney's office, which had yet to contact their lab and verify the report. In December of 2006, all charges were dropped against the accused. However, the use of false laboratory reports remains standard practice for the San Jose Police Department.[1]

This case involves a police detective fabricating a false lab report regarding physical evidence to obtain a suspect confession within the time frame parameters set for the present study. However, he was not employed as a forensic examiner in any capacity. Consequently, the data from this case was necessarily excluded from the present study. Specific criteria for inclusion in the present study are discussed in Chapter 8.

---

[1]In 1990, the same police department had been warned by the judiciary to cease the practice of creating phony lab reports. However, in 2002, "detective Juan Serrano [of the San Jose Police Department] described the use of ruse crime lab reports as 'standard procedure' at that time" (Griffy, 2007b).

INTERNAL TOLERANCE FOR CRIMINALITY

The hiring and retention practices of many law enforcement agencies suggest that there is an internal tolerance for some level of overt criminality in the culture. That is to say, being convicted of a crime does not always result in an automatic prohibition from law enforcement employment. Nor is termination from law enforcement employment automatic when an officer is arrested, convicted of crime, or is proved to have given false testimony (Spector, 2008).

First, many police agencies openly acknowledge the fact that they hire recruits with criminal records; however, they claim to avoid hiring those with felony convictions.

Consider the State of Georgia. Approximately one-third of police recruits out of the city of Atlanta have criminal records, and more than half have admitted to drug use. As reported in Eberly (2008):

> More than one-third of recent Atlanta Police Academy graduates have been arrested or cited for a crime, according to a review of their job applications. The arrests ranged from minor offenses such as shoplifting to violent charges including assault. More than one-third of the officers had been rejected by other law enforcement agencies, and more than half of the recruits admitted using marijuana.

A further investigation of state records revealed 1,384 officers with arrests and convictions for serious offenses that also remained certified to practice law enforcement with the Georgia Peace Officer Standards and Training Council (POST); many were still on active duty with police agencies (Moore, 2008). Law enforcement spokespersons in Atlanta cited shrinking budgets and fierce competition with other police agencies for the need to relax hiring standards, but also explained that it was common for many law enforcement agencies to hire applicants with misdemeanor convictions (Eberly, 2008).

Consider also the City of Milwaukee, Wisconsin. Currently, the City of Milwaukee Police Department allows the hiring of candidates with up to four misdemeanor convictions and two drunken driving offenses (Wooten, 2007). However, in responding to a Freedom of Information Request, the city refused to release the exact number of officers with criminal convictions, saying that such an effort would be too burdensome (Wooten, 2007). Despite a promise to make this data publicly available, the Milwaukee Fire and Police Commission has yet to do so (Barton, 2011).

Second, many police agencies find ways to retain brother officers convicted of fraud, false statements, and even violent crimes rather than fire them.

Consider the case of *U.S. v. Hayes* (2009). This litigation arose from federal legislation enacted in 1996: *Possession of Firearm After Conviction of Misdemeanor Crime of Domestic Violence, 18 U.S.C. §922(g)(9):* "As of September 30, 1996, it is illegal to possess a firearm after conviction of a misdemeanor crime of domestic violence. This prohibition applies to persons convicted of such misdemeanors at any time, even if the conviction occurred prior to the new law's effective date. A qualifying misdemeanor domestic violence crime must have as an element the use or attempted use of physical force or the threatened use of a deadly weapon."

Since that time, some law enforcement defendants have attempted to get around the consequences of this legislation by pleading "down to a plain simple assault not *called* domestic violence" (Rider, 2010), when charged with offenses that might cause them to lose their right to carry a firearm—and any related employment. A simple assault, for example, is a criminal charge without the predicate "domestic" descriptor.

Additionally, a percentage of law enforcement officers, and other government employees, faced the possibility of retroactively losing their guns and jobs in the resulting fallout from the 1996 legislation. These were individuals who had been convicted of violent offenses against their intimate partners, but not subsequently terminated by their law enforcement employers (May, 2005). Immediate reaction to the legislation by those in the law enforcement community included claims that it was unfair, as reported in Rodriquez (1997):

> A new federal law that makes it illegal for anyone convicted of domestic violence to carry a gun is threatening the jobs of dozens of police officers around the country.
>   Officers in Texas, Colorado, California, Minnesota and Michigan have been re-assigned or put on administrative leave as a result of their past arrests. The numbers are growing, and those affected are claiming the law is unfair and even unconstitutional.

Others in law enforcement have expressed gratitude that the existence of convicted domestic violence offenders among the ranks of law enforcement has been made an issue by the new legislation, considering such violations a firing offense (Davidow and Teichroeb, 2003).

In any case, *Hayes*, a ruling by the U.S. Supreme Court, closes any perceptual loophole: it holds that a domestic relationship need not be a consideration in the specific criminal conviction; only the actual relationship between the victim and the offender matters. If anyone is convicted of any crime that involves violence against a domestic partner, whether it is a misdemeanor or a felony, that person is banned from carrying a firearm by federal law. If one's profession requires carrying a firearm, then one must find other employment if so convicted. It remains to be seen whether law enforcement agencies will find a new loophole in this recent ruling to further retain those personnel with related convictions.

Consider the actions of the New Haven Police Department in the case of Police Officer Sam Streater, as reported in Kaempffer (2009). In this case out of Connecticut, Officer Streater was arrested and convicted of soliciting a known prostitute, Vanessa DiVerniero, by paying her $20 to have sex with him in his car while off duty. He was caught by a police sting operation being run in the neighborhood, and made false statements to fellow officers about his activities during the investigation. While he was suspended without pay for two weeks, he was not terminated. The New Haven Police Department made it clear that this is typical of how they handle such offenses, even when they involve law enforcement personnel (Kaempffer, 2009).

Consider that also, until recently, the Los Angeles County Sheriff's Office employed a more creative solution when sworn personnel engaged in criminal activity: law enforcement offenders were often sent to work in the Los Angeles County Jail. As explained in Leonard and Faturechi (2011): "For years, the department transferred problem deputies to the system's lockups as a way of keeping them from the public. Other deputies were allowed to remain working in the jails after being convicted of crimes or found guilty of serious misconduct." This included deputies with convictions related to fraud, loan sharking, death threats, assault, beating inmates, smuggling contraband into the jail, and falsified reports (Leonard and Faturechi, 2011).

Finally, consider the case of Ross Mirkarimi, the Sheriff of San Francisco (see Figures 4-2 and 4-3). He was recently convicted of a domestic violence offense involving his wife, a Venezuelan actress; however, he subsequently refused to resign from office and announced plans to run for re-election (Elias, 2012). As of this writing, Mirkarimi is serving three years' probation while still holding office, and the civilian Mayor of San Francisco suspended Sheriff Mirkarimi to pursue administrative charges of official misconduct. However, after an Ethics Commission Hearing, the board of supervisors reinstated Mirkarimi as sheriff despite his criminal conviction.

A tradition of hiring and retaining those with a criminal background, and failing to terminate members convicted of a crime subsequent to hiring, suggests some tolerance for criminality within the culture of law enforcement. This practice, often a violation of policy and the law, undermines the overall credibility of law enforcement agencies and the reputations of all those they employ. Some law enforcement agencies agree, including those in Illinois, as explained in Barton (2011):

SAN FRANCISCO
POLICE DEPARTMENT
MUGSHOT PROFILE

NAME:	ROSS MIRKARIMI
AKA:	,
AKA:	,
MONIKER:	
SF#:	
JAIL #:	
BOOKING DATE:	Jan 13 2012 4:43PM
DATE OF BIRTH:	·1961
PLACE OF BIRTH:	
SOCIAL SECURITY #:	
CII#:	
CA DRIVERS LIC #:	

PHYSICAL DESCRIPTION

SEX:	MALE
RACE:	WHITE
HEIGHT:	6'00"

273.5

FIGURES 4-2 and 4-3
Ross Mirkarimi during questioning at his Ethics Commission hearing, held at San Francisco City Hall on Thursday June 28, 2012. He was subsequently reinstated as sheriff, despite his criminal conviction.

An officer who has been convicted of a crime can be rendered useless as a prosecution witness—especially if dishonesty is involved, said Kenosha County Assistant District Attorney Richard Ginkowski, who once worked as a police officer in Iowa. The defense can use that information to cast doubt on the cop's testimony.

"If an officer is caught lying, that dilutes their credibility in other cases and makes them less effective as an officer," he said. "That's a significant concern."

That's one reason departments in many other states, including Illinois, preclude people convicted of certain misdemeanors—generally involving deception, drugs and abusive behavior—from carrying a badge and a gun.

"It's just overwhelming how people in communities really do believe law enforcement officers have to be held to this standard," said Kevin McClain, executive director of the Illinois Law Enforcement Training and Standards Board. "People feel that police officers should be models in society."

Not only are people convicted of those types of crimes barred from being hired as Illinois officers—working officers who are convicted of those crimes are automatically decertified under state law, which means they immediately lose their jobs and can't be rehired, McClain said. Any officer who fails to notify the state of a conviction—either during the application process or after hiring—can be charged with a felony.

It should not need mention that there is also hypocrisy in the practice of policing the citizenry with convicted criminals; it violates the ideal of personal integrity that is held up as a necessary hiring mandate within the law enforcement literature already cited. It also further nurtures a culture of tolerance for corruption, in accordance with the tenets of Social Learning Theory.

FRAUD DIAMOND THEORY: ASSESSING COMMON FORMS OF LAW ENFORCEMENT FRAUD

Fraud Diamond Theory states that in order for an act of occupational or employment fraud to occur, there must be a convergence of four elements: offender *motivation (aka pressure or need), opportunity, rationalization,* and *individual capability.* With respect to law enforcement culture, the literature is clear that it provides each of these elements to its members even when initially absent in a new recruit. In this section we review two of the most prevalent forms of law enforcement fraud in order to assess whether this model holds true when considering specific corrupt practices: *Improper Use of Government Databases* and *False Statements, Reports, and Testimony.* An exhaustive evaluation of every

Case Example:

Deborah Madden, SFPD Crime Lab

In early 2010, the San Francisco Police Department's crime lab suspended all drug testing and was forced to submit to an external audit owing to revelations that one of its veteran criminalists, Deborah Madden, had been stealing cocaine for personal use for a number of years—to feed her own substance abuse (see Figure 4-4). As reported in Burack (2012):

> In 2010, revelations that a department criminalist was pilfering drug evidence led to the dismissal of hundreds of drug cases. And in 2011, more than 100 more drug cases were dismissed after [Public Defender Jeff] Adachi's office discovered videos allegedly depicting officers illegally entering residences and falsifying police reports and stealing suspects' valuables.

Ms. Madden was not initially arrested for any crimes, but instead was given immunity, allowed to resign, and also allowed collect a pension while she continued to serve as an expert witness for the state in multiple criminal trials. As reported in Eskenazi (2011):

> Disgraced former crime lab technician Deborah Madden will not face any criminal charges, despite triggering a scandal that led to millions of dollars in city costs and a literal Get Out of Jail Free card for thousands of accused drug criminals. Madden is now free to begin drawing her city pension; with 29 years on the job, she's entitled to somewhere in the neighborhood of 75 percent of her $63,000 yearly salary.

This author experienced the hypocrisy of the prosecutor's office firsthand when testifying as an expert for the defense in *California v. Culton*, against Deborah Madden; the prosecution became furious when this author explained that he did not seek out information about the homicide scene directly from Ms. Madden, who processed it for evidence, because she was in fact a known fraud—and therefore unreliable. As reported in Burack (2011):

> The former San Francisco Police department criminalist whose alleged theft of drugs from the crime lab scandalized the department will be called soon to testify in a nearly 30-year-old murder case. Debbie Madden appeared at a pretrial court hearing Wednesday in the case of Dwight Culton, 61, accused of killing 43-year-old Joan Baldwin at a former auto body shop near the Hall of Justice on April 6, 1984.
>
> Madden, 61, will testify at Culton's trial, with immunity from prosecution for any statements she might make about her recently scrutinized activities at the lab, her attorney Paul DeMeester said Thursday. He said this was the first non-drug case in which she had been called to testify since leaving the department in 2009. Madden's alleged admission that she took small amounts

FIGURE 4-4

In 2010, Deborah Madden confessed to stealing cocaine from the San Francisco Police Department's crime lab, yet was allowed to resign, retained her pension, and was granted immunity from prosecution. The resulting scandal caused the temporary closure of the lab and resulted in the dismissal of hundreds of pending criminal cases.

Continued

Case Example: *Continued*

of cocaine from evidence at the lab in late 2009 could potentially be used by defense attorneys to impeach her credibility as a witness, even in a decades-old murder case.

DeMeester said the relatively recent accusations of Madden's misconduct at the drug lab "have nothing to do with what she did on the case in 1984." Madden was called to the scene of Baldwin's murder to collect blood evidence and later did some of the testing. "She is a material witness in this case, and her testimony is necessary for us to establish chain of custody," District Attorney's Office spokeswoman Erica Derryck said.

When still proffering her as a witness for the state, the prosecution routinely attempted to hide Ms. Madden's identity and by extension her duplicitous character; they placed her on the witness list under her maiden name, and routinely failed to discover her criminal history and laboratory drug theft to the defense as required by *Brady v. Maryland*. The prosecution argued that these were lawful tactics, reported in Begin (2010):

> The District Attorney's Office had no formal policy regarding releasing the criminal history of its expert witnesses to the defense, prosecutors told a judge Thursday. That information will be used to challenge evidence in a trial. The admission came as Superior Court Judge Anne-Christine Massullo is creating a framework for hundreds of future drug cases that could be revisited after a debacle at the San Francisco Police Department's crime lab that became public March 9.
>
> Documents released this week show top narcotics prosecutor Sharon Woo complained to her superiors in November of "disturbing" problems with the attendance of longtime lab technician Deborah Madden. While the chief attorney in the office, Russ Giuntini, relayed a message of concern to police, it did not include Madden's name.
>
> On Thursday, Massullo ordered the release of more documents to defense attorneys related

to the Police Department's investigation into Madden, who is suspected of taking cocaine from evidence samples at the crime lab. Massullo also pressed Woo for District Attorney Kamala Harris' policy on notifying defense attorneys of the criminal history of a witness.

> In 2008, Madden was convicted in San Mateo County on a count of misdemeanor domestic violence for throwing a cordless phone at her domestic partner's head. Despite the conviction and a subsequent internal investigation, the Police Department never informed the District Attorney's Office, which it's required to do under California law.
>
> "I don't believe there is a written policy," Woo said. "There is no written procedure. Our policy is to follow the law." The District Attorney's Office relies on the Police Department to provide information about one of its employees, Woo said.
>
> "Saying we rely on the police to tell us really isn't [sufficient] under this court's eyes," Massullo said.

When it became clear that local prosecutors had lost perspective regarding Ms. Madden, allowing her to essentially skate on one of the biggest lab scandals in the country at the time, the U.S. government stepped in and charged her with criminal violations of relevant federal statutes. As reported in Drumwright (2011):

> Felony drug charges were filed in federal court Thursday against Deborah Madden, the disgraced former technician at the San Francisco Police Department's crime lab. In a one-sentence indictment, federal prosecutors allege that Madden did "knowingly and intentionally acquire and obtain possession of, by misrepresentation, fraud, forgery, deception and subterfuge" cocaine from the lab.
>
> Madden, who has admitted to taking small amounts of drugs from the lab in 2009, is due to make an initial appearance before U.S. Northern District Court Judge Elizabeth D. Laporte on Wednesday. The drug scandal rocked the crime

Continued

Case Example: *Continued*

lab, which was temporarily shut down in March 2010. The incident led to the outsourcing of drug testing to other labs in the Bay Area.

Madden, 61, who has not been jailed on the charge, has never been prosecuted by The City. She did plead no contest in San Mateo County to charges that stemmed from San Mateo police finding 0.09 grams of cocaine during a search of Madden's home there.

In October of 2012, the federal case against Deborah Madden ended with a mistrial. This case serves to demonstrate that many of those suffused in law enforcement culture not only tolerate criminality, but are willing to actively conceal it to get what they want. Had the police department adopted a zero tolerance policy for criminal convictions, Ms. Madden's domestic violence conviction in 2008 would have removed her from the department and from casework, avoiding at least two years of misconduct. With respect to the rest, few better examples exist for the utter removal of crime lab management from the culture of police and prosecutors.

conceivable type of law enforcement fraud would be excessive, and is beyond the scope of the current research.

It should be noted that each of these examples involves either an administrative violation of law enforcement policy that can get a law enforcement employee suspended or terminated, or a criminal violation that can get the employee indicted, arrested, and even convicted of a crime. Whether the violation is administrative or criminal depends in some part on the nature of local criminal statutes and how they are applied, as we have learned from the previous sections.

Improper use of government databases

Law enforcement employees have rapid accessibility to information that the general public does not, as explained in Berkow (2004): "Police departments have access to national databases of the National Crime Information Center (NCIC) and the National Law Enforcement Telecommunication System (NLETS) and many other systems such as their state motor vehicle records, criminal warrant records, and wanted information." When logging in to these and other proprietary government databases, personnel are generally required to use a secure password and make a record of the ongoing case that their query is associated with. In other words, they must have a legitimate "need to know" that is attached to an official investigation.

Law enforcement employees frequently access government databases for personal reasons using false pretenses. For example, out of Michigan, Elrick (2001) reports:

> Over the past five years, more than 90 Michigan police officers,
> dispatchers, federal agents and security guards have abused the

Law Enforcement Information Network (LEIN), according to a Free Press examination of hundreds of pages of LEIN records and police reports.

In many cases, abusers turned a valuable crime-fighting tool into a personal search engine for home addresses, for driving records and for criminal files of love interests, colleagues, bosses or rivals.

This is similar to reports out of California, where officers are routinely found guilty of (Cassidy, 2009) "using law enforcement databases to meet women, investigate romantic rivals and keep tabs on ex-girlfriends." This includes abuse of the California Law Enforcement Telecommunications System (CLETS), which connects to the DMV, state, and federal law enforcement databases. Abuse of this system, which is a misdemeanor, is so common that there is actually a "CLETS MISUSE INVESTIGATION REPORTING FORM" included with the "CLETS POLICIES, PRACTICES and PROCEDURES" manual made available to subscribing agencies.

In a more severe case out of Maryland, Delores Culmer, a Montgomery County police officer, was charged with drug- and fraud-related offenses after using a police computer database. She used the database to help her fiancé, a drug trafficker, intimidate and keep track of his competition (News Release, 2011). She eventually pleaded guilty to conducting unauthorized warrant checks on her fiancé, a person who owed a drug-related debt to her sister, and vehicle checks on her fiancé's brother (Castaneda, 2011). She resigned from law enforcement and was sentenced to five months' home detention and two years' probation.

A pernicious aspect to this type of fraud is that it can continue even after retirement. Law enforcement agents retire to the private sector, or are terminated, but can continue to access law enforcement databases with unexpired passwords or through their relationships with former co-workers. The ability to achieve this kind of unauthorized access is a major consideration in the hiring of retired law enforcement agents by private security or insurance firms.

Law enforcement employees who engage in improper and illegal access of law enforcement databases tend to be *motivated* by personal gain; they have the *opportunity* by virtue of their law enforcement status and co-worker affiliations; they have cultural *rationalization* in the form of either noble cause or entitlement; and they have *individual capability* by virtue of their training and a culture that tolerates it in comportment with Social Learning Theory.

False statements, reports, and testimony

False statements, reports, and testimony are so common in law enforcement culture that police training officers actually developed their own term for what would eventually be required in the courtroom: "testilying" (McClurg, 1999; Mollen, 1994). As provided by the research presented in Dorfman (1999; p. 457): "Judges, prosecutors and defense attorneys report that police perjury is commonplace, and even police officers themselves concede that lying is a regular feature of the life of a cop." This kind of fraud occurs in all manner of contexts related to the work of law enforcement officers, whether it is a falsified timesheet related to overtime, sick days, or firearms qualification (e.g., Aseltine, 2011; Boyd, 2011; and Litz, 2011); a false statement in a report or affidavit about directly observing a suspect drop drugs, weapons, or other contraband (referred to as "dropsy" evidence; Capers, 2008; Cloud, 1996; Dorfman, 1999; and McClurg 1999); false testimony about finding evidence on a suspect when it was actually planted (referred to as "flaking"; Dorfman, 1999; see also the recent scandal involving the NYPD Brooklyn Narcotics Squad with respect to "flaking" innocent suspects with no criminal record in order to boost arrests for overtime, chronicled in Jarrett, 2011; Stelloh, 2011; and Yaniv, 2011); or false testimony in a pre-trial hearing, or before a grand jury, about the results of forensic testing to bolster an indictment prior to actually seeing the results (Smith, 2008). As reported in McClurg (1999; p. 394): "many police officers have come to believe that lying is a necessary and justifiable component of their jobs. 'Doing God's work' is how one officer defended the practice of falsification for the purpose of apprehending and convicting criminals."

Law enforcement employees who engage in fraudulent statements, reports, and testimony tend to be personally *motivated* by noble cause and peer pressure; they have the *opportunity* by virtue of their law enforcement status and a corresponding presumption of integrity; they have cultural *rationalization* in the form of either noble cause or an "Us versus Them" world view; and they have *individual capability* by virtue of their training, experience, and a culture that openly encourages it.

SUMMARY

Law enforcement organizations provide employees with the training, opportunity, and authority to commit acts of fraud on a variety of levels, which requires a high level of personal integrity to abjure. Law enforcement culture is often defined by traits that afford the motivations and rationalizations for a deviant internal subculture, actively cultivating fraud within its ranks. At the same time, law enforcement culture also furnishes otherwise lawful members with the skills, incentives, motivations, and rationalizations for ignoring, protecting, and even publicly defending their unlawful co-workers.[2] These employment circumstances and cultural features, in strong conformity with *Fraud Diamond Theory, Differential Association Theory*, and specifically *Social Learning Theory*, increase the likelihood that those in law enforcement will commit, tolerate, conceal, and even defend acts of overt fraud.

In addition, as Terrill, Paoline, and Manning (2003) explain (p. 104): "coercive behavior is implicitly, and perhaps even explicitly, viewed as a salient correlate of police culture." If this holds true within a given law enforcement agency, it stands to reason that any subordinate culture will ultimately be directed or forced into alignment with its values should there ever be a conflicting interest. Failure of the subordinate culture to align would be expected to result in the traditional peer group consequences and retaliation that law enforcement is known for and committed to (Cancino and Enriquez, 2004; Chin and Wells, 1998; and Cooper, 2009a). This reality places any forensic examiner employed by a law enforcement agency into a weak subordinate capacity within a culture that is opposed to the core tenets of scientific praxis.

---

[2]Although addressing these cultural features of law enforcement may seem dated to some, they are in step with the observations of modern law enforcement researchers as cited—as well as the observations of this researcher. Additionally, it is important to note that while the academic community may take these observations at face value as being established and uncomplex, criminal justice practitioners will likely not, especially those vested in the current model of law enforcement-aligned forensic science. There is a continued and persistent disconnect between those working in the justice system and the research that is published by those studying it. As this dissertation is written to be read by criminal justice practitioners and policymakers alike, a detailed and carefully referenced accounting, covering what may be obvious and simplistic to those in academia, is necessary.

CHAPTER 5

Fraud and Scientific Culture

"The scientific endeavor is based on vigilance, not trust."

Jonathan King (1999; p. 215)
Prof. of Molecular Biology, MIT

In the preceding chapter, we explored the culture of law enforcement—the first of two competing occupational environments that payroll and maintain the forensic sciences. This chapter explores the second culture associated with the forensic sciences—that of scientific inquiry. Specifically, this chapter establishes the nature of science and then defines its culture by identifying ideal cardinal traits from the literature. This leads to a discussion of the development of terms and definitions related to scientific fraud; the estimated frequency of scientific fraud; and the varying manifestations of scientific fraud in both research and clinical contexts. It is also demonstrated, by adducing case examples, that the existing literature on occupational scientific fraud is relevant for contextualizing the current research effort.

SCIENCE, SCIENTIFIC KNOWLEDGE, AND THE SCIENTIFIC METHOD

The classic definition of a *science* is provided in Thornton and Peterson (2007; p. 13): "an orderly body of knowledge with principles that are clearly enunciated," as well as being reality oriented and having conclusions susceptible to testing. Giddens (1991) further explains that science involves (p. 20) "the use of systematic methods of investigation, theoretical thinking, and the logical assessment of arguments, to develop a body of knowledge about a particular subject matter." In other words, the development of any field of study as a science requires building a knowledge base that is "accurate and systematized" (Ross, 1964; p. 66).

Scientific knowledge is understanding, enlightenment, or awareness that comes from examining events or problems through the lenses of analytical

Forensic Fraud. http://dx.doi.org/10.1016/B978-0-12-408073-7.00005-7

logic and the scientific method; it is necessarily less fallible than, and distinct from, common knowledge or mere observation (Judson, 2004; Popper, 2002; and Ross, 1964). The generation of scientific knowledge in a particular area (e.g., chemistry, biology, psychology, sociology, or criminology) leads to its development as a science. Suggested earlier, this process is intended to be ongoing and self-correcting (NAS, 2002; Popper, 2002; and Ross, 1964).

The *scientific method* is a systematic way to investigate how or why something works, or how something happened, with the development of hypotheses and subsequent attempts at falsification through testing (Cooley, 2004; DiFonzo and Stern, 2007; Giddens, 1991; Kennedy and Kennedy, 1972; Popper, 2002; and Thornton and Peterson, 2007). The scientific method may be regarded as a path to knowledge, involving steps that cannot be skipped. Initially, empirical information (e.g., observation and experience) identifies a question or a problem. This is developed into a testable hypothesis for which specific empirical data is identified and then systematically gathered. According to Popper (2002; p. 1): "[a] scientist, whether theorist or experimenter, puts forward statements, or systems of statements, and tests them step by step." Theory testing is generally accomplished by one of four means: logical comparison of conclusions for internal consistency; investigation of the logical form of a theory; comparison with other theories; and testing empirical applications of the theory with conclusions that can be derived from it (Popper, 2002). With sufficient testing, marked by a consistent failure to falsify, hypotheses can become working scientific theories (Popper, 2002; Raven and Johnson, 1986). Eventually, over time, scientific theories can survive to become scientific principles.

The scientific method is universally accepted as the best approach to knowledge building, as it (Dewey, 1995; p. 397)

> …is not just a method which it has been found profitable to pursue in this or that abstruse subject for purely technical reasons. It represents the only method of thinking that has proved fruitful in any subject—that is what we mean when we call it scientific. It is not a peculiar development of thinking for highly specialized ends; it *is* thinking so far as thought has become conscious of its proper ends and of the equipment indispensable for success in their pursuit.

The scientific method is therefore the definitive approach to logical inquiry, knowledge building, and problem solving used by scientists of every kind (DiFonzo and Stern, 2007; Popper, 2002). It must be pointed out that the opposite is also true. Any investigator or examiner who does not understand or use the scientific method as the foundation of inquiry is not engaging in scientific practice.

SCIENCE AS FALSIFICATION

Subsumed in the previous section, a cornerstone of the scientific method is *falsification*. This is achieved by subjecting a theory to repeated attacks in order to disprove it, which means testing it against case facts or alternative theories (Popper, 2002). Any study, method, or experiment designed only to confirm a hypothesis or theory is not, by definition, scientific. The scientific prohibition against seeking only proofs or confirmations was described by Sir Karl Popper (1902–1994), the noted Austrian-British psychologist, philosopher, and scientist (Popper, 1963; pp. 33–39):

SCIENCE AS FALSIFICATION
   These considerations led me in the winter of 1919–20 to conclusions which I may now reformulate as follows.

1. It is easy to obtain confirmations, or verifications, for nearly every theory—if we look for confirmations.
2. Confirmations should count only if they are the result of risky predictions; that is to say, if, unenlightened by the theory in question, we should have expected an event which was incompatible with the theory— an event which would have refuted the theory.
3. Every "good" scientific theory is a prohibition: It forbids certain things to happen. The more a theory forbids, the better it is.
4. A theory which is not refutable by any conceivable event is nonscientific. Irrefutability is not a virtue of a theory (as people often think) but a vice.
5. Every genuine test of a theory is an attempt to falsify it, or to refute it. Testability is falsifiability; but there are degrees of testability: Some theories are more testable, more exposed to refutation, than others; they take, as it were, greater risks.
6. Confirming evidence should not count except when it is the result of a genuine test of the theory; and this means that it can be presented as a serious but unsuccessful attempt to falsify the theory. (I now speak in such cases of "corroborating evidence.")
7. Some genuinely testable theories, when found to be false, are still upheld by their admirers—for example by introducing ad hoc some auxiliary assumption, or by reinterpreting the theory ad hoc in such a way that it escapes refutation. Such a procedure is always possible, but it rescues the theory from refutation only at the price of destroying, or at least lowering, its scientific status. (I later described such a rescuing operation as a "conventionalist twist" or a "conventionalist stratagem.")

One can sum up all this by saying that the criterion of the scientific status of a theory is its falsifiability, or refutability, or testability.

Falsification being an essential "criterion," scientific inquiry demands objectivity, doubt, and skepticism at every step. Useful stipulations along these lines are found in Kennedy and Kennedy (1972, p. 4):

> To be objective, an inquirer should be prepared to accept and record whatever facts he may encounter. He must not let personal feelings affect what he sees or hears. Although he does not need to like the nature of the information, he must be willing to investigate it. When such an investigation is begun, it must be carried through with a degree of skepticism. Skepticism does not imply cynicism or a distrust of the world. It only suggests that the [scientist] must be prepared to distinguish truth from the opinion or inclinations of others.

Science, consequently, does not seek confirmation of beliefs or ideas; it seeks eradication. Failing at this, hypotheses or theories that survive genuine attempts at falsification are sufficiently "accurate and reliable" to be considered scientific.

THE CARDINAL TRAITS OF SCIENTIFIC CULTURE

Some commentators have argued that *scientific culture* is an indefinite and disputed term "that is used to imply a variety of different things" (Cole, 2010; p. 439). This may be true at an applied level, where specific scientific constructs can be inconsistently defined or ineptly exercised by those without genuine scientific education or training. However, a careful examination of the scientific literature reveals the existence of consistent core scientific values, ideals, and prohibitions.

The scientific literature is replete with explanations of the requisite ethics and obligations for achieving trustworthy practice across the spectrum of scientific endeavor, whether in conducting research or engaging in clinical practice (e.g., Anderson, Martinson, and De Vries, 2007; Bosch and Titus, 2009; Dewey, 1995; Edwards and Gotsonis, 2009; Elgin, 2011; Hardwig, 1991; Judson, 2004; Kennedy and Kennedy, 1972; Martinson, Anderson, and de Vries, 2005; NAS, 2002 and 2009; ORI, 1995 and 2000; Popper, 1963 and 2002; Richardson, 2004; Ross, 1964; Stanbrook et al., 2011; Steneck, 2007a,b; and Titus, Wells, and Rhoades, 2008). This body of work, and that supporting it, collectively provides a unifying set of cultural objectives intended to distinguish scientists from other types of investigators. It also becomes clear that scientific culture is defined by not just accepted practices, but strict prohibitions. Specifically, all scientists must adhere to ethical guidelines and practice standards intended to fulfill and maintain what is referred to as "scientific integrity"; and they must also avoid intentional violations of that integrity (Jette, 2005; Judson, 2004; Martinson, Anderson, and de Vries, 2005; NAS, 2002 and 2009; Steneck, 2007a,b; and Titus, Wells, and Rhoades, 2008).

Robert Merton famously wrote of basic scientific norms, or "normative principles" in the 1940s, as explained in Anderson, Martinson, and De Vries (2007; p. 4):

> Merton (1942) identified four norms of science, which he expressed as principles of desirable behavior. He saw the normative principles as morally binding, but most other commentators now see them as representing ideals that are not binding on behavior (Hess, 1997; Ziman, 2000). They do, however, carry the weight of a group's near-consensus and therefore influence behavior. *Communality* refers to the shared ownership of scientific methods and findings. *Universalism* is the principle that a scientist's findings and body of work should be judged on the basis of their merit, without reference to the scientist's personal or other irrelevant characteristics. *Disinterestedness* represents the understanding that scientists' work should be free of self-interested motivation and pursuit of wealth. *Organized skepticism* requires that scientific findings be made available for scrutiny and that such scrutiny be performed in accordance with accepted scientific standards.

Subsequently, these norms (or their equivalent) have become generally accepted as the fundamental obligations of scientists to their employers, colleagues, students, and even the public at large (Anderson, Martinson, and De Vries, 2007; Hardwig, 1991; Jette, 2005; NAS, 2009; and Steneck, 2007a,b). For example, Steneck (2007b) advises that scientific culture is ultimately found in honest and unbiased reporting (p. xi): "Researchers who report their work honestly, accurately, efficiently, and objectively are on the right road when it comes to responsible conduct. Anyone who is dishonest, knowingly reports inaccurate results, wastes funds, or allows personal bias to influence scientific findings is not." Anderson, Martinson, and De Vries (2007; p. 4) "proposed two additional norms: *governance* as a mode of decision-making, and *quality* as an evaluative standard" intentionally consistent with Mertonian norms.

The National Academy of Sciences (aka the NAS)[1] offers more to the equation, describing a specific relationship between scientists and their employers. They observe that a culture of science exists as a function of both individual and institutional integrity. This begins with the institutional obligation to create an environment where scientific practice is encouraged and protected, and misconduct is not tolerated (NAS, 2002; p. 26):

---

[1]The NAS was formed and given Congressional authority to advise the United States federal government on scientific and technical matters in 1863. It has done so ever since.

The human contribution to the research environment is greatly shaped by each individual's professional integrity, which in turn is influenced by the individual's educational background and cultural and ethical upbringing. These result in values and attitudes that contribute to the formation of the individual's identity, unique personality traits, and ethical decision-making abilities. Because each researcher brings unique qualities to the research environment, the constants must come from the environment itself. Research institutions should consistently and effectively provide training and education, policies and procedures, and tools and support systems. Institutional expectations should be unambiguous, and the consequences of each individual's conduct or misconduct should be clear.

The NAS further describes scientific culture as being composed of honorable values and standards similar to those expected from lawful citizens in everyday life (NAS, 2009; p. 3):

Research is based on the same ethical values that apply in everyday life, including honesty, fairness, objectivity, openness, trustworthiness, and respect for others.

A "scientific standard" refers to the application of these values in the context of research. Examples are openness in sharing research materials, fairness in reviewing grant proposals, respect for one's colleagues and students, and honesty in reporting research results.

This is consistent with Edwards and Gotsonis (2009), which characterizes the culture of science as rewarding humility, openness, and criticism as it strives to refine itself through self-correction (p. 125):

The methods and culture of scientific research enable it to be a self-correcting enterprise. Because researchers are, by definition, creating new understanding, they must be as cautious as possible before asserting a new "truth." Also, because researchers are working at a frontier, few others may have the knowledge to catch and correct any errors they make. Thus, science has had to develop means of revisiting provisional results and revealing errors before they are widely used. The processes of peer review, publication, collegial interactions (e.g., sharing at conferences), and the involvement of graduate students (who are expected to question as they learn) all support this need. Science is characterized also by a culture that encourages and rewards critical questioning of past results and of colleagues. Most technologies benefit from a solid research foundation in academia and ample opportunity for peer-to-peer stimulation and critical assessment, review and critique through conferences, seminars, publishing, and more. These elements provide a rich set of paths through which new ideas and skepticism can travel and opportunities for scientists to step away from their day-to-day work and take a longer-term view. The scientific culture encourages cautious, precise statements and discourages statements that go beyond established facts; it is acceptable for colleagues to challenge one another, even if the challenger is more junior.

Self-correction can only come in an environment that embraces critical thinking and skepticism. As explained in Brookfield (1987), critical thinking requires strict adherence to logical analysis, and the discipline to scrutinize the strengths, weaknesses, and overall rationality of all arguments and assertions. It also requires (p. 6) "continual questioning of assumptions"; (p. 8) "challenging the importance of context"; (p. 9) "imagining and exploring alternatives" and "reflective skepticism"; and (pp. 11–12) "the ability to distinguish bias from reason and fact from opinion." Critical thinking necessitates doubt and proof, no matter the source of data or the strength of assertions about the integrity of findings. This means that scientists are prohibited from blindly accepting what they are told by anyone. The importance of this scientific norm is echoed in Gardenier (2011), which explains that (p. 3)

> [a]nalytic methodology cannot be divorced from the data. Both must be specifically congruent in structure, relevance, and assumptions. Even more important than any measure of confidence or significance in the output is the logic that the conclusions follow from the data....
>
> Scientists may mistakenly consider it an ethical obligation to accept data from colleagues or superiors for statistical analysis without detailed attention to all of the considerations above. That is incorrect. Without data integrity, it is impossible to achieve research integrity.

This advisory is universally applicable to any context where scientists are being asked to assume the integrity of information they are provided from any source: such assumptions are impermissible. Scientific integrity must be earned at all junctures and not presumed. When weaknesses exist, they must be acknowledged, considered, and then reported as a function of limits set against any reliable interpretation.

Scientific understanding is also intended to be regenerative—constantly evolving as new information is developed and assimilated. Consequently, the caution and humility advised for responsibly exploring "new truth" require acceptance that there is no such thing as absolute scientific certainty (Botkin, 2011). Scientists must therefore show an appreciation for exploring the limitations of their findings and inferences. They must also accept the need for clearly expressing those limitations to others, and for admitting that any scientific findings "are not absolute truths or immutable facts" (Inman and Rudin, 1999; p. 164).[2]

From all of this discussion, a consistent pattern of core scientific obligations associated with the establishment of scientific integrity is evident. As suggested by the NAS, these are appropriately divided into requisite values and practices associated with either individual scientists or their institution/ employer. This acknowledges the reality that every scientist has his own variable personality, education, abilities, and professional identity; and that (NAS, 2002; p. 4) "[s]ince each individual researcher brings unique qualities to the research environment, the constants must come from the environment itself."

Individual obligations to scientific culture

- Maintain an ethical professional character
- Embrace empiricism and the scientific method
- Maintain a disposition toward critical thinking and skepticism
- Maintain objectivity and disinterest toward predetermined outcomes
- Show humility toward inherent limitations and uncertainty of findings
- Use logical analysis and argumentation when interpreting findings
- Maintain honesty and precision in reporting, attributions, and authorship
- Maintain openness to peer review to enable independent validation
- Maintain transparency regarding personal conflicts of interest
- Demonstrate fairness in peer reviewing the work of others
- Report the misconduct of others
- Avoid reckless disregard for maintaining scientific integrity

Institutional obligations to scientific culture

- Employ qualified individuals with ethical professional character
- Provide mentorship and leadership promoting scientific literacy and integrity
- Provide clearly stated practice standards and ethical guidelines
- Provide opportunities for ongoing collaboration, education, and training
- Encourage peer review and self-correcting enterprise
- Quality control: Monitor and evaluate the environment for scientific integrity

---

[2]It comes as a surprise to many that nothing in science is 100% infallible and "if you thought before that science was certain—well, that is just an error on your part" (Feynman, 2001; p. 77).

- Maintain transparency regarding institutional conflicts of interest
- Place zero pressure on employees to produce results favoring the institution
- Base promotions and pay raises on scientific competence, not outcomes favorable to the institution
- Demand zero tolerance for misconduct; investigate all allegations and sanction appropriately
- Provide protection for whistleblowers; no negative consequences or reprisals
- Avoid reckless disregard for maintaining scientific integrity

While these obligations are not the set limit of what scientific culture requires, they are generally accepted as the basic starting point for building and preserving scientific integrity.

It is also agreed that "counternorms," antithetical to scientific culture, can develop in the context of (Mitroff, 1974; p. 585) "fierce, sometimes bitter competitive races for discovery" that involve inappropriate (Anderson, Martinson, and De Vries, 2007; p. 4) "personal" and "emotional commitment to theories and ideas." These include *secrecy, particularism, self-interestedness*, and *organized dogmatism*, to which have been added "*administration* as opposed to governance, and *quantity* as opposed to quality as an evaluative standard" (Anderson, Martinson, and De Vries, 2007; p. 4). As will be demonstrated, the failure of scientific norms within an occupational environment can incubate a culture of counternorms that provide for and even encourage fraud.

SCIENTIFIC FRAUD: TERMS AND DEFINITIONS

The literature is clear with respect to the obligations of scientists and their institutional employers. However, there is also general agreement that many of those operating within different scientific communities recklessly or intentionally fail to understand, uphold, and promote those obligations (Judson, 2004; Martinson, Anderson, and de Vries, 2005; Sovacool, 2008; and Titus, Wells, and Rhoades, 2008). This is in part because of human error, and the fact that (Anderson, Martinson, and De Vries, 2007; p. 3) "[scientific] norms represent ideal behavior, and so it is to be expected that scientists' actual behavior will fall short of perfect adherence to the norms." This is also, in part, due to acts of fraud (McDowell, 2010). The need to clearly distinguish fraudulent intent from inevitable human error has generated ongoing debate regarding the specified actions and motives that constitute scientific fraud. This has resulted in the development of specific terms and definitions that may be used to investigate the phenomenon.

The United States government employs a disproportionate number of scientists, and funds a significant amount of scientific research worldwide.[3]
It also requires any organization that receives government funding to have
policies and procedures in place for the reporting, investigation, and identification of any questionable research practices. As mandated in ORI (2009b;
p. 4): "[a]ll institutions receiving research funds from Public Health Service (PHS) agencies must have on file an assurance form with the Office
of Research Integrity (ORI). This assurance is to ensure that the institution
has in place policies and procedures for dealing with allegations of research
misconduct, has provided ORI with contact information for its assurance
official, and will submit an annual report to ORI identifying any activity
from the previous year requiring inquiries and investigations into allegations of possible research misconduct involving research supported by PHS
funds." To that end, the U.S. ORI has developed related terms and definitions in order to create uniformity and consistency during investigations
into scientific misconduct. These are intended to serve as a guide for institutions receiving government research money—facilitating their obligation
to report, investigate, and stem internal violations of scientific integrity
(Redman and Mertz, 2005).

The most serious violations of scientific integrity are referred to by the ORI
as *scientific misconduct*, which is defined as "fabrication, falsification,[4] or plagiarism (FFP) in proposing, performing, or reviewing research, or in reporting research results" (NAS, 2009; p. 3). As described, scientific misconduct is
a reference to *fraud*; it involves intentional misrepresentations by scientists
designed to secure an unfair or unlawful gain. In fact, the literature treats the
terms *scientific fraud* and *scientific misconduct* as essentially interchangeable.
However, the term *fraud* is fraught with legal implications[5]. As not all research
violations involve a crime, the term *misconduct* has been adopted as the official
substitute when dealing with actionable allegations in the context of internal institutional investigations (Catano and Turk, 2007; Resnick, 2003; and
Reynolds, 2004).

---

[3]In 2003, as reported in Sovacool (2008; p. 271): "between six and eight million scientists were
employed in research and development in the United States. Their activities— roughly 40% of the
world's R&D effort—constituted a $300 billion industry, accounting for roughly 3.2% of the entire
country's gross domestic product."

[4]Not to be confused with the Popperian concept of falsification associated with the scientific method.

[5]Despite the liabilities and legal tools available, scientific fraud is rarely criminalized except in extreme
or high-profile cases, even with recommendations from the scientific community that this is a necessary
reform (Bogner and Menz, 2006; Kline, 1993; Kuzma, 1992; Redman and Kaplan, 2005; and Resnick,
2003).

The major forms of scientific misconduct are operationalized in the ORI's "Policies on Research Misconduct" (ORI, 2009b; p. 5)[6]:

(a) Fabrication is making up data or results and recording or reporting them.
(b) Falsification is manipulating research materials, equipment, or processes, or changing or omitting data or results such that the research is not accurately represented in the research record.
(c) Plagiarism is the appropriation of another person's ideas, processes, results, or words without giving appropriate credit.
(d) Research misconduct does not include honest error or differences of opinion.

These concepts are further described in Reider (2010; p. 445): "The colloquial term for fabrication is 'dry-labbing,' making up results for experiments or trials that never occurred. … The term falsification is applied when research actually took place, but the results have been manipulated, modified, or edited so that the published work no longer accurately reflects the scientific findings." Though not listed by the ORI in a pedantic sense, it has been demonstrated that scientific misconduct also includes *ghost authorship, suppression of unfavorable results*, the *falsification of researcher credentials*, and *sexual harassment* when these actions have the potential to affect the results or interpretations of scientific inquiries (Krimsky, 2007; Parrish, 1996).

For the purposes of the present research, it bears explaining that *ghost authorship*, also referred to as *honorary* or *gift authorship*, is a common yet highly misleading practice, described in Krimsky (2007; p. 450): "Ghost authorship occurs when the person whose name appears on the publication was not involved either in doing the research, framing the ideas behind the article, or in writing the article. Alternatively, it also occurs when an individual who has made substantial contributions to the manuscript was not named as an author or whose contributions were not cited in the acknowledgments." Examples of ghost or gift authorship include giving a byline to a lab supervisor who has made no meaningful contribution to a given research publication; or a supervisor taking the research of a graduate assistant and publishing it under his own name without attribution.[7] Essentially the reverse of plagiarism, it is viewed as a dishonest practice that violates the covenant between the scientists and their intended readers, whether this includes supervisors, colleagues, policymakers, lawmakers, or members of the general public. The reasons are straightforward. First, it involves deception

---

[6]It is important to note that error is cleaved sharply from discussions of scientific misconduct in the literature as unintentional, expected, and on many levels unavoidable.
[7]Ghost/gift authorship is common in many research environments—a longstanding tradition in some circles that masquerades as legitimate scientific practice (Judson, 2004).

regarding what work was done and by whom; that is to say, it is a lie about accomplishment. Second, the purpose of the deception is to inappropriately enhance the credibility of an author or a publication; this illusion of credibility has the capacity to affect the beliefs and actions of others. The inherent dangers of giving anyone credit for work that he did not do, with respect to biasing outcomes and misrepresenting the true origins of reported findings, are discussed in Judson (2004); Lexchin (2007); Marusic, Katavic, and Marusic (2007); and NAS (2009).

Falsifying scientific credentials occurs when someone reports having scientific qualifications that she has not actually earned, or that do not actually exist. This includes padding an otherwise competent scientific resume with publications and certifications that are unearned or non-existent. It can also involve the fabrication of an entire pedigree, from formal education to work history. In either circumstance, fraud has occurred which may be considered to be a form of scientific misconduct—especially when the false credentials are material to employment, legal requirements for practice, promotions, or applications for grant money (Krimsky, 2007; ORI, 2009a; and Parrish, 1996).[8]

In many jurisdictions, there are criminal statutes that apply to instances of credential fraud, especially when used to gain a financial reward (e.g., employment, promotions, pay raises, and grants that can involves thousands or even millions of dollars). However, law enforcement generally shows little interest in responding to or initiating the prosecution of scientific fraudsters accused in such matters (Parrish, 1996). This may be due to the complicity of many law enforcement agencies with respect to condoning the use of "diploma mills" for officer advancement. In other words, the unwillingness of agencies or investigators to go after those engaged in credential fraud may in some instances reflect their own similar misconduct[9].

Irrespective of criminal charges, which are inconsistently applied at best, the violations discussed in this section are each consistent with ORI (2000), which provides that (p. 5) "'[s]cientific misconduct' or misconduct in science means fabrication, falsification, plagiarism, or other practices that seriously deviate from those that are commonly accepted within the scientific community for proposing, conducting, or reporting research." Admittedly, the last part of this definition has caused significant disagreement within the scientific community

---

[8]The ORI has a longstanding tradition of asserting scientific misconduct based largely on findings of credential falsification, despite the fact that it is not listed as one of the three major forms of research misconduct (Parrish, 1996).

[9]There is, especially among those seeking promotion into high-ranking positions, a tradition of using "diploma mills" that give officers college degrees based on "life experience," without coursework, for a fee (e.g., Clayton, 2003; Grolleau, Lakhal, and Mzoughi, 2008; Holguin, 2007; Hutchison, 1999; Schemo, 2008; and Stepankowski, 2009). This despite many states having laws that forbid using these kinds of fake degrees to gain employment, threatening fines and even imprisonment (Clayton, 2003).

(Judson, 2004; and Reynolds, 2004). It was criticized by some for being too ambiguous, while praised by others for recognizing the variety of fraud that can actually occur in scientific practice (Redman and Mertz, 2005; Resnick, 2003; Reynolds, 2004; Sovacool, 2008; and Weed, 1998). Subsequently, the language was changed to "[r]esearch misconduct means fabrication, falsification, or plagiarism in proposing, performing, or reviewing research, or in reporting research results" (DHSS, 2005; Sec. 93.103). This and related definitions are necessarily a starting point for the majority of publications examining the issue of scientific fraud.

THE BABBAGE TYPOLOGY

The concept of scientific fraud, and its examination, has significant history. Charles Babbage, the nineteenth century English mathematician, engineer, and inventor (he developed an original concept for a programmable computer; see Figure 5-1) was the first to publish a formal typology of scientific fraud (Judson, 2004). As explained in Babbage (1830; Ch.5, Section 3):

> There are several species of impositions that have been practised in science, which are but little known, except to the initiated, and which

FIGURE 5-1
Charles Babbage (1791–1871) was an English mathematician, philosopher, inventor, and mechanical engineer who originated the idea of a programmable computer. He was also the first to publish a formal typology related to scientific fraud.

it may perhaps be possible to render quite intelligible to ordinary understandings. These may be classed under the heads of hoaxing, forging, trimming, and cooking.

Scientific inquiries are more exposed than most others to the inroads of pretenders; and I feel that I shall deserve the thanks of all who really value truth, by stating some of the methods of deceiving practised by unworthy claimants for its honours, whilst the mere circumstance of their arts being known may deter future offenders.

As defined in Babbage (1830), *hoaxing* refers to frauds that are "intended to last for a time, and then be discovered, to the ridicule of those who have credited it"; *forging* refers to the behavior of one "who, wishing to acquire a reputation for science, records observations which he has never made"; *trimming* refers to "clipping off little bits here and there from those observations which differ most in excess from the mean, and in sticking them on to those which are too small; a species of 'equitable adjustment,' as a radical would term it, which cannot be admitted in science"; and *cooking* refers to giving "ordinary observations the appearance and character of those of the highest degree of accuracy."

Of cooking, Babbage further explains: "One of its numerous processes is to make multitudes of observations, and out of these to select those only which agree, or very nearly agree. If a hundred observations are made, the cook must be very unlucky if he cannot pick out fifteen or twenty which will do for serving up." Currently, this practice is referred to colloquially as *cherry-picking* (Chisum and Turvey, 2011).

The Babbage Typology survives in the modern scientific literature, echoed in the definition of scientific misconduct already discussed: fabrication, falsification, and plagiarism (aka FFP; ORI, 2009b). Forging is akin to fabrication—the invention of data or findings from tests not performed and observations not made. Trimming is akin to falsification—the alteration or manipulation of present elements to support predetermined results. Cooking is also akin to falsification, and is further accounted for in other forms of fraud detailed in the literature, including the self-explanatory *suppression of unfavorable results*.

The continued relevance of this typology will be demonstrated as we discuss the case examples in this chapter and those yet to come.

SCIENTIFIC FRAUD: FROM HIGH PROFILE TO MUNDANE

Scientific misconduct, synonymous in the literature with scientific fraud, is both pervasive and extensive (De Vries, Anderson, and Martinson, 2006;

Judson, 2004; Kline, 1993; Marshall, 2000; Reider, 2010; and Resnick, 2003). As reported in Martinson, Anderson, and de Vries (2005), the top 12 questionable research practices reported by scientists are (p. 737):

1. Falsifying or 'cooking' research data
2. Ignoring major aspects of human-subject requirements
3. Not properly disclosing involvement in firms whose products are based on one's own research
4. Relationships with students, research subjects or clients that may be interpreted as questionable
5. Using another's ideas without obtaining permission or giving due credit
6. Unauthorized use of confidential information in connection with one's own research
7. Failing to present data that contradict one's own previous research
8. Circumventing certain minor aspects of human-subject requirements
9. Overlooking others' use of flawed data or questionable interpretation of data
10. Changing the design, methodology or results of a study in response to pressure from a funding source
11. Publishing the same data or results in two or more publications
12. Inappropriately assigning authorship credit

Some high-profile examples from the past decade include:

■ The infamous Bell Labs scandal involving Jan Hendrick Schön (see Figure 5-2), described in Resnik (2003; pp. 123–124):

On September 25, 2002, a panel of independent investigators found that Jan Hendrick Schön, a 32-year-old physicist at Bell Laboratories, had fabricated or falsified data in 17 published papers, some of which had appeared in highly prestigious journals, including *Science, Nature,* and *Applied Physics Letters* (Service, 2002). The panel investigated a total of 25 papers with 20 coauthors. On November 1, 2002, Schön and 7 coauthors published a retraction of 8 papers that had been published in *Science* from 2000–2001 (Bao et al., 2002). The papers raised suspicions because they reported revolutionary breakthroughs in organic electronics, superconductivity, and nanotechnology.

Schön had even received a $3000 prize for his work, and *Technology Review* named him one of science's top young investigators (Service, 2002). Many scientists believe that Schön could have gotten away with his misdeeds if his papers had not been so sensational.

FIGURE 5-2
Jan Hendrick Schön, a physicist at Bell Labs, fabricated or falsified data in 17 published papers that reported phony revolutionary breakthroughs in organic electronics, superconductivity, and nanotechnology.

- In March of 2005, Dr. Eric T. Poehlman agreed to plead guilty to falsifying and fabricating research data in multiple federal grant applications and academic articles from 1992 to 2002 (ORI, 2005). His research focused on obesity, menopause, and aging. As reported in Interlandi (2006):

  Poehlman pleaded guilty to lying on a federal grant application and admitted to fabricating more than a decade's worth of scientific data on obesity, menopause and aging, much of it while conducting clinical research as a tenured faculty member at the University of Vermont. He presented fraudulent data in lectures and in published papers, and he used this data to obtain millions of dollars in federal grants from the National Institutes of Health—a crime subject to as many as five years in federal prison. Poehlman's admission of guilt came after more than five years during which he denied the charges against him, lied under oath and tried to discredit his accusers. By the time Poehlman came clean, his case had grown into one of the most expansive cases of scientific fraud in U.S. history.

- U.S. Attorney David V. Kirby explained (ORI, 2005): "This prosecution demonstrates that academic researchers will be held fully accountable for fraud and scientific misconduct. Dr. Poehlman fraudulently diverted millions of dollars from the Public Health Service to support his research projects. This in turn siphoned millions of dollars from the pool of resources available for valid scientific research proposals. As this prosecution proves, such conduct will not be tolerated." Dr. Poehlman was sentenced to one year and a day in federal prison, followed by two years of probation (Interlandi, 2006).
- In May of 2006, Hwang Woo-suk, the South Korean stem cell researcher, was put on trial and (Dorey, 2010; p. 16) "given a suspended custodial sentence for his part in fraudulent claims to have cloned the first human embryos and extracted stem cells from them." He had defrauded public and private contributors of around US $3 million, publishing his fabricated data and results throughout 2005 (Bogner and Menz, 2006).
- A 2009 report from the ORI revealed research fraud involving two surgeons experimenting with drugs intended to help prevent rejection of transplanted organs—using public money (Murdoch, 2009; p. 29):

In a series of studies designed to assess two anti-tissue-rejection drugs, former University of Alabama–Birmingham surgeons Judith Thomas and Juan Contreras carefully detailed experiments in which they replaced one kidney in rhesus monkeys with a foreign one and, a month later, removed the remaining native kidney. The new organs took, they reported. The drugs worked.

But according to a July report from the federal Office of Research Integrity, that second kidney was never removed from at least 32 of the 70 animals. The scientists denied intentional wrongdoing, but the promising drug has been deemed bogus. The experiments also cost taxpayers: The National Institutes of Health poured $23 million into the work over eight years.

These cases are not representative of typical scientific misconduct given the large scale, extensive publicity, and severe consequences involved. They are, however, the kinds of cases that get the attention of the media.

As a counterbalance, consider also the recent case studies of scientific misconduct published by the ORI between December 2010 and June 2011:

1. Hung-Shu Chang, Ph.D., a visiting post-doctoral fellow/endocrinologist at Washington State University, "engaged in research misconduct in research supported by National Institute of Environmental Health

Sciences (NIEHS), National Institutes of Health (NIH), grant R01 ES012974 … by fabricating and falsifying" experiments, data, and findings (ORI, 2010; p. 6). Dr. Chang's fraud was discovered when he returned home to Taiwan and subsequent researchers were unable to duplicate his data. They referenced his original data, which did not match his published work (Luiggi, 2010).

2. Elizabeth Goodwin, Ph.D., a former associate professor of genetics and medical genetics at University of Wisconsin–Madison, "engaged in scientific misconduct involving research supported by the National Institute of General Medical Sciences (NIGMS), National Institutes of Health (NIH), grants R01 GM051836 and R01 GM073183 … by falsifying and fabricating data that she included in grant applications" which misrepresented research findings and their origins (ORI, 2010; p. 7).

3. Sagar S. Mungekar, Ph.D., a former M.D./Ph.D. student at the New York University School of Medicine in the Sackler Institute of Graduate Biomedical Sciences, "engaged in research misconduct in research supported by National Institute of General Medical Sciences (NIGMS), National Institutes of Health (NIH), grants R01 GM35769, R01 GM55624, and T32 GM07308, and National Institute of Allergy and Infectious Diseases (NIAID), NIH, grant T32 AI007180 … by fabricating and falsifying data" related to tables and figures in his doctorate, and "also claimed to have constructed 53 different reporter plasmids with RNase E mutants, when sequencing data did not exist to support this claim" (ORI, 2011a; p. 6).

4. Meleik Goodwill, Ph.D., a former post-doctoral fellow, Wadsworth Center, N.Y.S. Department of Health, "engaged in research misconduct in research supported by National Institute of Environmental Health Sciences (NIEHS), National Institutes of Health (NIH), grant R21 ES013269-02 … by the fabrication of data for growth curves" and falsely labeled figures and articles in a publication that was ultimately retracted (ORI, 2011a; pp. 6–7).

5. Bengu Sezen, Ph.D., a former graduate student in the Department of Chemistry at Columbia University, "engaged in misconduct in science in research funded by National Institute of General Medical Sciences (NIGMS), National Institutes of Health (NIH), grant R01 GM60326 … based on evidence that she knowingly and intentionally falsified and fabricated, and in one instance plagiarized, data reported in three (3) papers and her doctoral thesis" (ORI, 2011a; p. 7).

6. Junghee J. Shin, Ph.D., a former graduate student at New York Medical College, "engaged in research misconduct in research supported by National Institute of Allergy and Infectious Diseases (NIAID), National Institutes of Health (NIH), grants R01 AI048856 and R01 AI043063 … by

falsifying data" in the form of figures, tables, and images in his published work (ORI, 2011b; p. 6).

7. Vipul Bhrigu, Ph.D., a former post-doctoral fellow with the University of Michigan Medical School, "engaged in research misconduct in research funded by National Cancer Institute (NCI), National Institutes of Health (NIH), grant R01 CA098730–05 "; and "knowingly and intentionally tampered with research materials, and switched the labels on culture dishes … to cause false results to be reported in the research record" (ORI, 2011b; p. 6). He also "tampered with laboratory research materials by adding ethanol to his colleague's cell culture media, with the deliberate intent to effectuate the death of growing cells, which caused false results to be reported in the research record" (ORI, 2011b; pp. 6–7). When the campus police became involved, he lied to them about his role and took no responsibility for what he had done. He came clean, however, when he was informed that his evidence-tampering activities in the lab had been recorded by video surveillance (ORI, 2011b).

8. Philippe Bois, Ph.D., a former post-doctoral fellow with the Department of Biochemistry at St. Jude Children's Research Hospital, "engaged in misconduct in science and research misconduct in research funded by National Institute of General Medical Sciences (NIGMS), National Institutes of Health (NIH), grant R01 GM071596, and National Cancer Institute (NCI), NIH, grants P30 CA021765, P01 CA071907, R01 CA072996, and R01 CA100603" when he "knowingly and intentionally falsified data reported in two (2) papers" (ORI, 2011b; p. 7).

These case examples serve a number of purposes, not the least of which is to demonstrate the mundane variety of fraud that is traditionally uncovered in scientific research settings. It is significant that the majority of fraud recently reported to and founded by the ORI involves newly minted laboratory subordinates, not supervisors. Only one instance involved a senior researcher (Elizabeth Goodwin). This is a stark contrast to the high-profile examples mentioned.

It is also significant that the majority of the cases during this time frame involved falsification and fabrication in tandem, with publication of the phony data under the aegis of multiple co-authors. This demonstrates that it is not unexpected to find multiple types of fraud being committed by a single individual within a group of honest but trusting researchers. Moreover, it is not uncommon for researchers to take the word of their colleagues at face value, without question or skepticism, past the point of publication. This type of faith is a violation of scientific integrity, as explained in King (1999; pp. 215–216): "In all of these efforts the criteria for professional scientific integrity were similar; even if the individual was your best friend, you asked to see the data; and if the data was in summary form, you asked to see the raw data. It was common to challenge a colleague's claim that he had carried out some procedure very carefully or precisely."

THE FREQUENCY OF SCIENTIFIC FRAUD

While numerous cases of scientific fraud are published in the literature and publicized by the media each year, assessments of overall frequency are wide ranging. The reason is that confirmed cases of scientific misconduct are often unreported; handled internally and not publicized; and handled without actual consequences save perhaps termination. For these reasons, reported cases of scientific fraud are considered merely the "tip of the iceberg" (Judson, 2004; Marshall, 2000; Redman and Mertz, 2005; Sovacool, 2008; Steneck, 2007a; and Weed, 1998). Still, some compelling studies have been published over the past decade, which begin to scrape the surface regarding incidence and prevalence in different scientific communities.

In a report by Geggie (2001), a survey of 194 newly appointed medical consultants working for seven separate hospitals revealed some interesting insights and attitudes with respect to research fraud: 55.7% of respondents reported observing some form of research misconduct; 5.7% admitted to prior acts of research misconduct; and 18% admitted to willingness or uncertainty regarding future acts of research misconduct.

Anderson, Martinson, and De Vries (2007) published a study regarding (p. 3) "normative dissonance in the research environment," defining normative dissonance as "inconsistency or lack of consonance between beliefs and behaviors related to norms." They conducted a survey of 3,247 U.S. scientists working on research funded by the National Institutes of Health, composed somewhat evenly of a mid-career sample (those who had received their first research grants between 1999 and 2001) and an early-career sample (those who had received post-doctoral training grants during 2000 or 2001). As explained in their methods section (Anderson, Martinson, and De Vries, 2007; p. 6), "[t]he questionnaire included items to measure subscription, enactment, and perceptions of other's typical behavior, each in terms of norms and counternorms." Their findings "reveal an uneasy tension in the research environment" (p. 13). They found that "[g]iven a choice between characterizing their own and others' behavior as normative or counternormative, most put themselves quite solidly on the normative side but other scientists on the opposite" (p. 8). Specific data includes the following (p. 8):

> In terms of their own behavior, most scientists still have higher norm than counternorm scores, though much larger percentages, 26 and 32%, have equal norm and counternorm scores, and 5 and 7% rate their own behavior as more counternormative than normative. Finally, and

most strikingly, a majority of researchers in the two samples, 61 and 76%, rank the typical behavior of scientists as more counternormative than normative.

In their discussion of findings, they argue their results (Anderson, Martinson, and De Vries, 2007; p. 12) "show that scientists do not just live in a world of normative dissonance: they are also subject to pressures and influences in their environments that compromise collective adherence to traditional norms." They also explained that normative dissonance provides otherwise principled scientists with a rationale to (p. 12) "align one's own behavior with others', instead of with one's principles, in cases where the two are opposed." The implications for building and maintaining a culture of scientific integrity at an institutional level, with respect to preventing misconduct, are significant.

In a disturbing report by Tilbert et al. (2008), a survey of 679 physicians revealed that 46%–58% prescribed placebo treatments to their patients on a regular basis—without necessarily telling them. Placebos that were reportedly prescribed included saline, sugar pills, over the counter analgesics, vitamins, and antibiotics. In the majority of cases, the phony "treatment" was described as beneficial, with the caveat that it was not typically used for treating the specific symptoms or condition at hand. Additionally, the study found that 62% of respondents believed that this practice was ethically permissible because of the outcome (Harris, 2008): "Everyone comes out happy: the doctor is happy, the patient is happy." This despite an advisory from the American Medical Association (AMA) discouraging the use of placebos by physicians when represented as helpful to their condition (Harris, 2008).

More recently, Fanelli (2009) offered the first ever meta-analysis of research regarding the frequency with which scientists fabricate, falsify, or commit other forms of scientific misconduct. It involves the examination of 21 different surveys conducted between 1986 and 2005. Fanelli's study revealed that 1.97% of scientists admitted to having fabricated, falsified, or modified data or results at least once (a low result was expected, as most scientists would not want to admit fraud in their own work); and 33.7% were willing to concede using other questionable research practices.[10] However, when asked about the behavior of colleagues, the same scientists reported 14.12% had falsified data or findings, and as many as 72% had engaged in other questionable research practices. The final analysis states (p. 9): "while surveys asking about colleagues are hard to interpret conclusively, self-reports

---

[10]Questionable research practices included things like trimming data and failing to report data that contradicted previous research.

systematically underestimate the real frequency of scientific misconduct. Therefore, it can be safely concluded that data fabrication and falsification—let alone other questionable research practices—are more prevalent than most previous estimates have suggested." These findings are consistent with Anderson, Martinson, and De Vries (2007), with respect to scientists reporting that they generally avoid misconduct while their immediate colleagues do not—by a wide margin.

FRAUD DIAMOND THEORY AND SCIENTIFIC MISCONDUCT

This section considers whether the previous research related to occupational fraud of a non-scientific nature, and specifically Fraud Diamond Theory, may be applied to the variety of fraud committed by scientists (see Chapter 2, "Occupational Fraud"). As previously referenced, Fraud Diamond Theory states that in order for an act of occupational or employment fraud to occur, there must be a convergence of four elements: offender *motivation (aka pressure or need)*, *opportunity*, *rationalization*, and *individual capability*. These elements are considered and discussed in the case examples that follow.

ANN MARIE GORDON, M.S., AND BARRY LOGAN, PH.D.[11]

Washington State Patrol Crime Lab

According to his professional resume, which lists a Ph.D. in Forensic Toxicology, Dr. Barry Logan became the Washington State Forensic Toxicologist in 1990. In 1999, he was hired to be the Director of the Washington State Patrol Forensic Laboratory Services Bureau—responsible for overseeing four full-service crime labs, two satellite labs, two latent print labs, and all of their combined 160 employees (see Figure 5-3). He served in both positions simultaneously until he resigned in 2008 (Johnson, 2008).

According to her professional resume, Ann Marie Gordon holds a B.A. in "Genetics" and an M.S. in "Microbiology and Immunology," both from the University of California at Berkeley. She was hired as a forensic toxicologist for the Washington State Toxicology Laboratory (WSTL) in 1998, and promoted to Laboratory Manager in 2000. She served in that position until 2007, when she resigned while still under investigation for laboratory fraud (Johnson and Lathrop, 2007).

Based on anonymous tips regarding fraudulent certifications of blood-alcohol-related tests from inside the WSTL, an investigation was launched that ultimately led to the dismissal of at least 100 criminal cases, and harm to the credibility of thousands more. According to a joint three-judge panel decision granting an "Order of Suppression" across multiple criminal cases (*Washington v. Amach, et al.*, 2008; Judge David Steiner, Judge Darrell Phillipson, and Judge Mark Chow), the findings of fact regarding accusations of fraud and misconduct by Ann Marie Gordon and Dr. Barry Logan are as follows, detailed in the section of the decision labeled "False Certifications" (pp. 3–4):

1. Ann Marie Gordon [AMG] became lab Manager at WSTL by appointment of Dr. Logan.
2. [In 2000] AMG informed Dr. Logan that her predecessor as lab manager had engaged in a practice of having other toxicologists prepare and test simulator solutions for him and yet certify that he had prepared and tested the simulator solutions.
3. AMG told Dr. Logan that she did not approve of this procedure and was then also informed by Dr. Logan that it was not acceptable for a toxicologist to engage in this practice.

ANN MARIE GORDON, M.S., AND BARRY LOGAN, PH.D.[11]
CONTINUED

FIGURE 5-3

Barry Logan, Director of the Washington State Patrol Forensic Laboratory Services Bureau, was accused of fraud and misconduct by a three-judge panel. He subsequently resigned and went to work in the private sector, without any known consequences from professional organizations where he holds membership.

4. Nonetheless, AMG did engage in this practice beginning in 2003. Ed Formoso was a lab supervisor; he prepared and tested simulator solutions for AMG from 2003 to 2007. This involved 56 simulator solution tests.

5. Each test was accompanied by a CrRLJ 6.13 certification that AMG had performed the test and that the test was accurate and correct.[12]

6. Melissa Pemberton was the quality control manager at the WSTL during a part of this time, and knew that AMG was not performing tests but was certifying them.

7. This deception was uncovered after two anonymous tips received by the Chief of the Washington State Patrol.

8. The first was received on March 15, 2007. Dr. Logan was directed by Assistant Chief Beckley to investigate this complaint.

9. Dr. Logan directed AMG and Formoso to investigate the complaint.[13]

10. AMG and Formoso discussed the procedure and agreed that Formoso would no longer perform tests on behalf of AMG.

11. AMG informed Dr. Logan that she did not perform the tests of the solutions but that she signed the forms indicating that she did.

12. AMG and Formoso prepared a report stating that there was no problem with the certifications and that no solution had left the lab with an incorrect solution in 20 years.

13. Dr. Logan, AMG, and Formoso knew, or should have known, that this report was incorrect and misleading, but took no steps to correct it or provide for another investigation.

14. Melissa Pemberton had run vials prepared for AMG by Formoso through the gas chromatograph along with her own sample, knowing that these were to be attributed to AMG, and that AMG would sign certificates alleging that she did this.

15. Dr. Logan was aware of this by August of 2007.

16. Dr. Logan and Pemberton both testified under oath that no one other that Formoso ever ran tests for AMG.[14]

The three-judge panel decision (*Washington v. Amach, et al.*, 2008) goes on to describe other significant problems with the WSTL under the direction of Dr. Barry Logan and the management of Ann Marie Gordon, including various "Defective and Erroneous Certification Procedures"; numerous detailed instances of "Software Failure, Human Error, Equipment Malfunction, and Violation of Protocols"; the ongoing use of "Improper Evidentiary Procedures"; the persistence of "Inadequate and Erroneous Protocols and Training"; the overall "Impact on Tests Conducted in the Field"; the WSTL's intentional "Nondisclosure of Machine Bias" to defendants, attorneys, or the public; and the WSTL's "Systematic Inaccuracy, Negligence, and Violation of Scientific Protocols"—all of which affected "Thousands of Tests." The judicial panel determined that all of this misconduct combined to create a "culture of compromise" in the WSTL. Furthermore, the panel explained that ongoing "ethical compromises" and "fraud" committed

Continued

ANN MARIE GORDON, M.S., AND BARRY LOGAN, PH.D.[11]
CONTINUED

by Ann Marie Gordon and her colleagues must have been known to others in their immediate work environment.[15]

Aside from describing false testimony (e.g., that no one other than Mr. Formoso ever ran tests for Ann Marie Gordon), the judicial panel also made it clear that Dr. Barry Logan was responsible for allowing a "culture of compromise" to develop. Additionally, the panel elicited inconsistent testimony from Dr. Logan in which he stated that he was not aware of the specific certifications that were being provided by his lab personnel in toxicology cases. However, the manual of laboratory protocols explaining these certifications in detail bears his signature on each protocol. Subsequently, and in accordance with other findings of fraud, negligence, incompetence, and error already mentioned, the judicial panel determined that Dr. Logan's ignorance, incompetence, and negligence as director prevented these problems from being identified, revealed, and corrected (*Washington v. Amach, et al.*, 2008; pp. 22–23).

Ann Marie Gordon resigned on July 20, 2007, only a few days after the investigation into her misconduct was initiated (Johnson and Lathrop, 2007). In 2008, the Office of the Medical Examiner for the County of San Francisco hired her as a forensic toxicologist. She worked in that system for two years, testifying under oath, before her history of fraud in Washington State was made known to local prosecutors and defense attorneys (Van Der Beken, 2010). She has since asserted her Fifth Amendment right to remain silent and not self-incriminate in subsequent court proceedings. She remains a member of the American Academy of Forensic Sciences (AAFS) in good standing, and as recently as 2011 hosted the annual meeting for The International Association of Forensic Toxicologists (TIAFT) in San Francisco, where she apparently enjoys the continued support of her peers (Verstraete, 2011).

Dr. Barry Logan resigned from the Washington State Patrol Forensic Laboratory in 2008, one year after the resignation of Ann Marie Gordon. Dr. Logan's resignation was necessary for "restoring public and judicial confidence," according to Washington State Patrol Chief John R. Batiste (Batiste, 2008). However, Dr. Logan himself strongly disagrees with the findings of the judicial panel in *Washington v. Amach, et al.* (2008) and takes only some responsibility for the problems that occurred under his management; he believes that the problems with the WSTL were "dramatically overstated" by defense attorneys (Johnson, 2008).[16]

Dr. Barry Logan remains a fellow of the American Academy of Forensic Sciences (AAFS) in good standing; became vice president of the AAFS subsequent to his resignation from the WSTL; and in early 2012, he was voted in as their president-elect (he had disappeared from their officer ranks for several years). He also remains a member in good standing of The International Association of Forensic Toxicologists (TIAFT), the Society of Forensic Toxicologists (SOFT), and the American Society of Crime Laboratory Directors (ASCLD). He is currently the National Director of Forensic Services for National Medical Services Labs, and continues to testify in major cases throughout the United States (Longo, 2011).

This case involved ongoing fraud by supervisory forensic scientists employed by an ASCLD-LAB (2011) accredited police forensic laboratory. It continued for a period of at least four years (2003–2007), involved hundreds of false certifications, and resulted in false testimony to conceal them. In terms of maintaining scientific integrity, the worst practice standards were embraced, acculturated, and then minimized by those involved upon public discovery. Not only did multiple high-ranking scientists certify lies about who had conducted testing bound for court under penalty of perjury, they did so knowing that it was unacceptable scientific practice. Furthermore, they conspired to conceal ongoing fraud and error from the courts, prosecutors, defense attorneys, criminal defendants, and the general public with reports and testimony denying it.

From a scientific misconduct point of view, these cases involved falsification of certifications and reports; a variation on ghost authorship; and the suppression of unfavorable evidence. From an occupational fraud perspective, there was opportunity to engage in fraud and conceal it by virtue of being in a trusted supervisory position; there was rationalization by virtue of a "culture of compromise"; there was motivation by virtue of pressure to maintain the illusion of supervisory competence; and there was individual capability by virtue of positioning, coercion of others to conform, the willingness to deceive others in order to prevent detection, and ego manifested in the unwillingness to accept personal responsibility once the facts were brought to light. This is consistent with the necessary elements of Fraud Diamond Theory.

It is of significant concern that an enduring culture of fraud, incompetence, and compromise was created and sustained during the overlapping tenures of Barry Logan

ANN MARIE GORDON, M.S., AND BARRY LOGAN, PH.D.[11]
CONTINUED

and Ann Marie Gordon. Of equal concern, however, is the complicity of the criminal justice and forensic science communities in general, both of which continue to employ and protect these examiners without significant consequence. This is demonstrated by the failure to suspend or revoke professional memberships; the failure to disclose the history of false certifications by supervisors in Ms. Gordon's new employment environment; the downplaying of fraud by supervisors in Ms. Gordon's new employment environment;

and the failure of ASCLD-LAB to suspend or revoke the certification of the WSTL.

These law enforcement-employed criminalists, having committed their acts within the parameters and time frame set for this study (2000–2010), were both included in the final data set. Impact data was not replicated for both individuals, to prevent duplication in the data. See Chapter 8, "Forensic Fraud, 2000–2010: Data and Frequency," for details regarding inclusion criteria and data collected.

[11]All documents, exhibits, and testimony referenced in this case example can be found archived online at "KING COUNTY, 3 JUDGE PANEL RULING," url: http://www.waduicenter.com/?page_id= 470. Cited as Washington v. Amach, et al. (2008).

[12]The record is clear that the forms signed by Ann Marie Gordon indicate they are signed "under penalty of perjury" (McEachran, 2008; O'Brien, 2007; and Washington v. Amach, et al., 2008; p. 20).

[13]The wrongness of directing those committing fraud to investigate themselves was not lost on the panel, which they referred to as (Washington v. Amach, et al., 2008; p. 23) "a situation screaming with irony."

[14]Dr. Logan testified before the three-judge panel in Washington v. Amach, et al. (2008) from January 7 to 9, 2008.

[15]Dr. Barry Logan had a history of hiring known forensic frauds to work for the Washington State Patrol Forensic Laboratory, including Charles Vaughan, a former criminalist with the Oregon State Police crime lab made infamous over his role in the Boots and Proctor wrongful conviction case (Teichroeb, 2004a); and Arnold Melnikoff, former Director of the Montana State Crime Laboratory (from 1970 to 1989), made

infamous for misrepresenting the evidence in multiple rape and murder cases that were eventually overturned (Bohrer, 2002). In 2003, the Washington State Patrol issued a report recommending that Mr. Melnikoff be terminated for a three-year track record of incompetence and reaching conclusions that were "weak or unsupported by sufficient data" (Geranios, 2003; see also Chapter 7, "Forensic Fraud: Prior Research").

[16]In April of 2008, the Washington State Forensic Investigations Council (FIC) wrote a report condemning fraud among Dr. Logan's subordinates at the crime lab. However, it did not hold Dr. Logan himself accountable (McEachran, 2008). Composed of appointees from the law enforcement community with a mandate to preserve and protect the lab system, the FIC ignored the court's findings of fraud in Washington v. Amach, et al. (2008). It also did not appear to hold Dr. Logan accountable for the negligence it agrees occurred under his supervision—failing to adequately supervise Ann Marie Gordon and others, failing to know what certifications were being provided by lab employees to the courts, and failing to be aware of ongoing fraud and error despite the fact that everyone else in the lab was aware of it.

RAYMOND COLE, CRIMINALIST

San Diego County Sheriff's Crime Laboratory

This case involves the falsification of relevant scientific credentials by a criminalist in a law enforcement forensic laboratory accredited by ASCLD-LAB (2011). As described in Strumpf (2006), it was Raymond Cole's job to "explain to judges and jurors how alcohol and drugs impair drivers and how the police measure levels of intoxication." He also gave training in related instrumental analysis to forensic scientists and police officers.

According to the official memo from the Office of the District Attorney in San Diego County (Rodriguez, 2006): "Ray Cole was a criminalist employed by the San Diego County Sheriff's Crime Laboratory who has testified as a prosecution witness in a number of criminal prosecutions from 1974 to January 2006." If not read carefully, this language

might leave the impression that the number of times Mr. Cole testified was not actually in the thousands. As more accurately explained in Moran (2006): "A criminalist who testified for San Diego prosecutors in possibly thousands of drunken-driving cases falsely described his background on his résumé for years, which could imperil some convictions." This is consistent with Strumpf (2006), which reports that the number is in the thousands, but that officials don't see it as the government's job to find and review each case:

> According to testimony from a 2003 DUI trial, Cole estimated he'd testified "well over 4,000 times" during his career, but representatives of [District Attorney Bonnie] Dumanis, [City

Continued

RAYMOND COLE, CRIMINALIST *CONTINUED*

Attorney Mike] Aguirre and the crime lab all say they have no way of tracking those cases. Instead, they put the responsibility for unearthing the trail of their expert witness on defense attorneys.

[Justin Brooks, a professor at California Western School of Law and head of the California Innocence Project] said the government, not defense attorneys, should be responsible for notifying individuals in whose cases Cole testified. "I don't think it's practical or appropriate as a solution," he said, noting that during the past 30 years, many defense attorneys may have moved, quit, retired or died.

The memo from the Office of the District Attorney in San Diego County goes on to relate that (Rodriguez, 2006) "[t]he Sheriff's Crime Laboratory has informed us there was an error on Mr. Cole's resume that may have been provided in discovery in those cases. Mr. Cole's resume stated that his 1957 undergraduate degree was in premedical studies. His actual degree was in Political Science." If not read carefully, this description provided by the Office of the District Attorney might leave the false impression that this act of deliberate fraud was akin to an unintentional clerical error or a bookkeeping mistake. However, the nature of the false information could only have been offered to support employment as a forensic scientist and subsequently bolster the credibility of related expert testimony in court. It served no other purpose. As Mr. Cole had no actual science background, and gained employment and credibility as a criminalist based initially on false credentials, this meets the threshold definition of fraud and not error.

However, other law enforcement representatives have also shown interest in minimizing Mr. Cole's fraud, which was discovered during an internal audit. According to Chris Morris, head of the criminal division in the San Diego City Attorney's Office (Moran, 2006): "The strength of his testimony was based on his years as a criminalist, not whatever his course of study was back in the 1950s." While this may have been true later in Mr. Cole's career, his initial employment was achieved under false pretenses. Moreover, each time the phony resume was offered to the court, as evidence of Mr. Cole's background and credibility, it involved a new deception to protect the initial fraud. The fact that he lied consistently to the court and also deceived his employers for 30 years makes his fraud worse, not better, with respect to the strength of professional credibility.[17]

Greg Thompson, the San Diego County Sheriff's Crime Laboratory's director of forensic services, explained that

"[w]hen Cole was hired in 1974, a degree in science was not a requirement for the job." This additional attempt to minimize Mr. Cole's fraud is an admission that the County has not always been in the practice of hiring scientists, or those with a scientific background, to perform forensic casework at the crime lab. This admission does not speak well of employment standards, or the remaining personnel, at the crime lab. Again, it would suggest that things are much worse, and certainly does not excuse repeated credential fraud in court.

Defending himself, Mr. Cole explained that he never actually testified under oath regarding the phony degree; that he only listed it on his resume (which was provided to the court, prosecutors, and defense attorneys every time he testified). This attempt to excuse fraudulent conduct suggests that he does not feel he has done anything wrong—that the ends (e.g., his good work for the police and subsequent testimony in court) justify the means (e.g., obtaining employment and court acceptance as a forensic expert by means of fraud). Consequently, Mr. Cole's rationalization appears akin to a noble cause justification.

From a scientific misconduct point of view, this case involved falsification of scientific credentials in a context where they were material to both initial employment and ongoing expert forensic testimony. From an occupational fraud perspective, there was opportunity to engage in the fraud and conceal it by virtue of being in a trusted position; there was rationalization by virtue of a noble cause; there was motivation by virtue of the need for employment and demonstration of expertise in the courtroom; and there was individual capability by virtue of positioning, the willingness to deceive others in order to prevent detection, and ego manifested in the unwillingness to accept personal responsibility once the facts were brought to light. This is consistent with the necessary elements of Fraud Diamond Theory.

This criminalist's fraud, having been committed while employed by a law enforcement ASCLD-LAB accredited crime lab, was revealed within the parameters and time frame set for this study (2000–2010). It was therefore included in the final data set. See Chapter 8 for details regarding inclusion criteria and data collected.

---

[17]It should be noted that current employment application guidelines for San Diego County require an affirmation that all information provided by the applicant be true; that providing any false or incomplete information can lead to denial of the application or termination subsequent to employment (San Diego County, 2011). In other words, the County takes resume fraud seriously, and considers it a termination offense. This is consistent with the language on most employment application forms.

EDWARD J. WOLFRUM

Audio Graphic Services, Royal Oak, Michigan

This case involves a private consultant operating out of Royal Oak, Michigan. Through his company, Audio Graphic Services, Mr. Edward J. Wolfrum provides forensic analysis of audio recordings. As provided in the appellate court decision affirming his conviction (*Idaho v. Edward J. Wolfrum*, 2007):

> In 2000, Wolfrum testified as an expert witness on behalf of a defendant in a Cassia County criminal case. He testified that in his opinion, an audio recording upon which the State relied as evidence of the defendant's guilt had been altered by editing. As part of his qualifications as an expert witness, Wolfrum testified that he held a Ph.D. in advanced mathematics from the "Michigan Institute of Technology." Wolfrum was later charged with perjury because he held no such degree.

Mr. Wolfrum testified to holding an advanced degree to bolster his forensic expertise from an institution that does not exist. He was subsequently arrested and tried for the crime of *perjury*, a violation of Idaho Code § 18-5401, which provides that perjury is committed by a person who, having taken an oath to testify truthfully, "willfully and contrary to such oath, states as true any material matter which he knows to be false" (*Idaho v. Wolfrum*, 2007).

In his defense of the perjury charge, Mr. Wolfrum testified that when he erroneously referred to the "Michigan Institute of Technology," he actually meant the Michigan Technological University—a well-known institution of higher education. According to the court record from Mr. Wolfrum's perjury trial (*Idaho v. Wolfrum*, 2007): "the registrar from Michigan

Technological University (MTU) testified that the institution had no record of Wolfrum ever attending or being registered at MTU, much less having received a degree, and that the institution offered no graduate degree in advanced mathematics."

Mr. Wolfrum was convicted of perjury, and subsequently failed in his appeal. He was not and is not a member of any relevant professional forensic organizations and continues to own and operate Audio Graphic Services. Though numerous services are offered and referenced on the company's website at www.audiographicservices.com, forensic analysis is not among them.

From a scientific misconduct point of view, this case involved falsification of scientific credentials in a context where they were material to expert forensic testimony. From an occupational fraud perspective, there was opportunity to engage in the fraud and conceal it by virtue of being in a trusted position; there was rationalization by virtue of a possible financial incentive; there was motivation by virtue of the need for demonstrating expertise in the courtroom; and there was individual capability by virtue of the willingness to deceive others in order to prevent detection, and ego manifested in the unwillingness to accept personal responsibility once the facts were brought to light. This is consistent with the necessary elements of Fraud Diamond Theory.

The fraud of this independent forensic expert, committed in the course of physical evidence examination and related courtroom testimony, was revealed within the parameters and time frame set for this study (2000–2010). It was therefore included in the final data set. See Chapter 8 for details regarding inclusion criteria and data collected.

These case examples, which are representative of the sample in the present study, suggest that the previous research related to occupational fraud of a non-scientific nature, and specifically Fraud Diamond Theory, may be successfully applied to fraud committed by scientists. They also suggest the utility of scientific misconduct as a construct for classifying cases of forensic fraud. At the same time, they further demonstrate the limited nature of a "bad apple" approach to understanding occupational fraud; all but Wolfrum evidence an abiding connection to employment cultures that permit, minimize, and ultimately fail to criminalize fraud by its members.

SUMMARY

Scientific culture is defined by a history of consistently referenced practices, values, obligations, and prohibitions intended to achieve and protect scientific integrity. They include honesty, use of the scientific method, skepticism, objectivity, transparency, and a host of other related scientific ideals and norms. The development of these scientific norms has involved the corresponding generation of specific terms and definitions related to the investigation, identification, and remedy of scientific misconduct (referred to commonly as scientific fraud). These prohibitions, with a history that goes back to at least the 1830s, include fabrication (aka forging or dry-labbing); falsification (aka cooking); suppression of unfavorable results (aka cherry-picking); plagiarism; ghost authorship (aka honorary or gift authorship); falsification of scientific credentials; and the reckless disregard for practice standards that ensure scientific integrity.

Scientific misconduct is both pervasive and extensive. High-profile cases reported in the media over the past decade have generally involved years of ongoing misconduct by those operating at a supervisory level; millions of dollars misappropriated in each instance; and cultural environments where prior subordinate attempts to abide with basic standards of scientific integrity had been discouraged or punished. In contrast, recently reported cases of scientific misconduct tended to be more mundane: they generally involved student researchers or newly minted scientists engaged in both fabrication and falsification past the point of publication. They also tended to occur without the knowledge of more senior co-authors who uncritically accepted the integrity of the fraudster's data and findings—a common violation of scientific norms.

Despite the steady volume of cases involving scientific misconduct that are published in the literature and publicized by the media each year, assessments of overall frequency are inconsistent. The reason is that confirmed cases of scientific misconduct are often unreported; are handled internally and not publicized; and do not always involve consequences for those responsible. As a result, the reported and known cases of scientific fraud are considered merely the "tip of the iceberg" (again, this is a problem with most crime data).

The "iceberg" theory of estimated frequency is consistent with research from multiple studies which have found that the vast majority scientists believe themselves to be generally engaged in ethical and honest scientific practice (or generally unwilling to self-report misconduct). These scientists also reported being surrounded by a majority of colleagues that regularly engaged in data fabrication, falsification, and other questionable research practices. This same research goes on to suggest that scientists exist predominantly in a state of "normative dissonance," subject to "counternormative" pressures and influences within their work environments that can eventually weaken adherence to traditional scientific norms.

In the context of the present study, the body of research related to occupational fraud of a non-scientific nature, and specifically Fraud Diamond Theory, was successfully applied to cases of fraud committed by scientists in their work environment. Additionally, the case examples adduced in this chapter were instructive as to the relationship between fraud, science, and employment culture. Not only did they suggest the relevance of occupational and scientific fraud research to instances of forensic fraud, they also suggested the weaknesses inherent in a "bad apple" approach to understanding occupational fraud.

CHAPTER 6

Contrasting Scientific Integrity with Law Enforcement Culture

"Persons acquire patterns of criminal behavior in the same way they acquire patterns of lawful behavior—through learning in interaction with other persons."

Criminologist Donald R. Cressey, Ph.D. (1919–1987)

(Cressey, 1952; p. 43)

In the preceding chapters, we explored the occupational environments of law enforcement and science as they relate to fraud. Given that we are examining the phenomenon of forensic fraud by scientific examiners who are most often employed by law enforcement agencies, these were critical first steps. Primarily, we established how fraud presents and is regarded in each of these professional cultures, as well as the methods used in fraud assessment. This exploration of the literature also confirmed the values and consequent pressures that necessarily exist within scientific and law enforcement cultures, all of which constrain members to conform.

The current chapter contrasts the established values of law enforcement culture against those required for scientific integrity, and theorizes at the potential impact on the forensic examiner. Specifically, there is a discussion of scientific fraud in light of *Routine Activities Theory, Differential Association Theory,* and *Role Strain* to contextualize the relevance of focusing on cultural and institutional traits as they influence acts of workplace fraud. Using these criminological constructs, we can juxtapose scientific and law enforcement cultures in an informed manner. This reveals the strain that law enforcement alignment can bring to bear upon the already stressed forensic examiner. Based on this comparison of traits and values, and in the light of related criminology theory, it is argued that scientific integrity is essentially incompatible with law enforcement culture.

DISPENSING WITH "BAD APPLE" THEORY

Before a meaningful discussion of relevant criminological theory can be had, it is necessary to dispense with the traditional explanations provided by those

97

responsible for managing issues of fraud and error within the law enforcement and forensic science communities.

To avoid personal responsibility and institutional liability for instances of employee misconduct, those in a supervisory or leadership role are known for making declarations that focus primarily on individual examiner impurity and the conduct of isolated "bad apples." This approach toward explaining misconduct, which ignores supervisory, environmental, and cultural factors, is referred to as *Rotten Apple*, *Bad Apple*, or *Bad Actor* theory (Adams and Pimple, 2005; Judson, 2004; Marshall, 2000; Resnick, 2003; and Sovacool, 2008). In this paradigm, it is argued that the problem of misconduct within a given agency or institution is all but solved by identifying, retraining, punishing, or terminating one or two troubled (or "rogue") individuals (Judson, 2004).

Supervisory law enforcement authorities, in response to accusations of fraud and error, are known for these kinds of defensive assertions—dismissively suggesting that any known instances of forensic fraud are isolated to a "few rogue practitioners" or "bad apples" (Budowle, 2007; Chemerinsky, 2005; Collins and Jarvis, 2007; Dorfman, 1999; Jarrett, 2011; Martinelli, 2006; Olsen, 2002; Pyrek, 2007; Taylor, 2011; Taylor and Doyle, 2011a,b; and Thompson, 2009). These claims are useful because they protect the reputations of remaining employees and the overall image of the institution; at the same time, they require no further action, investigation, or responsibility on the part of remaining supervisors. As explained in Sovacool (2008; p. 280):

> To blame only a few individual violators or institutions divides the scientific community into the guilty and the innocent, and heaps large amounts of contempt on the few singled out as violators. It therefore creates the illusion of solidarity among the scientific community, reaffirming their central virtue. And by isolating a few behaviors as corrupt, it stamps all others as blameless. In this way the interests of corporate and government patrons of science are less likely to come under attack.

The rationale for invoking Bad Apple Theory to explain scientific misconduct is provided in Judson (2004; p. 26): "The grandees of the scientific establishment regularly proclaim that scientific fraud is vanishingly rare and that perpetrators are isolated individuals who act out of a twisted psychopathology. As a corollary, they insist that science is self-correcting." Certainly, there are internal causes and motives that compel particular examiners to engage in misconduct, including financial stasis, financial gain, ego, vanity, professional advancement, the need to conceal incompetence, apathy, addictions, and other mental infirmity (Judson, 2004; Kumar, 2010; Redman and Mertz, 2005; and Weed, 1998). Yet these elements are only part of the overall equation. Researchers have found that focusing on individual "bad apples" without consideration of how they were planted or grown in a particular environment provides an incomplete understanding of the problem at best.

Scientific fraud is conceived in the literature as arising largely from three factors acting separately or in concert: individual examiner impurity (e.g., a personal lack of ethics or integrity); localized institutional failure; and structural crisis within a scientific community at large (Sovacool, 2008). Adams and Pimple (2005) further explain that acts of scientific misconduct (p. 229) "require both internal states (propensity) as well as external resources (opportunity)." This is consistent with the environmental and employment constraints described in Dorey (2010; p. 17): "There is no reason to think that scientists are fundamentally different from other human beings when it comes to the pursuit of fame and financial reward.… The pressure in terms of 'publish or perish' and the increasing difficulty of getting jobs and grants funded certainly adds to the problem."

It is also generally agreed that individual propensity is less of a factor in scientific misconduct than external situational strains—including the pressure to publish, competition for funding, lack of adequate training or supervision, lack of opportunities for quality mentoring, mentors setting bad examples, or working in an environment that tolerates or encourages misconduct as a means to an end (Adams and Pimple, 2005; Judson, 2004; Marshall, 2000; Redman and Mertz, 2005; Resnick, 2003; Sovacool, 2008; and Weed, 1998). Therefore, as explained in Judson (2004; p. 149): "The lesson must be that the laboratory, its hierarchy, and the larger institutional setting—factors that can be analyzed, anticipated, perhaps modified— may make such conflicts between an individual's intellectual and personal motives more likely, or less likely." Breaches of scientific integrity, including acts that fall within the parameters of scientific misconduct, are primarily the result of institutional failures to uphold scientific values and nurture scientific culture; such breaches are therefore the institution's responsibility to detect, investigate, and correct (Adams and Pimple, 2005; De Vries, Anderson, and Martinson, 2006; Franzen, Rödder, and Weingart, 2007; Jette, 2005; Judson, 2004; Kline, 1993; Martinson, Anderson, and de Vries, 2005; NAS, 2002; Redman and Kaplan, 2005; Sovacool, 2008; and Weed, 1998).

Ultimately, as provided in Judson (2004; p. 28): "that fraud is almost always the work of isolated, twisted individuals seems inherently unlikely." Moreover, given the dearth of solid research into the specific causes, origins, and frequencies of scientific fraud, there is a lack of empirical "evidence" to support the general assertion of *Bad Apple Theory*; as argued in Judson (2004; pp. 26–27): "The grandees make these claims as a matter of faith.... Their claims about science are unscientific." It is argued in this dissertation, and consistent with the scientific literature presented in this section, that corrupt individuals cannot be hired, or retained, by any employer without some level of institutional or environmental negligence, apathy, tolerance, or even encouragement. Consequently, it is inappropriate to place the blame for misconduct solely on bad or rotten apples, to marginalize the suggestion of systemic corruption, or to close ranks in order to protect the appearance of institutional integrity.

RELEVANT CRIMINOLOGICAL THEORY: ROUTINE ACTIVITIES THEORY, DIFFERENTIAL ASSOCIATION THEORY, AND ROLE STRAIN

The choice to commit an act of fraud does not occur in a vacuum: by definition, the perpetrator willfully follows a path that leads them to intentionally deceive others. The question becomes the degree to which they were constrained or encouraged by their environment along the way. In other words, in order to understand the causes of forensic fraud, as with any other potentially criminal act, one needs to first establish and understand the relationship between the motivated perpetrator and the environment that allows fraud to occur. Specifically, once the level of "individual examiner impurity" has been established, the influence of localized institutional failure, as well as any structural crises within a scientific community at large, must also be assessed. This requires the employment of criminological theories appropriate to the task.

In the present research, Routine Activities Theory, Differential Association Theory, and Role Strain proved valuable to the development of our thesis statements. These criminological theories embrace and support the premise that crime is a function of individual choice shaped heavily by environmental factors. A brief discussion of each is necessary.

In their foundational research describing what has come to be known as *Routine Activities Theory* (RAT), criminologists Cohen and Felson (1979) explain (p. 604): "the convergence in time and space of three elements (motivated offenders, suitable targets, and the absence of capable guardians) appears useful for understanding crime rate trends. The lack of any of these elements is sufficient to prevent the occurrence of successful direct-contact predatory crime." In other words, RAT proposes that (Sasse, 2005; p. 547) "victimizations occur when there is a convergence in space and time of a motivated offender, a suitable target, and an absence of a capable guardian."[1,2]

This theory of crime is well suited to assist with the present study of causality and prevention related to forensic fraud: in accordance with Judson (2004), it focuses on the location or place (e.g., workplace) where a crime occurs, and corresponding institutional responsibility, as opposed to theories that empha-size primarily the personality traits of the individual (Reid, 2003).

Differential Association Theory (DAT; aka Differential Association-Reinforce-ment) was first published in 1947 by Edwin Sutherland, a sociological crimi-nologist, as a means to (Vold and Bernard, 1988; p. 210) "organize the many diverse facts known about criminal behavior into some logical arrangement," or as Cressey (1952) explains, to provide (p. 43) "a general theory of crime causation." DAT, in association with Social Learning Theory discussed in Chap-ter 4, "Fraud in Law Enforcement Culture," proposes that criminal behaviors, crime-specific techniques, criminal motives, and corresponding rationaliza-tions for violating the law are not genetic; that they are learned through direct social interaction with others; and that criminal values vary, depending on an individual's perception of related social, cultural, and peer attitudes (Jeffery, 1965; Matsueda, 2006; Reid, 2003; Sutherland, 1947; and Vold and Bernard, 1986). As explained in Cressey (1952; p. 43): "persons acquire patterns of criminal behavior in the same way they acquire patterns of lawful behavior—through learning in interaction with other persons." As an adjunct to this the-ory, the propensity for criminal behavior is maintained by material and social consequences, or their absence (Jeffery, 1965). This theory of crime is also well suited to assist with the present study of causality and prevention related to forensic fraud: it provides that the development criminal patterns by an indi-vidual are a reflection of their contact with those who accept, rationalize, and engage in criminal activity—including supervisors and workmates (Matsueda, 2006; Ruiz-Palomino and Martinez-Canas, 2011).

Related to DAT, *General Strain Theory* suggests that criminogenic propensity arises "from the failure of institutions, families and other structures to provide for the functional and affective needs of individuals" (Donegan and Danon,

---

[1]Variations of this theory (e.g., Rational Choice Theory and the theory of crime prevention by environmental design) have been developed by the criminologist Ronald Clarke and his colleagues, who have empirically tested its salience under a wide variety of crime-related conditions (see generally Clarke and Felson, 2004; and Clarke, Newman, and Shoham, 1997).
[2]It bears mentioning that Routine Activities Theory (formalized in 1979) is remarkably similar to, if not simply a broader application of the concepts in, Fraud Triangle Theory (formalized in 1953; discussed in Chapters 2, "Occupational Fraud," and 4, "Fraud in Law Enforcement Culture"). However, Fraud Triangle Theory has not been subjected to the same empirical testing, hence our greater reliance on Routine Activities Theory when considering the present data.

2008; p. 4). This can result in personal feelings of alienation, which in turn can manifest as anti-social or even criminal behavior. In this paradigm, criminal behavior is viewed as an individual response to external sources of stress or strain (Akers, 2000; Colvin, Cullen, and Vander Ven, 2002).

Role Strain, as a part of General Strain Theory, posits that individuals experience difficulty when required to fulfill competing or contradictory role demands (Goode, 1960; Hecht, 2001; and Kennedy and Kennedy, 1972). Specifically, it provides that individual strain increases when "demands associated with one role interfere directly with one's ability to satisfy the demands of another role" (Hecht, 2001; p. 112). In an employment context, employee role obligations are prescribed by institutional policy and supervisory instruction; however, these can be contradicted or even contravened by directives from multiple supervisors, work overload, and pressure from workmates to conform with adverse cultural norms (Pettigrew, 1968). Individuals experiencing role strain continually bargain with themselves regarding which of their competing role demands to satisfy, and tend to seek out options that reduce or alleviate the anxiety caused by strain (Goode, 1960).

The theory of Role Strain can be used "to illuminate the problem of structurally determined tension and conflict in organizations" (Pettigrew, 1968; p. 206). This includes role strain within a law enforcement context where cultural loyalty is highly valued, direct supervision is often inadequate or absent, and role demands continuously shift from one ambiguous situation to the next (Kennedy and Kennedy, 1972; Maahs and Pratt, 2001).

The same argument applies to a scientific community, where an examiner's desire to maintain scientific integrity may be in conflict with professional and institutional pressures (Dorey, 2010; Martinson, Anderson and de Vries, 2005). For example, in a clinical or university setting, there may be pressure on scientists to continuously publish research in order to sustain employment, achieve advancement, or secure and maintain funding. Stressing quantity over quality can thin the actual science in some publications to unacceptable levels, or even encourage ghost/gift authorship. In forensic laboratories, the same kind of quantity over quality pressure can be applied to maintain increasing caseloads or reduce backlogs despite staff or budgetary shortfalls—which may cause some to cut corners, ignore protocols, and then to conceal what hasn't been done. Additionally, in a forensic science context, there are numerous examples of law enforcement employers pressuring scientists to report findings that are in accordance with suspect theories, or of law enforcement-aligned scientists perceiving pressure to avoid the appearance of helping the defense.[3]

---

[3]Examples provided later in this chapter.

Applying these criminological theories as a lens to the present research, we will juxtapose scientific values and law enforcement culture to "illuminate" institutional responsibility (RAT), workmate pressure (DAT), and subsequent examiner role strain as they contribute to the problem of forensic fraud in the subsequent sections of this chapter.[4]

OVERT PRESSURE TO CONFORM

Over the past decade, the subconscious influences on forensic examiners to bias their efforts in favor of law enforcement theories have slowly been acknowledged in the literature. These influences are referred to as observer effects. *Observer effects* are present when the results of a forensic examination are distorted by the employment context and mental state of forensic examiners, to include subconscious expectations and desires imposed by their employers, supervisors, and workmates (Cooley and Turvey, 2011; Dror, Charlton, and Peron, 2006; Edwards and Gotsonis, 2009; Risinger et al., 2002; and Saks et al., 2003). Observer effects are governed by fundamental principles of cognitive psychology asserting that subconscious needs and expectations, which are heavily influenced by external pressures and expectations, work to shape both examiner perception and interpretation. As the term *subconscious* implies, this happens without the awareness of the forensic examiner. In the context of a forensic examination, this includes a distortion of what is recognized as evidence, what is collected, what is examined, and how it is interpreted. However, subconscious forms of bias are beyond the scope of the present research.

Presently, we are concerned with forensic examiners who perceive overt institutional, supervisory, or workmate pressure to conform with biased values and norms (e.g., in 1995, the acknowledgment of Dr. Fred Whitehurst, FBI whistleblower, in sworn testimony, that "there was a great deal of pressure put upon me to bias my interpretation," as reported in Hsu, Jenkins, and Mellnick, 2012). Specifically, we are concerned with the differential association and subsequent role strain that law enforcement alignment and influence can bring to bear upon forensic examiners. It is theorized that these circumstances make conscious acts of fraud by law enforcement-employed or -affiliated forensic examiners more likely.

At this point, some examples of the kinds of overt pressure suffered by law enforcement-employed and -affiliated forensic examiners within the temporal scope of the present research are appropriate.

---

[4]Additional related discussions can also be found in Chapter 7, "Forensic Fraud: Prior Research," and Chapter 10, "Conclusions and Recommendations."

KATHLEEN LUNDY, FORENSIC SCIENTIST

FBI Crime Laboratory

Kathleen Lundy held a B.S. in metallurgy and was employed as a forensic scientist by the FBI crime laboratory; as part of her work, she would routinely testify that bullets or bullet fragments associated with a crime were "chemically" and "analytically indistinguishable," or "consistent with," boxes of ammunition found in the possession of law enforcement suspects (*Ragland v. Commonwealth of Kentucky*, 2006). The chemical test that she used in these cases is referred to as comparative bullet lead analysis (aka CBLA). As described in Giannelli (2007; pp. 199–200):

> In *Ragland v. Commonwealth*, a Kentucky murder case, Lundy got herself in trouble while testifying at a pretrial admissibility hearing. She stated that the elemental composition of a .243 caliber bullet fragment removed from the victim's body was "analytically indistinguishable" from bullets found at the home of the defendant's parents. Lundy further testified that the Winchester Company purchased its bullet lead in block form prior to 1996 and then remelted it at its manufacturing plant. During cross-examination at trial, however, Lundy admitted that she knew prior to the hearing that Winchester had purchased its lead in billet form in 1994. This was not a minor point. Millions more bullets could have the same "source" if they were last melted by a secondary smelter instead of by Winchester. Lundy subsequently admitted to her superiors that she had lied, and on June 17, 2003, she pleaded guilty to testifying falsely and was sentenced to a suspended ninety-day jail sentence and a $250 fine.

Further detail regarding the circumstances of Ms. Lundy's false testimony, and the pressure she was under, was reported in Solomon (2003):

> FBI lab scientist Kathleen Lundy, an expert witness in murder trials who performs chemical comparisons of lead bullets, was indicted by Kentucky authorities earlier this year on a charge of misdemeanor false swearing after she acknowledged she knowingly gave false testimony in a 2002 pretrial hearing for a murder suspect.

Lundy informed her FBI superiors of the false testimony a couple of months after it occurred. By that time she had corrected her pretrial testimony at the trial and had been questioned about it by defense lawyers.

Federal authorities decided not to prosecute her, but Kentucky prosecutors brought the misdemeanor charge.

In memos and a sworn affidavit, Lundy stated she had an opportunity to correct her erroneous testimony at the hearing, but didn't. "I had to admit it was worse than being evasive or not correcting the record. It was simply not telling the truth," Lundy wrote in a memo to a superior. "I cannot explain why I made the original error in my testimony … nor why, knowing that the testimony was false, I failed to correct it at the time," Lundy wrote in a subsequent sworn affidavit. "I was stressed out by this case and work in general."

Lundy also said she was increasingly concerned that a former lab colleague, retired metallurgist William Tobin, was beginning to appear as a defense witness in cases and openly questioning the FBI's science on gun lead. "These challenges affected me a great deal, perhaps more than they should have. I also felt that there was ineffective support from the FBI to meet the challenges," Lundy wrote.

While Kathleen Lundy pleaded guilty to false swearing and lost her job at the FBI crime laboratory, she had already testified as an expert in CBLA for the FBI in more than a hundred cases. As of this writing, those cases have all come under review, and at least three convictions secured with her testimony have been overturned. Ultimately, subsequent to being declared junk science by the National Academy of Sciences in 2004 (NAS, 2004), the FBI acquiesced and put an end to all CBLA casework in their lab.

While this case involves an admission to fraud by a single forensic examiner, it involves years of questionable science and similarly aggressive testimony from other forensic examiners working for the same agency. The circumstances of this case comport with RAT (e.g., a motivated

Continued

KATHLEEN LUNDY, FORENSIC SCIENTIST *CONTINUED*

offender without proper supervision) and DAT (e.g., learning by example to give false testimony about match probabilities). They also reveal the strain experienced by the forensic examiner to stay the course with respect to the certainty of findings and testimony despite the fact that she knew the evidence did not warrant it. This pressure, the examples set by FBI supervisors and co-workers, and the lack of institutional support perceived, cannot be discounted when considering her decision to commit fraud on multiple occasions.

This law enforcement-employed forensic examiner, having committed her acts of fraud within the parameters and time frame set for this study (2000–2010), was included in the final data set. See Chapter 8, Forensic Fraud, 2000–2010: Data and Frequency," for details regarding inclusion criteria and data collected.

LYNN SCAMAHORN, FORENSIC SCIENTIST

Indiana State Police Crime Lab—Evansville

David Camm, a former Indiana State Police trooper, was arrested for killing his wife, Kimberly, 35; son, Bradley, 7; and daughter, Jill, 5. He was tried and convicted for all three murders in March of 2002. In 2004, however, the Indiana Court of Appeals overturned these convictions. He was charged and tried again in 2006.

Lynn Scamahorn is a forensic scientist and DNA criminalist with the Indiana State Police Evansville Regional Laboratory. In February of 2006, she took the stand for the prosecution in the second trial of David Camm. Under oath, she reportedly broke down and recounted being pressured during the first trial to change her findings, specifically that "former Floyd County Prosecutor Stan Faith cursed and shouted at her and threatened to charge her with obstruction of justice if she wouldn't testify as he expected" (Zion-Hershberg, 2006). As further reported in Zion-Hershberg (2006):

> Scamahorn said that during a break in her testimony in the first trial, Faith took her to his office and closed the door.
>
> She said she believes he wanted to influence her to testify that she had found Camm's DNA on the sweat shirt....
>
> "I felt that was something I could not say," Scamahorn said, adding that the evidence she found on the sweat shirt didn't support that conclusion.
>
> ...Scamahorn said yesterday that Faith was asking her about DNA evidence that was actually inconclusive and might have contained DNA from several people, including Camm. But

she couldn't determine whose it was, Scamahorn said. "He wanted me to say David Camm was on the sweat shirt, but I couldn't," Scamahorn said.

> Faith also wanted her to say more about unidentified bodily fluids on another piece of evidence than was supported by her tests, Scamahorn said.
>
> She said she has felt no pressure to influence her testimony from Owen or from Keith Henderson, the current Floyd County prosecutor. "It has been more of a team effort," Scamahorn said.
>
> She also said … that she told Faith he could talk with her immediate supervisor if he felt she was testifying improperly. But Faith said he would contact a colonel in the state police several ranks above her supervisor, Scamahorn said. She said she took it "as a threat" to her continued employment.
>
> In a telephone interview, Faith denied threatening Scamahorn in any way. He said he recalled his conversation with her during a break in the first trial. But, he said, they were discussing her reluctance to say that a bodily fluid found on some of the evidence was that of an unknown female.

In a letter of complaint to her supervisor (F. Joseph Vetter, First Sergeant and Manager of the Indiana State Police Evansville Regional Laboratory), written only a few days after her testimony in the first trial, Lynn Scamahorn provided

Continued

LYNN SCAMAHORN, FORENSIC SCIENTIST *CONTINUED*

specific details regarding the pressure applied by the prosecutor's office (Scamahorn, 2002):

> On Friday February 8, 2002 at a break, Mr. Faith called me into his office. There were no witnesses as it was only Mr. Faith and myself. Questioning was now on defense cross and recross stage. Mr. Faith shut the door to his office and began yelling at me very loudly using foul language. I felt it was totally inappropriate behavior and it was extremely unsettling to me due to the fact that I had to go back on the stand after break. Mr. Faith was upset at the fact that he wanted me to state that a stain was identified as vaginal secretions or saliva. To which (on the stand) I said that it could be. Mr. Faith was not satisfied with this answer. He said how could I let the defense lead me all over the place and when he (Mr. Faith) questioned me that I tried to second guess him and was so "damned literal." Mr. Faith stated that he felt I was being biased. Mr. Faith also wanted me to make a statement that David Camm could be included on the sweatshirt and the DNA types clearly do not include David Camm and I felt this is not something that could be stated. I told Mr. Faith that I could not make a statement of identity for vaginal secretions or saliva due to the fact that there is not an identifying test for these types of stains. To which Mr. Faith replied that I was being "told how to testify" and this was a "Class D Obstruction of Justice." I told Mr. Faith that he was welcome to contact my supervisor at Indianapolis ISP Laboratory, Paul Misner and discuss this. Mr. Faith said he would not call Indianapolis, he would call Brackman. Mr. Faith stated that he would open his own laboratory and his analyst could "say whatever they wanted." I told Mr. Faith that if he felt I was being biased then I apologized but restated that I could not testify to the things he wanted me to. He then said "They have been horrible to you over this." At this point I excused myself to the restroom to be able to go back on the stand. After coming out of the restroom, I asked Detective Sean Clemons from Sellersburg district to sit with me so that Mr. Faith would be less likely to yell at me again.

It is important to note that the forensic examiner in this case properly reported overt pressure and threats from an external law enforcement agency (the Floyd County Prosecutor's office) to change DNA interpretations mid-trial. This is the very definition of role strain. However, she had the character to ignore these threats and testified in accordance with the evidence as she perceived it. She also filed an immediate notification of these threats with her own police laboratory manager in order to make a record of the prosecutor's misconduct.

This example does not involve fraudulent behavior by a forensic examiner. Rather, this example serves to demonstrate that extreme pressure to conform exists, that role strain is real, and that there is an ethical way to handle it. In accordance with DAT, it also suggests the culture that the Floyd County Prosecutor's office expected and intended to create with respect to the forensic personnel in its employ, and begs the question regarding the possibility of other forensic examiners under similar pressure to conform.

ROBERT STITES, BLOODSTAIN ANALYST

Private Law Enforcement Consultant

Robert Stites was a retired police officer who testified as an expert in bloodstain pattern analysis for the prosecution in both of David Camm's murder trials (see previous example, "Lynn Scamahorn"). During the second trial, however, Mr. Stites admitted to falsely testifying about his education, training, and experience during the first, as reported in Kozarovich (2006):

[Defense attorney Stacy Uliana] read from the transcript of the first trial where Stites said he had testified as a blood-stain-pattern expert three previous times, but on Wednesday he admitted he had never testified as a blood stain expert.

Continued

ROBERT STITES, BLOODSTAIN ANALYST *CONTINUED*

Stites also told the previous jury he was pursuing his master's degree and Ph.D., though he hadn't been accepted to any program and wasn't taking any classes at the time. In fact, Uliana said, Stites' only degree is in economics, not forensics or blood-stain analysis. At the time of the murders, he had not taken the basic, 40-hour blood analysis course, the defense noted. There are no required standards or tests for crime scene reconstructionists.

Uliana even pointed out that Stites had failed basic college chemistry, which drew a sharp objection from Floyd County Prosecutor Keith Henderson.

Under cross-examination, Uliana also determined the Camm murder scene was the first one Stites had processed as a crime scene specialist without his mentor Rod Englert.

Mr. Stites admitted to being without bloodstain training or experience, and without scientific background or credentials, while testifying under oath to precisely the opposite. From a scientific misconduct standpoint, he gave false testimony about his education, training, and experience. It is unclear, however, whether he also gave false or misleading testimony regarding his findings. In any case, there were no consequences to this examiner for his false testimony.

While this case involves an admission to fraud by a single forensic examiner, it is significant that it occurred in an employment environment reported to be suffused with pressure and strain from the prosecutor's office, which comports with DAT and Role Strain theory (see the preceding example involving Lynn Scamahorn).

This law enforcement employed forensic examiner, having committed his acts of fraud within the parameters and time frame set for this study (2000–2010), was included in the final data set. See Chapter 8 for details regarding inclusion criteria and data collected.

DANIELLE WIELAND, CRIMINALIST

Orange County Sheriff's Department Crime Lab

In 2005, police arrested 20-year-old James Ochoa for robbery and carjacking near a Buena Park nightclub in Orange County, California. Although DNA found on evidence from the crime scene did not match him, Mr. Ochoa was pressured by the district attorney to accept a two-year plea, mid-trial, or face life in prison should the jury find him guilty. While Mr. Ochoa was sitting in prison for a crime that he did not commit, the unknown DNA sample from the scene was matched to the actual offender, a career criminal already serving time in Los Angeles (Moxley, 2008b).

Mr. Ochoa was subsequently released from prison and filed a civil complaint for damages related to wrongful arrest, prosecution, and conviction. During a deposition for that case, Danielle Wieland, a DNA criminalist for the Orange County Sheriff's Department crime lab, testified that prosecutors had pressured her to "alter key exculpatory evidence" (Moxley, 2008a).[5] As further reported in Moxley (2008a):

Wieland performed numerous tests to determine if Ochoa's DNA could be found on items the

bandit inadvertently left at the crime scene: a black baseball cap, a gray plaid long-sleeve shirt and a BB gun. There was also DNA left in the stolen car that didn't belong to the two victims. All of the sheriff's department tests excluded Ochoa as a DNA contributor. Two other crime-lab officials independently double-checked and confirmed Wieland's results. In her official records, she recorded "no [Ochoa] match."

...On Oct. 14, 2005, [prosecutors] asked to meet with Wieland before she shared her findings with defense attorney Scott Borthwick, a young Santa Ana-based lawyer who'd taken the case pro bono because he thought officials were railroading Ochoa. In those meetings—one by phone, two more in person—a deputy district attorney asked Wieland to do something she knew was not supported by the science and possibly outright unethical: Tell Borthwick that Ochoa's DNA had been found on the shirt.

Continued

DANIELLE WIELAND, CRIMINALIST *CONTINUED*

In a civil deposition taken last month for Ochoa's wrongful-prosecution lawsuit, Ochoa attorney Patricio A. Marquez of Morrison & Foerster asked Wieland, "Did anyone ever exert pressure on you to change your [DNA] conclusions?"

"Yes," Wieland replied. "Camille Hill from the DA's office … She called me and asked me to change the conclusion that Mr. Ochoa was eliminated from [DNA found on] the left cuff of the shirt."

According to the transcript, Hill told Wieland she "didn't care" about the crime lab's findings. "I want him [Ochoa] not excluded," Wieland recalls Hill saying.

…In a subsequent face-to-face confrontation, Hill arrived with four other DA staffers including Deputy District Attorney Christian Kim, who was assigned to Ochoa's case. They argued that eyewitness and police-dog identifications of Ochoa as the bandit (sloppy and tainted, respectively) must have been right.

Wieland brought her own crime-lab colleagues as backup. According to Wieland's deposition, "We kind of went back and forth [with the DA's office] on why we felt the sample was eliminated as a contributor. And it ended up with us pretty much not backing down and saying he's still excluded, still eliminated."

Hill, a veteran prosecutor and DNA expert who once worked as a forensic specialist for the Houston Police Department, thinks this is a non-story. She describes herself as a "lawyer/scientist" and defends her contact on the Ochoa case with Wieland. "I, in no way, did anything unusual," Hill tells the *Weekly*. "About every week, we ask the crime lab to reconsider findings. Sometimes, they make changes."

In 2008, Mr. Ochoa's civil complaint successfully resulted in a payment from the State of California for nearly $30,000 (Moxley, 2008b).

It is important to note that, in this case, the forensic examiner perceived overt pressure and threats from an external law enforcement agency (the Orange County Prosecutor's office) to suppress exculpatory DNA evidence. This is, again, the definition of role strain in an employment context that threatens to encourage fraud (and punish ethical behavior), in comportment with DAT. As with the prior example from Indiana, this forensic examiner had the character, and perceived sufficient institutional support, to ignore these threats and testified in accordance with the evidence as she found it.

This example does not involve fraudulent behavior by a forensic examiner, but rather serves again to demonstrate that extreme pressure to change findings and testimony exists, that role strain is real, and that there is a proper way to respond.[6] It also suggests the culture that the Orange County Prosecutor's office expected and intended to create with respect to the forensic personnel in its employ. Specifically, it demonstrates that at least one prosecutor, Camille Hill (a former forensic scientist from the embattled Houston Police Department Crime Lab), viewed herself as a "lawyer/scientist." In that capacity, which is rife with conflict, it is significant that Ms. Hill admitted her office requests the crime lab to reconsider its scientific findings on a regular basis. This, again, would seem to be the very definition of inappropriate pressure, creating role strain for the forensic examiners working in that employment environment.

---

[5]*It is significant to note that this evidence did not come out during the trial of Mr. Ochoa. Had Mr. Ochoa not been exonerated at a later date, not filed a civil complaint, and not deposed Ms. Weiland, this example of prosecutorial misconduct would not have been made public.*

[6]*Indeed, had the forensic scientists in these cases lacked the character to maintain the integrity of their findings, we would likely never have learned of it.*

These examples, which are representative of cases revealed in the present study, are primarily intended to demonstrate the overt cultural hazards suffered upon forensic examiners employed by law enforcement agencies. Some experience differential association and strain by virtue of their agency's cultural tendencies and failings; others experience differential association and strain from the intense pressure placed on them by prosecutors to align their testimony with desired results.

CONTRASTING SCIENTIFIC VALUES AND LAW ENFORCEMENT CULTURE

Using the criminological theories described previously in this chapter as a guide, and with the full understanding that there can be intense strain placed on law enforcement-employed forensic examiners, this section juxtaposes the cardinal traits of law enforcement culture with those required for scientific integrity, as revealed in Chapters 4, "Fraud in Law Enforcement Culture," and 5, "Fraud and Scientific Culture," respectively.

In Chapter 4, it was established that law enforcement organizations provide their employees with the training, opportunity, and authority to commit acts of fraud on a variety of levels. This demands a high level of personal integrity to avoid corruption. However, law enforcement culture is often locally defined by traits that afford the motivations and rationalizations for a deviant internal subculture, actively cultivating fraud within its ranks. Law enforcement culture also provides otherwise lawful members with the skills, incentives, motivations, and rationalizations for ignoring, protecting, and even defending their unlawful co-workers. In light of RAT and DAT, these employment circumstances and cultural facets increase the likelihood that those employed by law enforcement agencies will commit, tolerate, conceal, and even defend acts of overt fraud.

In Chapter 5, the culture of science was defined by a history of consistently referenced practices, values, obligations, and prohibitions intended to achieve and protect scientific integrity. Ideal traits for reliable scientific practice include honesty, use of the scientific method, skepticism, objectivity, transparency, and a host of other related scientific norms. At the same time, scientific integrity prohibits the fabrication of results (aka forging or dry-labbing), falsification of data (aka cooking), suppression of unfavorable results (aka cherry-picking), plagiarism, ghost authorship (aka honorary or gift authorship), falsification of scientific credentials, and the reckless disregard for established practice standards. Therefore, in order for scientific integrity to prevail, it must be nurtured and maintained by examiners and institutions that understand the obligations required.

As shown in Table 6-1, there is almost complete direct conflict between the reality of one and the needs of the other. Law enforcement culture promulgates a noble cause belief system that tolerates corruption at variable levels depending on localized leadership and norms; alternatively, scientific integrity demands zero tolerance for misconduct of any kind. Law enforcement culture is authoritative and coercive, training officers to take charge, solve problems, and maintain control on a continuum of force that includes handcuffs and firearms; alternatively, scientific integrity demands that examiners achieve results through empirical research and analytical logic while embracing overall

Table 6-1 Law Enforcement Culture Versus Scientific Integrity	
Law Enforcement Culture	**Scientific Integrity**
▪ A "noble cause" belief system/varied toleration for corruption	▪ Zero tolerance for misconduct
▪ Authoritative/coercive	▪ Logical, empirical, and fair
▪ Masculinity and aggression	▪ Humility re: limits of findings
▪ Group loyalty/solidarity	▪ Critical thinking/skepticism
▪ Deception as a viable tool	▪ Honesty in reporting
▪ Isolation/"Us versus Them"	▪ Openness to peer review and independent validation
▪ Secrecy/"code of silence" toward error and misconduct	▪ Transparency of errors/reporting of all misconduct
▪ Punishment/ostracism for those who break the "code of silence"	▪ Protection for whistleblowers
▪ Project and protect image of professional integrity	▪ Project and protect image of professional integrity

fairness, without the use of threats or coercion of any kind. Law enforcement culture is essentially masculine and aggressive in its approach to problem solving; alternatively, scientific integrity demands conservative humility and the consideration of alternatives. Law enforcement culture rewards members for unwavering group loyalty and solidarity regardless of the circumstances; alternatively, scientific integrity demands that the findings of others be questioned, to the point of skepticism being a scientific virtue. Law enforcement culture embraces the use of differing levels of deception as a means to an end, lawful and otherwise; alternatively, scientific integrity demands honesty at all levels of reporting. Law enforcement culture instills an "Us versus Them" mentality in its members, creating a sense of isolation from the community and hostility toward outsiders; alternatively, scientific integrity requires examiners to welcome peer review and external inquiry as a necessary part of any validation process. Law enforcement culture is marked by an overall secrecy, or "code of silence," with respect to the errors and misconduct of its membership; those who break this code are punished and in extreme cases ostracized. Scientific integrity mandates transparency of all methodology, including errors, as well as the reporting of any and all misconduct; those who report misconduct, referred to as "whistleblowers," are theoretically entitled to absolute protection without sanction.

However, law enforcement culture and scientific integrity do share one significant trait: the need to project and protect an overall image of integrity. Both must maintain the appearance of integrity to outsiders in order to sustain institutional functionality. Without the appearance of integrity, neither institution could receive outside funding, offer believable reports or testimony, maintain liability insurance, or keep the faith of supervisors and the general public. When the perception of institutional integrity disappears, institutional functionality erodes, sometimes slowly, until the institution itself becomes unsustainable.

On this issue, the demands of law enforcement and science differ primarily with respect to the means by which the perception of integrity is achieved and maintained. Law enforcement sustains this perception through the afore-mentioned culture of secrecy, the "code of silence," and the punishment or blacklisting of any detractors. Additionally, as previously described, Bad Apple Theory is invoked when institutional integrity is questioned, and anyone not closing ranks is suddenly found outside of them. In this paradigm, secrecy is essential, and the outcome is all that matters—that the perception of institu-tional integrity remains defensible for lack of public evidence to the contrary. Scientific integrity, on the other hand, can only be secured by using the *scien-tific method*, which regards secrecy and cronyism as anathema to trustworthi-ness (*Frye v. United States*, 1923; Judson, 2004; Kennedy and Kennedy, 1972; and Popper, 2002). For the scientific examiner, a strict adherence to scientific methodology is more important than any actual outcome, given that scientific examination seeks reliable knowledge and not merely the confirmation of pre-conceived ideas. In a scientific paradigm, outcomes are less important than the methods of inquiry that are being observed.

As mentioned previously, the overall conflict that exists between law enforce-ment culture and scientific integrity is significant because of the fact that (Thorn-ton and Peterson, 2007; p. 2) "[m]ost forensic examinations are conducted in government-funded laboratories, usually located within law enforcement agencies, and typically for the purpose of building a case for the prosecution." Edwards and Gotsonis (2009) warn us further that (pp. 183–184) "[t]he major-ity of forensic science laboratories are administered by law enforcement agen-cies, such as police departments, where the laboratory administrator reports to the head of the agency. This system leads to significant concerns related to the independence of the laboratory and its budget" as well as "cultural pressures caused by the different missions of scientific laboratories vis-à-vis law enforce-ment agencies."

Forensic examiners employed under these conditions are continuously exposed to a culture where members are encouraged (or instructed) to commit, toler-ate, conceal, or defend acts of overt misconduct—often for years.[7] They also experience variable pressure to conform to, and take sides with, the localized

---

[7]For example, even as this text is in its final stages, a new scandal involving the FBI has emerged wherein the results of unfavorable task force findings regarding forensic casework under review since the late 1990s have been intentionally suppressed and concealed, harming an untold number of criminal defendants (Hsu, Jenkins, and Mellnick, 2012).

ethos of law enforcement institutions from their supervisors and workmates.[8] Given the theories of RAT, DAT and Role Strain, continuous exposure to, and pressure from, law enforcement culture increases the likelihood that subordinate forensic examiners will also commit, tolerate, conceal, and even defend acts of overt fraud.

SUMMARY

Breaches of scientific integrity, including acts that fall within the parameters of scientific misconduct, are primarily the result of institutional failures to uphold scientific values and nurture scientific culture; these breaches are therefore an institution's responsibility to detect, investigate, and correct. More specifically, corrupt individuals cannot be hired, or retained, by any employer without some level of institutional negligence, apathy, tolerance, or encouragement. It is therefore inappropriate, and even misleading, to blame forensic fraud solely on "bad apples."

Three criminological theories have proved useful for understanding forensic fraud as a cultural and environmental issue: Routine Activities Theory, Differential Association Theory, and Role Strain.

Routine Activities Theory makes misconduct and criminality more likely among law enforcement professionals and their subordinate forensic examiners given their employment training and constant opportunities; their fierce cultural loyalty, tolerance for misconduct, and code of silence; and their lack of consistent supervision.

Differential Association Theory goes deeper, providing that the development of criminal patterns by an individual is necessarily a reflection of disproportionate contact with those who accept, rationalize, and engage in criminal activity. Evidence of forensic fraud by even a single examiner suggests that this person learned from either the present employment culture, or a previous one, that such behavior is institutionally acceptable on some level. Moreover, ongoing fraud, and fraud by multiple forensic examiners, is evidence of willful institutional and supervisory negligence—if not ongoing cultural pressure to commit acts of fraud.

Role Strain is often high within a law enforcement context, where cultural loyalty is highly valued, direct supervision is often inadequate or absent, and role

---

[8]Some of these forensic examiners are actually little more than "cops in lab coats," without any formal scientific education, grounding, or investment (Findley, 2008; Giannelli, 2003; Moreno, 2004). See also case example "Robert Stites" in this chapter.

demands continuously shift from one ambiguous situation to the next. The strain from multiple and competing role obligations is even higher for forensic examiners. The reason is that most are meant to uphold values and ideals that are in direct conflict with law enforcement culture while working subordinate to or alongside of it.[9]

Under the contextual weight of law enforcement employment, alignment, and cultural pressures, and given full consideration of the criminological theories discussed in this chapter, it is theorized that the already fragile ideals of scientific integrity necessary for objective forensic examinations are more likely to crack, or shatter, in the absence of sufficient institutional safeguards.

---

[9]It bears mentioning that, as discussed in Chapter 5, the requisite traits for scientific integrity are ideals, and that scientific misconduct outside law enforcement influence is not difficult to find. The scientific endeavor is fraught, as discussed, with all manner of strain. Imposing law enforcement culture on a scientist adds additional and unnecessary strain.

CHAPTER 7

Forensic Fraud: Prior Research

"While there have always been bad labs, their shoddy work has been difficult to detect because the worst labs tend to be found in jurisdictions that have historically shielded crime labs from external scrutiny."

William Thompson, J.D., Ph.D.
Department of Criminology, Law & Society
University of California at Irvine
(Thompson, 2006; p. 11)

The preceding chapter contrasted the established values of law enforcement culture against those required for scientific integrity, and theorized at the potential impact on the forensic examiner in light of relevant criminological theory. This was supported by literature reviews related to general occupational fraud, law enforcement culture, and scientific integrity. It was also established that the already-fragile ideals of scientific integrity necessary for objective forensic examinations are essentially incompatible with law enforcement culture.

Because we have reviewed the literature related to fraud, law enforcement culture, and scientific integrity, the present chapter provides the final pillar required to support and contextualize the present research effort: a review of the literature that has addressed the issue of forensic fraud. First, it suggests why there is a dearth of attention paid to the subject, resulting in the overall absence of direct empirical research. Then it reviews the nature of the limited (and indirect) studies that do exist, both ideographic and nomothetic. Finally, based on the relevant literature, a typology of forensic fraud is discussed and expounded with case examples.

BACKGROUND: PUBLIC EMPLOYEE RESTRICTIONS AND FEAR OF RETALIATION

Forensic fraud has an undeniably devastating impact: it destroys the reputations of the forensic examiners involved, if not their careers; it erodes public

Forensic Fraud. http://dx.doi.org/10.1016/B978-0-12-408073-7.00007-0

confidence in the institutions where they are employed; it can result in overturned convictions, individual and institutional liability, and costly civil judgments; and it is corrosive to the collective faith in the justice system as a whole. However, as mentioned in previous chapters, there is a perception that problems related to fraud and error in the forensic sciences are primarily the result of a "few rogue practitioners" or "bad apples"—primarily owing to the public assurances of crime lab managers and supervisors (Budowle, 2007; Collins and Jarvis, 2007; Giannelli, 2007; Olsen, 2002; Pyrek, 2007; Taylor and Doyle, 2011a,b; and Thompson, 2009). Despite the fact that "Bad Apple Theory" is contradicted by established criminological theories relating to fraud and corruption (see Chapter 6, "Contrasting Scientific Integrity with Law Enforcement Culture"), criminal justice professionals and the public they serve tend to accept this explanation insomuch as they offer little in the way of resistance to it. Consequently, and despite the broad spectrum of harm that can result, forensic fraud is given relatively narrow recognition or attention in the published forensic literature.

The dearth of literature disclosing and examining cases of forensic fraud may be the result of general ignorance regarding the nature and scope of the problem. This state of overall blindness is perhaps made possible by two factors working in concert: (1) institutional secrecy protected by law, and (2) employees operating under strict contractual obligation and related general self-interest. In other words, the lack of professional and public awareness regarding forensic fraud, and the resulting absence of any meaningful data or research, may be a result of the reality that those who have direct knowledge also have a vested interest, if not a contractual obligation, to keep it from becoming public.

Government (aka public) institutions, including law enforcement agencies and their respective crime laboratories, generally have written policies and rules of conduct that restrict the speech of their employees—in and outside the workplace. Consider that law enforcement policies are adapted from, or draw heavily on, the "Model Policy on Standards of Conduct" developed by the International Association of Chiefs of Police, which states (IACP, 2012):

1. Officers shall not, under color of authority,
   a. make any public statement that could be reasonably interpreted as having an adverse effect upon department morale, discipline, operation of the agency, or perception of the public;
   b. divulge or willfully permit to have divulged, any information gained by reason of their position, for anything other than its official, authorized purpose; or
   c. unless expressly authorized, make any statements, speeches, or appearances that could reasonably be considered to represent the views of this agency

An example of an adapted standard comes from the Seattle Police Department's Policy and Procedure Manual (SPD, 2012):

IV. Communication and Confidentiality
  A. Through Chain of Command
    1. Employees shall direct communications through their chain of command unless directed otherwise. If an employee believes they have information of such a sensitive nature as to require communication outside the chain of command, the employee may communicate directly with any higher-ranking officer, including the Chief of Police, and at that point the responsibility for any further dissemination of that information lies with the higher-ranking officer.
  B. Representation of the Department
    1. Responsibility for management of the Department and promulgation of policy and budget rests with the Chief of Police.
    2. Employees shall not disseminate information concerning their personal interpretations of Department policy, investigations, crime patterns, budget, deployment or other opinions that could be construed as representing the Department or the Chief of Police. Subordinate employees may be granted authority to represent Department issues on a case-by-case basis, but only following delegation by their chain of command. Specific employees (e.g., Media Relations Officers) may be granted broad authority to represent Department issues outside their chain of command, or on behalf of the Chief of Police (or his designee).

This kind of language is a part of most government employee contracts, intended to maintain the confidentiality of sensitive issues, to provide for operational authority, and to help maintain overall agency effectiveness.

A careful read of these regulations makes it clear that government employees with concerns or grievances regarding co-workers, supervisors, or other internal matters must report them only within the institutional chain of command. Having done this, they are forbidden from pursuing such matters themselves or speaking out about them publicly—lest they harm the "operation of the agency, or perception of the public." Consequently, unless a matter of public interest is involved (which is a subjective standard at best), government employees can be punished, and even terminated, for violating these and related administrative policies (Ronald, 2007).

Restrictions on employee speech have a longstanding tradition within government agencies, and currently enjoy coverage from the United States Supreme Court, which holds that (*Garcetti, et al. v. Ceballos*, 2006): "When public employees make statements pursuant to their official duties, they are not speaking as citizens for First Amendment purposes, and the Constitution does not insulate their communications from employer discipline." In a work environment where punishment, termination, and loss of employee benefits (e.g., wages, medical coverage, and pensions) can result from sharing internal matters outside the chain of command, institutional secrecy is all but assured except in perhaps the most extreme cases (Diehl, 2011; Papandrea, 2010; and Wright, 2011).[1]

In sum, government employees who are in a position to have direct knowledge, and an applied understanding, of forensic fraud do not enjoy unfettered freedom of speech. They are contractually bound to report such violations strictly within their chain of command. They are also contractually bound to refrain from speech that harms the image or effectiveness of their agency. By abiding with their employment contracts and keeping agency secrets, they preserve its image to the public, their professional reputation within the community, and their continued employment prospects.[2] As a consequence, what is publicly known about the nature and scope of forensic fraud is best viewed as the tip of the iceberg—as has been suggested in previous chapters.

To alleviate the tendency to maintain institutional secrecy, forensic examiners working for crime labs or law enforcement agencies that receive federal funding are meant to enjoy immunity from employer retaliation when acting as a whistleblower (Giannelli, 2007). As explained in a report from the Innocence Project (IP, 2009; p. 4):

> In 2004, Congress established an oversight mechanism within the Paul Coverdell Forensic Science Improvement Grant Program, which provides federal funds to help improve the quality and efficiency of state and local crime labs and other forensic facilities. In order to receive the federal funds, applicants are required to designate independent external government entities to handle allegations of serious negligence or misconduct affecting the quality of forensic analysis in facilities that receive Coverdell grants, and those oversight entities must also have a process for handling such allegations.

---

[1]Concern regarding retaliation against public employees, and the resulting culture of secrecy, is something that the U.S. Supreme Court generally acknowledged and warned against when ruling on anti-retaliation legislation subsequent to the *Garcetti* decision in *Crawford v. Metro. Government of Nashville et al.* (2009), arguing: "if an employee reporting discrimination in answer to an employer's questions could be penalized with no remedy, prudent employees would have a good reason to keep quiet about Title VII offenses [e.g., employer retaliation in the form of discrimination, unlawful employment practices and sanction, unlawful investigations of employees, and procedural denial]."

[2]It was only recently revealed, for example, that the results of unfavorable task force findings regarding forensic casework under review since the late 1990s have been intentionally suppressed and concealed the U.S. Department of Justice and the FBI, harming an untold number of criminal defendants (Hsu, Jenkins, and Mellnick, 2012).

This immunity is theoretical, however, because agencies don't always under-stand, abide, or enforce required whistleblower protections. This can result in a whistleblower who is initially terminated or otherwise sanctioned, who must then bear any legal costs of proving his status and asserting related protections. As reported in Maier (2003):

> ...forensic scientists who levy charges of incompetence or corruption against their labs often find themselves unemployed. Former FBI forensic expert Whitehurst was suspended, then fired, before settling in 1997 for a $1.46 million payment in a lawsuit for wrongful discharge. Elizabeth Johnson, former director of a DNA lab in the Harris County Medical Examiner's Office in Texas, now often works as a consultant for criminal-defense teams, but she found herself unemployed in 1997 after failing to be a "team player" and link a murder suspect's blood to the scene of a crime. She was vindicated in a jury trial and settled for $375,000. When DNA lab worker Laura Schile called attention to serious problems in Oklahoma, she found herself under investigation and resigned in 2001 because of a "hostile work situation."

A more recent example includes Donald Mikko, chief of the firearms branch at the U.S. Army Criminal Investigation Laboratory (see Figure 7-1). As reported in Taylor (2012a,b):

> Earlier this month, the U.S. Army Criminal Investigation Laboratory warned its firearms branch chief, Donald Mikko, in a memo of its plans to fire him, in part for talking to a McClatchy Newspapers reporter.
> As part of an internal investigation, Mikko was interrogated for about four hours and questioned about his contacts with McClatchy, according

FIGURE 7-1
Donald Mikko, chief of the firearms branch at the U.S. Army Criminal Investigation Laboratory. In May of 2012, he resigned after 21 years of service. The lab's director, Larry Chelko, also resigned, even though the lab was still under investigation by The Office of Special Counsel.

to his attorney, Peter Lown. The Army Criminal Investigation Command, which oversees the lab, launched the inquiry after McClatchy published a story late last year about the lab losing evidence.

McClatchy has written more than a dozen stories about the lab since last March; the stories included details of the misconduct of two former analysts who made serious errors during DNA and firearms testing and who later were found to have falsified and destroyed documents when confronted with the problems.

As a result of McClatchy's articles, Senate Judiciary Committee Chairman Patrick Leahy, D- Vt., and Sen. Charles Grassley of Iowa, the committee's top-ranking Republican member, urged the military to look into the lab's handling of the misconduct by one of the analysts. An investigation by the Pentagon's inspector general is ongoing.

...The Criminal Investigation Command, abbreviated as CID, says it's never targeted anyone for talking to the news media, and it's asserted that McClatchy's series of stories has overblown isolated mistakes and misconduct that shouldn't reflect on the lab's overall reputation.

As of this writing, the outcome for Donald Mikko remains uncertain, and his career remains in jeopardy. However, it is clear that without his efforts the ongoing problems of fraud and error at the U.S. Army Criminal Investigation Laboratory would have remained hidden from public and congressional scrutiny.

Whatever the circumstance, public employees understand that successful lawsuits are personally expensive and don't always end well—a problem compounded by the strain of suspension or termination. This weighs heavily on any decision to come forward with allegations against an employer or fellow employees. The outcome of any administrative complaint, investigation, or subsequent legal proceeding is never guaranteed—regardless of the evidence—and can cost more than the uncertain outcome is worth to the individual.

This state of affairs deprives the research community at large of complete or easily referenced data sources, hampering meaningful independent study. For example, consider the NAS Report—perhaps the most important comprehensive investigation and review of the forensic sciences published in history. While full of important findings and suggested reforms related to the forensic sciences, the NAS Report provides little direct coverage of forensic fraud. It does explain that (Edwards and Gotsonis, 2009; pp. 44–48):

- there have been many major crime lab scandals involving both fraud and error;
- a disturbing number of forensic scientists refuse to concede the possibility of error in their methods, and are "resistant" to the findings of research critical of the forensic sciences;

- explanations of scientific limitations, demonstrations of scientific rigor, and transparency of methodology are often absent in forensic science work product; and,
- while the community perception appears to be that forensic fraud is rare, the absence of community "openness" has severely hampered in-depth study of error, bias, and fraud committed by forensic science practitioners.

Ultimately, however, the NAS Report avoided addressing the issue of forensic fraud by sidestepping to the issue of practitioner error. It suggested that unintentional error within the forensic science community is the more common and immediate concern. However, it also conceded that there is currently no research to accurately demonstrate the rate or scope of either forensic fraud or forensic error (Edwards and Gotsonis, 2009). This makes the need for actual research in both areas critical to the scientific health and credibility of the forensic sciences.

This is not to say that the subject of forensic fraud has been entirely ignored in the professional literature, but rather that it has been limited with respect to available data and those who are able and willing to voice critical opinions.

IDEOGRAPHIC RESEARCH: LOOSELY REFERENCED CASE STUDIES

The vast majority of research published in relation to the subject of forensic fraud has been ideographic in nature. That is to say it consists primarily of peer-reviewed articles and textbooks that touch anecdotally on specific high-profile cases resulting from individual examiner misconduct. Such cases are generally adduced in order to highlight a relevant issue, or demonstrate a significant condition or failing within the forensic science community. Commonly cited cases include those described in following sections (cited alphabetically).[3]

Jacqueline Blake, DNA analyst

Jacqueline Blake was a forensic examiner for the FBI Crime Laboratory's DNA Analysis Unit; she held a bachelor's of science degree in Biology. As explained in Murphy (2007), Ms. Blake (p. 733) "pled guilty to falsifying reports of 'negative controls'—the data used to demonstrate that no contamination has taken place during testing." Her acts of fraud at the FBI Crime Lab spanned five years, leading up to her resignation in 2002, and involved at least 103 cases

---

[3]Data included and excluded from the present study are described as such.

(Botluk, 2007; Cooley, 2004; DiFonzo, 2005; Giannelli, 2007; Murphy, 2007; OIG, 2004; and Pyrek, 2007).

This law enforcement-employed forensic examiner, having committed her acts of fraud within the time frame parameters set for this study (2000–2010), was included in the final data set. See Chapter 8, "Forensic Fraud, 2000–2010: Data and Frequency," for details regarding inclusion criteria and data collected.

Ralph Erdmann, coroner

Ralph Erdmann was a coroner from Texas who, in 1992, pleaded no contest to falsifying at least six autopsies in Dickens, Hockley, and Lubbock counties for the prosecution. He falsified results regarding forensic examinations and testing that were never performed (aka dry-labbing), and gave related false testimony in court proceedings to facilitate criminal convictions. He was subsequently convicted, received ten years' probation, and moved to Washington State. There, Mr. Erdmann violated his probation by keeping a "cache of firearms" and was returned to serve out his time in Texas (Underwood, 1997). Mr. Erdmann was reportedly well known among his contemporaries for tailoring autopsy results to fit law enforcement needs and theories (Cooley, 2007a; Giannelli, 1997; and Giannelli and McMunigal, 2007).

This law enforcement-employed forensic examiner, having committed his acts of fraud outside the time frame parameters set for this study (2000–2010), was properly excluded from the final data set. See Chapter 8 for details regarding inclusion criteria and data collected.

Joyce Gilchrist, forensic scientist

Joyce Gilchrist was a forensic scientist for the Oklahoma City Police Department crime laboratory (see Figure 7-2). Her reputation for pro-police and pro-prosecution bias was well known by supervisors, co-workers, and professional organizations early in her career, which began in the 1980s (Giannelli and McMunigal, 2007).[4] This included withholding exculpatory findings from the defense, testifying beyond the accepted limits of science, falsely reporting findings, and contaminating evidence to prevent testing (Cooley, 2007a). However, her scientific misconduct went unchecked and by many counts was even rewarded within the local prosecutorial system that she served (Giannelli, 2007). As reported in Raeder (2007), Ms. Gilchrist was (p. 1421) "an African-American forensic chemist, known as 'Black Magic' for her ability to sway juries with evidence only she could see."

---

[4]Over the years, multiple complaints were filed against American Academy of Forensic Sciences member Joyce Gilchrist, none of which resulted in sanctions or expulsion.

FIGURE 7-2
Joyce Gilchrist, a forensic scientist for the Oklahoma City Police Department crime laboratory, known by the nickname "black magic." She was fired in 2001 for giving false testimony in multiple criminal trials, and then sued in civil court.

Things came to a head, however, after the 2001 DNA exoneration of Jeffrey Pierce. He was convicted of rape in 1986, based almost entirely on the work and testimony of Ms. Gilchrist. As explained in IP (2009; p. 29):

> …the Oklahoma State Bureau of Investigation conducted a review of cases assigned to Gilchrist from 1980 to 1997. Of the 1,600 cases reviewed, they identified nearly 200 that warranted further review. A 2001 FBI review of her work also found errors in five of the eight cases randomly reviewed. Gilchrist testified in 11 cases in which the defendant has already been executed. She has contributed to at least three other wrongful convictions overturned through DNA testing. Gilchrist was terminated in 2001 after 21 years with the lab.

Subsequent to this case review, Ms. Gilchrist's fraud and misconduct have resulted in multiple overturned verdicts, retrials, and millions of dollars in settlement payments to the wrongfully convicted (Cooper, 2009b; Greiner, 2005).

This law enforcement-employed forensic examiner, having committed her acts of fraud or having had them revealed within the time frame parameters set for this study (2000–2010), was included in the final data set. See Chapter 8 for details regarding inclusion criteria and data collected.

David Harding, latent print examiner

A New York State Trooper and fingerprint supervisor with the Troop C Forensic Unit, David Harding confessed to planting fingerprint evidence in numerous cases in order to secure convictions during the application process for a job with the Central Intelligence Agency. He also implicated his partner, Trooper Robert Lishansky, and admitted to burning physical evidence to protect fellow officers from consequences in a wrongful shooting investigation (Moenssens, 1993). As reported in Young (1996; p. 466): "New York State Trooper David Harding, after pleading guilty to perjury charges, justified his acts of fabricating evidence, using fabricated evidence to obtain confessions, and testifying falsely about evidence at trial by saying that he had acted 'because of a stern belief the defendant was a danger to society.'" See also *Chamberlain v. Mantello* (1997); Cooley (2004); and Risinger et al. (2002).

This law enforcement-employed forensic examiner, having committed his acts of fraud outside the time frame parameters set for this study (2000–2010), was properly excluded from the final data set. See Chapter 8 for details regarding inclusion criteria and data collected.

Arnold Melnikoff, laboratory director

Arnold Melnikoff was employed by the Department of Justice Crime Laboratory in Montana from 1970 to 1989, where he eventually became the director. During that time, his testimony helped secure the conviction of Jimmy Ray Bromgard for the rape of an eight-year-old girl (Cooley and Oberfield, 2007). As explained in Olsen (2002): "During Bromgard's 1987 trial, Melnikoff claimed hairs found in the girl's bedclothes were virtually indistinguishable from those of the defendant—though experts agree such evidence is not that precise." This level of certainty with respect to hair comparison testimony was standard for Mr. Melnikoff.

In 1989, Mr. Melnikoff was hired by Barry Logan to work at the Washington State Patrol Crime Lab; he worked there as a forensic chemist performing drug tests, among other duties (Olsen, 2003). However, his work in Montana came under fire as the cases worked their way through the appellate system, resulting in multiple lawsuits from wrongfully convicted defendants (Cooley, 2004; Cooley and Oberfield, 2007). This included the Bromgard case. In 2002, DNA evidence exonerated Mr. Bromgard after 15 years in prison (Olsen, 2003). Consequently, reviews of Mr. Melnikoff's casework in Montana and Washington State were conducted. As reported in Geranios (2003):

> The State Patrol reviewed 100 cases completed by Melnikoff from 1999 to 2002 and found that his work on drug analysis did not meet professional standards.
>
> "The review of the cases did not necessarily reflect any mistakes that would have changed the basic conclusions drawn from the analysis," according to a patrol report obtained through a state public records act request. "It is just that often the work product was weak or unsupported by sufficient data to reach clear conclusions."

Mr. Melnikoff, a charter member of the American Society of Crime Lab Directors (ASCLD), also admitted to previously fabricating statistics to bolster his hair comparison testimony (Olsen, 2003). Ultimately, based on a review of his "incompetent" and "sloppy" work in their lab system, and his prior false testimony, the Washington State Patrol determined that Arnold Melnikoff should be terminated (Geranios, 2003). His appeal for termination was denied in 2005.

This law enforcement-employed forensic examiner, having committed his acts of fraud outside the time frame parameters set for this study (2000–2010), was properly excluded from the final data set. See Chapter 8 for details regarding inclusion criteria and data collected.

Fred Zain, forensic chemist

Fred Zain was a forensic chemist for the West Virginia State Police Crime Laboratory from 1980 to 1989, after which he resigned and took a job as chief of evidence for the Bexar County Medical Examiner in Texas (Chan, 1994). As reported in McMunigal (2007; p. 437): "An investigation of Fred Zain, the former head serologist at the West Virginia State Police Crime Laboratory … showed that between 1979 and 1989, he falsified test results in as many as 134 cases, almost always in favor of the prosecution." At least 10 defendants had their convictions overturned as a consequence. Among the most widely publicized cases of forensic fraud, Mr. Zain's pro-prosecution bias and tendency to dry-lab favorable results are referenced repeatedly in the literature (Castelle, 1999; Connors et al., 1996; Cooley, 2004; Edwards and Gotsonis, 2009; Giannelli, 2007; Risinger et al., 2002; and Starrs, 1993).

This law enforcement-employed forensic examiner, having committed his acts of fraud outside the time frame parameters set for this study (2000–2010), was properly excluded from the final data set. See Chapter 8 for details regarding inclusion criteria and data collected.

The literature referencing these case studies is authored primarily by legal scholars aligned with the criminal defense bar. These commentators seek, ostensibly, to evaluate forensic science and its role in the justice system; they are, after all, in a unique and altogether unenviable position to experience the direct impact of forensic fraud.[5] Their collective view of the profession

---

[5]Despite the scientific literacy of a select few, it must be conceded that the vast majority of attorneys have a very limited understanding of forensic science; have no real understanding of how to cross-examine forensic scientists effectively with respect to establishing the limitations of their methods and conclusions; and often demonstrate limited interest in learning either. This holds true regardless of their courtroom alignment.

and its practitioners is dim to say the least. First, legal scholars tend to view the truly objective forensic examiner as an exception; they contend that many if not most are "guns for hire," selling opinions to the highest bidder (Barkacs, Browne,. and Williamson, 2002). Second, they tend to view the problem of laboratory fraud as endemic (Castelle, 1999). Third, given the parade of high-profile DNA exonerations involving fraudulent examiners, hidden evidence, and misleading interpretations, they have come to accept that forensic fraud cannot always be averted or "unmasked" by the limited due process afforded at trial (Imwinkelried, 2003). This leads them to the inescapable conclusion that the vast majority of forensic fraud passes undetected through the courtroom, and that any public estimates of its frequency are low (Castelle, 1999).

MONOGRAPHS: CASE STUDIES WITH A THEME

Separate from literature that references well-known cases of forensic fraud with a few lines in order to craft a much larger position, there are other works that focus on its occurrence as an important symptom of the overall infirmity of forensic science practice. While providing in-depth reviews spanning multiple case examples, these research efforts do not attempt statistical analysis and inference. Rather, they are anthologies with a theme, telling a story associated with a particular case, type of evidence, practice, or institution.[6] Significant examples from the past two decades are described in the following sections.

Mountebanks

First published in 1982, the *Forensic Science Handbook*, by the renowned forensic scientist Dr. Richard Saferstein, has generally included chapters reviewing cases of forensic fraud. These tend to emphasize the responsibility of forensic science to court proceedings through the exploration of examiner ethics and misconduct. The *Handbook* is currently in its second edition and exists as a three-volume series. Chapter 1, written by James Starrs, Professor of Law and Forensic Sciences at The George Washington University, is titled "Mountebanks Among Forensic Scientists" (Starrs, 2004). Chapter 2, written by Charles Midkiff, formerly of the Bureau of Alcohol, Tobacco, and Firearms (BATF) National Laboratory Center, and Adjunct Professor in the Department of

---

[6]It is worth noting that there are a number of Australian monographs written for this same purpose, reviewing flawed or biased forensic science and the resulting miscarriages of justice (e.g., Crowley and Wilson, 2007; Moles, 2004; Sangha, Roach, and Moles, 2010; and Wilson, 1992).

Justice, Law, and Society at American University, is titled "More Mountebanks" (Midkiff, 2004). A "mountebank" is a charlatan or a fake—a word derived from an Italian saying that means "climb the bench" (suggesting a desire to get on a platform and attract an audience).

Convicted by juries, exonerated by science

The work of Connors, Lundregan, Miller, and McEwen (1996) was among the first modern efforts to report on the subject of wrongful convictions revealed by forensic science, providing an early review of 28 cases that were overturned using DNA evidence. It included a number of cases that involved fraud and misconduct committed by forensic scientists working for the police and prosecution. This watershed report, titled *Convicted by Juries, Exonerated by Science: Case Studies in the Use of DNA Evidence to Establish Innocence after Trial* (Connors et al., 1996), revealed that (pp. xvi–xvii):

> A second important issue is the number of cases in which there was misconduct on the part of the prosecution's scientific experts. For example, the forensic serologist who testified against Gary Dotson failed to disclose that, because the alleged victim was also a type B secretor, the fraction of the male population that could have contributed the semen found on the vaginal swabs exceeded 60 percent, making the serological evidence in the case probative of very little. In this instance, the prosecution's expert witness failed to volunteer potentially exculpatory information but did not actually lie under oath.

As further detailed in Giannelli (2007; pp. 186–187):

> Gary Dotson was convicted of the rape of Cathleen Webb.... Six years later she recanted, stating that she had fabricated the charge.... Subsequent DNA tests excluded Dotson as the source of the crime-scene semen.... At Dotson's 1979 trial, Timothy Dixon [a forensic scientist employed by the Illinois Department of Law Enforcement] testified that seminal material found in Webb's panties matched Dotson's blood type.... He failed to disclose, however, that Webb's own vaginal discharges, not necessarily semen, could have caused the stains.... Years later when a *Washington Post* reporter asked Dixon why he had not spoken up. He replied: "I guess I wasn't asked."

The Gary Dotson exoneration underscores the games that some forensic examiners for prosecution will play in order to keep and maintain the agendas of their employers—by refusing to acknowledge that omitting information and leaving a false impression with reports or testimony is in itself a deceptive practice.[7]

Of note, an additional three cases reviewed in Connors et al. (1996) involved overt forensic fraud committed by the aforementioned Fred Zain, ensuring his continued place in the literature that would follow.[8]

Tainting evidence: the FBI crime lab

In 1995, the FBI Crime Laboratory suffered the first of numerous scandals that would plague it until the present day, resulting from allegations by one of its own: Dr. Fred Whitehurst—a 20-year FBI veteran with a Ph.D. in chemistry. A whistleblower, Dr. Whitehurst reported that FBI evidence examiners were being pressured to cut corners and skew test results in favor of prosecutorial efforts. As explained in Peterson and Leggett (2007; pp. 646–647):

> …in 1995, Dr. Frederic Whitehurst, a scientist employed in the FBI laboratory, leveled charges of sloppy work, flawed report writing, and perjured court testimony affecting the explosives, chemistry-toxicology, and materials analysis units of the laboratory. Under the supervision of Michael R. Bromwich, the United States Justice Department's Inspector General, and with the assistance of an external blue ribbon panel, an extensive eighteen-month investigation ensued, which uncovered very serious problems. The investigation did not substantiate most of Whitehurst's allegations but did find numerous instances of "testimonial errors, substandard analytical work, and deficient practices." The Inspector General's final report, issued in

---

[7]It is worth mentioning that the current research effort revealed a number of cases where this kind of fraudulent examiner behavior was evident. Most notably, this included the North Carolina State Bureau of Investigation's Crime Lab, where an audit of the lab "determined that the practice of not reporting results of more sophisticated blood tests was sanctioned by some analysts. In 1997, it became written policy. That policy remained in effect as recently as 2003" (Locke, Neff, and Curliss, 2010). As further reported in Locke, Neff, and Curliss (2010):

> In serology, police use rudimentary presumptive tests at crime scenes to determine where blood might be. Those tests are fallible, prone to giving false positives. So analysts depend on more sophisticated, confirmatory tests to determine whether a substance is, in fact, blood.
> Before 1997, the serology unit operated without report-writing guidelines. Analysts set their own criteria until 1997; that policy sanctioned the practice of not reporting negative or inconclusive results of confirmatory tests.

This crime lab scandal involved evidence and findings withheld in over 230 cases, false and biased testimony, and resulted in the closure of the lab's bloodstain unit. It also resulted in the termination of two fraudulent examiners: Duane Deaver and Gerald Thomas. Data from both individuals was collected and included in the present study.

[8]This report served as an important precursor to the book *Actual Innocence* by Scheck, Neufeld, and Dwyer (2000), which details the stories of ten men wrongfully convicted and then exonerated by DNA with the help of the Innocence Project in New York.

1997, made numerous recommendations aimed at maintaining the independence of scientists in the crime laboratory and at protecting them from the influence of field investigators while conducting laboratory examinations, writing reports, and delivering testimony.

Dr. Whitehurst subsequently sued the FBI as a whistleblower, eventually reaching a $1.46 million settlement for wrongful termination.

The scandal made public by Dr. Whitehurst, and the Inspector General's investigation that followed, preceded the publication of *Tainting Evidence: Inside the Scandals at the FBI Crime Lab* (Kelly and Wearne, 1998). This detailed effort levied a scathing indictment of FBI Crime Laboratory culture and ongoing misconduct. It included a litany of specific failings by FBI agents and laboratory personnel in their casework related to high-profile investigations such as the Unabomber, Ruby Ridge, the first World Trade Center bombing in 1993, and the O.J. Simpson trial.

Law reviews: chronicles from the defense bar

Since the late 1990s, which included the first FBI Crime Laboratory scandal and the advent of DNA exonerations already mentioned, there have been a spate of law review articles focusing on scientific ethics and the fraud committed by forensic examiners employed within publicly funded crime labs. As discussed previously, these law reviews are primarily the work of the criminal defense bar. They are crafted using details from crime lab scandals occurring across the country in an effort to expose the partiality of forensic scientists working for the police, and the subsequent potential fallibility of what is often presented as irrefutable physical evidence of guilt at trial. A list of devoted legal scholars and their major publications focusing primarily on forensic fraud and misconduct includes (in chronological order by author):

- "The Abuse of Scientific Evidence in Criminal Cases: The Need for Independent Crime Laboratories" (Giannelli, 1997); "False Credentials" (Giannelli, 2001); "Fabricated Reports" (Giannelli, 2002); and "Prosecutors, Ethics, and Expert Witnesses" (Giannelli and McMunigal, 2007)
- "Scientific Evidence and the Ethical Obligations of Attorneys" (Saks, 2001) and "Ethics in Forensic Science: Professional Standards for the Practice of Criminalistics" (Saks, 2003)
- "Reforming the Forensic Community to Avert the Ultimate Injustice" (Cooley, 2004) and "Forensic Science and Capital Punishment Reform: An 'Intellectually Honest' Assessment" (Cooley, 2007b)
- "The Crimes of Crime Labs" (DiFonzo, 2005) and "Devil in a White Coat: The Temptation of Forensic Evidence in the Age of CSI" (DiFonzo and Stern, 2007)

- "More than Zero: Accounting for Error in Latent Fingerprint Identification" (Cole, 2005) and "The Prevalence and Potential Causes of Wrongful Conviction by Fingerprint Evidence" (Cole, 2006)
- "Beyond Bad Apples: Analyzing the Role of Forensic Science in Wrongful Convictions" (Thompson, 2009)

These law review articles, and others like them, essentially seek to chronicle and broadcast the fraud, misconduct, and error related to forensic examiners and any resulting crime lab scandals that might be relevant to litigation. They also contextualize what has been publicly revealed about forensic fraud for the purposes of better understanding, and negotiating, the role that forensic scientists play in court. Ironically, they often include suggested reforms that would serve to make the forensic sciences more scientific (e.g., more valid, reliable, and impartial methodology; scientific education; and laboratory independence from law enforcement)—an effort that has been generally absent from the forensic science community itself (Edwards and Gotsonis, 2009).

Forensic science under siege

As an antidote to the critiques from the defense bar, and their coverage of ongoing forensic laboratory scandals and related instances of forensic fraud, a journalist named Kelly Pyrek wrote a book titled *Forensic Science Under Siege* (Pyrek, 2007). Ms. Pyrek researched the criticisms levied against the forensic sciences by interviewing various high-profile forensic science practitioners,[9] the majority of whom were "stakeholders" (e.g., crime lab directors and senior members of organizations invested in the current forensic system). As provided in the "Preface," the "siege" mentioned in the title is part of a battle over ownership, leadership, and the precise mandates of reliable forensic science practice (pp. xiii–xiv):

> …engaged in battle most frequently are social scientists and legal scholars vs. forensic practitioners in a tussle over, if you will, ownership rights: Who owns forensic science, who has the right to dictate to it, and who will ultimately assume leadership over a field with immense power and strategic access to all three levels of U.S. government—legislative, judicial, and executive. The feud is triggered by allegations of errors, fraud, and malfeasance on the part of forensic service providers that undermine criminal justice, and fueled by disagreements over a diverse plank of issues ranging from the very definition of science and its purpose, to the admissibility of forensic evidence in a court of law, to the effects of a significant paradigm shift

---

[9]This researcher was interviewed by Ms. Pyrek for her book, and was quoted accurately in numerous sections.

some commentators say is occurring at the nexus of law and science—
the place where forensic science lives.

   One very important argument that we will explore is the allegation
by critics that forensic science is deficient in scientific methodology
and rigor—with the extremists asserting that it is utterly lacking in
science altogether—and the response from forensic practitioners,
stunned by the charges, that forensic science was born from and is
steeped in the traditional sciences.

The conclusion of this work is that forensic science is practiced by well-mean-
ing examiners in need of more funding; that the few laboratory errors reported
are expected and manageable; that the rare occurrence of forensic fraud is the
result of a small number of "rogues" and "cowboys"; and that the forensic science community is better served when built up than torn down in the media.

It bears mentioning that two years after the publication of *Forensic Science
Under Siege* (Pyrek, 2007), the NAS Report on the forensic sciences concluded
that there was an absence of scientific education, methodology, and research
in the majority of the forensic sciences; that many forensic science stakeholders are too attached to the current broken system to fix it; that many forensic
scientists are resistant to criticisms and reforms; and that actual rates of forensic fraud and error are unknown for lack of any research efforts from within the
community—suggesting the need for a major overhaul of the forensic sciences
(Edwards and Gotsonis, 2009).

NOMOTHETIC RESEARCH: GROUP STUDIES

There have been few group studies examining questions related to the reliability and validity of scientific expert testimony, and only one specific to the
nature and frequency of forensic fraud. Moreover, the existing research has not
come from those associated with the stakeholders of forensic science. This is
likely due to the liability issues discussed at the beginning of this chapter, in
combination with the absence of an overall scientific research culture in the
forensic sciences (Edwards and Gotsonis, 2009; Mnookin et al., 2011).

Empirical research addressing the issue of forensic fraud has come, largely,
from legal scholars associated with the Innocence Project.[10] This should not be
much of a surprise, owing to the following: the advent of DNA exonerations

---

[10]As provided in the "Mission Statement" on the Innocence Project's website at www.innocenceproject.
org: "The Innocence Project was founded in 1992 by Barry C. Scheck and Peter J. Neufeld at the
Benjamin N. Cardozo School of Law at Yeshiva University to assist prisoners who could be proven
innocent through DNA testing. To date, 300 people in the United States have been exonerated by DNA
testing, including 17 who served time on death row."

identified the issue of forensic fraud and misconduct as a significant contributor to wrongful criminal convictions (Connors et al., 1996); the Innocence Project has a vested interest in exposing forensic fraud and misconduct in order to overturn wrongful convictions; and the Innocence Project has amassed a large database of case evidence and expert transcripts related to criminal defendants exonerated by DNA, ripe for study (300 exonerated defendants, as of the writing of this dissertation).

Saks and Koehler (2005)

In a study of 86 DNA exoneration cases provided by the Innocence Project, Saks and Koehler (2005) reported the following frequency data: forensic testing errors in 63%; police misconduct in 44%; prosecutorial misconduct in 28%; and false or misleading testimony by forensic experts in 27%. They also reported surprise regarding the findings related to forensic testing, explaining that (p. 893):

> It was not surprising to learn that erroneous convictions sometimes occur, and that new science and technology can help detect and correct those mistakes. Nor was it surprising to learn … that erroneous eyewitness identifications are the most common contributing factor to wrongful convictions. What was unexpected is that erroneous forensic science expert testimony is the second most common contributing factor to wrongful convictions, found in 63% of those cases. These data likely understate the relative contribution of forensic science expert testimony to erroneous convictions. Whereas lawyers, police, and lay witnesses participate in virtually every criminal case, forensic science experts participate in a smaller subset of cases—about 10 to 20% of criminal cases during the era when these DNA exonerations were originally tried.

This data suggests, according to the authors of the study, that forensic scientists are the courtroom witnesses most likely to present "misleading or fraudulent testimony" (p. 893).

Gross et al. (2005)

In a broader study of 340 exonerations between 1989 and 2003, 196 of which did not involve DNA evidence, Gross et al. (2005) found the following: "In 5 [1.5%] of the exonerations that we have studied there are reports of perjury by police officers. In an additional 24 [7%] we have similar information on perjury by forensic scientists testifying for the government" (p. 19). This study relied only in part on cases from the Innocence Project, explaining that (p. 2) "[m]ost of the exonerations we include in this database are listed on one or more [of] the web sites that are maintained by three organizations: The Death Penalty Information Center … the Innocence Project at Cardozo Law School … and the Center on Wrongful Convictions at Northwestern University Law

School." While this is significantly fewer than the frequency of forensic fraud and error identified in Saks and Koehler (2005), the authors concede that their findings underestimate the problem due to the fact that (p. 19) "[d]etecting a deliberate lie is harder; there may be no simple way to tell if a statement was false, and if so whether the falsehood was intentional." Moreover, the authors did not have access to complete case materials and transcripts, making their findings regarding fraud and error incidental to the purpose of the study—which was to get an initial estimate of the nature and occurrence of wrongful convictions in the United States.

Garrett and Neufeld (2009)

In the first published study of scientific testimony by prosecution experts in cases where the defendant was eventually exonerated, Garrett and Neufeld (2009) reviewed the transcripts from 137 trials. They found that (pp. 1–2):

> ...in the bulk of these trials of innocent defendants—82 cases or 60%—forensic analysts called by the prosecution provided invalid testimony at trial—that is, testimony with conclusions misstating empirical data or wholly unsupported by empirical data. This was not the testimony of a mere handful of analysts: this set of trials included invalid testimony by 72 forensic analysts called by the prosecution and employed by 52 laboratories, practices, or hospitals from 25 states. Unfortunately, the adversarial process largely failed to police this invalid testimony. Defense counsel rarely cross-examined analysts concerning invalid testimony and rarely obtained experts of their own. In the few cases in which invalid forensic science was challenged, judges seldom provided relief.

Examining trial testimony did not reveal the entire picture, however. The authors discovered, upon evaluating "post-conviction review, investigations, or civil discovery" (p. 14), that 13 (10%) of the 137 cases also involved withholding of exculpatory evidence. This included 3 cases that did not involve invalid testimony. Consequently, 85 (63%) of the 137 cases under review involved either invalid scientific testimony or the withholding of exculpatory evidence.

The nature of invalid forensic science testimony reported in Garrett and Neufeld (2009) included

- Non-probative evidence presented as probative
- Exculpatory evidence discounted
- Inaccurate frequency or statistic presented
- Statistic provided without empirical support
- Non-numerical statements provided without empirical support
- Conclusion that evidence originated from defendant without empirical support

With respect to the types of forensic examinations that involved invalid testimony in the 137 cases reviewed (with 10 cases involving more than one type of forensic examination), Garrett and Neufeld (2009) reported the following frequency data:

- Serology: 100 cases reviewed; 57 cases involved invalid testimony
- Hair comparison: 65 cases reviewed; 25 cases involved invalid testimony
- Bite mark comparison: 6 cases reviewed; 4 cases involved invalid testimony
- DNA testing: 11 cases reviewed; 3 cases involved invalid testimony
- Fingerprint comparison: 13 cases reviewed; 1 case involved invalid testimony
- Shoe print comparison: 3 cases reviewed; 1 case involved invalid testimony
- Voice comparison: 1 case reviewed; 1 case involved invalid testimony
- Soil comparison: 6 cases reviewed; 0 cases involved invalid testimony

While not delving into the issue of intent such that accusations of fraud might be levied beyond examiner ignorance and incompetence, this study (1) identifies invalid scientific testimony and the withholding of exculpatory evidence, as significant factors in wrongful convictions; and (2) identifies those specific forensic science examinations and testimony that have caused the most harm to innocent defendants.

Turvey (2003)

There has been only one previously published study specific to assessing instances of forensic fraud. It was a descriptive review of limited frequency data related to 42 forensic examiners who had been determined to have committed one or more acts of forensic fraud. These examiners were divided into three types: *Simulators*, *Dissemblers*, and *Pseudoexperts* (Turvey, 2003). This study was broad in its scope: it included forensic examiners from many different forensic disciplines, from multiple countries, and from as far back as 1981.

Simulators, the largest group, were forensic examiners who physically manipulated physical evidence or forensic examinations; this involved fabrication or destruction of findings. This group was composed of 17 (41%) forensic examiners: 13 (31%) examiners were involved in dry-labbing results and 4 (10%) examiners had been involved in planting evidence. Simulators involved in dry-labbing, by evidence type, were reported as follows (Turvey, 2003):

- Autopsy results: 3
- Drug tests: 3
- Serological tests: 2

- DNA tests: 2
- Fingerprint comparisons: 2
- Psychological assessments: 1

Simulators involved in planting evidence, by evidence type, were reported as follows (Turvey, 2003):

- Fingerprints: 2
- Biological material: 2

Dissemblers were forensic examiners who exaggerated, embellished, lied about, or otherwise misrepresented their actual findings. This group was composed of 15 forensic examiners (36% of all cases). Dissemblers, by evidence type, were reported as follows (Turvey, 2003):

- Serological evidence: 4
- Arson/explosive evidence: 3
- DNA evidence: 3
- Hair and fiber comparison: 2
- Footwear comparison: 1
- Lead bullet analysis: 1
- Social science research: 1

Pseudoexperts were forensic examiners who fabricated or misrepresented expert credentials. This group was composed of 13 forensic examiners (31% of all cases). The most commonly falsified expert credentials were college diplomas, found in 8 (19%) cases. Pseudoexperts, by credential type, were reported as follows (Turvey, 2003):

- College education: 8
- Professional certifications: 4
- Work experience: 4
- Professional affiliations: 3

A significant finding of this study was that the majority of forensic examiners committing fraud did so while employed in government agencies such as police departments (14%) and police crime labs (57%). When the study considered those forensic examiners working privately (26%), 3 worked almost exclusively for law enforcement and the prosecution. In other words, in 34 (81%) of 42 total cases, forensic fraud was committed on behalf of the prosecution, and most often by law enforcement-employed crime laboratory personnel (Turvey, 2003).

While limited in descriptive depth (e.g., no impact data, limited employer data, and limited examiner data), and overly broad with respect to the sampling of different kinds of forensic examiners, these preliminary findings provided assistance with shaping the framework and dimensions of the current dissertation.[11]

SUMMARY

There is an overall dearth of professional literature related to forensic fraud. The majority of existing research is found primarily in the form of ideographic case studies and monographs authored by those from the criminal defense bar. This is a consequence of the absence of a research culture within the forensic sciences created in part by the punitive disincentives for reporting, gathering, and publishing data regarding fraud that exists for public employees.

Larger-scale empirical research associated with forensic fraud has tradition-ally been indirect, arising from the examination of forensic science testimony in relation to wrongful convictions. In these studies (authored primarily by legal scholars with access to court transcripts), expert perjury, invalid scientific testimony, and the withholding of exculpatory evidence have been identified as significant contributing factors to proven miscarriages of justice. They also identify specific types of forensic examination and related areas of testimony that have caused the most harm to innocent defendants.

Turvey (2003) provided preliminary descriptive frequency data regarding a limited international sample of fraudulent examiners from multiple forensic disciplines over roughly a 30-year period ($n = 42$), and also suggested a typol-ogy. However, the current study aims to provide a more reliable and focused analysis of forensic fraud and its significant correlates—examining data related to forensic fraud at a level that has not been explored previously. This will include, in subsequent chapters, descriptive frequency data for cases included in the final sample ($n = 100$), correlation matrices, and multiple hierarchical regression analysis.

---

[11]It should be acknowledged that 23 of 42 cases in Turvey (2003) fell within the parameters of the current study. Consequently, further data was gathered for these 23 cases for inclusion with other cases identified for the dissertation.

CHAPTER 8

Forensic Fraud, 2000–2010: Data and Frequency

"The legal community now concedes, with varying degrees of urgency, that our system produces erroneous convictions based on discredited forensics."

Pamela R. Metzger (Metzger, 2006; p. 491)
Associate Prof. of Law, Tulane University

This chapter describes the methods used to identify and gather data for the original research presented in this text, along with initial frequency results. First, data sources are discussed with respect to availability and reliability. Second, the data parameters are laid out, establishing the criteria used for including and excluding instances of forensic fraud. Some case examples are provided. Finally, the variables collected and examined are defined, and frequency results from the final data set are presented. These frequency results, being useful as limited preliminary assessments, provide the basis for more complex and reliable correlation analysis, and related discussion, in subsequent chapters.[1]

SOURCES OF DATA

As mentioned in the preceding chapter, there is an overall absence of research-oriented culture within the forensic sciences (Mnookin et al., 2011). This may have been created, in part, by the punitive disincentives for reporting, gathering, and publishing data regarding fraud that exist for public employees; and in part by the desire to limit liability among forensic science stakeholders. These circumstances combine to make identifying, parsing, and gathering forensic fraud data a significant challenge.

---

[1]Methods of data analysis and findings are presented and discussed in Chapter 9, "Multivariate Analysis of Forensic Fraud, 2000–2010."

Ultimately, however, the following data sources were identified and searched for information and viable data.

Media accounts

Newspaper databases were routinely searched to identify cases of potential forensic fraud using combinations of the terms *crime lab, fraud, forensic, expert, perjury, scientist, technician, resigned, suspended, scandal, terminated, fired, charlatan,* and *phony* (e.g., Factiva, Westlaw, and Google news). However, media accounts were not considered reliable sources of final data. Rather, they were used to direct this author toward related court records, official agency records and press releases, official audit reports, and peer-reviewed literature.

Discovery material and author's case files

As part of this author's work as a forensic scientist since 1996, a large amount of discovery material has been accumulated from a variety of agencies that documents the length and breadth of forensic fraud committed by various forensic examiners. Those cases having entered the justice system, that discovery material is now part of the public record. This includes internal disciplinary memoranda, forensic examination reports, sworn testimony, expert resumes, court transcripts, internal audit reports, and interviews conducted by members of various government agencies.

Court records

This author has gathered court records, filings, testimony, and decisions from sources in the public domain, including media outlets (i.e., records provided as part of Freedom of Information Act requests), appellate court decisions from Westlaw, and government-affiliated websites (indicated in the "References" section).

Agency records

This author has gathered public records available directly from the websites of law enforcement agencies, government crime laboratories, and media outlets; these records include press releases, subpoenas, indictments, arrest warrants, interdepartmental memoranda, and incident reports.

Audit reports

Some of the police agencies and government crime laboratories involved in this study were subject to internal or independent audits revealing forensic fraud, the results of which have been made public (e.g., departmental websites, independent auditor websites, or media websites).

Peer-reviewed literature

A number of cases of forensic fraud have been researched by others and published in the professional literature, as cited in the preceding chapter.

Save media accounts, the data sources used for the dissertation were deemed sufficiently reliable for the present study to the extent that law enforcement agents, government agencies, and the courts have also relied upon them to make decisions regarding employee misconduct, penalties, and institutional liability.

It should be noted that the nature of these data sources limits the study to those cases in the public domain. For liability purposes, this is desirable, as privacy is always a concern. However, it did confine the sample size. This is addressed in the next section.

PARAMETERS FOR THE CURRENT DATA SET

The present study focuses on the identification of cases involving forensic fraud in the United States. The goal was to render a data set that would provide a sufficient sample size, and a sufficiently narrow group of like forensic examiners, in order to enable the meaningful application of results relevant to questions raised in the thesis (see Chapter 1, "Introduction"). To that end, the following parameters were observed.

Time frame and region

The fraud occurred, or was revealed, in the United States within the years 2000–2010. This criterion narrows the time frame and region of the study to a relevant scope in the post-DNA era. Regional limitations were imposed to maintain the relevance of findings within similar justice systems; the results of an international study might not be reliably interpreted or applied within the culture and conditions of a single nation's legal framework. Temporal limitations were set to keep the study relevant to the post-DNA era, where convictions and exonerations may be argued to be more reliable given the forensic tools and evidence available.

In every case, the forensic examiners, their employer, and/or the justice system also experienced some or all of the consequences related to the fraud within the years 2000–2010. This means that the following scenarios are possible: fraud was committed and revealed during the years 2000–2010; fraud was committed prior to, and then revealed during, the years 2000–2010; or fraud was committed prior to and within the years 2000–2010, during which time it was subsequently revealed.

Physical evidence

Forensic examiners committed fraud related to their collection, preservation, examination, interpretation, and/or testimony regarding physical evidence.

This criterion excludes many different kinds of forensic examiners (e.g., forensic accountants, forensic criminologists, and forensic mental health professionals), and focuses on the classic forensic sciences associated with crime laboratory work (Turvey and Petherick, 2010). It also excludes cases in which non-forensic criminal justice professionals were found to have been involved in physical evidence-related fraud (e.g., tampering with, or planting of, evidence, committed by attorneys, police officers, and correctional officers).[2]

External decree

Forensic fraud was determined by a judgment or decree external to this author. That is to say, this author had no part in evaluating or determining whether forensic fraud actually occurred. Cases included in the sample required a judgment or decree of fraud levied against the forensic examiner in the form of court rulings; employer determinations; and/or the public statements and admissions of the forensic examiner.

Research efforts using these parameters uncovered 32 crime labs experiencing significant crises across the United States between the years 2000 and 2010.[3] These same efforts also revealed 170 different forensic examiners alleged to have committed fraud in the course of their casework to varying degrees. Of these 170 examiners identified, 70 were excluded, as they ultimately fell outside research parameters. Exclusions are discussed in the next section.

The final sample size ($n = 100$) comprises a representative number of those forensic examiners committing fraud within the parameters of the study that were made public.[4] In fact, it is reasonable to infer that these cases were identifiable because they were made public. An apt analogy would be to imagine that all cases of forensic fraud are like an unknown volume of water boiling in a pot over a fire—a pot that we are not allowed to open. When the pot boils over, we can observe a volume of water being released as

---

[2]Evidence planting, or "flaking," committed by law enforcement professionals (e.g., police and prosecutors) was found to be a regular and therefore predictable occurrence, some of which has been referenced in prior chapters. Evidence concealment was also regular and predictable. This area is ripe for study, with data that is easily accessible. As such, and given the number of Ph.D.s in Criminal Justice that one finds in academia, a serious question regarding why this research has not been conducted must be raised.

[3]Myriad cases of forensic fraud have been revealed in multiple lab scandals since the completion of the present study. Consequently, Chapter 11, "Crime Labs in Crisis, 2011–2012: Update and Discussion," offers an update and detailed discussion based on those cases brought to light from 2011 to 2012.

[4]Data-gathering efforts closed when 100 examiners had been identified as having committed forensic fraud, hence the round number. It should be noted that it would have been difficult to find very many more fraudulent that fit the parameters of the study, given the constraints on data collection already described. As mentioned, these efforts also identified 70 examiners that fell outside the current parameters.

either liquid or gas. What can be observed can also be sampled and measured using various instruments. The measure of the water remaining in the pot is unknown. When the pot boils over with respect to incidents of forensic fraud spilling into the public domain, we can observe and study those cases with some expectation that they are representative of what remains unseen. This reality limits implications of the present study to known cases, and forces us to acknowledge that the characteristics of unreported and undiscovered cases, which could be many, remain unknown. However, this limitation is true of any study involving any criminal behavior: only the known and reported cases can be sampled for examination. Consequently, this is not a legitimate argument for avoiding the study of crime, only a limitation regarding the interpretation of results. Additionally, the acknowledgment of this limitation grants that there are more cases of fraud out there that have not been made public, which further makes a key assertion of this research—that fraud is a serious problem requiring the immediate attention of the forensic science community.

EXCLUDED CASES

In the very early stages of conception, this research had broader parameters, including the study of forensic examiners engaged in fraud across every major forensic discipline (e.g., forensic accounting, criminal profiling, and forensic psychology). However, it was soon understood that such an approach is not appropriate given the narrow issues of concern in the thesis. The reason is in part due to the differing professional constraints across forensic disciplines, differing professional standards, and that some forensic disciplines would have been overrepresented.[5] Consequently, the parameters of this study were attenuated as described in the previous section.

Ultimately, data from 70 examiners alleged to have committed forensic fraud identified in the initial stages of research was excluded. The reason is that in-depth examination of reliable data sources revealed an exclusionary criterion

---

[5]For example, unlike forensic scientists working with physical evidence, forensic mental health professionals (e.g., psychologists, psychiatrists, and counselors) are licensed and regulated by state boards in the jurisdictions where they work. Some individual states keep open public records regarding those professionals that have lost their licensure, often with detailed explanations as to why. In the case of forensic mental health professionals, a quick search of available state licensure databases reveals numerous cases of fraud related to billing (e.g., examinations or assessments that did not take place) and the fabrication of results related to non-existent forensic evaluations. The prevalence of this fraudulent activity combined with the ease of gathering data would have caused this group to be overrepresented against other forensic examiners.

regarding the examiner. None of these cases involved multiple exclusionary criteria. Exclusions break down as follows.

Pre-2000 and post-2010

Twenty-five forensic examiners committed forensic fraud that was discovered and disposed of prior to the year 2000. Therefore, these cases fall outside the temporal parameters established for the present study.

International

Twenty-five forensic examiners committed forensic fraud in justice systems outside the United States (e.g., England, Canada, Australia, Barbados, Israel, and India). Therefore, these cases fall outside the regional parameters established for the present study.

Other forensic professionals

Fourteen forensic examiners committed fraud while working in forensic professions unrelated to preservation, examination, interpretation, and/or testimony regarding physical evidence. This includes the following professions: forensic mental health (6), criminal profiling (5),[6] forensic accounting (2), and forensic sociology (1). Therefore, these cases fall outside the employment parameters established for the present study.

Unproved allegations

Six forensic examiners were alleged to have committed forensic fraud; however, those allegations had not been sufficiently investigated, or they did not hold up to official scrutiny. Resolutions included the following: accused but still under investigation (2); tried in court and acquitted (1); accused and expelled from a professional organization, but later reinstated and allowed to resign (1); arrested with the charges later dropped (1); and admission to error but not fraud, without follow-up investigation (1). Under the circumstances described, these cases fall outside the "decree" parameter established for the present study.

The following case examples are representative of those that were excluded from the present study.

---

[6]The parameters of the present study required this researcher to exclude five law enforcement experts describing themselves generally as behavioral analysts (aka criminal profilers), three of which were employed by, or affiliated with, the FBI. Three of these five falsified their credentials in professional resumes and subsequent expert testimony; one of them falsely testified to examining evidence that he had not; one resigned public office amid allegations of wrongdoing; and none have been sanctioned by any authority, including those who are active members of the American Academy of Forensic Sciences (AAFS). See: *Drake v. Portuondo* (2006) and Turvey (2011) for discussion regarding most of these forensic examiners.

HOWARD B. OLLICK, FORENSIC TOXICOLOGIST

Independent Forensic Examiner

Howard B. Ollick offered his services as a forensic toxicologist in private practice. However, it was eventually revealed by opposing counsel (a prosecutor) that his resume contained false and misleading information—including a fake Ph.D. According to Fitzgerald (1998a):

> [Prosecutor Tony] Loe noticed a discrepancy between two of Ollick's resumes. In one, Ollick wrote he had a bachelor of science degree from the school of education at Ohio State University; in the other, it was a bachelor of arts from the school of business administration at Ohio State.
>
> …Ollick also claimed he had earned a doctorate in organic chemistry from FAU in 1973, but the university does not offer that degree. In fact, FAU's registrar found no record of his attending the university or receiving a degree there.

In reality, Mr. Ollick was not an expert in forensic toxicology, but rather he was a laboratory technician licensed by the Florida Department of Health. Mr. Ollick was tried and found guilty of forging his credentials and falsifying his education. He was sentenced to prison for three years (Fitzgerald, 1998b).

This case involved a forensic examiner falsifying his credentials in relation to both evidence examination and expert testimony regarding the interpretation of physical evidence. However, his acts of fraud were committed, revealed, and dealt with prior to 2000, placing them outside the scope of the present study. Consequently, Mr. Ollick's years of credential fraud across hundreds of cases were excluded from the present data set.

DIPLOMA FRAUD

Washington State Patrol

In March of 2008, Dixie E. Randock, 59; Steven K. Randock Sr., 67; and their daughter, Heidi K. Lorhan, 39; of Spokane, Washington, pleaded guilty to conspiracy to commit wire and mail fraud. They admitted to jointly creating a string of at least 127 fictional educational institutions out of their home. Over a period of ten years, they sold more than 8,000 bogus credentials to "students" all over the world from any one of their diploma mills with names such as "Saint Regis University" and "Robertstown University." As detailed in Morlin (2008):

> At least 300 of the buyers worked for the federal government, including in positions in the Justice Department, the State Department, various military branches and even the White House, it has been disclosed in previous court hearings.
>
> The only publicly announced criminal prosecution of a purchaser involves a former deputy U.S. marshal supervisor who worked in Spokane and bought a degree from Saint Regis. He pleaded guilty to lying on a promotion application and awaits sentencing.

The discoveries in this case led to an audit of the rank and file in the Washington State Patrol (WSP), to check for fraud with respect to claims of academic achievement in higher education. Like many law enforcement agencies, the WSP offers promotions and pay raises based in part on educational accomplishments. As a result of the audit, nine WSP officers were placed on leave under accusations of fraud for having purchased falsified diplomas in order to get increased pay and inevitably enhance courtroom testimony (Sullivan, 2008).[7] Ultimately, none of those officers were charged with crimes or terminated—unlike the U.S. marshal described above.

This incident involved multiple instances of credential fraud by multiple law enforcement officers during the time frame set for the present study. However, these officers were not assigned primarily as forensic personnel, and the fraud did not involve or impact physical evidence examination. Consequently, these cases were excluded from the present data set.

---

[7]Diploma mills commonly target government employees, especially those in law enforcement, offering classroom credit for life experience. It is well known within the law enforcement community that presenting this kind of college diploma as evidence of having completed a higher education requirement is tantamount to fraud. However, the practice is so widespread within the higher ranks that it often goes uninvestigated or unpunished.

MIGUEL RIVERA, LATENT PRINT EXAMINER

Los Angeles Police Department (LAPD)

Scientific Investigation Division, Latent Print Unit (LPU)

During 2007–2008, the LAPD's LPU was involved in a fingerprint misidentification scandal resulting in multiple overturned cases, the termination of one examiner, the suspension of three others, and the replacement of two supervisors (Rubin and Winton, 2008; Winton, 2009).[8] The subsequent investigation of the LPU by the LAPD's Audit Division revealed that "[e]rroneous identifications pose an immediate and extensive risk, liability, and exposure to the department"; "[q]uality assurance processes are insufficient and require immediate improvement"; and "[m]orale and the professionalism of the LPU and LPU staff need improvement to support an effective working environment" (LAPD, 2008; pp. 5–7). Further inquiry revealed "that errors were partly the result of the unit's being marred by inadequate training, antiquated facilities, poor supervision, careless handling of evidence and other shortfalls" (Winton, 2009). Though the LAPD was clearly responsible for recklessly creating an environment where the mandates of good science were largely ignored, there was no clear evidence reported of examiner fraud; rather, there was systemic incompetence, ineptitude, and apathy.

In 2009, Miguel Rivera, one of the LAPD's highest-ranking latent print examiners, and a unit supervisor, was charged with sexual assault (Rubin and Winton, 2009). This case involved criminal activity by a forensic examiner during the time frame established for the present research. However, his crimes were not known to be related to his work as a latent print examiner, and were not known to involve acts that fit the definition of forensic fraud.

Consequently, given the absence of specific instances of forensic fraud in either of these related scandals (only ignorance, incompetence, and criminality), the data from these cases was properly excluded from the present study.

---

[8]*The LAPD's Latent Print Unit employs almost 80 civilian examiners (Rubin and Winton, 2008).*

LARRY STEWART, FORENSIC SCIENTIST

Secret Service Forensic Services Laboratory

In 2004, Martha Stewart was put on trial for conspiracy, obstruction, and making false statements regarding the illegal sale of some stocks. She was convicted of multiple counts. Larry Stewart (no relation to Martha), a forensic scientist with the Secret Service Forensic Services Laboratory, and a witness for the prosecution against Martha Stewart, was accused of multiple counts of perjury related to his expert testimony regarding ink analysis that had been performed (Smilon, Hadad, and Gaffney, 2004; see Figure 8-1). He was put on trial and ultimately acquitted of those charges (McClam, 2004).

This case involved a forensic examiner accused of giving false testimony related to his examination of physical evidence, and put on trial for perjury, during the time interval of interest in the present study. However, a federal jury acquitted him at trial; the criminal allegations against him were ultimately unproved. Consequently, and out of an abundance of caution, this forensic examiner was excluded from the present data set (see also the discussion of perjury provided in Chapter 1).

FIGURE 8-1
Larry Stewart of the Secret Service Forensic Services Laboratory, during the 2004 trial of Martha Stewart

KEVIN REED, FIREARM AND TOOL MARK EXAMINER

Detroit Police Department, Forensic Services Laboratory

Police officer Kevin Reed was the co-author of "a firearms evidence report in the case that ultimately led to the closure of the department's crime lab" (Schmitt, 2009). An employee of the crime laboratory, Mr. Reed gave conflicting testimony regarding tests that were supposed to have been run on multiple shell casings before a conclusion could be reached as to their origin. As reported in Schmitt (2009):

> At one point, Reed said he helped work on a June 6, 2007, report by his colleague Officer Tenisha Bridgewater. The report found that all the casings came from the same weapon in the May 27, 2007, killings of Detroiters DeAngelo Savage, 33, and Tommy Haney, 38. That was later found inaccurate.
>
> Bridgewater testified that she never signed the report but didn't know why. She also said that she was told to rush the report, though she couldn't recall who gave her that order. "I'm pretty sure I was supposed to sign it, yes," she told defense attorney Marvin Barnett. "I believe it's the legal process of it."
>
> Jarrhod Williams, 22, was on trial in the Detroit killings a year ago when prosecutors offered to let him plead no contest to second-degree murder and serve 12 years in prison. He took the deal but withdrew the

plea after Barnett hired firearms expert David Balash, who discovered the shell casings came from two weapons.

This case prompted an audit of the Detroit Police Department crime laboratory by the Michigan State Police, which determined that 10% of the firearms examinations contained "significant errors" (MSP, 2008; p. 3), as well as 42% rate of non-compliance with laboratory practice standards (far below the 100% compliance requirement). It also determined that not only was the cost of a 10% lab error rate unacceptable, but that it had a serious impact on the justice system (p. 3):

> In total, this equates to approximately 10% of the completed firearms cases having significant errors. On average, the DPD firearms unit analyzes 1,800 cases per year. If this 10% error rate holds, the negative impact on the judicial system would be substantial, with a strong likelihood of wrongful convictions and a valid concern about numerous appeals.

High-ranking officers agreed that the Detroit Police Department Forensic Services Laboratory suffered from "numerous errors made by multiple examiners," and that the errors found at the lab were "indicative of a systemic problem" (Patton, 2008). Consequently, the Detroit Police Department closed its entire crime lab and had it condemned (see Figure 8-2).

FIGURE 8-2
Inside the shuttered Detroit Police Department Forensic Services Laboratory in 2011—its motto literally in ruins.

Continued

KEVIN REED, FIREARM AND TOOL MARK EXAMINER
CONTINUED

While employees and supervisors from the shuttered lab claimed that physical evidence had been properly secured and shipped elsewhere for analysis or storage, the reality was different. An investigative effort by local journalists revealed (Neavling, Ashenfelter, and Damron, 2011): "Thousands of rounds of live ammunition, sealed evidence kits and case files—some containing Social Security numbers of rape and assault victims—lay amid rubble in a crime lab abandoned by Detroit police two years ago." Eventually, the Detroit

Police conceded that this was true and reportedly went to work remedying the situation.

This case involved at least one forensic examiner who gave inconsistent testimony in a multiple-murder trial. However, it is unclear from the record whether that testimony was a result of incompetence or intentional deception. As forensic fraud was not established with certainty, and there is no evidence of sanction or termination, this forensic examiner was excluded from the present data set.

The present study also excludes cases in which non-forensic-evidence-related law enforcement personnel were found to have engaged in fraud related to the physical evidence. As suggested previously, typical cases encountered by this author included police officers or jail officers stealing cash/drugs, tampering with physical evidence, and planting physical evidence.[9] These cases did not involve forensic examiners and therefore did not meet the initial threshold for potential viability. They were also not counted as part of the original 170 potentially viable cases identified.

The only police officers included in the present data set were those employed by or affiliated with a law enforcement crime laboratory, and those whose primary duties were related to the collection, preservation, and testing of forensic evidence. This includes evidence technicians and crime scene investigators. These professionals, with varying levels of scientific education (some with none), hold a broad range of forensic responsibilities related to the processing and presumptive field testing of physical evidence. In many cases, they are called to testify in court (or before a grand jury) and offer what can only be described as expert scientific testimony regarding how physical evidence is collected, preserved, and examined. This is commonly a prelude to opinion testimony regarding the results of presumptive field tests for drugs or biological evidence—without didactic qualification as an expert.

---

[9]In recent years, there has been a steady stream of major law enforcement scandals involving conspiracies by multiple members of different police units to "flake," or plant, drug evidence on innocent suspects for financial incentives, including departments in Brooklyn (Yaniv, 2011); Dallas (Emily, 2009); Oakland (Lee, 2009); and St. Louis (Patrick, 2009).

VARIABLES AND FREQUENCY RESULTS

Variables were extracted from the final sample ($n = 100$) and assigned to one of four categories: *employee, employer, evidence,* and *impact.*

Employee variables

Employee variables are composed of traits specific to the forensic examiner. They include examiner education, general job description, supervisory status, history of fraud, history of criminality, history of addiction, and their general approach to fraud.

Examiner education was divided into four weighted categories, from those with zero higher education to those with a graduate-level science background (M.S. or Ph.D.). Frequency results for this variable are as follows: ED0[10]: $n = 36$; ED1[11]: $n = 12$; ED2[12]: $n = 26$; and ED3[13]: $n = 26$. See Figure 8-3.

The largest individual education category is composed of those forensic examiners with no formal higher education of any kind (ED0; 36%). However, if we combine forensic examiners holding an undergraduate education in the sciences (ED2; 26%) with those holding a graduate-level education in the sciences (ED3; 26%), this becomes the majority group by a narrow margin ($n = 52$, or 52%). More significant, however, is that if we compare all forensic examiners holding no formal higher education in the sciences (ED0 + ED1 = 48%) with all forensic examiners who do (ED2 + ED3 = 52%), the representation all but evens out. This begins to suggest that higher education in the sciences, by itself, may not be a significant variable in relation to forensic fraud in general.[14]

Forensic examiners were assigned to only one of five general job descriptions: *laboratory criminalist* (JLAB), *technician* (JTEC), *law enforcement examiner*

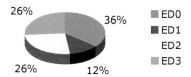

26%   36%   ■ ED0
        ■ ED1
          ED2
26%   12% ■ ED3

FIGURE 8-3
Examiner science education

---

[10]Zero college education.
[11]Undergraduate education, non-science.
[12]Undergraduate education, science oriented.
[13]Graduate-level education, science oriented.
[14]For discussion, see Chapter 9.

(JLEX), *medicolegal examiner* (JMED), and *digital evidence examiner* (JDIG). Then they were also classified regarding their *supervisory status* (JSUP), with the notion that supervisors might have more access, privacy, and therefore opportunities to commit fraud. Frequency results for job description variables are as follows: JLAB[15]: $n = 53$; JMED[16]: $n = 23$; JTEC[17]: $n = 15$; JLEX[18]: $n = 7$; JDIG[19]: $n = 2$; and JSUP[20]: $n = 56$. See Figure 8-4 for detail excluding the JSUP variable.

The largest individual category by job description is composed of those forensic examiners who work in a crime laboratory of some kind (JLAB; 53%). This is followed distantly by those forensic examiners who work in the medicolegal professions (JMED; 23%). Those forensic examiners working directly for law enforcement agencies and not affiliated with a crime laboratory (JTEC and JLEX) could be combined to make a single group. However, they would still rank the same with respect to overall frequency. The smallest category, by a wide margin, is composed of those examiners who work with digital evidence (JDIG: 2%).

While sheer frequency suggests that being a supervisor may not be a significant variable, by itself, in relation to forensic fraud (JSUP; 53%), it is difficult to speculate regarding the potential meaning of the other job description variables. They could be a function of the ratio of full-time crime laboratory personnel to other full-time positions found among other employers. They could also be a

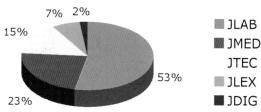

FIGURE 8-4
Examiner job description

---

[15]Laboratory criminalists.

[16]Forensic pathologists, coroners, forensic nurses, and medicolegal death investigators.

[17]Police technicians with evidence collection, preservation, testing, and reporting duties (e.g., crime scene technicians and evidence technicians).

[18]Police officers or employees, unaffiliated with a crime lab or crime scene unit, who have come to be relied upon as experts in evidence examination and/or interpretation (e.g., officers with arson or drug sniffing canines, narcotics officers, and some police bloodstain experts).

[19]Experts in the interpretation of digital evidence, including computer hard drives and any related digital files.

[20]Examiners acting in a supervisory capacity, as either a unit manager or a laboratory manager of some kind.

function of cultural accountability, suggesting that forensic fraud is more easily identified in crime laboratories because of the scientific nature of the work, procedural transparency, and a higher frequency of audits. As discussed in prior chapters, law enforcement culture is more closed, secretive, and punitive toward those who speak out, demanding loyalty over honesty. Whichever the case may be, correlation with evidence, employer, and outcome variables is required before the significance of any of these variables can even be guessed at.[21]

Before examiner history was assessed, it was established whether the forensic fraud in question represented an isolated (single) incident, or whether it was known to be part of an ongoing pattern of fraudulent behavior. Only 18 examiners were found to be involved in isolated incidents of fraud. That is to say, 82% of the forensic fraud in this study was determined to be part of an ongoing pattern of fraud by the examiner, often involving multiple examiners, prior to its discovery. This is a significant finding given that, as discussed in previous chapters, forensic fraud is routinely presented as an isolated event, blamed on the lone examiners (aka "bad apples").[22]

Forensic examiners were assessed for a known *history of addiction* (ADDx), a *history of fraud* (FRDx), and a *history of other criminal convictions* (CRMx). Frequency results for examiner history variables are as follows: ADDx: $n = 23$; FRDx: $n = 21$; and CRMx: $n = 17$. Some examiners fell into more than one category. See Figure 8-5.

The frequency with which these variables occur, separately and in concert, suggests that they may be significant in relation to forensic fraud—and may also hint at direct preventative measures.[23]

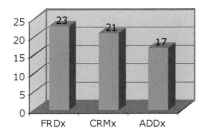

FIGURE 8-5
Examiner history

---

[21]For discussion, see Chapter 9.
[22]This is discussed further in Chapter 10, "Conclusions and Recommendations," in the context of other related findings.
[23]For discussion, see Chapter 9.

Adapted from, and consistent with, typologies provided in Babbage (1830), NAS (2002), ORI (2009b), and Turvey (2003), forensic examiners were cross-categorized as having used one or more of three general approaches to committing fraud, referred to as *Simulators,*[24] *Dissemblers,*[25] and *Pseudoexperts.*[26]

Simulators are those examiners who physically manipulate physical evidence or related forensic testing. This means that they physically fabricate, tamper with, or destroy evidence. As the name suggests, they are trying to create the appearance that something happened when it did not, or create the appearance that nothing happened at all when in fact it did. This approach to fraud also describes those examiners engaging in evidence suppression by concealing its existence (e.g., hide it in a desk drawer, hide it on the evidence shelf, remove it from the evidence log).

Dissemblers are those examiners who exaggerate, embellish, lie about, or otherwise misrepresent findings. They are not tampering with the evidence; they are simply not telling the truth about it. *Dissemblers* exist on a continuum from those who lie outright about the significance of examination results to those who intentionally present a biased or incomplete view.

Pseudoexperts are those examiners who fabricate or misrepresent their credentials. They are also referred to as fakes, phonies, charlatans, and mountebanks. Pseudoexperts exist on a continuum of severity as well, from those with valid credentials who misrepresent a credential or an affiliation, to those with no valid credentials at all.

Frequency results for examiner fraud type variables are as follows: Simulators (SIM): $n = 90$; Dissemblers (DIS): $n = 57$; and Pseudoexperts (PSE): $n = 27$. See Figure 8-6.

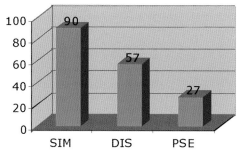

FIGURE 8-6
Examiner approach to fraud

---

[24]Also referred to as *forging* (Babbage, 1830) or *fabrication* (ORI, 2009b).
[25]Also referred to as *trimming* and *cooking* (Babbage, 1830), or *falsification* (ORI, 2009b).
[26]Also referred to as *falsifying credentials* (ORI, 2009b).

The frequency of these variables evidences that Simulators are the most common (90%), evidencing that this is the most frequently used approach by fraudulent forensic examiners. Pseudoexperts are the least common, yet still proportionately high (27%), evidencing that this approach is found in more than a quarter of all cases of forensic fraud. Given this frequency distribution, it is clear that these variables may be significant in relation to forensic fraud when correlated with other evidence, employer, and impact variables. Correlation with employee, employer, and impact variables is necessary before more reliable interpretations can be made.[27]

Employer variables

Employer variables are composed of traits specific to the agencies and institutions where the fraudulent examiners in this study worked. They include employer independence from law enforcement, lab accreditation, and the involvement of an audit.

Employers were divided into four weighted categories in relation to their *independence from law enforcement*: crime labs within law enforcement agencies (ELAW), public crime labs within government agencies (EPUB), private crime labs (EPLI), and self-employed examiners (EIE). Frequency results for these variables are as follows: ELAW: 76; EPUB: 5; EPLI: 9; and EIE: 8. See Figure 8-7.

The frequency of these variables evidences that crime labs within law enforcement agencies represent the largest of all employer groups (ELAW: 78%). As most crime labs are publicly funded (as part of either law enforcement or some other government agency), this might not be entirely unexpected. However, the low frequency of other publicly funded crime labs initially correlated with fraud in the present sample (5%) suggests that crime labs operating within law enforcement agencies might be associated with a particular type of fraud. This could in turn suggest that employer independence from law enforcement may

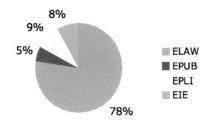

FIGURE 8-7
Employers

---

[27]For discussion, see Chapter 9.

have a significant relationship to forensic fraud, when correlated with other evidence, employer, and impact variables.[28]

Employers were evaluated with respect to whether they were *accredited*. The primary accrediting agency associated with forensic science laboratories is the American Society of Crime Lab Directors (ASCLD). Of the employers in the present study, 45% (n = 45) were accredited by ASCLD. No employers were accredited by any other agency. This somewhat even frequency distribution suggests that accreditation may not have a significant relationship to forensic fraud; however, this preliminary inference ultimately proves inaccurate in light of multivariate hierarchical regression results.[29]

Employers were finally evaluated with respect to whether they uncovered the fraudulent examiner during an *internal investigation* or *audit*. Of the employers in the present study, 54% (n = 54) discovered the fraudulent examiner during an internal investigation or audit. This relatively even frequency distribution suggests that the potential for internal investigations and audits may not have a significant relationship to forensic fraud; however, again, this preliminary inference ultimately proves inaccurate in light of multivariate hierarchical regression results.[30]

Evidence variables

Evidence variables are composed of the different kinds of physical evidence that forensic examiners committed fraud in relation to. These evidence types included DNA (DNAEV); biological evidence other than DNA (BIOEV); money (CASHEV); chain of custody (CHNEV); drug weights or amounts (DRG1EV); drug test results (DRG2EV); education, training, and experience (EDEXEV); fingerprint evidence (FNGEV); and firearms and ballistics evidence (BALEV). In some cases, forensic examiners committed fraud in relation to more than one evidence type. Frequency results for these variables are as follows: CHNEV: n = 59; EDEXEV: n = 30; BIOEV: n = 28; DRG1EV: n = 24; DRG2EV: n = 17; DNAEV: n = 9; CASHEV: n = 8; BALEV: n = 5; and FNGEV: n = 4. See Figure 8-8.

The frequencies of these variables demonstrate that chain of custody is the most common form of evidence affected by fraudulent examiners (CHNEV; 59%). This was followed a distant second by forensic examiners who lied about their credentials (EDEXEV; 30%). Firearms/ballistics evidence (BALEV; 5%) and fingerprint evidence (FNGEV; 4%) were the least likely to be associated with forensic fraud.

---

[28]For discussion, see Chapter 9.
[29]For discussion, see Chapter 9.
[30]For discussion, see Chapter 9.

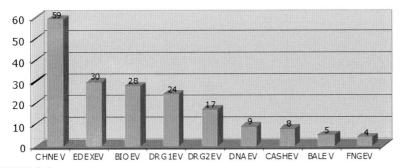

FIGURE 8-8
Frequency of fraud by evidence type

The frequency of these variables' evidence is consistent with chain of custody being necessarily associated with at least one other form of evidence, causing it to be more recurrent than others. The other forms of evidence are generally distributed in such a fashion as to suggest that some may also have a somewhat significant relationship to forensic fraud. Correlation with employee, employer, and impact variables is necessary before more reliable interpretations can be made.[31]

Impact variables

Impact variables are composed of consequences to employees, employers, and cases that have entered the justice system.

Traits associated with the severity of *consequences to forensic examiners* were divided into weighted categories for analysis. These included, in order of increasing severity, examiners who were promoted (PROM); retained without consequence or change (RET); transferred to a different department (TRAN); encouraged to resign (RES); terminated (TERM); held civilly liable in a lawsuit (CIVL); convicted of a crime (CONV); and those who committed suicide (SUIC). Frequency results for these variables are as follows: PROM: $n = 1$; RET: $n = 37$; TRAN: $n = 6$; RES: $n = 32$; TERM: $n = 38$; CIVL: $n = 15$; CONV: $n = 48$; and SUIC: $n = 2$. See Figure 8-9. Note that some examiners suffered multiple consequences (e.g., retained and held civilly liable; resigned and held civilly liable; resigned and convicted; and terminated and convicted).

The frequencies of these variables begins to suggest that being convicted of a crime, as well as having committed forensic fraud, is not, by itself, a significantly correlated factor: it is just about as likely to occur as not (CONV; 48%). Other variables evidence varying levels of significance. Correlation with

---

[31]For discussion, see Chapter 9.

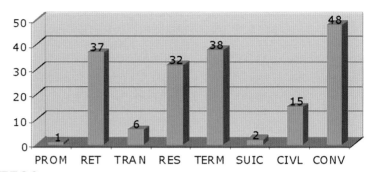

FIGURE 8-9
Examiner consequences

employee, employer, and evidence variables is necessary before more reliable interpretations can be made.[32]

Employer consequences were assessed by considering the number of cases each was required to review (REV) and the number of labs ultimately shut down subsequent to the discovery of fraud (SHUT—in a few cases, the closure was temporary). Consequences to the justice system overall were assessed by additionally considering the number of cases that have been overturned to date as a direct consequence of the fraud (OVER). Frequency results for these variables are as follows: REV: 42,042; OVER: 5,443; and SHUT: 9.

The frequency of these variables evidences a significant impact with respect to expenses necessarily related to reviewing cases and hiring/training new employees incurred by employers; and a significant impact on the financial cost and credibility to the justice system related to cases that must be overturned and perhaps even retried. As the actual expense incurred for each case reviewed, overturned, and retried varies widely across agencies and jurisdictions, along with the variable costs related to lab closures and outsourcing evidence examination, it is not possible to reliably estimate the total impact revealed in this study in actual dollars. This is to say nothing of the financial costs related to civilly litigating wrongful convictions and the liability that is generally incurred as a result—which can result in civil judgments that average around half a million dollars per case or more (Bernhard, 2004; not including legal fees and the average cost of $25,000 per year to board a prisoner). This issue would require separate study, but it is safe to infer that the actual cost in dollars and credibility would be substantial.

---

[32]For discussion, see Chapter 9.

SUMMARY

Research efforts described in this chapter revealed 170 different forensic examiners alleged to have committed fraud in the course of their casework. Of these 170 forensic examiners, data from 70 were excluded, as they ultimately fell outside research parameters. Variables were extracted from the final sample ($n = 100$) and assigned to one of four categories: *employee, employer, evidence,* and *impact.* The frequencies for some of these variables suggest a potentially significant relationship with forensic fraud, whereas others show little potential significance.

Ultimately, these descriptive frequencies provide a shallow first look at the relationships that might exist in the present data. They have utility in that they offer preliminary inferences about where to look for more significant results. In order to more completely and reliably determine the statistical significance of these variables in relation to each other, evidence, employer, and impact variables are correlated using multivariate regression analysis in the next chapter.

CHAPTER 9

Multivariate Analysis of Forensic Fraud, 2000–2010

"Statistics are like a bikini. What they reveal is suggestive, but what they conceal is vital."

Aaron Levenstein
Associate Prof. Emeritus of Business at Baruch College (1961–1981)

This chapter presents the results of multivariate analysis performed on frequency data discussed in the preceding chapter. As will be demonstrated, that frequency data was useful but preliminary. First, the statistical methodology used is discussed in brief. Second, correlation matrices and Hierarchical Multiple Regression Analyses are presented and discussed for each of the three dependent variable sets: *approach to fraud*, *evidence type*, and *consequences*. Finally, the limitations of these results are considered, as well as immediate recommendations for additional related research.

STATISTICAL METHODS

As mentioned in the preceding chapter, variables were extracted from the final sample of fraudulent examiners ($n = 100$) and assigned to one of four categories: *employee*, *employer*, *evidence*, and *impact*. For the analyses presented in this chapter, the variables in these categories were appropriately separated with respect to cause and effect (Feinberg, 2007). Independent variables (aka causal or explanatory variables) in this study are those associated with *examiners* and their *employers*. Dependent variables (aka effect or response variables) are those associated with the examiner's *approach to fraud*; the *evidence* associated with the approach to fraud; and the *impact* of the fraud on the examiner, the employer, or the justice system.

Independent variables are first examined using correlation matrices, requiring one matrix for each of the three dependent variable sets (approach to fraud, evidence, and impact). A correlation matrix provides the statistical correlations between all pairs of data sets. This is the usual first stage for data analysis

Forensic Fraud. http://dx.doi.org/10.1016/B978-0-12-408073-7.00009-4

involving multiple variables. It is intended to reveal both anticipated and unanticipated relationships of a statistically significant nature.

Because this research involves multiple independent variables, it was decided that a multivariate analysis was the next appropriate step. After consideration was given to the data, the final sample size, and the goals of the research, a hierarchical multiple regression analysis was used.[1] Hierarchical multiple regression estimates the statistical relationship between a set of independent variables and individual or grouped dependent variables (Cohen et al., 2003).[2] By definition, any findings reported to have "statistical significance" are unlikely to have occurred by chance—meaning that differences are likely the result of test variables causally interacting with each other (Aiken and West, 1991). This allows for more reliably informed theorization regarding the nature of that interaction, some of which is offered here and is then followed up on in Chapter 10, "Conclusions and Recommendations."

CORRELATION MATRICES

A correlation matrix provides the statistical correlations between all pairs of data sets—summarizing all possible relationships (Grimm and Yarnold, 1995). As explained earlier, this reveals both anticipated and unanticipated relationships of a statistically significant nature. When the correlation is between the variable and itself, the values are in agreement, creating a diagonal consisting of 1s. Correlation matrices are presented in Tables 9-1 through 9-3.

As indicated in the three correlation matrices provided (Tables 9-1 through 9-3), there are multiple employer and examiner variables that are significantly correlated with a number of approach, evidence type, and impact variables at the .01** and .05* level. The presence of significant correlations indicates that these variables affect each other in a manner that is noteworthy, requiring a

---

[1]In the early stages of this research, another form of multivariate analysis was considered, referred to as smallest space analysis (SSA). However, it was eventually understood that SSA requires researchers to make initial assumptions about the distance between variables in order to present them graphically. Then, the data from SSA graphs is interpreted based on the distance between variables that are presented. In essence, SSA allows the researcher to assume the nature of the distance-relationships that the researcher is purporting to reveal, and then to present them as though they are something that has been generated via statistical analysis. Therefore, while useful for presenting presumed but untested theoretical relationships, SSA does not provide for the discovery of unknown statistical relationships (see generally Bloombaum, 1970; Guttman and Greenbaum, 1998; and Kumar and Ryan, 2009). Given that the examination of the data in the present study is an exploratory effort and that a priori assumptions about the relationships between variables must be made when employing SSA, it was decided that presenting data via SSA would be premature, if not misleading.

[2]While this methodology is not particularly creative, nor should it be, it offers the best hope of revealing and exploring the statistical relationships between the variables of known forensic fraud cases.

more in-depth investigation and discussion.[3] As this is presented in the next section, detailed discussion here would be premature.

HIERARCHICAL MULTIPLE REGRESSION ANALYSIS AND DISCUSSION

Hierarchical multiple regression is used to estimate the relationship between a set of independent variables and individual or grouped dependent variables (Cohen et al., 2003). It involves a sequence of simultaneously conducted analyses, as explained in Grimm and Yarnold (1995; p. 52):

> The first analysis in the series contains one or more predictors. The next analysis adds one or more new predictors to those used in the first analysis. The next analysis adds new predictors to those used in the second analysis, and so on. The change in R^2 between consecutive analyses in this series represents the proportion of variance in the criterion that is shared exclusively with the newly added variables. Thus, hierarchical analysis is one way of calculating semipartial correlations....

Hierarchical multiple regression indicates whether a set of independent variables explains a percentage of the variance in a dependent variable at a significant level. It can also indicate the corresponding predictive importance of independent variables.

Hierarchical multiple regressions are presented in Tables 9-4 through 9-6. Some discussion of results is presented here, and then followed up on in Chapter 10.

Hierarchical multiple regression analysis of examiner approaches to fraud

Hierarchical multiple regression analysis demonstrates that, in the present sample, sets of employer characteristics, examiner characteristics, and situational factors explained a statistically significant portion of the variance in examiner approach to fraud (see Table 9-4). Each statistically significant result is presented and discussed next.[4]

---

[3]Original frequency data was extracted from the final sample of fraudulent examiners ($n = 100$). However, ten additional cases were omitted from regression analysis in this chapter owing to extreme values on the "Cases Reviewed" variable—some in the thousands. These outliers skewed the distribution to such a degree that the assumption of normality necessary for regression analysis could not be met.
[4]Though there is undeniable tedium in the repetition of pro forma discussion points throughout this chapter, this format is necessary for brevity, clarity, and transparency. This will allow others to more capably evaluate these findings for empirical integrity.

Table 9-1 Employer and Examiner Variables Correlated with *Approach to Fraud*

		Employer Independence	Accredited Lab	Internal Audit	JLAE	JTEC	JLEX	JMED
Employer Independence	Pearson Correlation	1						
Accredited Lab	Pearson Correlation	−.339**	1					
	Sig. (2-tailed)	.001						
Internal Audit	Pearson Correlation	−.417**	.296**	1				
	Sig.(2-tailed)	.000	.005					
JLAB	Pearson Correlation	−.185	.701**	.200	1			
	Sig.(2-tailed)	.081	.000	.059				
JTEC	Pearson Correlation	−.191	−.223*	.212*	−.420**	1		
	Sig.(2-tailed)	.071	.034	.045	.000			
JLEX	Pearson Correlation	−.008	−.228*	−.095	−.273**	−.110	1	
	Sig.(2-tailed)	.942	.030	.373	.009	.303		
JMED	Pearson Correlation	.261*	−.449**	−.293	−.599**	−.241*	−.157	1
	Sig.(2-tailed)	.013	.000	.005	.000	.022	.141	
Isolated Incident	Pearson Correlation	.349**	−.202	−.289**	−.178	.032	−.022	.217*
	Sig.(2-tailed)	.001	.056	.006	.094	.767	.835	.040
Science Education	Pearson Correlation	.055	.239*	−.228*	.249*	−.366**	−.120	.132
	Sig.(2-tailed)	.610	.024	.032	.019	.000	.263	.218
History of Addiction	Pearson Correlation	−.098	−.056	.179	−.148	.252*	−.138	.071
	Sig.(2-tailed)	.358	.598	.091	.165	.017	.194	.503
Criminal History	Pearson Correlation	.121	−.181	−.010	−.194	−.002	.008	.170
	Sig.(2-tailed)	.255	.088	.929	.068	.986	.939	.109
History of Fraud	Pearson Correlation	.187	−.111	−.202	−.093	−.058	−.138	.134
	Sig.(2-tailed)	.078	.296	.056	.382	.589	.194	.208
Dissembler	Pearson Correlation	−.004	.339**	-.003	.490**	−.406**	.054	−.259*
	Sig.(2-tailed)	.971	.001	.978	.000	.000	.614	.014
Pseudoexpert	Pearson Correlation	.217*	−.148	−.357**	−.161	−.192	.223*	.132
	Sig.(2-tailed)	.040	.164	.001	.129	.070	.035	.214
Simulator	Pearson Correlation	−.441**	.234*	.591**	.255*	.208*	−.205	−.267*
	Sig.(2-tailed)	.000	.026	.000	.015	.049	.052	.011

**Correlation is significant at the .01 level (2-tailed).
*Correlation is significant at the .05 level (2-tailed).

Isolated Incident	Education	History of Addiction	Criminal History	History of Fraud	Dissembler	Pseudoexpert	Simulator
1							
.213*	1						
.046							
−.259*	−.217*	1					
.014	.041						
−.215*	−.291**	.454**	1				
.042	.006	.000					
−.191	−.217*	.133	.379**	1			
.072	.041	.212	.000				
−.123	.257*	−.152	−.058	−.097	1		
.247	.015	.153	.589	.363			
−.074	−.115	−.330**	−.071	.151	−.086	1	
.491	.285	.002	.508	.156	.422		
−.324**	−.200	.348**	.156	−.005	.090	−.472**	1
.002	.060	.001	.142	.961	.397	.000	

Table 9-2 Employer and Examiner Variables Correlated with *Evidence Types*

		Employer Independence	Accredited Lab	Internal Audit	JLAE	JTEC	JLEX	JMEC	Isolated Incident	Science Education	History of Addiction
Employer Independence	Pearson Correlation	1									
	Sig.(2-tailed)										
Accredited Lab	Pearson Correlation	−.339**	1								
	Sig.(2-tailed)	.001									
Internal Audit	Pearson Correlation	−.417**	.296**	1							
	Sig.(2-tailed)	.000	.005								
JLAB	Pearson Correlation	−.185	.701**	.200	1						
	Sig.(2-tailed)	.081	.000	.059							
JTEC	Pearson Correlation	−.191	−.223*	.212*	−.420**	1					
	Sig.(2-tailed)	.071	.034	.045	.000						
JLEX	Pearson Correlation	−.008	−.228*	−.095	−.273**	−.110	1				
	Sig.(2-tailed)	.942	.030	.373	.009	.303					
JMED	Pearson Correlation	.261*	−.449**	−.293**	−.599**	−.241*	−.157	1			
	Sig.(2-tailed)	.013	.000	.005	.000	.022	.141				
Isolated Incident	Pearson Correlation	.349**	−.202	−.289**	−.178	.032	−.022	.217*	1		
	Sig.(2-tailed)	.001	.056	.006	.094	.767	.835	.040			
Science Education	Pearson Correlation	.055	.239*	−.228*	.249*	−.366**	−.120	.132	.213*	1	
	Sig.(2-tailed)	.610	.024	.032	.019	.000	.263	.218	.046		
History of Addiction	Pearson Correlation	−.098	−.056	.179	−.148	.252*	−.138	.071	−.259*	−.217*	1
	Sig.(2-tailed)	.358	.598	.091	.165	.017	.194	.503	.014	.041	
Criminal History	Pearson Correlation	.121	−.181	−.010	−.194	−.002	.008	.170	−.215*	−.291**	.454**
	Sig.(2-tailed)	.255	.088	.929	.068	.986	.939	.109	.042	.006	.000
History of Fraud	Pearson Correlation	.187	−.111	−.202	−.093	−.058	−.138	.134	−.191	−.217*	.133
	Sig.(2-tailed)	.078	.296	.056	.382	.589	.194	.208	.072	.041	.212
DNA Evidence	Pearson Correlation	−.155	.315**	.178	.326**	−.137	−.089	−195	−.074	.156	−.172
	Sig.(2-tailed)	.145	.002	.094	.002	.198	.404	.065	.488	.143	.104
Money	Pearson Correlation	−.135	−.248*	.284**	−.297**	.235*	−.078	.210*	.062	−.297**	.155
	Sig.(2-tailed)	.204	.018	.007	.004	.026	.467	.047	.560	.005	.145
Biological/Non-DNA	Pearson Correlation	.114	.044	−.214*	.087	−.176	.141	−.008	.075	.223*	−.312**
	Sig.(2-tailed)	.285	.680	.042	.414	.096	.185	.943	.480	.036	.003

Criminal History	History of Addiction	DNA Evidence	Money	Biological/ Non-DNA	Chain of Custody	Education and Experience	Drug1(Weights/ Amounts	Drug 2 (Test Results)
1								
.379**	1							
.000								
−.143	−.172	1						
.179	.104							
.219*	.053	−.097	1					
.038	.619	.364						
−.189	−.066	−.034	−.175	1				
.074	.539	.754	.099					

Continued

Table 9-2 Employer and Examiner Variables Correlated with *Evidence Types* —Cont'd

		Employer Independence	Accredited Lab	Internal Audit	JLAE	JTEC	JLEX	JMEC	Isolated Incident	Science Education	History of Addiction
Chain of Custody	Pearson Correlation	−.320**	.166	.493**	.132	.279**	−.229*	−.184	−.203	−.183	.377**
	Sig.(2-tailed)	.002	.119	.000	.217	.008	.030	.083	.055	.085	.000
Education and Experience	Pearson Correlation	.239*	−.156	−.467**	−.182	−.216*	.102	.250*	.012	−.020	−.298**
	Sig.(2-tailed)	.023	.142	.000	.086	.041	.340	.017	.911	.851	.004
Drug1 (Weights/ Amounts)	Pearson Correlation	−.257*	−.046	.277**	−.249*	.446**	−.147	.038	−210*	−.163	.745**
	Sig.(2-tailed)	.015	.666	.088	.018	.000	.166	.721	.047	.126	.000
Drug2 (Test Results)	Pearson Correlation	−.026	.161	.149	.339**	.079	−.110	−.241*	−.205	.091	.020
	Sig.(2-tailed)	.810	.130	.161	.001	.460	.303	.022	.052	.395	.853

**Correlation is significant at the .01 level (2-tailed).
*Correlation is significant at the .05 level (2-tailed).

Table 9-3 Employer and Examiner Variables Correlated with *Impact*

		Employer Independence	Accredited Lab	Internal Audit	JLAB	JECT	JLEX	JMED
Employer Independence	Pearson Correlation	1						
	Sig. (2-tailed)							
Accredited Lab	Pearson Correlation	−.339**	1					
	Sig. (2-tailed)	.001						
Internal Audit	Pearson Correlation	−.417**	.296**	1				
	Sig. (2-tailed)	.000	.005					
JLAB	Pearson Correlation	−.185	.701**	.200	1			
	Sig. (2-tailed)	.081	.000	.059				
JTEC	Pearson Correlation	−.191	−.223*	.212*	−.420**	1		
	Sig. (2-tailed)	.071	.034	.045	.000			
JLEX	Pearson Correlation	−.008	−.228*	−.095	−.273**	−.110	1	
	Sig. (2-tailed)	.942	.030	.373	.009	.303		
JMED	Pearson Correlation	.261*	−.449**	−.293**	−.599**	−.241*	−.157	1
	Sig. (2-tailed)	.013	.000	.005	.000	.022	.141	
Isolated Incident	Pearson Correlation	.349**	−.202	−.289**	−.178	.032	−.022	.217*
	Sig. (2-tailed)	.001	.056	.006	.094	.767	.835	.040
Scientific Education	Pearson Correlation	.055	.239*	−.228*	.249*	−.366**	−.120	.132
	Sig. (2-tailed)	.610	.024	.032	.019	.000	.263	.218
History of Addiction	Pearson Correlation	−.098	−.056	.179	−.148	.252*	−.138	.071

Criminal History	History of Addiction	DNA Evidence	Money	Biological/Non-DNA	Chain of Custody	Education and Experience	Drug1(Weights/Amounts)	Drug 2 (Test Results)
.172	−.010	−.173	.243*	−.109	1			
.106	.922	.103	.021	.307				
−.099	.168	.008	−.200	.176	−.680**	1		
.353	.114	.941	.058	.098	.000			
.343**	.036	−.184	.134	−.333**	.354**	−.324**	1	
.001	.733	.083	.208	.001	.001	.002		
.085	.020	−.137	−.119	−.248*	.215*	−.216*	−.077	1
.424	.853	.198	.263	.019	.042	.041	.469	

Isolated Incident	Scientific Education	History of Addiction	Criminal History	History of Fraud	Cases Reviewed	Cases Overtuned	Lab Shut Down	Consequence Severity
1								
.213*	1							
.046								
−.259*	−.217*	1						

Continued

Table 9-3 Employer and Examiner Variables Correlated with *Impact* —Cont'd

		Employer Independence	Accredited Lab	Internal Audit	JLAB	JECT	JLEX	JMED
	Sig. (2-tailed)	.358	.598	.091	.165	.017	.194	.503
Criminal History	Pearson Correlation	.121	−.181	−.010	−.194	−.002	.008	.170
	Sig. (2-tailed)	.255	.088	.929	.068	.986	.939	.109
History of Fraud	Pearson Correlation	.187	−.111	−.202	−.093	−.058	−.138	.134
	Sig. (2-tailed)	.078	.296	.056	.382	.589	.194	.208
Cases Reviewed	Pearson Correlation	−.056	.232*	.271**	.394**	−.081	−.125	−289**
	Sig. (2-tailed)	.599	.028	.010	.000	.449	.241	.006
Cases Overturned	Pearson Correlation	−.097	.104	.162	.072	.097	−.052	−.121
	Sig. (2-tailed)	.364	.330	.128	.500	.362	.625	.258
Lab Shut Down	Pearson Correlation	.039	.165	−.044	.326**	−.137	−.089	−.195
	Sig. (2-tailed)	.717	.120	.677	.002	.198	.404	.065
Consequence Severity	Pearson Correlation	−.022	−.280**	.083	−.325**	.267*	.012	.107
	Sig. (2-tailed)	.838	.008	.443	.002	.012	.909	.323

**Correlation is significant at the .01 level (2-tailed).
*Correlation is significant at the .05 level (2-tailed).

Table 9-4 Hierarchical Multiple Regressions of Employer, Job Description, and Examiner Variables on *Approaches to Fraud*

	Dissemblers β (sr)	Pseudoexperts β (sr)	Simulators β (sr)
STEP 1—EMPLOYER			
Employer Independence	.10 (.09)	.07 (.06)	−.23 (−.21)*
Accredited Lab	.42 (.38)**	−.03 (−.03)	.01 (.01)
Internal Audit	−.10 (−.09)	−.31 (−.28)**	.49 (.44)**
R^2	.15**	.10**	.39**
STEP 2—JOB DESCRIPTION			
JLAB	.34 (.09)	−.74 (−.20)*	.46 (.12)
JTEC	−.24 (−.09)	−.58 (−.21)*	.29 (.10)
JLEX	.07 (.04)	−.07 (−.04)	−.04 (−.02)
JMED	−.09 (−.03)	−.52 (−.17)	.20 (.06)
ΔR^2	.17**	.10**	.06**
STEP 3—EXAMINER			
Isolated Incident	−.09 (−.08)	−.27 (−.22)*	−.03 (−.03)
Scientific Education	.12 (.09)	−.23 (−.19)*	−.04 (−.03)
History of Addiction	−.04 (−.03)	−.31 (−.25)**	.17 (.14)
Criminal History	.09 (.07)	−.13 (−.10)	.12 (.10)
History of Fraud	−.09 (−.08)	.03 (.03)	.07 (.06)
ΔR^2	.02**	.16**	.08**
Total ΔR^2	.34**	.36**	.53**

Note: N = 90. *p < .05, **p < .01, ΔR^2 represents the change in the amount of variance in the dependent variable accounted for in the set of predictors at each step of the regression. Total R^2s are not identical to the sum of R^2 and the changes in R^2 due to rounding.

Isolated Incident	Scientific Education	History of Addiction	Criminal History	History of Fraud	Cases Reviewed	Cases Overturned	Lab Shut Down	Consequence Severity
.014	.041							
-.215*	-.291**	.454**	1					
.042	.006	.000						
-.191	-.217*	.133	.379**	1				
.072	.041	.212	.000					
-.234*	-.113	.114	.045	-.072	1			
.027	.293	.283	.672	.498				
-.104	-.048	.347**	.104	-.067	.259*	1		
.331	.658	.001	.331	.532	.014			
-.167	-.052	.009	.061	.100	.223*	-.069	1	
.116	.630	.932	.566	.349	.035	.518		
-.263*	-.367**	.360**	.342**	.237*	.066	.136	-.139	1
.013	.000	.001	.001	.026	.539	.206	.195	

Dissemblers

Employer characteristics ($R^2 = .15**$), Job Description characteristics ($\Delta R^2 = .17**$), and Examiner characteristics ($\Delta R^2 = .02**$) all accounted for a statistically significant portion of the variance found in Dissemblers, $F(12,76) = 3.24$, $p < .01$. Put another way, the Employer, Job Description, and Examiner characteristics in the present study resulted in a total R^2 of $.34**$, accounting for 34% of all variance found among Dissemblers.

In Step 1 (Employer characteristics), statistically significant results are observed for Dissemblers based on Laboratory Accreditation ($sr = .38**$); significantly more Dissemblers were correlated with accredited forensic laboratories. This finding suggests that if a forensic laboratory is accredited, fraudulent examiners are significantly more likely to exaggerate, embellish, lie about, or otherwise misrepresent findings than to falsify credentials or dry-lab their results.

One way to interpret this finding is to infer that the structure and accountability necessary to achieve laboratory accreditation may be effective at preventing the unqualified (Pseudoexperts) from gaining employment at accredited labs, and at ensuring that physical evidence gets examined without direct tampering from Simulators—in other words, that there are some positive and constructive results of laboratory accreditation. This is a reasonable interpretation.

However, this finding also demonstrates that laboratory accreditation does not eliminate forensic fraud. In fact, it may be used to infer that laboratory accreditation actually encourages forensic examiners to commit a particular kind of fraud—to lie about the results of their examinations for fear of committing documented error or failing their proficiencies. As will be discussed later in this chapter, this interpretation is supported by findings demonstrating that laboratory accreditation is significantly related to increased falsification of only one kind of evidence: DNA.

In Step 2 (Job Description characteristics), statistically significant results are observed for Dissemblers based on a combined ΔR^2 of .17**, accounting for 17% of all variance found among Dissemblers. While the combined ΔR^2 is significant, examination of individual variables (JLAB, JTEC, JLEX, and JMED) is not revealing. Consequently, Step 2 variables represent what may be referred to as a pool of variance. That is to say, these variables are important as a group in relation to Dissemblers, but it is likely that there is insufficient sample size to magnify and reveal which are significant factors on their own. Further study is needed to determine which Job Description characteristics are significantly correlated with Dissemblers.

In Step 3 (Examiner characteristics), statistically significant results are observed for Dissemblers based on a combined ΔR^2 of .02**, accounting for 2% of all variance found among Dissemblers. While the combined ΔR^2 is significant, examination of individual variables (Isolated Incident, Science Education, History of Addiction, Criminal History, and History of Fraud) is not revealing. Consequently, Step 3 variables represent a pool of variance. That is to say, these variables are important as a group in relation to Dissemblers, but it is likely that there is insufficient sample size to magnify and reveal which are significant factors on their own. Further study is needed to determine which Examiner characteristics are significantly correlated with Dissemblers.

Pseudoexperts

Employer characteristics (R^2 = .10**), Job Description characteristics (ΔR^2 = .10**), and Examiner characteristics (ΔR^2 = .16**) all accounted for a statistically significant portion of the variance found in Pseudoexperts, $F(12,76)$ = 4.15, $p < .01$. Put another way, the Employer, Job Description, and Examiner characteristics in the present study resulted in a total R^2 of .36**, accounting for 36% of all variance found among Pseudoexperts.

In Step 1 (Employer characteristics), statistically significant results are observed for Pseudoexperts based on Internal Audits (sr = −.28**); in the present sample, significantly fewer Pseudoexperts are revealed in association with Internal Audits. This finding may suggest that internal audits are not effective at revealing those who falsify their credentials—that audits are more often focused on reviewing cases and protocols, and not hiring practices or examiner resumes. Alternatively, it may suggest that the kinds of forensic laboratories imposing internal audits are less likely to hire examiners with phony qualifications in the first place.

In Step 2 (Job Description characteristics), statistically significant results are observed for Pseudoexperts employed as laboratory criminalists (JLAB, sr = −.20*) and technicians (JTEC; sr = −.21*); in the present sample, those examiners employed as laboratory criminalists or technicians are significantly less likely to falsify their credentials. With respect to JLAB examiners, this may reflect the reality that laboratory positions require a demonstration of knowledge, skill, and ability that are not easily faked; these examiners are hired primarily based on the presentation verification of scientific credentials in biology or chemistry. With respect to JTEC examiners, this may reflect the reality that police technicians are generally not expected to be educated in the sciences, and subsequently rely primarily on training and experience acquired on the job when writing reports and giving testimony.

In Step 3 (Examiner characteristics), statistically significant results are observed for Pseudoexperts with respect to Isolated Incidents (sr = −.22*), Scientific Education (sr = −.19*), and a History of Addiction (sr = −.25**). In the present sample, Pseudoexperts are significantly more likely to engage in prolonged fraud involving multiple instances of falsification; they are significantly less likely to have a scientific education; and they are significantly less likely to have a history of addiction. Pseudoexperts are significantly more likely to have engaged in prolonged fraud involving multiple instances of credential falsification owing to the time it generally takes to uncover their activity;[5] also, they tend to commit fraud more frequently: each time they apply for a job or a promotion, or testify under oath (by either commission or omission). Pseudoexperts are significantly less likely to have a scientific education, as this tends to be the very type of credential that they are falsifying. Though it is not immediately apparent why Pseudoexperts are significantly less likely to have a history of addiction, it may have something to do with avoiding additional deviant behavior that draws unwanted attention or scrutiny (this is offered as one possibility only; further study is necessary to develop a more complete set of possible explanations).[6]

Simulators

Employer characteristics ($R^2 = .39**$), Job Description characteristics ($\Delta R^2 = .06**$), and Examiner characteristics ($\Delta R^2 = .08**$) all accounted for a statistically significant portion of the variance found in Simulators, $F(12,76) = 7.36$, $p < .01$. Put another way, the Employer, Job Description, and Examiner characteristics in the present study resulted in a total R^2 of .53**, accounting for 53% of all variance found among Simulators.

---

[5]Pseudoexperts examined in the present study were generally uncovered by opposing counsel at trial, and not by their employers. This reflects a lack of resume checking and verification by some employers. It also necessarily results in a subset of fraudsters that will have committed credential fraud multiple times prior to discovery.

[6]See also Step 3 (Examiner characteristics), under Education and Experience later in this chapter, for a discussion of related results.

In Step 1 (Employer characteristics), statistically significant results are observed for Simulators in relation to Employer Independence from law enforcement (sr = −.21*) and Internal Audits (sr = .44**). In the present sample, Simulators represent the most frequent approach to committing forensic fraud (90%).[7] Simulators are also significantly less likely to be found in association with non-law enforcement employers, and significantly more likely to be discovered in association with Internal Audits.

Simulators are significantly less likely to be found in association with non-law enforcement employers. Given that law enforcement employers comprise 78% of our sample, this might cause some to argue that law enforcement is overrepresented, which would in turn result in a higher correlation with forensic fraud. However, no other approach to fraud is significantly correlated with this variable. This suggests that the finding is not necessarily a function of employer overrepresentation in the sample. It also supports the argument that increased employer independence from law enforcement significantly reduces the frequency of Simulators. Conversely, it supports the argument that law enforcement affiliation is significantly associated with an increased frequency of Simulators.

Simulators are also significantly more likely to be discovered in association with internal audits. It could be argued that this may be a feature of overrepresentation in the sample (SIM = 90%). However, given that internal audits are not significantly associated with Dissemblers either way (DIS = 57%), this interpretation seems less likely. Rather, it appears consistent with the argument that internal audits are most effective at revealing when physical evidence has been fabricated, tampered with, or destroyed by forensic examiners—as discussed previously.

In Step 2 (Job Description characteristics), statistically significant results are observed for Simulators based on a combined ΔR^2 of .06**, accounting for 6% of all variance found among Simulators. While the combined ΔR^2 is significant, examination of individual variables (JLAB, JTEC, JLEX, and JMED) is not revealing. Consequently, Step 2 variables represent what may be referred to as a pool of variance. That is to say, these variables are important as a group in relation to Simulators, but it is likely that there is insufficient sample size to magnify and reveal which are significant on their own. This is consistent with a similar observation made with regard to Dissemblers at Step 2. Further study is needed to determine which Job Description characteristics are significantly correlated with Simulators.

In Step 3 (Examiner characteristics), significant results are observed for Simulators based on a combined ΔR^2 of .08**, accounting for 8% of all variance found among Simulators. While the combined ΔR^2 is significant, examination

---

[7]As with all approaches to fraud discussed in this section, it must be remembered that these are not exclusive categories. Fraudulent examiners often employ multiple approaches.

of individual variables (Isolated Incident, Science Education, History of Addiction, Criminal History, and History of Fraud) is not revealing. Consequently, Step 3 variables represent a pool of variance. That is to say, these variables are important as a group in relation to Simulators, but it is likely that there is insufficient sample size to magnify and reveal which are significant on their own. Further study is needed to determine which Examiner characteristics are significantly correlated with Simulators.

Hierarchical multiple regression analysis of fraud impact

Hierarchical multiple regression analysis demonstrates that some of the sets of employer characteristics, examiner characteristics, and situational factors explained a significant portion of the variance in the impact of fraud on examiners, employers, and the justice system (see Table 9-5). Each statistically significant result is presented and discussed next.

Table 9-5 Hierarchical Multiple Regressions of Employer, Job Description, and Examiner Variables on *Impact of Fraud*

	Severity of Consequences β (sr)	Cases Reviewed β (sr)	Cases Overturned β (sr)	Labs Shut β (sr)
STEP 1—EMPLOYER				
Employer Independence	−.08 (−.07)	.18 (.10)	−.02 (−.02)	.08 (.07)
Accredited Lab	−.34 (−.32)**	.19 (.17)	.05 (.05)	.21 (.20)
Internal Audit	.14 (.13)	.27 (.24)*	.14 (.12)	−.07 (−.07)
R^2	.07*	.11*	.03	.04
STEP 2—JOB DESCRIPTION				
JLAB	−.58 (−.16)	.51 (.14)	.03 (.01)	.53 (.14)
JTEC	−.17 (−.06)	.08 (.03	.09 (.03)	.13 (.05)
JLEX	−.26 (−.13)	.04 (.02)	−.01 (−.01)	.05 (.02)
JMED	−.35 (−.11)	.03 (.01)	−.03 (−.01)	.08 (.03)
ΔR^2	.06*	.10**	.01	.09
STEP 3—EXAMINER				
Isolated Incident	−.19 (−.16)	−.15 (−.12)	.02 (.02)	−.15 (−.12)
Science Education	−.14 (−.11)	−.16 (−.12)	.02 (.02)	−.15 (−.12)
History of Addiction	.17 (.13)	.09 (.07)	.38 (.31)**	−.01 (−.01)
Criminal History	.11 (.08)	.04 (.03)	.00 (.00)	.06 (−.04)
History of Fraud	.08 (.07)	−.12 (−.10)	−.09 (−.08)	.03 (.02)
ΔR^2	.17**	.06*	.12	.06
Total ΔR^2	.30**	.27**	ns	ns

Note: *p < .05, **p < .01, ΔR^2 represents the change in the amount of variance in the dependent variable accounted for in the set of predictors at each step of the regression. Total R^2s are not identical to the sum of R^2 and the changes in R^2 due to rounding. ns = findings not significant.

Severity of consequences

Employer characteristics (R^2 = .07*), Job Description characteristics (ΔR^2 = .06*), and Examiner characteristics (ΔR^2 = .17**) all accounted for a statistically significant portion of the variance found in the Severity of Consequences, $F(12,76)$ = 3.07, p < .01. Put another way, the Employer, Job Description, and Examiner characteristics in the present study resulted in a total R^2 of .30**, accounting for 30% of all variance found with respect to the Severity of Consequences.

In Step 1 (Employer characteristics), statistically significant results are observed for Severity of Consequences and Accredited Labs (sr = −.32**); in the present sample, more severe consequences to the forensic examiner were associated with non-accredited labs. This finding suggests that accredited labs respond to examiner fraud with less severe consequences. This may be the result of the accreditation process itself, which requires laboratory protocols and guidelines for examiner conduct be clearly preserved in written form; that agency responses to misconduct be carefully tiered; and that extreme consequences, like termination and criminal charges, be considered last. In unaccredited agencies, there exists greater discretion on the part of supervisors to levy sanctions that can result in more severe internal and external consequences. Alternatively, accredited forensic laboratories may be less likely to impose severe consequences on fraudulent examiners for fear of increasing the impact of fraud on supervisor and agency reputations, incurring audits, and ultimately harming accreditation.

In Step 2 (Job Description characteristics), statistically significant results are observed for Severity of Consequences based on a combined ΔR^2 of .06**, accounting for 6% of all variance found related to Severity of Consequences. While the combined ΔR^2 is significant, examination of individual variables (JLAB, JTEC, JLEX, and JMED) is not revealing. Consequently, Step 2 variables represent what may be referred to as a pool of variance. That is to say, these variables are important as a group in relation to the severity of examiner consequences, but it is likely that there is insufficient sample size to magnify and reveal which are significant on their own. Further study is needed to determine which Job Description characteristics are significantly correlated with increased or decreased Severity of Consequences.

In Step 3 (Examiner characteristics), statistically significant results are observed for Severity of Consequences based on a combined ΔR^2 of .17**, accounting for 17% of all variance found within this variable set. While the combined ΔR^2 is significant, examination of individual variables (Isolated Incident, Science Education, History of Addiction, Criminal History, and History of Fraud) is not revealing. Consequently, Step 3 variables represent a pool of variance. That is to say, these variables are important as a group in relation to the severity of examiner consequences, but it is likely that there is insufficient sample size to magnify and reveal which are significant on their own. Further study is needed to determine which Examiner characteristics are significantly correlated with increased or decreased Severity of Consequences.

Cases reviewed

Employer characteristics (R^2 = .11*), Job Description characteristics (ΔR^2 = .10**), and Examiner characteristics (ΔR^2 = .06*) all accounted for a statistically significant portion of the variance found in the number of Cases Reviewed, $F(12,76)$ = 2.34, $p < .01$. Put another way, the Employer, Job Description, and Examiner characteristics in the present study resulted in a total R^2 of .27**, accounting for 27% of all variance found with respect to the number of Cases Reviewed.

In Step 1 (Employer characteristics), statistically significant results are observed for Cases Reviewed and Internal Audits (sr = .24**); significantly more cases were reviewed by employers that were also conducting internal audits. This finding is expected, given that it is the nature of an internal audit to reveal cases that have been reviewed, or are in need of review. Those employers not conducting audits are therefore far less likely to identify cases that are in need of review for lack of a directed effort.

In Step 2 (Job Description characteristics), statistically significant results are observed for Cases Reviewed based on a combined ΔR^2 of .10**, accounting for 10% of all variance found within this variable. While the combined ΔR^2 is significant, examination of individual variables (JLAB, JTEC, JLEX, and JMED) is not revealing. Consequently, Step 2 variables represent what may be referred to as a pool of variance. That is to say, these variables are important as a group in relation to the number of cases reviewed, but it is likely that there is insufficient sample size to magnify and reveal which are significant on their own. Further study is needed to determine which Job Description characteristics are significantly correlated with an increased or decreased number of Cases Reviewed. This is consistent with a similar observation made with regard to Severity of Consequences at Step 2.

In Step 3 (Examiner characteristics), statistically significant results are observed for Cases Reviewed based on a combined ΔR^2 of .06*, accounting for 6% of all variance found within this variable. While the combined ΔR^2 is significant, examination of individual variables (Isolated Incident, Science Education, History of Addiction, Criminal History, and History of Fraud) is not revealing. Consequently, Step 3 variables represent a pool of variance. That is to say, these variables are important as a group in relation to the number of cases reviewed, but it is likely that there is insufficient sample size to magnify and reveal which are significant on their own. Further study is needed to determine which Examiner characteristics are significantly correlated with an increased or decreased number of Cases Reviewed. This is consistent with a similar observation made with regard to Severity of Consequences at Step 3.

Cases overturned

Employer characteristics (R^2 = .03), Job Description characteristics (ΔR^2 = .01), and Examiner characteristics (ΔR^2 = .12) did not account for a statistically significant portion of the variance found in the number of Cases Overturned, $F(12,76)$ = 1.18, *ns*. This was not entirely unexpected, given that the decision to overturn a case (e.g., dropping criminal charges and vacating convictions) is a legal matter, or a judicial response, generally external to the authority of the employer or the examiner.

While the overall model did not account for statistically significant variance with respect to the number of cases overturned, History of Addiction (sr = .31**) did (see Table 9-5, Step 2). In other words, examiners with a history of addiction were significantly correlated with an increased number of overturned cases. This is likely a result of the fact that examiners with a history of addiction are also related to a significantly higher frequency of cases involving altered drug weights and amounts (DRG1; see Table 9-6). Examiners discovered committing acts of fraud, in combination with a history of addiction, are more likely to lose overall credibility with the court. Subsequently, prosecuting attorneys and judges would be more likely to support overturning cases where the findings of such examiners played a role.

Labs shut

Employer characteristics (R^2 = .04), Job Description characteristics (ΔR^2 = .09), and Examiner characteristics (ΔR^2 = .106) did not account for a statistically significant portion of the variance found in the number of Labs Shut (aka laboratory closures), $F(12,76)$ = 1.44, *ns*. This was not entirely unexpected, given that the decision to shut down a forensic laboratory, whether temporarily or permanently, is generally external to the authority of those actually working for, or directly supervising, the lab.[8] In some instances, this decision was made by a chief of police regarding an internal forensic division; in others it was made by an organization such as ASCLD-LAB, which suspended or revoked laboratory accreditation resulting in a de facto closure until accreditation could be reinstated.

---

[8]In the present sample, the number of laboratory managers coming forth to declare that their own labs were so badly managed or so rife with error that they must be closed was zero. And while laboratory employees do have the ability to be whistleblowers, they are not in charge of how seriously their allegations are taken, or how thoroughly their allegations are investigated.

Hierarchical multiple regression analysis of evidence affected

Hierarchical multiple regression analysis demonstrates that some of the sets of employer characteristics, examiner characteristics, and situational factors explained a statistically significant portion of the variance in the type of evidence affected by forensic fraud (see Table 9-6). Each statistically significant result is presented and discussed next.

DNA

Employer characteristics ($R^2 = .08^*$) accounted for a statistically significant portion of the variance found in the DNA evidence, $F(12,76) = 3.39$, $p < .05$.

Table 9-6 Hierarchical Multiple Regressions of Employer, Job Description, and Examiner Variables on *Evidence Affected*

	DNA EV β (sr)	Money EV β (sr)	Chain EV β (sr)	EDEX EV β (sr)	Drug1 EV β (sr)	Drug2 EV β (sr)	Bio EV β (sr)
STEP 1—EMPLOYER							
Employer Independence	−.03 (−.02)	−.13 (−.11)	−.15 (−.13)	.05 (.04)	−.23 (−.20)	.08 (.07)	.06 (.06)
Accredited Lab	.28 (.26)*	−.41 (−.38)**	−.04 (−.04)	−.01 (−.01)	−.21 (.19)	.14 (.13)	.13 (.12)
Internal Audit	.09 (.08)	−.36 (−.32)**	.46 (.42)	−.44 (−.39)**	.26 (.23)*	.14 (.13)	−.22 (−.20)
R^2	.08*	.23**	.28**	.22**	.14**	.04	.06
STEP 2—JOB DESCRIPTION							
JLAB	.10 (.03)	−.18 (−.05)	.34 (.09)	−.67 (−.18)	−.21 (−.06)	.51 (.14)	.52 (.14)
JTEC	−.12 (−.04)	.01 (.00)	.35 (.13)	−.52 (−.19)*	.32 (.12)	.10 (.04)	.25 (.09)
JLEX	−.04 (−.02)	−.10 (−.05)	.01 (.00)	−.17 (−.09)	−.09 (−.05)	.02 (.01)	.38 (.20)
JMED	−.07 (−.02)	.11 (.04)	.22 (.07)	−.38 (−.12)	.11 (.03)	.03 (.01)	.38 (.12)
ΔR^2	.03	.05**	.05**	.06**	.16**	.10	.06
STEP 3—EXAMINER							
Isolated Incident	−.05 (−.04)	.21 (.17)	.03 (.03)	−.21 (−.17)	−.01 (−.01)	−.19 (−.16)	−.11 (−.09)
Science Education	.08 (.06)	−.15 (−.12)	.00 (.00)	−.20 (−.16)	.15 (.12)	.17 (.14)	.12 (.10)
History of Addiction	−.17 (−.13)	−.05 (−.04)	.21 (.17)	−.24 (−.19)*	.61 (.50)**	−.06 (−.05)	−.24 (−.20)
Criminal History	.04 (.03)	.17 (.13)	.12 (.09)	−.17 (−.14)	.10 (.08)	.17 (.13)	−.06 (−.05)
History of Fraud	−.12 (.10)	.05 (.04)	.05 (.04)	.04 (.03)	−.02 (−.02)	.02 (.01)	.01 (.01)
ΔR^2	.04	.07**	.08**	.12**	.38**	.06	.08
Total ΔR^2	.08*	.35**	.41**	.40**	.68**	ns	ns

Note: *$p < .05$, **$p < .01$, ΔR^2 represents the change in the amount of variance in the dependent variable accounted for in the set of predictors at each step of the regression. Total R^2s are not identical to the sum of R^2 and the changes in R^2 due to rounding. ns = findings not significant.

Put another way, the Employer characteristics in the present study resulted in a total R^2 of .08**, accounting for 8% of all variance found with respect to the DNA evidence.

In Step 1 (Employer characteristics), statistically significant results are observed for DNA evidence and Accredited Labs (sr = .26*); accredited forensic laboratories in the current sample were more likely to suffer from forensic fraud that involves DNA evidence. Consistent with previously discussed findings regarding accreditation being significantly associated with Dissemblers, this result may reflect the certainty and finality of DNA evidence and its analysis, all of which must be carefully documented. The majority of fraud related to DNA involves dry-labbing, concealing error, or cutting corners out of laziness or to maintain individual examiner proficiencies—not to help acquit or convict a particular suspect. As mentioned earlier in this chapter, these results may, in concert, be used to support the argument that laboratory accreditation may encourage dissembling (aka falsification) of DNA evidence.

This is further consistent with no significant variations observed for DNA relative to Job Description characteristics (Step 2) and Examiner characteristics (Step 3), suggesting that DNA-related fraud is more likely a function of workplace culture. Accredited labs require close monitoring of examiner proficiencies, and it is possible that fear of error may compel more DNA examiners to commit fraud than others in order to push through high volumes of casework and/or maintain their individual certifications and proficiencies (this is offered as one possibility only; further study is necessary to develop a more complete set of possible explanations).

Money

Employer characteristics (R^2 = .23**), Job Description characteristics (ΔR^2 = .05**), and Examiner characteristics (ΔR^2 = .07**) accounted for a statistically significant portion of the variance observed in relation to Money-related fraud, $F(12,76)$ = 3.28, $p < .01$.

In Step 1 (Employer characteristics), statistically significant results are observed for Money Evidence in relation to Laboratory Accreditation (sr = −.38**) and Internal Audits (sr = −.32**). Accredited laboratories experience significantly less forensic fraud related to money evidence, and internal audits reveal significantly less forensic fraud related to money evidence. These two findings may be related, as laboratory audits are more likely to be conducted by laboratories seeking or maintaining accreditation. As an aggregate, these findings may suggest that accredited labs (and by extension those that might actually audit the evidence) experience less money-related fraud (e.g., theft of money from evidence and subsequent misreporting) because of clearer protocols and higher examiner accountability.

In Step 2 (Job Description), statistically significant results are observed for Money evidence based on a combined ΔR^2 of .05**, accounting for 5% of all variance found within this variable. While the combined ΔR^2 is significant, examination of individual variables (JLAB, JTEC, JLEX, and JMED) is not revealing. Consequently, Step 2 variables represent what may be referred to as a pool of variance. That is to say, these variables are important as a group in relation to the number of cases reviewed, but it is likely that there is insufficient sample size to magnify and reveal which are significant on their own. Further study is needed to determine which Job Description characteristics are significantly correlated with Money evidence.

In Step 3 (Examiner characteristics), statistically significant results are observed for Money evidence based on a combined ΔR^2 of .07**, accounting for 7% of all variance found within this variable. While the combined ΔR^2 is significant, examination of individual variables (Isolated Incident, Science Education, History of Addiction, Criminal History, and History of Fraud) is not revealing. Consequently, Step 3 variables represent a pool of variance. That is to say, these variables are important as a group in relation to money-related fraud, but it is likely that there is insufficient sample size to magnify and reveal which are significant on their own. Further study is needed to determine which Examiner characteristics are significantly correlated with Money evidence.

Chain of custody

Fraud related to Chain of Custody evidence holds statistically significant promise as a dependent variable, but revealed little in the current study. Employer characteristics (R^2 = .28**), Job Description characteristics (ΔR^2 = .05**), and Examiner characteristics (ΔR^2 = .08**) accounted for a significant portion of the variance observed in relation to Chain of Custody-related fraud, $F(12,76)$ = 3.28, $p< .01$.

In Step 1 (Employer characteristics), statistically significant results are observed for Chain of Custody evidence based on a combined ΔR^2 of .28**, accounting for 28% of all variance found within this variable. In Step 2 (Job Description), significant results are observed for Chain of Custody evidence based on a combined ΔR^2 of .05**, accounting for 5% of all variance found within this variable. In Step 3 (Examiner characteristics), significant results are observed for Chain of Custody evidence based on a combined ΔR^2 of .08**, accounting for 8% of all variance found within this variable. Consequently, the combined variables in each Step (1–3) represent three separate pools of significant variance. However, it is likely that there is insufficient sample size to magnify and reveal which are the significant variables within each Step's pool. Further study is needed to determine which Employer, Job Description, and Examiner characteristics are significantly correlated with Chain of Custody evidence.

Education and experience

Employer characteristics (R^2 = .22**), Job Description characteristics (ΔR^2 = .06**), and Examiner characteristics (ΔR^2 = .12**) accounted for a statistically significant portion of the variance observed in relation to false presentation of Education and Experience, $F(12,76)$ = 4.23, $p < .01$.

In Step 1 (Employer characteristics), statistically significant results are observed for false presentation of Education and Experience in relation to Internal Audits (EDEX EV, sr = –.39**). That is to say, those labs conducting internal audits tend to reveal significantly less fraud related to examiner education and experience. This was not unexpected, as internal audits are generally focused on specific complaints or concerns with respect to casework and protocols, not necessarily examiner qualifications. Credential fraud is generally revealed through cross-examination or research by opposing counsel; it is largely a surprise to an employer that has not done its own due diligence, and not as a function of an internal audit or investigation. This is consistent with previously discussed findings related to Pseudoexperts shown in Table 9-4.

In Step 2 (Job Description), statistically significant results are observed for false presentation of Education and Experience in relation to forensic technicians (e.g., evidence technicians and crime scene investigators; JTEC, sr = –.19**). That is to say, forensic technicians are significantly less likely to falsify their credentials than those serving in other capacities. This is likely related to Step 2 characteristics for Pseudoexperts (see Table 9-4), reflecting the reality that police technicians are generally not expected to be educated in the sciences, and subsequently rely primarily on training and experience acquired on the job when writing reports and giving testimony. As a consequence, they do not generally experience cultural or work-related pressure to falsify or inflate their credentials.

In Step 3 (Examiner characteristics), statistically significant results are observed for false presentation of Education and Experience in relation to an examiner History of Addiction (sr = .19*). Those engaged in credential fraud are significantly less likely to have a history of addiction. This is likely related to Step 3 characteristics for Pseudoexperts (see Table 9-4), reflecting the reality that those engaging in credential fraud do not tend to engage in activity that might draw unwanted attention or cause a review of their work.

Drug1 evidence

Employer characteristics (R^2 = .14**), Job Description characteristics (ΔR^2 = .16**), and Examiner characteristics (ΔR^2 = .38**) accounted for a statistically significant portion of the variance observed in relation to false presentation of Drug1 evidence (i.e., falsifying drug weights or amounts), $F(12,76)$ = 13.60, $p < .01$.

In Step 1 (Employer characteristics), statistically significant results are observed for Drug1 evidence in relation to Internal Audits (sr = .23). That is to say, those employers conducting internal audits were significantly more likely to reveal Drug1-related fraud. This was expected, as an audit generally involves a physical inventory and retesting of evidence; this requires weighing and counting what exists (and finding out what is missing). Moreover, it is fairly difficult to physically replace drug evidence without committing even more acts of fraud.

In Step 2 (Job Description), statistically significant results are observed for Drug1 evidence based on a combined ΔR^2 of .16**, accounting for 16% of all variance found within this variable. While the combined ΔR^2 is significant, examination of individual variables (JLAB, JTEC, JLEX, and JMED) is not revealing. Consequently, Step 2 variables represent what may be referred to as a pool of variance. That is to say, these variables are important as a group in relation to Drug1 evidence, but it is likely that there is insufficient sample size to magnify and reveal which are significant on their own. Further study is needed to determine which Job Description characteristics are significantly correlated with Drug1 evidence.

In Step 3 (Examiner characteristics), significant results are observed for Drug1 evidence in relation to an examiner History of Addiction (sr = .50**). That is to say, those examiners engaged in Drug1 fraud were significantly more likely to have a history of addiction. This was not unexpected, as the examiners engaged in Drug1 fraud were generally stealing drugs from the lab to manage an addiction—though a few were selling them.

Drug2 evidence

Employer characteristics (R^2 = .04), Job Description characteristics (ΔR^2 = .10), and Examiner characteristics (ΔR^2 = .06) did not account for a statistically significant portion of the variance observed in relation to false presentation of Drug2 evidence (i.e., falsifying drug test results), $F(12,76)$ = 1.61, *ns*. Given that fraud related to Drug2 evidence occurs in 17% of all cases in the present sample (n = 100), this may suggest that Drug2-related fraud exists as a cultural or systemic problem within the forensic science community, distributed evenly regardless of employer-, job description-, or employee-related variables.

Biological evidence

Employer characteristics (R^2 = .06), Job Description characteristics (ΔR^2 = .06), and Examiner characteristics (ΔR^2 = .08) did not account for a statistically significant portion of the variance observed in relation to false presentation of non-DNA-oriented Biological evidence (BioEV; e.g., hair evidence and serological tests), $F(12,76)$ = 1.52, *ns*. Given that fraud related to non-DNA-oriented Biological evidence occurs in 28% of all cases in the sample (n = 100), this may suggest that BioEv-related fraud exists as a cultural or systemic problem within the forensic science community, distributed evenly regardless of employer-, job description-, or employee-related variables.

IMMEDIATE RECOMMENDATIONS FOR RELATED RESEARCH

Hierarchical multiple regression analyses presented in Tables 9-4 through 9-6 revealed numerous "pools of variation," each suggesting immediate recommendations for additional related research to determine the nature of potentially significant relationships between specific variables examined in the present study.[9]

1. In Table 9-4, Job Description characteristics (JLAB, JTEC, JLEX, and JMED) combine to account for 17% of all variance among Dissemblers. This evidences that one or more are significantly correlated with that particular approach to fraud. Further study is required to reveal which.

2. In Table 9-4, Examiner characteristics (Isolated Incident, Science Education, History of Addiction, Criminal History, and History of Fraud) combine to account for 2% of all variance found among Dissemblers. This evidences that one or more are significantly correlated with that particular approach to fraud. Further study is required to reveal which.

3. In Table 9-4, Job Description characteristics (JLAB, JTEC, JLEX, and JMED) combine to account for 6% of all variance found among Simulators. This evidences that one or more are significantly correlated with that particular approach to fraud. Further study is required to reveal which.

4. In Table 9-5, Job Description characteristics (JLAB, JTEC, JLEX, and JMED) combine to account for 6% of all variance found related to Severity of Consequences to the examiner. This evidences that one or more are significantly correlated with that particular approach to fraud. Further study is required to reveal which.

5. In Table 9-5, Examiner characteristics (Isolated Incident, Science Education, History of Addiction, Criminal History, and History of Fraud) combine to account for 17% of all variance found related to Severity of Consequences to the examiner. This evidences that one or more are significantly correlated with that particular approach to fraud. Further study is required to reveal which.

6. In Table 9-5, Job Description characteristics (JLAB, JTEC, JLEX, and JMED) combine to account for 10% of all variance found related to Cases Reviewed. This evidences that one or more are significantly correlated with that particular approach to fraud. Further study is required to reveal which.

---

[9]Future research suggested by the findings of this study in general are presented in Chapter 10, "Conclusions and Recommendations."

7. In Table 9-5, Examiner characteristics (Isolated Incident, Science Education, History of Addiction, Criminal History, and History of Fraud) combine to account for 6% of all variance found related to Cases Reviewed. This evidences that one or more are significantly correlated with that particular approach to fraud. Further study is required to reveal which.

8. In Table 9-6, Job Description characteristics (JLAB, JTEC, JLEX, and JMED) combine to account for 5% of all variance found related to Money. This evidences that one or more are significantly correlated with that particular approach to fraud. Further study is required to reveal which.

9. In Table 9-6, Examiner characteristics (Isolated Incident, Science Education, History of Addiction, Criminal History, and History of Fraud) combine to account for 7% of all variance found related to Money. This evidences that one or more are significantly correlated with that particular approach to fraud. Further study is required to reveal which.

10. In Table 9-6, Employer characteristics (Employer Independence, Accredited Lab, and Independent Audit) combine to account for 28% of all variance related to Chain of Custody evidence. This evidences that one or more are significantly correlated with that particular approach to fraud. Further study is required to reveal which.

11. In Table 9-6, Job Description characteristics (JLAB, JTEC, JLEX, and JMED) combine to account for 5% of all variance related to Chain of Custody evidence. This evidences that one or more are significantly correlated with that particular approach to fraud. Further study is required to reveal which.

12. In Table 9-6, Examiner characteristics (Isolated Incident, Science Education, History of Addiction, Criminal History, and History of Fraud) combine to account for 8% of all variance related to Chain of Custody evidence. This evidences that one or more are significantly correlated with that particular approach to fraud. Further study is required to reveal which.

13. In Table 9-6, Job Description characteristics (JLAB, JTEC, JLEX, and JMED) combine to account for 16% of all variance related to Drug1 evidence. This evidences that one or more are significantly correlated with that particular approach to fraud. Further study is required to reveal which.

Again these research recommendations are those explicitly suggested by the current data, in order to gain a greater understanding of the relationships that the current data suggests.

LIMITATIONS

The present study is not without important limitations. First, there is the sample size. While it is the best available representation of known cases of forensic fraud, it was also small enough to conceal the relevance of some significant variables within, referred to as "pools of variation" (this limitation was also discussed previously).[10] While several major variables significantly affecting forensic fraud were revealed, specific lesser variables will remain hidden until further research can be performed with larger or more focused sample sizes. Second, while statistically significant correlations have been identified between certain examiner-, employer-, evidence-, and impact-related variables that allow for prediction and even potential manipulation, these cannot necessarily be interpreted causally. Further study is necessary to develop a more complete set of causal possibilities for the results at hand.

---

[10]See Chapter 8, "Forensic Fraud, 2000–2010: Data and Frequency," for a discussion regarding the limitations of using known data in crime-related research.

CHAPTER 10

Conclusions and Recommendations

"One who fraudulently makes a misrepresentation of fact, opinion, intention, or law for the purpose of inducing another to act or to refrain from action in reliance upon it, is subject to liability to the other in deceit for pecuniary loss caused him by his unjustifiable reliance upon the misrepresentation."

American Law Institute (1965), Vol. 2, p. 55

Forensic fraud is no small problem for the justice system, as has been demonstrated by the research that has been compiled and presented in this work. Beyond the conviction of innocent defendants, which has been tabulated in part by the published research conducted through the Innocence Project, it can also destroy careers and create immense financial liability for law enforcement agencies, individual examiners, and the municipalities that employ them. It also creates incalculable expense for the justice system in general. Forensic fraud is therefore not something to be disregarded, minimized, or otherwise ignored. It is a serious problem that requires the close attention of any professional community intersecting with the forensic sciences.

To that end, the purpose of this study was to develop a preliminary understanding of forensic fraud by examining whether and how cultural factors, workplace conditions, and examiner traits interact with each other to make specific types of fraud more or less likely. In this chapter, results presented in previous chapters are discussed and conclusions rendered in consideration of relevant criminological theory. First, the significant findings of major importance in the present study are summarized and related to the theses set forth in Chapter 1, "Introduction." Second, reforms suggested in the forensic literature prior to the current study are reviewed and evaluated—including those from the NAS Report. Third, specific forensic reforms suggested by the results of the present study are offered. Finally, future research into the phenomenon of forensic fraud is recommended.

183

SIGNIFICANT AND RELEVANT FINDINGS: A SUMMARY

In the current study, we began with two central thesis statements. First, that forensic fraud tends to be the result of cultural, pathological, and systemic causes rather than the narrow motives of single individuals, as the circumstances surrounding are allowed to develop and persist by those in the immediate forensic environment. Second, that although private (e.g., defense) forensic practitioners are routinely characterized as biased or mercenary, those working on behalf of the state (e.g., the police and the prosecution) are responsible for a substantial amount, if not the majority, of known cases of forensic fraud. The research compiled and presented in this study offers both theoretical and empirical support for these statements.

Theoretical support

To demonstrate the validity of these hypotheses, we sought theoretical support from the related professional literature.

In Chapter 2, "Occupational Fraud," it was established that occupational fraud is viewed predominantly through the lens of *Fraud Triangle Theory*, asserting that it is the result of situational motivation, opportunity, and rationalization—often tied to the individual perception of unfairness or an affiliation with a deviant employee sub-group. Some researchers have begun to use Fraud Diamond Theory, which adds the element of individual capability. Generally, however, the management of employee fraud is considered the responsibility of the employer, who is best situated to control the workplace by reducing motivators, opportunities, and conditions that can lead to pro-fraud rationalizations. Furthermore, it was established that there are no reliable employee variables that are suitable for use as predictors of fraud in the workplace: anyone can commit fraud, and those that do cannot be reliably distinguished from anyone else. This removes support for focusing exclusively on employee variables when looking for causes or correlations. Consequently, this literature provides initial theoretical support for the notion that any form of occupational fraud tends to be the result of cultural, pathological, and systemic causes—including fraud committed by forensic examiners.

In Chapter 3, "Forensic Science: A Primer," it was established that the majority of forensic examiners work for law enforcement or government agencies, and almost exclusively for the police and prosecution. These employment conditions require consideration of both law enforcement culture and the mandates of scientific integrity when researching environmental factors associated with forensic fraud—given the existence of competing cultural pressures, *Differential Association Theory*, and potential *Role Strain*. Consequently, this literature lays a foundation for theoretical support of the notion that forensic fraud tends to occur on behalf of law enforcement, and that it tends to be the result of cultural, pathological, and systemic causes.

In Chapter 4, "Fraud in Law Enforcement Culture," it was established that law enforcement organizations provide employees with the training, opportunity, and authority to commit acts of fraud on a variety of levels, which requires a high level of personal integrity to evade. It was further established that law enforcement culture is often defined by traits that afford the motivations and rationalizations for a deviant internal subculture, actively cultivating fraud within its ranks. At the same time, law enforcement culture also furnishes otherwise lawful members with the skills, incentives, motivations, and rationalizations for ignoring, protecting, and even publicly defending their unlawful co-workers. These employment circumstances and cultural features, in conformity with *Differential Association Theory, Social Learning Theory*, and *Role Strain*, increase the likelihood that those in law enforcement will commit, tolerate, conceal, and even defend acts of overt fraud. Forensic examiners being largely employed by law enforcement agencies, this literature provides theoretical support for the notion that forensic fraud can be the result of cultural, pathological, and systemic causes.

In Chapter 5, "Fraud and Scientific Culture," it was established that scientific integrity requires honesty, use of the scientific method, skepticism, objectivity, transparency, and a host of other well-established scientific norms. It also prohibits fabrication (aka forging or dry-labbing); falsification (aka cooking); suppression of unfavorable results (aka cherry-picking); plagiarism; ghost authorship (aka honorary or gift authorship); falsification of scientific credentials; and the reckless disregard for practice standards that ensure scientific integrity. However, it was established that scientific misconduct (i.e., fraud) remains both pervasive and extensive—mandating an employer's obligation to create a workplace environment where scientific practice is encouraged and protected, and fraud is not tolerated. As previously explained, *Differential Association Theory* and *Social Learning Theory* help to explain how the capacity to commit fraud is transmitted within groups and remains pervasive. Consequently, this literature provides theoretical support for the notion that forensic fraud is primarily the result of cultural, pathological, and systemic causes that are the responsibility of the employer to manage.

In Chapter 6, "Contrasting Scientific Integrity with Law Enforcement Culture," it was established that scientific misconduct is primarily the result of institutional failures to uphold scientific values and nurture scientific culture; they are an institution's responsibility to detect, investigate, and correct.

More specifically, it was established that corrupt individuals cannot be hired, or retained, by any employer without some level of institutional negligence, apathy, tolerance, or even encouragement. It is therefore inappropriate, and even misleading, to blame forensic fraud solely on bad apples. It was also established that the mandates of scientific integrity are incompatible with law enforcement values and cultural pressures—making the employment or alignment of forensic examiners with law enforcement inappropriate. Though fraud exists in the scientific community without the influence of law enforcement culture, the imposition of that culture on the requirements of scientific integrity can only make things worse, and not better.

Empirical support: findings in the current study

In Chapter 7, "Forensic Fraud: Prior Research," it was established that there is an overall dearth of professional literature related to forensic fraud, demonstrating the need for the present research effort. However, preliminary empirical support for the notion that known instances of forensic fraud tend to originate from law enforcement-aligned examiners, and that it tends to be the result of cultural, pathological, and systemic causes, was suggested by the research associated with wrongful convictions, as well as a limited descriptive study of forensic fraud by Turvey (2003).

Based on the findings in the current sample of data related to fraudulent examiners, there is significant empirical support for the thesis statements in this study, summarized in the following section.[1] Additionally, it will be shown that the absence of significant findings for certain variables was also relevant.

Frequency data

In Chapter 8, "Forensic Fraud, 2000–2010: Data and Frequency," frequency data for the current study established the following:

Examiner History: 23% ($n = 23$) of the forensic examiners in this study were determined to have a history of addiction; 21% ($n = 21$), a history of fraud; and 17% ($n = 17$), a history of other criminal convictions. These findings combine to indicate that a large percentage of forensic fraud was committed by forensic examiners who were not properly screened by employers during the hiring process. Arguably, this kind of history should be an employment disqualifier for anyone seeking a career in the criminal justice system (CCLRTF, 2009; see Chapter 3 for discussion). That so many forensic examiners in the present sample were negligently hired and then retained, despite a history of addiction, criminal convictions, or both, suggests a lack of due diligence by

---

[1]Findings of statistical significance unrelated to the theses of this study were reported in Chapters 8 and 9, but are not discussed here.

employers.[2] Consequently, these findings generally point toward the existence of unchecked systemic factors in employment culture.

Pseudoexperts: 27% ($n = 27$) of forensic examiners in this study were lying about some or all of their education, training, and experience, and subsequently classified as Pseudoexperts. That so many forensic examiners in the present sample were negligently hired and retained while providing this kind of false information on their resumes, or in expert testimony, suggests a further lack of due diligence by employers with respect to tracking either. Consequently, these findings generally point toward the existence of unchecked systemic factors in employment culture.

Examiner Education: 52% ($n = 52$) of forensic examiners in this study had an undergraduate or graduate-level science education; and 48% ($n = 48$) had a non-science education or no education. This finding suggests, and subsequent hierarchical multiple regression analyses agree, that having a formal science education is unrelated to almost all of the approach-, impact-, or evidence-related variables under examination.[3] That is to say, forensic examiners committing fraud were about as likely to have a formal scientific education as not, suggesting that the causes of forensic fraud are not related to current scientific education models one way or another. Consequently, this finding supports focusing on cultural or systemic causes and remedies under the current conditions.[4]

However, this is not to say that having a science education is completely unrelated to the problem of forensic fraud. In some cases, the data revealed examiners possessing no science education that committed errors and then attempted

---

[2]Far from being a mere value judgment regarding the employability of those with a criminal history or a history of addiction, the issue is one of trustworthiness and liability. Bank robbers should not be allowed to work at banks; drug addicts should not be allowed to work with drugs; and child molesters should not be allowed to work with children. To allow otherwise is to invite transgression and liability. More to the point, those with a history of lying, which is inextricable from criminal conduct and addiction, cannot be trusted to give sworn expert testimony in court under oath. Those who are allowed to do so are viewed with disdain by any trier of fact. The importance of upholding this criterion is often lost on those working outside or only indirectly with the justice system, who may be unaccustomed to having to give their word under penalty of perjury. It is, nevertheless, a matter that the court takes very seriously.

[3]With the anticipated exception of increased scientific education being significantly correlated with fewer Pseudoexperts, as this is the type of credential that the majority of Pseudoexperts are lying about possessing—see Chapter 9 for discussion.

[4]Given the variety of scientific educational backgrounds associated with the forensic sciences, and the varied hiring policies of different forensic employers, it is not possible to make meaningful recommendations regarding forensic science education based on the data gathered in the present study. This becomes even more complex when dealing with international education, not all of which is equal despite uniform-sounding degrees and titles. Further study that accounts for this variability as it relates to the phenomenon of forensic fraud is therefore recommended.

to cover them up with acts of fraud. The precise nature and frequency of this particular forensic fraud sub-type was not explored in the present research, suggesting the need for further study. In any case, this comes back to agencies hiring properly qualified scientists in the first place, and creating a scientific culture where deficiencies in education and training may be recognized and addressed as opposed to ignored.

Supervisory Status: 56% (n = 56) of the forensic examiners in this study were determined to be working in a supervisory capacity. It was theorized that supervisors might have more access, more privacy, and therefore more opportunities to commit fraud. This frequency suggests, and hierarchical multiple regression analyses agree, that supervisory status is unrelated to any of the approach-, impact-, or evidence-related variables under examination. Those committing forensic fraud were about as likely to be supervisors as not. Consequently, this finding generally points away from examiner-related causes.

Isolated Incidents: 82% (n = 82) of the forensic examiners in this study were determined to be involved in an ongoing pattern of fraud, often involving multiple examiners, prior to discovery. This finding is an empirical refutation of *Bad Apple Theory*[5] as a primary explanation for fraud within the present data. Consequently, this finding generally points toward the existence of unchecked systemic factors in employment culture.

Law Enforcement Labs: 78% (n = 78) of the forensic examiners in this study were employed directly by law enforcement agencies. The corresponding low frequency of other publicly funded (aka government) crime labs initially correlated with fraud in the present sample (5%; n = 5) begins to suggest that crime labs operating within law enforcement agencies might be associated with a particular type of fraud. In any case, this finding supports the theory that those working on behalf of the police and the prosecution (though not necessarily the government in general) are responsible for a substantial amount, if not the majority, of the known cases of forensic fraud.

Examiners Retained: 37% (n = 37) of the fraudulent examiners in the present study were initially retained by their respective employers without severe consequences despite their misconduct; of these, the weightiest involved examiners being reassigned or temporarily suspended. This evidences employer negligence, and indifference to scientific integrity, as there is no reasonable justification for permanently retaining an examiner who has committed forensic fraud. Examiner fraud should result in automatic termination, as the examiner can no longer be trusted to give reliable evidence in court and his continued employment is a toxic example to other employees. Yet, consistent with law

---

[5]See Chapter 6 for a discussion regarding the theoretical refutation of Bad Apple Theory.

enforcement culture in general, there seems to be a tolerance for forensic examiner misconduct by more than one-third of the employers in the present study.[6] Consequently, this finding generally points toward the existence of unchecked systemic factors in employment culture.

Impact: The actions of the 100 forensic examiners in the present study resulted in at least the following consequences, conservatively: 42,042 cases reviewed for potential by forensic laboratory employers; 5,443 criminal cases dismissed or overturned; and 9 forensic laboratories closed, either temporarily or permanently. In addition, 38% ($n = 38$) of fraudulent examiners were terminated, and 32% ($n = 32$) eventually resigned. These findings evidence a significant impact with respect to expenses necessarily related to reviewing cases and hiring/training new employees incurred by employers; a significant impact on the financial cost and credibility to the justice system related to cases that must be overturned and perhaps retried; a significant impact on forensic services as laboratory caseloads must be shifted due to suspensions, terminations, and closures; and a significant impact on the financial cost to those individuals, agencies, and governments that incur civil liability.[7]

Hierarchical multiple regression analyses

In Chapter 9, "Multivariate Analysis of Forensic Fraud, 2000–2010," hierarchical multiple regression analyses revealed significant correlations between

---

[6]See Chapter 4, the section titled "Internal Tolerance for Criminality." Relevant to this concern, there is an ongoing scandal related to the forensic sciences at a national level involving the Bureau of Alcohol, Tobacco, and Firearms (B-ATF). Kenneth Melson was pressured to resign from the B-ATF in 2011, after serving only two years as its interim director, for supervisory negligence regarding the infamous "Fast and Furious" operation (Serrano, 2011). The details of this affair, involving the illegal sale of guns by those working for U.S. law enforcement agencies such as the B-ATF and FBI to drug cartels operating in Mexico, are still being investigated and revealed as of this writing. However, it is known that one of those guns was an AK-47 used to kill Border Patrol Agent Brian Terry, whose family has filed a lawsuit against the U.S. Department of Justice and the B-ATF for $25 million. Mr. Melson is a former prosecutor, and as of this writing remains a Distinguished Fellow and past President of the American Academy of Forensic Sciences (AAFS), and serves as a Board Member for the American Society of Crime Laboratory Directors Laboratory Accreditation Board (ASCLD-LAB). Despite being pressured to resign during an ongoing investigation by the U.S. Congress into confirmed criminal activity that he supervised and sanctioned, Mr. Melson was subsequently appointed as Senior Advisor to the Assistant Attorney General for the Office of Legal Policy (OLP), to specialize in forensic science policy issues at the Department of Justice. That Mr. Melson remains so prominent a fixture in the forensic science community under these circumstances further suggests a community tolerance for criminality and misconduct by those forensic science organizations involved (e.g., the AAFS and ASCLD-LAB). It also demonstrates the extent to which these organizations are inappropriately aligned with law enforcement agencies and prosecutors over actual scientists.

[7]As discussed in Chapter 8, the actual impact in dollars cannot be reliably calculated from the present data and would require separate study.

employer, job description, and employee variables related to examiner approach, the impact of fraud, and evidence affected.[8]

Employer independence

Significant correlations regarding Employer Independence, relevant to the theses of this study, are as follows (see also discussion provided in Chapter 9):

1. As mentioned, Simulators represent the most frequent approach to committing forensic fraud (90%; $n = 90$).
2. Increased employer independence from law enforcement is associated with a significantly reduced frequency of Simulators.
3. Conversely, increased law enforcement dependence (i.e., affiliation) is associated with a significantly increased frequency of Simulators.
4. Independence from law enforcement is not associated with a significant increase or reduction in the frequency of other approaches to fraud.

These findings provide explicit empirical support for the thesis that those working on behalf of the state, specifically the police and the prosecution, are responsible for a substantial amount, if not the majority, of known cases of forensic fraud. These findings also support the assertion that the culture of law enforcement has a significant and potentially corrupting effect on the forensic examiners that it employs.

Laboratory accreditation

Significant correlations regarding Laboratory Accreditation, relevant to the theses of this study, are as follows (see also discussion provided in Chapter 9):

1. If a forensic laboratory is accredited, fraudulent examiners are significantly more likely to exaggerate, embellish, lie about, or otherwise misrepresent results.
2. Laboratory accreditation is significantly correlated to increased falsification of only one kind of physical evidence: DNA.
3. Accredited laboratories are significantly less likely to impose severe consequences on fraudulent examiners.

These findings provide explicit empirical support for the thesis that forensic fraud tends to be the result of cultural, pathological, and systemic causes rather than the narrow motives of single individuals, as the circumstances surrounding it must be allowed to develop and persist by those in the immediate forensic environment.

---

[8]Significant findings unrelated to the thesis statements put forth in this study are not summarized here, but are presented and discussed in Chapter 9.

Internal audits

Significant correlations regarding Internal Audits, relevant to the theses of this study, are as follows (see also discussion provided in Chapter 9):

1. Internal Audits are significantly correlated with an increase in the number of cases under review; as this is generally the purpose of an audit, this finding was expected.
2. Significantly more Simulators are revealed in association with Internal Audits, demonstrating their effectiveness with identifying this type of forensic fraud.
3. Significantly fewer Pseudoexperts, and related Education and Experience fraud, are revealed in association with Internal Audits. This may reflect that audits are more often focused on reviewing cases and protocols, and not hiring practices or examiner resumes. Alternatively, this may suggest that the kinds of forensic laboratories imposing Internal Audits are less likely to hire examiners with phony qualifications in the first place.
4. While Internal Audits are significantly correlated with identifying more Drug1 evidence-related fraud (e.g., weights and amounts), they are significantly correlated with identifying fewer cases of fraud related to Money and Biological (non-DNA) evidence.

These findings provide explicit empirical support for the thesis that forensic fraud tends to be the result of cultural, pathological, and systemic causes rather than the narrow motives of single individuals, as the circumstances surrounding it must be allowed to develop and persist by those in the immediate forensic environment.

History of addiction

Significant correlations regarding Examiner History of Addiction, relevant to the theses of this study, are as follows (see also discussion provided in Chapter 9):

1. Examiners with a history of addiction were significantly correlated with Drug1 evidence related to fraud (e.g., weights and amounts).
2. Examiners with a history of addiction were significantly correlated with an increased number of overturned cases.

A history of addiction is something that can be screened for by an employer both prior to and during examiner employment. Therefore, these findings provide explicit empirical support for the thesis that forensic fraud tends to be the result of cultural, pathological, and systemic causes rather than the narrow motives of single individuals, as the circumstances surrounding it must be allowed to develop and persist by those in the immediate forensic environment.

Drug2 and biological evidence

There was a noteworthy absence of any significant correlations between the Independent variables in this study, and Drug2 and Biological (non-DNA, aka BioEV) evidence (detailed discussion provided in Chapter 9; see Table 9-6). This may suggest that Drug2- and BioEV-related fraud exist as cultural or systemic problems within the forensic science community, distributed evenly regardless of employer, job description, or employee-related variables. The failure to significantly correlate either of these types of evidence suggests empirical support for the thesis that forensic fraud tends to be the result of cultural, pathological, and systemic causes rather than the narrow motives of single individuals.

PRE-NAS REPORT REFORM IN THE LITERATURE

In Chapter 7, it was established that the majority of research relating to forensic fraud is found primarily in the form of ideographic case studies and monographs authored by those from the criminal defense bar. It was also found that the few larger empirical research efforts associated with forensic fraud have the same origins, indirectly resulting from the examination of forensic science testimony in relation to wrongful convictions. It should come as no surprise that this community has also suggested a number of corresponding reforms.

Leading up to the NAS Report (Edwards and Gotsonis, 2009; discussed in the next section), many criminal justice reformers have called upon the forensic science community to become more scientific—to behave honestly, fairly, and with humility toward the evidence. Their research has focused primarily on exposing the lack of empirical research in the forensic sciences, as well as problems associated with examiner bias, general scientific ignorance, and unintentional error, all of which contribute to incompetent and overconfident examiner interpretations (e.g., Cole, 2005 and 2006; Dror, Charlton, and Peron, 2006; Findley, 2008; Heller, 2006; Murphy, 2007; Peterson and Leggett, 2007; and Saks et al., 2003). Some criminal justice reformers, however, have been specific regarding concerns over the issue of abusing the forensic sciences, including the problem of examiner fraud (e.g., Cooley, 2007a, 2007b; Cooley and Oberfield, 2007; DiFonzo, 2005; DiFonzo and Stern, 2007; Giannelli, 1997, 2007; and Thornton and Peterson, 2007). While consistently revealing the absence of scientific education, empirical research, or even a scientific culture in forensic science practice, these and related efforts have also chronicled the lack of forensic parity between the defense and the prosecution, while calling for due process from the courts.

However, some criminal justice reformers have advocated the complete separation of forensic science practice from law enforcement oversight and control—arguing that science aligned with law enforcement cannot achieve the independence and impartiality that scientific practice requires (Chisum and Turvey, 2006; Cooley, 2007b; Giannelli, 1997, 2007; Kirk and Bradford, 1965; Starrs, 1993; and Ungvarsky, 2007).

THE NAS REPORT: LACK OF SCIENCE AND ERROR OVER FRAUD

As mentioned in the first chapter of this work, the National Academy of Sciences Report on forensic science (Edwards and Gotsonis, 2009; aka the NAS Report) presents the findings of a Congressionally funded system-wide investigation and review of forensic science disciplines and crime laboratory practice. It was initiated by the U.S. Congress in response to the endless publication of critical legal reviews regarding the bias and lack of science in forensic practice; the ongoing occurrence of highly publicized forensic frauds, blunders, and crime lab scandals nationwide; and the ever-increasing number of DNA exonerations sourced back to flawed or misleading forensic evidence documented by groups such as the Innocence Project. The NAS Report represents the first major effort to investigate the forensic science community by actual scientists—and to recommend related reforms.

However, the NAS Report ultimately avoids addressing the issue of forensic fraud directly. Instead, it focuses on the issues of scientific integrity and related forensic error. It does so by suggesting that developing scientific culture and managing unintentional error within the forensic science community are the more common and immediate concerns. However, it concedes that there is currently no research to accurately demonstrate the rate or scope of either forensic fraud or error. In that spirit, the NAS Report provides the following conclusions and suggested reforms:

1. The forensic science community is fragmented and broken, without a single voice or purpose; it cannot identify, let alone fix, its own problems. As explained in the NAS Report: "The forensic science enterprise lacks the necessary governance structure to pull itself up from its current weaknesses. Of the many professional societies that serve the enterprise, none is dominant, and none has clearly articulated the need for change or presented a vision for accomplishing it," (Edwards and Gotsonis, 2009; p. 16). Nor has the adversarial process been adequate to the task. Consequently, the NAS Report recommends that the federal government step in to mandate and manage forensic science reforms—by forming a National Institute of Forensic Science (NIFS).

2. Forensic science and law enforcement are culturally incompatible, with separate missions in the justice system. Therefore, publicly funded crime

labs should be "independent of or autonomous within law enforcement agencies" (Edwards and Gotsonis, 2009; p. 184). Specifically, the NAS Report recommends that "[t]o improve the scientific bases of forensic science examinations and to maximize independence from or autonomy within the law enforcement community, Congress should authorize and appropriate incentive funds to the National Institute of Forensic Science (NIFS) for allocation to state and local jurisdictions for the purpose of removing all public forensic laboratories and facilities from the administrative control of law enforcement agencies or prosecutors' offices" (Edwards and Gotsonis, 2009; p. 24). This would result in separate administration and separate budgets—so that those working in crime labs would experience less pressure or constraint from the will of those in law enforcement.

3. The majority of the forensic science community lacks standardized terminology and report writing requirements. This results in forensic reporting that is unclear and in many cases incomplete. Consequently, the NAS Report recommends that standardized terminology and reporting must be developed and mandated through the NIFS.

4. Many forensic examiners perform examinations and testify regarding subsequent findings with an inappropriately high degree of certainty. The NAS Report recommends, "research is needed to address issues of accuracy, reliability, and validity in the forensic science disciplines" (Edwards and Gotsonis, 2009; p. 22). This because there is an absence of scientific research supporting the accuracy, reliability, and validity of many of the forensic sciences (excluding DNA).

5. The NAS Report recommends empirical research into the frequency and nature of examiner bias and error, in order to "develop standard operating procedures (that will lay the foundation for model protocols) to minimize, to the greatest extent reasonably possible, potential bias and sources of human error in forensic practice" (Edwards and Gotsonis, 2009; p. 24). This because there is an overall dearth of scientific research into examiner bias and error in forensic practice.

6. The NAS Report recommends research into the development of "tools for advancing measurement, validation, reliability, information sharing, and proficiency testing in forensic science and to establish protocols for forensic examinations, methods, and practices," (Edwards and Gotsonis, 2009; pp. 24–25). This because there is an overall dearth of scientific research into such tools, owing to an overall scientific ignorance that they are necessary in the first place.

7. The NAS Report recommends, "laboratory accreditation and individual certification of forensic science professionals should be mandatory, and all forensic science professionals should have access to a certification

process" (Edwards and Gotsonis, 2009; p. 25). This because laboratory accreditation is currently voluntary, and the practice of forensic science does not generally require examiner certification. The NAS Report argues that accreditation and certification are necessary for levying scientific standards and providing professional accountability.

8. The NAS Report recommends that forensic laboratories develop and adopt quality assurance and control procedures. It explains that "quality control procedures should be designed to identify mistakes, fraud, and bias; confirm the continued validity and reliability of standard operating procedures and protocols; ensure that best practices are being followed; and correct procedures and protocols that are found to need improvement" (Edwards and Gotsonis, 2009; p. 26). This because current quality assurance and control procedures are inconsistently attended or entirely absent in the majority of forensic laboratories. This acknowledges that mistakes, bias, and fraud are not intentionally screened for, let alone identified and managed, in the majority of forensic laboratories.

9. Currently, there is no uniform code of ethics across forensic science disciplines. The NAS Report recommends that the NIFS "should establish a national code of ethics for all forensic science disciplines and encourage individual societies to incorporate this national code as part of their professional code of ethics. Additionally, NIFS should explore mechanisms of enforcement for those forensic scientists who commit serious ethical violations" (Edwards and Gotsonis, 2009; p. 26). These because existing professional codes of ethics are non-existent, inadequate, or selectively enforced within the majority of forensic science organizations.

10. In order to practice forensic science competently, the forensic examiners must first be educated and trained as scientists. As explained in the NAS Report (Edwards and Gotsonis, 2009; pp. 26–27):

Forensic science examiners need to understand the principles, practices, and contexts of scientific methodology, as well as the distinctive features of their specialty. Ideally, training should move beyond apprentice-like transmittal of practices to education based on scientifically valid principles. In addition to the practical experience and learning acquired during an internship, a trainee should acquire rigorous interdisciplinary education and training in the scientific areas that constitute the basis for the particular forensic discipline and instruction on how to document and report the analysis. A trainee also should have working knowledge of basic quantitative calculations, including statistics and probability, as needed for the applicable discipline.

This position asserts that the current model of learning on the job from others within the broken forensic system, often from those without scientific education or training, provides an inadequate foundation for the performance of forensic examinations. This position also acknowledges that forensic examinations are commonly performed by non-scientists (often wearing a badge), without attendance to scientific integrity, and then presented inappropriately in court with the aura of scientific legitimacy.

11. The NAS Report recommends that graduate programs intersecting with the forensic sciences be developed and funded, to increase educational opportunities for aspiring forensic scientists, provide for continuing education opportunities, and nurture a research culture in the forensic science community. Currently, there are many forensic science programs operating out of schools of criminal justice aligned with or taught by current and former law enforcement professionals. Such models are vocational rather than scholarly. In other words, these programs are designed to produce police officers, correctional officers, crime scene technicians, or bench criminalists for police crime labs. This is reflected by the types of instructors employed—too many are criminal justice practitioners, not objective scientists or academic scholars. In this environment, research is not supported, funded, or viewed as necessary within forensic science. The NAS Report explains that (Edwards and Gotsonis, 2009; pp. 230–231):

> Many forensic degree programs are found at small colleges or universities with few graduate programs in science and where research resources are limited. The lack of research funding has discouraged universities in the United States from developing research-based forensic degree programs, which leads to limited opportunities to attract graduate students into such programs. Only a few universities offer Ph.D.-level education and research opportunities in forensic science, and these are chemistry or biology programs with a forensic science focus.

> Most graduate programs in forensic science are master's programs, where financial support for graduate study is limited. In addition, the lack of research funds means that universities are unlikely to develop research programs in forensic science. This lack of funding discourages top scientists from exploring the many scientific issues in the forensic science disciplines. This has become a vicious cycle during which the lack of funding keeps top scientists away and their unavailability discourages funding agencies from investing in forensic science research. Traditional funding agencies have never had a mission to support forensic science research.

This acknowledges the absence of strong scientific practitioners in the forensic sciences, and the need for establishing Ph.D. forensic science programs that would both attract them and simultaneously generate quality research. This educational model is something that just about every other scientific discipline benefits from.

12. The NAS Report recommends a complete overhaul of the Medicolegal Death Investigation System, from the development of consistent national educational requirements for forensic pathologists, to increased funding (e.g., money for modernization of facilities and equipment, accreditation efforts, and examiner certifications). Currently "requirements for practitioners vary from nothing more than age and residency requirements to certification by the American Board of Pathology in forensic pathology" (Edwards and Gotsonis, 2009; p. 28). This acknowledges a reality that most criminal justice practitioners are aware of but generally choose to ignore: that cause and manner of death determinations are often made by ignorant and unqualified personnel, without even the most basic understanding of science or forensic science. Yet these practitioners, by virtue of job title alone, are afforded the undeserved attention and respect of the court.

13. The NAS Report recommends "a new broad-based effort to achieve nationwide fingerprint data interoperability" (Edwards and Gotsonis, 2009; p. 31). As an adjunct, it recommends funds for retraining current fingerprint examiners, and "training new fingerprint examiners to gain the desired benefits of true interoperability" (p. 32). This acknowledges the fact that the documentation and interpretation of fingerprint evidence are not sufficiently standardized; that fingerprint examiners are inadequately trained; and that fingerprint databases do not always communicate with each other effectively (if at all) as a result.

The recommendations of the NAS Report are broad in scope and characterized by generally negative observations regarding the current state of the forensic science community. They accurately recognize an unhealthy alignment with law enforcement; an absence of properly educated scientists; an absence of scientific research into methodology, bias, error, and fraud; an absence of mechanisms for identifying error and fraud; and an absence of consistent practice standards, ethical guidelines, and accountability to manage those forensic examiners who would violate the mandates of scientific integrity. Most important to the present research, the NAS Report does not deny the problem of forensic fraud. Rather, it is subsumed with recommendations regarding bias and error, which are considered of greater immediate concern in the current environment of forensic disrepair.

In general, the NAS Report has enjoyed support in the professional literature that has responded, with multi-disciplinary agreement, to focus on reducing bias, develop scientific education requirements and practice standards, and embrace a research culture in the forensic science community (Chisum and Turvey, 2011; Giannelli, 2010; Lentini, 2009; Mnookin et al., 2011; and Saks, 2010). However, and despite this professional agreement, there is no evidence that the recommendations of the NAS Report are being embraced and applied to any significant degree. This is to say that there has been no development or funding of a NIFS from which the majority of the recommended reforms must flow; law enforcement remains in direct control of the majority of forensic science practitioners; and the vast majority of forensic examiners still lack a formal science education.

FORENSIC REFORM SUGGESTED BY THE CURRENT RESEARCH

The questions for the present research are whether the recommendations of the NAS Report, and the related professional literature, are sufficient to address and manage the problem of forensic fraud, and whether there are further specific reforms suggested by the empirical findings in the present study.

The NAS Report appears written in the belief that forensic science can benefit most from scientific research, standardization, laboratory accreditation, and examiner certification. It suggests that by teaching scientific values to practitioners and providing them with clear scientific guidelines, bias, fraud, and error can be reduced. It seems, in essence, to suggest that the majority of those employing forensic examiners, as well as those performing forensic examinations, have generally honest (though often uninformed and misguided) intentions. The present research offers no reason to doubt this.

However, making rules does not ensure that they will always be followed—only that it will be clear to all when they have been broken, and that the consequences can be prescribed in advance. Consequently, the recommendations of the NAS Report do not specifically address how forensic fraud, necessarily involving forensic examiners with the worst intentions, is best identified and managed. Though they do suggest that it can and should be.

Institutional hiring and retention policies

The present research findings indicate that forensic fraud might be significantly curtailed by the development of more rigorous hiring and retention practices. This includes the following, which are not standard for many employers of forensic examiners:

Scientific Education Requirement: In comportment with the NAS Report, forensic examiners must have at least an undergraduate scientific education. This would assist with the employer's obligation to screen for Pseudoexperts and promote a culture that embraces scientific integrity. It could also potentially help to reduce the kinds of scientific errors that some examiners feel the need to conceal with fraudulent behavior.

Resume Verification: Forensic employers must engage in a comprehensive vetting process prior to hiring any new personnel. This must include the verification of every aspect of the prospective employee's resume, from acquiring official college transcripts and reviewing educational qualifications, to direct verification of any certifications and publications. Employee retention must also be dependent upon verification of any updates to employee resumes. The employer has a duty to keep and maintain documentation regarding the verification of each item on an employee's resume, to enable production upon request as part of any timely discovery package before trial (aka Brady material, Brady package). Again, this would assist with the employer's obligation to screen for Pseudoexperts and promote a culture that embraces scientific integrity.

Criminal Background Check: Prior to hiring any new personnel, applicants must be required to submit to a thorough criminal background investigation—in and out of state. This must be done to screen candidates for disqualifiers, such as those who are on parole, those who are convicted felons, and those with a history of disqualifying misdemeanors (e.g., theft, domestic violence conviction, drug-related convictions, and fraud-related convictions). This would assist with the employer's obligation to screen for those with a history of criminality, and promote a culture that embraces scientific integrity.

Medical and Mental Health History: Prior to hiring any new personnel, applicants must be required to submit to a medical and mental health evaluation, to screen for those with a history of mental disturbance (and related medication), substance abuse, and addiction. This is common practice for many high-security companies and law enforcement agencies. Once an employee is hired, it can be extremely difficult to terminate that employee with a previously unacknowledged mental health or substance abuse problem. For what should be obvious reasons, such individuals should not be trusted with the custody of physical evidence that can include controlled substances, nor should they be relied upon to perform forensic examinations and give expert testimony under oath. As discussed in the preceding chapter, this is one of the most significant issues revealed in association with forensic fraud by the present study. This would assist with the employer's obligation to screen for those with a history of addiction, and promote a culture that embraces scientific integrity.

Mandatory Drug Testing: Employers should adopt a zero tolerance policy with respect to substance abuse, and require all employees to refrain from illegal drug use as part of their employment contracts. As an adjunct, employers should require all forensic examiners to submit to random on-the-spot drug testing without pre-notification of any kind. Again, this is one of the most significant issues revealed in association with forensic fraud by the present study. This would assist with the employer's obligation to screen for those with addiction problems, and promote a culture that embraces scientific integrity.

Criminalizing Expert Resume Fraud: Currently, it is not necessarily illegal for an expert to commit resume fraud (see Chapter 1, discussion regarding perjury). Nor does resume fraud necessarily result in the termination of an employee or her expulsion from a professional organization. Criminalizing expert resume fraud would create a powerful disincentive to provide false information on one's expert resume. It would also furnish employers and professional organizations with a powerful tool for expelling those without professional integrity.

Reforms to institutional culture

The present research findings indicate that forensic fraud might be significantly curtailed by the development of specific reforms within institutional culture. This includes the following, which are not standard for many employers of forensic examiners:

Forensic Autonomy: In comportment with the NAS Report, forensic science examinations must be separated from law enforcement alignment, administration, and oversight. This given the cultural conflicts discussed previously, and that institutional independence from law enforcement is correlated with a significantly reduced frequency of Simulators.

Such an arrangement does not necessarily mean privatizing forensic science. It could simply mean passing legislation to separate all the existing government forensic laboratory systems from law enforcement budgets, oversight, and chains of command. Related policy and legislation should preclude anyone working for any law enforcement agency from serving in the capacity as a forensic examiner, or from supervising anyone who is a forensic examiner: such work should be the sole province of trained scientists, given the many conflicts of interest between law enforcement and scientific culture already discussed.

This should be done despite the costs that will be associated, given the financial liabilities of forensic fraud that have already been established related to the cases in this study. With respect to additional government costs, this could necessitate the building and maintenance of separate and up-to-date facilities that are often mandated as part of accreditation requirements anyway. With respect to free market or chain of custody concerns, it should be noted that many government-funded forensic laboratories already sub-contract to private companies for the examinations that they do not provide, or when there is a backlog (e.g., DNA analysis, toxicological analysis, and blood alcohol testing).

Transparency: In general comportment with the NAS Report, forensic examiners and employers must embrace the concept of complete scientific transparency with respect to all methods and findings. Ideally, this would include transparency with respect to any evidence in custody; examinations and related results; and any prior examiner testimony, resumes, certifications, and proficiencies—all of which employers have a responsibility to collect, store, and maintain to enable production upon request as part of any timely discovery package before trial. In short, federal legislation should be passed making all documents and communications generated by any forensic laboratory a public record—to end any lack of compliance with evidence discovery and admissibility rulings held by the U.S. Supreme Court in *Brady v. Maryland* (1963) and *Melendez-Diaz v. Massachusetts* (2009). This requirement would help reduce and reveal Pseudoexperts and Dissemblers.

Accreditation: The NAS Report recommends laboratory accreditation as one of several measures necessary to achieve and maintain scientific accountability. However, as discussed, laboratory accreditation is not significantly correlated with any decreases in forensic fraud. In fact, the opposite is observed in the present findings. Laboratory accreditation is significantly correlated with an increased frequency of Dissemblers and DNA-related fraud, as well as being significantly correlated with decreased severity in examiner consequences. Ultimately, the results of the present study can be used only to suggest that present laboratory accreditation efforts may actually do more harm than good when it comes to the specific problem of forensic fraud.[9] Given the cost that is associated with laboratory accreditation, and the cachet that it is used to imply, this finding raises questions about its overall efficacy.

Mandatory Comprehensive Independent Audits: In general comportment with the NAS Report, employers should submit themselves, and their employees, to

---

[9]One could argue that laboratory accreditation is not intended to address the issue of forensic fraud, but rather it is intended to reduce examiner error and increase overall accountability within the forensic community, and this would be a fair comment. However, there is no research to suggest that accredited forensic laboratories experience less error than unaccredited forensic laboratories. Consequently, any assertions about the effectiveness of accreditation with respect to reducing examiner error and increasing accountability are not based on anything that has been empirically verified.

comprehensive audits from independent external non-law enforcement organizations. As discussed, many audits are conducted in response to case-specific
complaints, and are therefore goal oriented as opposed to being all-inclu-
sive. Specifically, they are associated with a significantly increased frequency
of fraud cases related to drug weights and amounts. However, they tend to
be associated with revealing significantly fewer Pseudoexperts, significantly
fewer cases of money-related fraud, and significantly fewer cases of biological
evidence (non-DNA)-related fraud. This means that the majority of forensic
fraud is discovered by other mechanisms—such as complaints from co-workers or cross-examination by opposing counsel. Comprehensive audits, involving the spontaneous independent review of forensic examination results,
physical evidence inventories, examiner resumes, and any related testimony
could help identify both fraud and error earlier in the process, reducing any
damaging effects. They would also help to better preserve institutional reputations relating to scientific integrity, allowing the justice system to correctly
perceive that forensic fraud is being identified and managed owing to institutional efforts, rather than as the result of legal review or whistleblowers.

Zero Tolerance for Fraud: Forensic employers, professional organizations, and
employees have an obligation to adopt a zero tolerance policy with respect to
forensic fraud. Currently, this is not the case: forensic employers often retain
fraudulent examiners; ASCLD-LAB rarely revokes the accreditation of labs
employing fraudulent examiners[10]; forensic science organizations such as the
American Academy of Forensic Sciences (AAFS) infrequently expel fraudulent

---

[10]ASCLD-LAB generally prefers not to suspend or revoke laboratory accreditation. This was explained by
then-chair Don Wyckoff when defending the decision not to suspend the accreditation of the FBI crime
lab subsequent to the Brandon Mayfield scandal, which admittedly involved a systemic problem with
the way that fingerprint examinations were being performed at the time (Wyckoff, 2005; p. 39):

> The suspension of a laboratory's accreditation, without complete review of facts, does little to
> support a laboratory that must immediately deal with QA issues and, in fact, shows that ASCLD/
> LAB really does not abide with its stated objective of trying to improve the quality of service to
> the criminal justice system. Had ASCLD/LAB's first response been to suspend accreditation, the
> right to due process would have been violated.
>
> …Because the ASCLD/LAB accreditation program is voluntary and our goal is to encourage
> every forensic laboratory to subject its operation to the scrutiny of accreditation, the process
> discussed above is routinely carried out in a confidential manner.

It is relevant to note that despite numerous such scandals over the past decade, the FBI crime lab has
not had its ASCLD-LAB accreditation suspended or revoked. As Mr. Wyckoff explains, the mission
of ASCLD-LAB is to "support a laboratory" through voluntary accreditation (presumably, the logic
is that if labs fear losing accreditation, they are less likely to pay the costs associated with achieving
and maintaining it). This is not to say that suspension or revocation never happens, but that it is rare
when forensic fraud is concerned. Ultimately, this researcher finds it difficult to agree that the forensic
science community is best served by the continued accreditation of forensic laboratories with systemic
problems.

examiners;[11] and, mentioned in previous chapters, whistleblowers are often punished by employers when the law is meant to protect them. This collective unwillingness to act when action is required supports the findings of the NAS Report (Edwards and Gotsonis, 2009), which found that some law enforcement agencies are (p. 18) "too wedded to the current 'fragmented' forensic science community, which is deficient in too many respects"; and that the forensic science community is disjointed, and (p. 16) "lacks the necessary governance structure to pull itself up from its current weaknesses." This general inaction creates an environment of tolerance for fraud within the forensic science community.

A series of related remedies are necessary to help begin to alleviate these deficiencies. First, forensic employers and professional organizations have an obligation to develop and maintain a public registry of forensic examiners who have resigned or been terminated in relation to fraudulent activity. This would include a clear description of institutional measures taken to review affected cases and prevent future fraud of a similar nature. Second, forensic laboratories should be prohibited from employing examiners with a criminal history, or a history of forensic fraud or other misconduct. Third, forensic organizations should adopt strict policies requiring the public expulsion of any member who has a criminal history, or a history of forensic fraud or other misconduct.

These remedies, providing for enhanced transparency and accountability, would go a long way in preventing fraudulent examiners from transferring to other jurisdictions—a problem identified in multiple cases within the present study. Primarily, however, they would help to restore and maintain confidence in affected agencies and organizations. While they may seem extreme to the uninitiated, they are actually common in the sciences with respect to the publications of the U.S. Office of Research Integrity already cited, and the various state databases that publicly catalog the revocation of certifications or credentials of licensed professionals (e.g., attorneys, school teachers, and medical health-care professionals).

---

[11]The present research effort identified only a single case involving a professional forensic science organization permanently censuring a forensic examiner for false or misleading testimony in the public domain within the established parameters—*Dougherty v. Haag et al.* (2008), involving the Association of Firearm and Tool Mark Examiners (AFTE). However, numerous cases were identified involving fraudulent examiners that remained members in good standing within their respective professional organizations, most commonly the AAFS. It is worth noting that the AAFS, in a 2004 memo from then-president Ronald Singer, responding to an ethics complaint against a law enforcement bloodstain expert where no action was taken, has conceded, "under our current Bylaws, it is not unethical to be ignorant" (Singer, 2004). The fallacies inherent in this position are discussed at length in Cooley (2011). Also, given that professional organization membership data was not available for many of the forensic examiners included in the study, this variable was not examined—though perhaps it should be in the future.

FUTURE RESEARCH

The discussions regarding necessary forensic reforms in this chapter lead to a recognition that there are many areas where future research efforts should focus in order to help anticipate and limit the frequency of forensic fraud. These include

1. More general research into the areas of bias, fraud, and error in relation to potentially mitigating employer and examiner variables—as suggested by the NAS Report. Specific recommendations would include research into correlates of bias, fraud, and error related to Drug2 and Biological (non-DNA) evidence.
2. Examination of correlates between fraud and a higher degree of scientific education. Specifically, the data revealed examiners possessing no science education who committed errors and then attempted to cover them up with acts of fraud. The precise nature and frequency of this particular forensic fraud sub-type was not explored in the present research, suggesting the need for further study.
3. Examination of correlates between fraud, fraud types, and examiner affiliation with specific professional organizations and ethical codes (or their absence)—to assess efficacy and impact.
4. Examination of correlates between the presence or absence of specific resume variables not investigated by the present research (e.g., specific degree types, the absence of degree titles, the presence of media appearances, and the absence of training dates) and forensic fraud, in order to suggest red flags for use during the hiring process.
5. Examination of correlates between specific addictions, medications, or mental health variables not covered by the present research and forensic fraud, in order to better inform the employee vetting process.
6. Examination of correlates between specific forms of criminal activity, drug abuse and forensic fraud, in order to better inform preventative policies and auditing efforts.
7. Examination of correlates between the specific traits of accredited and non-accredited forensic laboratories not examined in the present study, to better understand how accreditation impacts different incarnations of forensic fraud.
8. Examination of correlates between the results of internal and external forensic laboratory audits, in order to better inform preventative policies and future auditing efforts.

Although these research recommendations may seem relatively unambitious, they reflect two important realities: first, they are the areas of research explicitly suggested by the current data, in order to gain a greater understanding of the relationships that the current data suggests; second, more ambitious research should not be undertaken until more basic and foundational research has been completed to address the many years of empirical neglect that have been demonstrated.

Consequently, these research recommendations, in combination with the specific recommendations for future research necessary to understand the findings of the present study discussed in the prior chapter, provide the forensic science community with significant direction and opportunity for examining the complex phenomenon of forensic fraud in the years to come.

SUMMARY

Forensic fraud is a major concern for the criminal justice system. It results in a significant cost from retesting evidence, overturned cases, dismissed cases, and civil actions for wrongful convictions. It can also simultaneously destroy the lives of innocent defendants, the careers of the forensic examiners involved, and the credibility of their employers and co-workers by association. This to say nothing of eroding public confidence in the justice system and those working within it.

Prior to the publication of the NAS Report, a persistent group of criminal justice reformers consistently worked to reveal the absence of scientific education, research, or culture in forensic science practice. They also chronicled the lack of forensic parity between the defense and the prosecution, while calling for due process from the courts. Some of these even called for the separation of forensic science practice from law enforcement oversight.

In 2009, the publication of the NAS Report included the observations that the forensic science community suffered an unhealthy alignment with law enforcement; an absence of properly educated scientists; an absence of scientific research into methodology, bias, error, and fraud; an absence of mechanisms for identifying error and fraud; and an absence of consistent practice standards, ethical guidelines, and accountability to manage those forensic examiners who would violate the mandates of scientific integrity. It also acknowledged the problem of bias, fraud, and error in forensic fraud—and the corresponding lack of sufficient empirical research to suggest informed management strategies.

In the wake of the NAS Report and its watershed findings, the current study is a first exploratory effort into the phenomenon of forensic fraud. Though preliminary, it has yielded results that suggest the immediate importance of specific reforms. It supports the assertion that forensic fraud tends to be the result of cultural, pathological, and systemic causes rather than the narrow motives of single individuals, as the circumstances surrounding it must be allowed to develop and persist by those in the immediate forensic environment. It also supports the assertion that although private (e.g., defense) forensic practitioners are routinely characterized as biased or mercenary, those working on behalf of the state (e.g., the police and the prosecution) are responsible for a substantial amount, if not the majority, of known cases of forensic fraud. Additionally, it is fair to say that *Routine Activities Theory*, *Differential Association Theory*, and *Role Strain Theory* provided useful insights into cultural and other environmental influences brought to bear on the forensic examiner.

Of further significance, this study has also revealed specific areas of future research that would add to the current body of literature relevant to our understanding of how to anticipate and manage the occurrence of forensic fraud.

CHAPTER 11

Crime Labs in Crisis, 2011–2012: Update and Discussion

Research parameters for the study presented in this work limited data collection efforts to the end of December of 2010. This cap provided for a decade's worth of fraud-related crime lab scandals to analyze and contemplate. Since that time, from January 2011 to December 2012, fraud and other forms of misconduct have continued to occur in the forensic science community. In some ways it is worse than ever before. Specifically, at least 12 crime laboratories in the United States have experienced significant and newly discovered crises related to examiner fraud, negligence, and error in just the past two years[1]—many with dramatic, extensive, and expensive consequences.

In this final chapter, we discuss these crises and their origins. When appropriate, and when there is sufficient information, we also assess whether and how established misconduct comports with the 2000–2010 findings. Then we also discuss whether the reforms suggested in prior chapters might have made a difference. It bears mentioning that some of these laboratories are experiencing fall out from prior and ongoing scandals; others are in administrative limbo, with internal investigations continuing while decision makers strive to avoid answering questions or making tough decisions. These circumstances will be made clear, especially when they are related to past incidents of forensic fraud that were included in our 2000–2010 study.

This inventory of forensic laboratories in crisis is presented alphabetically for ease of reference, save the Department of Public Health drug lab in Jamaica Plain. That particular scandal ranks among the worst in history for a variety of reasons. It also involves some of the clearest documentation of systemic fraud made available on the public record. It is therefore discussed last.

---

[1]Other crime labs around the country have experienced smaller scandals related to terminations for criminal activity unrelated to lab work, or those involving allegations and lawsuits from former employees, but these do not necessarily rise to the level of "significant" and are in some cases unsubstantiated.

Forensic Fraud. http://dx.doi.org/10.1016/B978-0-12-408073-7.00011-2

LAB CRISIS #1: AUSTIN POLICE DEPARTMENT CRIME LABORATORY (APDCL), TEXAS

Since 2010, the Austin Police Department Crime Laboratory (APDCL) has suffered under the cloud of multiple accusations of misconduct: two of these have come from within, and one has come from a private forensic lab. In each instance, and despite the seriousness and similarities of the allegations, investigators have recommended clearing the lab of any wrongdoing. However, laboratory responses and the reasoning behind these recommendations leave a great deal to be desired.

Cecily Hamilton, DNA analyst

In early 2010, Cecily Hamilton (see Figure 11-1), a DNA analyst with the APDCL, made a formal written complaint to her supervisors regarding poor supervision, poor quality control, incompetent examiners, and possible cheating on proficiency tests. For example, as reported in Kreytak (2010):

> Cecily Hamilton said that one day in 2008 she looked into the office of Cassie Carradine, her supervisor at the Austin Police Department DNA lab, and saw Carradine speaking with fellow forensic scientist Diana Morales and using a calculator.
>
> Hamilton claimed that Morales was being tested to see whether she should be allowed to conduct independent DNA analysis at the lab and suspected that Carradine was helping Morales with her computations.

Hamilton also claimed that when ASCLD-LAB (the American Society of Crime Laboratory Directors Laboratory Accreditation Board) sent investigators to review the work in her unit, she was sent home and barred from communicating with them until their audit was complete. She further complained that at

FIGURE 11-1
Former Austin Police Department Crime Lab DNA analyst Cecily Hamilton, whistleblower.

least three of the laboratory supervisors lacked a science background or education, including lab manager William Gibbens.

Hamilton's allegations were investigated internally and, in late March, they were determined to be "unfounded" by lab manager William Gibbens (Gibbens, 2010; TFSC, 2011). Hamilton, who claims that her work environment became increasingly hostile after the complaint, and that officials gave copies of the complaint to those involved prior to conducting any investigation, resigned in May of 2010 (Kreytak, 2010).

Debra Stephens, forensic drug chemist

Debra Stephens, a forensic chemist who had been fired from the APDCL for insubordination, filed a complaint with the Travis County District Attorney's Office regarding crime lab misconduct in 2011. It was first dismissed, and then later reopened, as reported in TFSC (2012):

> On December 27, 2011, Debra Stephens, a former employee in the drug chemistry section of the APDCL, submitted a letter to Travis County District Attorney Rosemary Lehmberg, in which she raised significant concerns about APD controlled substance cases "being analyzed without regard to proper laboratory procedures and without regard to policies required under the accreditation inspection guidelines." In the letter, Ms. Stephens cited 23 specific cases in which she alleged results were issued without regard to laboratory procedure.
>
> Ms. Stephens previously filed a complaint with the Commission in April 2011, outlining various broad-based quality concerns and personnel issues, which she argued led to her wrongful termination. On September 8, 2011, the Commission dismissed Ms. Stephens' original complaint because it did not specify an allegation of negligence or misconduct that would substantially affect the integrity of the results of a forensic analysis conducted by the laboratory, as required by the Commission's enabling statute.
>
> On January 13, 2012, the Commission voted to re-open Complaint #11-07, in light of the new information submitted by the complainant to the Travis County District Attorney in December 2011. On March 9, 2012, Ms. Stephens submitted an additional letter describing concerns regarding the laboratory, including allegations regarding laboratory security and alleged cheating on a proficiency exam. On February 28, 2012, she submitted responses to a DPS audit and statements made by the APDCL manager during a TFSC Complaint Screening Committee meeting. The Commission also solicited feedback from the APDCL regarding the allegations filed by Ms. Stephens.

In that letter of complaint, Ms. Stephens alleged that laboratory supervisors were unqualified, in violation of city policy and ASCLD-LAB accreditation guidelines, and that proper testing procedures were not being followed within the lab in order to cut corners and save time. For example, she wrote (Stephens, 2011):

> Beginning in 2005, the Texas Legislature required that evidence presented in criminal courts in Texas must come from laboratories that have achieved some level of accreditation. The Austin [P]olice Department Crime Laboratory was inspected in order to achieve this certification, in spite of the fact that the administrators of the laboratory did not possess the credentials required by inspectors. So from this point forward, the accredited laboratory was managed by non-scientists and unqualified personnel. Not only did these administrators not meet the qualifications of federal investigators, but they also did not meet the qualifications of the City of Austin personnel policies. In promoting these individuals, police administrators did not follow proper procedures by posting these job openings or by interviewing any qualified candidates. And they did whatever they could to conceal this information.
>
> The evidence I am providing to you documents that controlled substance analysis cases are being analyzed without regard to proper laboratory procedures and without regard to policies required under the accreditation inspection guidelines. Laboratory policies require that the evidence analyzed must be reviewed and approved prior to the dissemination of the laboratory reports (Exhibit #1). The case files I have attached show that these results are being reported and charges are being filed prior to any analysis being conducted at all (Exhibit #2). Not only does this violate laboratory policy, but it violates scientific methods at the most basic level. I believe that these unqualified police administrators have covered up this evidence when it was presented to quality control and quality assurance personnel. And these are not isolated cases. I have provided a list of cases I discovered that had been released in violation of these policies (Exhibit #3). I would estimate that there are hundreds of other cases dating back to 2005 that were analyzed without regard to laboratory protocols in "rush" case requests that I was unable to identify using my limited access to files in the database.
>
> The danger of violating these procedures not only could result in the erroneous analysis of items of evidence, but the false conviction of individuals charged based on the results of these analyses. There appears to be a rush to report results.

In response to these allegations, Pat Johnson, the Deputy Assistant Director of the Texas Department of Public Safety Crime Lab, wrote a memo to Buddy Meyer, an Assistant District Attorney of Travis County in January of 2012 which, in essence, minimized Debra Stephens' complaints as an exaggeration. However, it would be hard to characterize this memo as a denial. Mr. Johnson's main argument appeared to be the following: given that ASCLD-LAB did not see any problems with the APD Crime Laboratory and its management during its most recent audit, there must not be any serious problems (Johnson, 2012).

Integrated Forensic Laboratories (IFL), Euless, TX

IFL, a private forensic laboratory,[2] was retained by the defense to examine three separate cases in which they identified significant APDCL reporting issues and non-compliance with respect to court orders. Subsequently, they filed a formal complaint against the APDCL with the Texas Forensic Science Commission (TFSC). These complaints are summarized in the TFSC investigative report on the matter (TFSC, 2012):

(1) *Crack Cocaine case* (IFL 1108165/APD L10-12068): IFL alleged that APDCL's results were inconsistent with previous results reported by the laboratory and also inconsistent with results reported by IFL. IFL also expressed concern that APDCL did not appear to have conducted an investigation when a significant difference in weight was noted from initial testing in October 2010 to subsequent testing in August 2011. IFL expressed doubt that a 42% reduction in evidence weight could be attributable to degradation of the sample over time, specifically the breakdown of cocaine base to benzoylecgonine.

(2) *Marihuana/Tetrahydrocannabinols case* (IFL Case # 1111143/APD #L-1013202): Immediately after finishing the crack cocaine case, IFL received another case reported by APDCL. The lab reported the evidence as material other than marihuana containing tetrahydrocannabinols. In Texas, this category is a PG1 group and carries a stiffer penalty compared to marihuana, a PG3 group. On re-examination of this case, IFL determined the material was comprised almost entirely of cystolithic trichomes, non-cystolithic trichomes, and glandular trichomes. IFL raised concerns regarding the discrepancy between reporting "marihuana" vs. "material other than marihuana containing tetrahydrocannabinols." Initially, IFL was concerned the discrepant results indicated the material may not have been properly examined by APDCL. After learning about differences in the way crime laboratories in Texas report material with

---

[2]IFL is accredited by ASCLD-LAB and the Texas Department of Public Safety.

these characteristics (differences not attributable to laboratory error), IFL asked the Commission for guidance and further clarification regarding the two categories to encourage consistency from laboratory to laboratory across Texas.

(3) *IFL Case #XXXXXXXX (redacted case number/pending criminal case):* IFL received a court-ordered request to reweigh a large number of MDMA tablets. However, APDCL cut the tablets in half and sent only half of the tablets to IFL. APDCL claims standard operating procedure was to retain half of the exhibit, in case there is a disagreement with the defense laboratory regarding results. IFL asserted this was inconsistent with the court order and the prior practice of APDCL, and IFL was unable reweigh the tablets per the court order because only half of the evidence was sent.

In April of 2012, the TFSC voted to consider the allegations of Debra Stephens and the complaint filed by IFL jointly, as part of a single overall investigation into potential negligence and misconduct at the APDCL.

Texas Forensic Science Commission Report—2012

In July of 2012, "[a]fter a months-long investigation into the Austin Police Department's crime lab, a panel of the Texas Forensic Science Commission on Thursday voted to recommend that the full commission declare that the lab committed no professional negligence or misconduct" (George, 2012). It was explained that some of what was alleged did in fact occur; and concerns regarding drug weight discrepancies lacked sufficient information to make a judgment; however, none of what could be proved met the TFSC definition of negligence or misconduct, and the overall seriousness and impact had been exaggerated (George, 2012; TFSC, 2012).

For example, the TFSC Report explained that (TFSC, 2012) "the Commission recognizes that the practice of discarding notes, (regardless of whether the notes are subsequently entered into a laboratory's electronic case management system) does not constitute 'best practice' in the forensic discipline. The Commission strongly discourages forensic practitioners in Texas from engaging in this practice under any circumstances." With respect to the issue of cutting pills in half, thereby failing to comply with a court order to allow for reweighing, the TFSC Report explained that (TFSC, 2012) "[t]he interpretation of a court order falls outside the scope of the Commission's jurisdiction...."

As of this writing, the official word from the Texas Forensic Science Commission is that all is well within the walls of the APDCL. This determination is suspect, however, given their admission that they were not able to investigate the allegations fully, and that some were outside their jurisdiction.[3] Consequently, this author is concerned that the issues raised by the separate yet consistent Hamilton, Stephens, and IFL complaints are the first in a series of seismic red flags forecasting something much worse that is yet to be fully revealed. The APDCL could do with more scientific leadership and not less; and their over-all sloppiness and inability to comply with basic court orders suggest a lack of interest in accountability and scientific integrity. These conditions ensure future error, further complaints, and greater scandal.

However, it should also be noted that this author's research did not connect this crime lab to any publicly known instances of forensic fraud from 2000 to 2010.

LAB CRISIS #2: CONNECTICUT DEPARTMENT OF EMERGENCY SERVICES & PUBLIC PROTECTION (DESPP), DIVISION OF SCIENTIFIC SERVICES LABORATORY

In August of 2011, the accreditation for the Connecticut State Police Crime Laboratory in Meriden expired. The American Society of Crime Laboratory Directors Laboratory Accreditation Board (ASCLD-LAB) declined to grant it a second six-month extension (Staff, 2011). As reported in Kovner (2012):

> The lab, once the province of internationally known criminalist Henry C. Lee, was slammed in two federal audits last year and lost its professional accreditation. As a result, the lab lost its access to the national DNA database of convicted offenders, maintained by the FBI. Postings to the data bank, known as CODIS, is one of the most important functions of any American crime lab. Officials said that both accreditation and access to CODIS may be restored by next month.

As a consequence of losing access to CODIS, criminal investigations were delayed and criminal trials were put on hold (McQuaid, 2011).

---

[3]Another issue: Retesting was conducted on drug samples by National Medical Services, aka NMS, at the request of the TFSC. According to TFSC (2012): "Because the NMS re-testing confirmed the results of the APDCL reports, and no report (preliminary or otherwise) was issued externally containing incorrect information (or information that would otherwise impact the report's integrity) Commissioners concluded the practice does not meet the definition of professional negligence." However, the director of NMS is now Dr. Barry Logan—the defrocked former Director of the Washington State Patrol Crime Lab; he was forced to resign after being accused of giving false testimony by a three-judge panel in relation to concealing falsified drug test certifications (See Chapter 5, "Fraud and Scientific Culture"). Consequently, any result coming out of NMS is impossible to trust, in the opinion of this author.

A "Full Assessment Report" prepared by ASCLD-LAB, subsequent to an on-site inspection one month later, identified no fewer than 40 items requiring correction. These "Corrective Action" items included problems related to managerial confusion regarding protocols; lack of required protocols; lack of examiner compliance with existing established protocols; inadequate existing protocols; improper, inconsistent, or non-existent documentation related to evidence tests and results; poorly or improperly trained personnel; the absence of required documentation related to examiner education, qualification, and competency; and the failure to maintain examination records in order to support conclusions (Gonsowski, 2011). As reported in O'Leary (2012):

> The critical audit raised questions about supervision, reporting of case results, evidence control, data security, quality assurance and validation techniques for DNA test results.
>
> [Crime policy chief Michael Lawlor] said previously that personality conflicts between the lab staff and the accreditation auditors "got out of hand," which led to a breakdown in communication.
>
> The audit called attention to the backlog of 3,812 DNA cases alone, a 400 percent increase in this type of testing in the past six years. At the same time, the number of scientists dropped by 10 percent and the overall workload for the lab increased 25 percent since 2005. The state estimates that 35 positions were needed to fully staff the lab.
>
> In other words, the Connecticut State Police Crime Laboratory was suffering on all levels with respect to leadership, management, quality control, and casework. As the result of a lack of communication with, and a perceived lack of respect for, ASCLD-LAB auditors, ASCLD-LAB punished the lab in the only way that it could. It made an example of them.

In February of 2012, ASCLD-LAB voted to restore the Connecticut State Police Crime Laboratory's accreditation (O'Leary, 2012). Over the next ten months, it was made independent from law enforcement; the lab's director, Ken Zercie, retired; and a new director was appointed (see Figure 11-2), as reported in a press release from the Office of the Governor (Mallory, 2012):

> Dr. [Guy] Vallaro, a nationally renowned expert in forensic sciences, currently serves as Director of the state forensic laboratory for the Commonwealth of Massachusetts. He was recommended following a nationwide search by a committee established by Commissioner Bradford and will begin the position on December 28.
>
> "A decade of neglect led to the unwelcome news last year that the state crime lab's accreditation had been withdrawn. Evidence processing backlogs had become a major problem for Connecticut's prosecutors and police. This was not fair to them, and was a betrayal of our state's commitment to victims of crime. Dr. Vallaro is the perfect

FIGURE 11-2
Massachusetts State Police crime lab director, Dr. Guy Vallaro (center), speaking at a press conference regarding the Annie Dookhan scandal in the fall of 2012 (see the Jamaica Plain Crime Lab scandal, end of chapter); Dr. Vallaro was tapped in 2012 by the State of Connecticut to take over its troubled crime lab in Meriden.

> leader to restore our lab to what it once was: the envy of the nation," Governor Malloy said. "With the recent reorganization of administrative functions, new protocols, and the appointment of Dr. Vallaro as its Director, Connecticut will have the best crime lab in the country."
>
> As a result of legislation signed into law by Governor Malloy in June that reorganized its administrative functions, the state crime lab now functions independent of the Connecticut State Police, and the position of Director will report directly to the DESPP [Department of Emergency Services & Public Protection] Commissioner, similar to the rank of a deputy commissioner.

It is unclear whether or not the Meriden crime lab has turned itself around and escaped this crisis altogether. Only time will tell. However, it is clear that some necessary first steps have been taken, in comportment with the kinds of recommendations made in this work: first, the lab has been separated from law enforcement culture and oversight; second, new leadership with a strong scientific orientation has been brought in. What is needed now is competent polices based in good science; transparency to afford greater lab accountability; and personnel adequate to the task.

It should be noted that this author's research did not connect this crime lab to any publicly known instances of forensic fraud from 2000 to 2010.

LAB CRISIS #3: DETROIT POLICE DEPARTMENT FORENSIC SERVICES LABORATORY, MICHIGAN

This ongoing scandal stems from events that began unfolding in 2007, as discussed previously in the case example of Kevin Reed, a firearm and tool mark examiner for the Detroit Police Department Forensic Services Laboratory (DPFSL; see Chapter 8, "Forensic Fraud, 2000–2010: Data and Frequency"). Because of errors in an evidence report made by Officer Reed, Jarrhod Williams pleaded no-contest to second-degree murder charges related to a 2007 shooting; he believed that all of the 42 shell casings discovered at the scene had been matched to a single gun—his. In fact this was not the case. Michigan State Police reviewed the case after a defense expert determined that two separate guns had been used, and they agreed with this independent finding.

As previously mentioned, this case prompted an audit of the DPFSL by the Michigan State Police.[4] It was determined that 10% of the firearms examinations contained "significant errors" (MSP, 2008; p. 3), as well as 42% rate of non-compliance with laboratory practice standards (far below the 100% compliance requirement). It was also determined that the cost of a 10% lab error rate not only was unacceptable, but had a serious impact on the justice system (p. 3):

> In total, this equates to approximately 10% of the completed firearms cases having significant errors. On average, the DPD firearms unit analyzes 1,800 cases per year. If this 10% error rate holds, the negative impact on the judicial system would be substantial, with a strong likelihood of wrongful convictions and a valid concern about numerous appeals.

High-ranking officers agreed that the DPFSL suffered from "numerous errors made by multiple examiners," and that the errors found at the lab were "indicative of a systemic problem" (Patton, 2008). Consequently, the Detroit Police Department closed the entire lab and had it condemned (see Figures 11-3a and 11-3b). Its evidence-testing responsibilities were largely absorbed by the state police. By 2009, investigators had determined that at least 147 different cases required retesting, and defense attorneys had identified 30 more involving evidence that had been mishandled in some fashion.

While employees and supervisors from the shuttered DPFSL claimed that physical evidence had been properly secured and shipped elsewhere for analysis or storage, the reality was different. An investigative effort by local journalists revealed (Neavling, Ashenfelter, and Damron, 2011) that "[t]housands of rounds of live ammunition, sealed evidence kits and case files—some containing Social Security numbers of rape and assault victims—lay amid rubble in a crime lab abandoned by Detroit police two years ago." Eventually, the Detroit Police conceded that this was all true and reportedly went to work remedying the situation.

---

[4]Michigan State Police forensic labs are accredited by ASCLD-LAB, while the DPFSL was not.

FIGURES 11-3a and 3b

Case files with confidential identifying victim and suspect information, as well as hazardous vials of blood, were found abandoned and unsecured at the Detroit Police Department Forensic Services Laboratory. They had been left there from the fall of 2008 until at least the summer of 2011.

In the debris left behind at the DPFSL, investigators also found more than 11,000 untested rape kits. The extreme consequences of failing to immediately test rape kits, and instead shelving and then losing track of them, continue to be felt in this ongoing scandal, as reported by Burns (2012a):

> ...[S]tate police found 11,303 dusty rape kits upon the shelves.
> Some of them had been there for decades, their contents—and the horror stories of the women who provided them—forgotten for years.
> Though raised from the oblivion of the crime lab, the kits remain far from being processed. "I can't even speculate," Wayne County Prosecutor Kym Worthy said when asked how long it may take. "A long time … It's too depressing to think about how long it's going to take."
> Worthy spoke about numerous problems crippling the Detroit justice system at a Wayne State University Seminar called, "City Under Siege: A University Forum on the Crime Crisis in Detroit." Some in the crowd gasped when she spoke of the untested rape kits.

> "We have usually a woman who was raped, they went to a police department to report their rape and they willingly went to a rape kit exam—so three- to four-hour extensive exam, literally every orifice of your body is looked at and scoped and examined—and hoping … we can get some DNA and hopefully that produces a trial," Worthy said.
>
> She said 600 of the kits have been tested. The most recent "wave" of 200 resulted in the detection of 21 serial rapists among 153 test results.
>
> One of the test kits contained DNA belonging to Shelly A. Brooks, 43, a serial rapist and killer arrested in 2006. "Shelly A. Brooks killed and raped five more women after the date on this rape kit," Worthy said. "So that means if the rape kits were analyzed in a timely fashion perhaps, perhaps these five women would still be alive."

It is important to note that it is common practice in many police departments and crime labs to shelve rape kits without any examination or testing unless a viable suspect is identified during the police investigation; though such practices save money in the short term, they are investigatively unsound, working against the identification of criminals and the prevention of crime (Savino and Turvey, 2011).

The Detroit Police Department as a whole has been in a state of crisis since at least 2008, with respect to inadequate leadership, sex scandals, forensic failings, and instances of high-level ongoing criminal enterprise. Aside from the ongoing crime lab scandal and evidence backlogs, this includes the following:

- In 2010, Ralph Godbee took over as the Chief of the Detroit Police Department. Former Chief Warren Evans was fired by Mayor Dave Bing earlier that same year for misconduct, including an inappropriate sexual relationship with Lt. Monique Patterson of the sex crimes unit (White, 2012).
- William Rice, the former head of the Detroit Police Department Homicide Division, is going on trial with his girlfriend for charges related to at least 18 crimes, including running a criminal enterprise, drug dealing, drug possession, and mortgage fraud—all committed from 2006 to 2011 while he was still a cop (Burns, 2012b).
- James Moore, a Commander with the Detroit Police Department, was demoted as the result of an incident that occurred in the summer of 2012; it is alleged that he assaulted a female subordinate in public and on video. It is considered a domestic incident as he is reported to also be romantically involved with her, and the incident occurred in relation to the birthday of Moore's son (Kiertzner, 2012).
- In the fall of 2012, Chief Godbee (also a reverend) resigned amidst another sex scandal involving multiple female subordinates, including a married Internal Affairs investigator and the same Lt. Monique Patterson

mentioned above in relation to former Chief Evans (Hunter and Feretti, 2012).

These and other scandals within the Detroit Police combine to suggest a department out of control, with ethically bankrupt leadership creating a culture that is marked by entitlement, permissiveness, and in extreme cases, criminality. Ultimately, as evidenced by the research provided in this work, no scientific endeavor can survive under such conditions. And while outsourcing forensic services to state law enforcement agencies is a necessary short-term solution, it adds too much to an already-strained laboratory system. Given the character of this department, combined with the irresponsible tolerance for unacceptably high error rates within their lab, an external audit of DPFSL casework was long overdue.

In addition, as the termination of "scientific" services from within this broken department has led to further revelations about misplaced and forgotten evidence, closing the DPFSL was clearly a necessary step. However, it was not followed up with a thorough and complete investigation into concerns regarding related misconduct; the lab closure effectively ended any internal investigation into wrongdoing, leaving defense attorneys to sort things out for themselves. Consequently, the occurrence of this scandal and the related law enforcement response serve to reinforce the research findings presented in this work regarding law enforcement culture.

Hopefully, future decision makers will exercise better judgment by creating a new lab that is independent from the corrupted culture of local law enforcement; with regular independent audits; high transparency and accountability; and scientific leadership overseeing the work of actual scientists. Failing at this, history seems very likely to repeat itself in Detroit.

LAB CRISIS #4: EL PASO POLICE DEPARTMENT CRIME LABORATORY (EPDCL), TEXAS

As the result of an audit conducted in June of 2011, ASCLD-LAB suspended the El Paso Police Department Crime Laboratory's accreditation across the board until September 2, 2011 (see Figure 11-4). The suspension required that the EPDCL cease all casework involving instrumental analysis until the competence of its forensic examiners could be demonstrated; that they come up with a plan for fixing the numerous problems identified at the lab within 14 days; and that they submit to a more extensive ASCLD-LAB audit of forensic casework from the past six months to identify any potential errors (Keaton, 2011).

A "Full Assessment Report" prepared by ASCLD-LAB identified no fewer than 18 issues requiring immediate correction. These "Corrective Action" items

FIGURE 11-4
Police Chief Greg Allen during a press conference in 2011, discussing the EPDCL's ASCLD-LAB accreditation.

included EPDCL problems related to lack of consistent language and clarity in report writing; lack of proper record-keeping and data retention for comparison and interpretation of spectrometer findings; lack of definitions related to "acceptable ranges for retention time comparisons with known standards" with respect to toxicology samples; lack of examiner competency with respect to identifying drug samples; lack of proper documentation in controlled substance reports; lack of security with respect to both the laboratory and the evidence storage room; lack of appropriate and competent technical review by qualified, experienced examiners with respect to drug identification; use of laboratory equipment by unqualified personnel; lack of clear qualification and authorization of personnel to "perform sampling, testing, issuing test reports, giving opinions and interpretations and operating laboratory equipment" with respect to controlled substances; examiner incompetence with respect to controlled substance quantitative analysis and related lab policy; lack of minimum competency standards and testing for forensic examiners analyzing controlled substances; insufficient documentation with respect to using and interpreting results from the mass spectrometer; and analysts with significantly flawed deductive reasoning capabilities, as evidenced by failed proficiencies and follow-up questioning (Fox, 2011). In response, city officials investigated whether closing the police lab and outsourcing casework to the state or a private company might be a more cost-effective option (Schladen, 2011).

The EPDCL regained ASCLD-LAB accreditation early 2012, but then voluntarily withdrew from their accreditation program in November of that same year. This because it had already begun to outsource all of its forensic casework—a solution which the El Paso City Council made permanent in late August of 2012, as reported in Hunt (2012):

The crime lab failed the accreditation process which left the lab, which tests substances such as marijuana, cocaine and other controlled substances, out-sourcing its operations and delaying some drug cases.

City Council voted 6 to 1 to hire Integrated Forensic Laboratories (IFL) the group hired temporarily to help with that out-sourcing, as a permanent in-house option.

It will cost about half-a-million dollars a year or $2.5 million over the next five years.

This series of decisions, including the installment of IFL's five year contract, has rendered the EPDCL essentially non-existent as a forensic entity. It has, in effect, privatized forensic testing at the El Paso Police Department.

It is worth noting that IFL, which featured in the Austin Police Department Crime Laboratory scandal mentioned previously, is a private forensic lab in Texas run by Ralph Keaton. This is the same Ralph Keaton currently serving as Executive Director for ASCLD-LAB. This is also the same Ralph Keaton who prepared the audit report regarding in the EPDCL (Keaton, 2011). At the very least, this conflict of interest with respect to serving multiple competing roles in the same lab scandal, one of which profits from it by securing a multi-million dollar contract, serves to demonstrate just how small and incestuous the forensic science community can be.

There can be no question that the EPDCL was suffering, culturally, under the management of law enforcement. Furthermore, the El Paso City Council ulti-mately took the view that the problems within it were so bad (i.e., systemic) that they could only be solved by shutting down the lab and outsourcing examinations to a private company. Consequently, the occurrence of this scan-dal and the mechanism by which it was resolved serve to reinforce the research findings presented in this work.

However, it should also be noted that this author's research did not connect the EPDCL to any publicly known instances of forensic fraud from 2000 to 2010.

LAB CRISIS #5: DEPARTMENT OF PUBLIC SAFETY (DPS) CRIME LABORATORY, HOUSTON, TEXAS

In May of 2012, it was revealed by the Texas Department of Public Safety that a forensic chemist had made errors in multiple cases involving drug evidence (see Figure 11-5). The chemist, Jonathan Salvador, had worked in the Texas DPS crime lab system since 2006, and has examined more than 4,500 cases, as reported in Flake (2012):

On Friday, DPS alerted district attorney offices using the lab that errors in drug evidence analysis conducted by one scientist were found. That

FIGURE 11-5
The Texas Department of Public Safety crime lab in Houston, completed in 2011, at a cost of around $19 million. The logo for the Texas DPS contains a star (a law enforcement badge), and the words *Courtesy, Service,* and *Protection.*

scientist has been suspended while an internal investigation is being conducted, DPS spokesman Tom Vinger stated in an email to The Courier Tuesday.

While reanalyzing evidence in 100 of the employee's most recent cases, "we identified errors in two other cases," the DPS alert states.

DPS personnel discovered an issue with the DPS–Houston Crime Lab employee's work in February, and immediately began an investigation and suspended the drug analyst, Jonathan Salvador, who began working for the lab in 2006, Vinger stated.

When DPS began retesting a sampling of the analyst's work, two errors were discovered. Because of those additional errors, DPS is advising prosecutors in Montgomery, Harris, Fort Bend, Galveston, Brazoria and Matagorda counties that it is "prudent" to review the employee's entire body of work from early 2006....

There are 3,009 analyses—representing 1,281 individual defendants—that could be affected, First Assistant District Attorney Phil Grant said. "It's every controlled substance case, from misdemeanors to felonies," he said. "We don't expect any more. My understanding is this is his entire caseload."

In cases that the prosecutor, defense attorney and judge determine need retesting, DPS will perform that testing, Grant said.

Subsequently, it was made public that this case indeed involved forensic fraud; however, a grand jury failed to indict Salvador for criminal charges brought by the district attorney, as reported in Wrigley (2012):

This spring, an analyst at the DPS Crime Lab in Houston was found to have substituted evidence using a drug from another case to validate what he was testing. He was no-billed by a grand jury of any criminal misconduct. He resigned in July, but the fallout from that mishandling continues.

As of this writing, it is unclear why the grand jury refused to indict and what evidence was actually presented to them. As such, it would be unhelpful to speculate further, at least until more information has been made public. Surely, this will be fodder for the defense bar, and documentation regarding Mr. Salvador's actions will be drawn out in future legal proceedings. Even if the state drops every outstanding case involving his work, those defendants who have already been convicted could file appeals and request discovery that would bring much to light—perhaps even providing the basis for civil action. Therefore, the final determination of his misconduct, and any related legal consequences, must be resigned to future editions of this work.

However, it is worth noting that the Texas Department of Public Safety crime lab system as a whole is no stranger to scandal. This includes forensic fraud committed by *Dianna Boyd Monaghan*, a fingerprint examiner convicted of false reporting related to dry-labbed tests in 13 different cases while working for the Austin DPS crime lab (Osborne, 2001); *Jesus Hinojosa*, a laboratory technician convicted of crimes related to stealing cocaine from the DPS Jersey Village crime lab, falsifying evidence-related logs, and then selling the cocaine on the street (Rogers, 2008); and *Vanessa Nelson*, a DNA Unit Chief from the embattled Houston Police Department crime lab who resigned while under investigation for fraud and misconduct—she was immediately (and inexplicably) hired by the DPS crime lab in McAllen (Quaintance, 2008). Data related to the established fraud committed by each of these individuals was gathered and integrated into the 2000–2010 study.

LAB CRISIS #6: IDAHO STATE POLICE FORENSIC SERVICES LABORATORY, POCATELLO

In 2011, a scandal broke at the Idaho State Police Forensic Services Laboratory (ISPFSL) in Pocatello, involving fraud and other misconduct by at least three of its forensic examiners: Skyler Anderson (a lab manager), Shannon Larson, and Lamora Lewis. As reported in Morrin (2011):

> ...[T]hree memos ... give details on an Idaho State Police investigation into its own drug lab in Pocatello. The memos give details on broken policies and protocols, investigators say, lab workers committed over several years.
>
> One memo says some of the employees "... hid the unauthorized display drugs from auditors to avoid detection of this practice." Another memo says when a worker was questioned she "climbed

up on the drug bench, lifted the ceiling tiles, and pulled out a box of drugs."

ISP investigators discovered a third lab worker violated policies as well saying "(she) deliberately kept the GHB secreted within the lab."

ISP has refused to comment on the matter saying it is an internal personnel issue. All three lab workers involved have resigned as a result of the scandal. They are not facing criminal charges since they are legally authorized to handle the drugs as long as they don't leave the lab.

In accordance with *Brady v. Maryland*, these memos were discovered to the office of the public defender and a number criminal defendants. They were made an issue on appeal in *U.S. v. Ellingford* (2011), referred to as "Newly Discovered Evidence":

> The newly discovered evidence in this case is a recent Idaho State Police administrative investigation of several employees of the Idaho State Forensic Laboratory located in Pocatello. Laboratory employees admitted to maintaining a box of undocumented "display drugs." The box contained a cache of unusual controlled substances that lab scientists kept to train new employees and to show students during tours. Employees kept the box after changes to laboratory accreditation regulations in 2007 should have led to its destruction. See Exhibit E (Dkt. 122-2) at p. 2. Rocklan McDowell, a former Laboratory employee who processed the drug samples in this case and testified as a Government witness, admitted that he knew of the existence of the box, and hid the box to prevent its discovery and destruction during annual audits. Id. at pp. 14–18.

The appellate court concluded that the evidence of examiner misconduct did not justify vacating Mr. Ellingford's conviction, as it was unrelated to the evidence and issues specific to his case. However, this misconduct was related to maintaining the laboratory's ASCLD-LAB accreditation, as it hid the evidence from auditors whenever they came around. This comports with the findings in the present research—namely that laboratory accreditation is associated with increased fraudulent behavior (e.g., examiners commit fraud to maintain certifications related to accreditation).

As a consequence of the ISP's investigation into these three lab employees, all were first placed on leave and then allowed to resign without criminal charges being brought against them. This is of concern, as it is a crime to give false information to police investigators in the course of an official investigation, and the specific deceptions noted occurred multiple times. Unfortunately, allowing the employees to resign effectively ended the internal investigation, which prevents further information from being developed related to potential criminal charges—which is often the point of taking such a course of action. Scandals are bad for everyone, and ending them swiftly and without publicity is often the preferred method of disposal.

However, it should also be noted that this author's research did not connect the ISPFSL to any other publicly known instances of forensic fraud from 2000 to 2010.

LAB CRISIS #7: INDIANA STATE DEPARTMENT OF TOXICOLOGY

The Indiana State Department of Toxicology (ISDT), which was run out of the Indiana University School of Medicine for more than 50 years until June of 2011, had been experiencing problems documented internally for almost a decade. These included overworked examiners, excessive case backlogs, and drug identification error. However, these long-term and wide-spread issues were not disclosed by the lab, or its supervisors, until the results of an external audit were made public by investigative journalists and the lab's former director, Michael Wagner, as reported in Alesia and Evans (2011a):[5]

> Soon after Michael Wagner took over as director in August 2008, he told Steve Johnson and Deborah Reasoner of the Indiana Prosecuting Attorneys Council [IPAC] that he had found problems at the lab and planned to launch an audit of test results. IPAC, however, made no effort to notify its members, much less defense attorneys.
>
> In February 2009, Wagner told a group of deputy prosecutors and police officers not to move ahead with cases involving tests from 2007 and 2008 without having him review the files and perhaps retest samples. He said he had found errors that made him unwilling to testify to those results in court.
>
> In March 2010, Johnson told the Governor's Council on Impaired & Dangerous Driving that prosecutors have "great concern about the reliability of tests." …
>
> Last month, The Star revealed that an audit showed 200 out of 2,000 positive marijuana test results from 2007 to 2009 shouldn't have been reported to prosecutors because of errors. That audit is continuing into other categories such as cocaine and alcohol—results that might suggest even more problems.

---

[5]This author has read the complete public archive of original memos, emails, and reports made available regarding this scandal at www.indystar.com and agrees that this summary of findings is more than a fair assessment.

Johnson expressed "grave concern" over the first wave of audit results. But he told The Star that he did not think what they knew previously about the possibility of bad results warranted disclosure.

Defense attorneys, however, say that any hint of a problem with something as vital as test results should have been disclosed. "When somebody hands the prosecution evidence that testing might be unreliable, you can't hide that," said John Tompkins, a prominent Indianapolis defense attorney who concentrates on DUI cases. Tompkins and [Larry] Landis [head of the state public defenders council] are among those who fear some convictions might be tainted—a sobering possibility that could lead to the re-examination of hundreds of cases, and convictions being overturned, all at a huge cost to taxpayers. That alone would be reason for prosecutors to be concerned about information regarding the audit becoming public.

Wagner, who's still a faculty member at the IU School of Medicine, which runs the lab, said "absolutely" some people might be in jail because of lab errors and that it's "a strong concern."

Landis said he knew nothing about an audit until last summer when he was informed by former Marion County Prosecutor Scott Newman, who was hired by IU to look into various problems at the lab. Fearing that he would be made a scapegoat for those problems, Wagner said he secretly recorded conversations to protect himself. He shared the recordings with The Star because he said he thought it was important for the public to know the truth. In his first interview since resigning in May—under pressure, he says, from IU officials—Wagner said the lab's problems are longstanding and systemic.

The publicly funded state lab, in Indianapolis, has been operated by Indiana University since 1957. Its job is not to favor the prosecution or defense but to provide scientifically accurate results. According to testimony at a 2008 congressional hearing, more than 85 percent of such labs have accreditation from groups such as the American Society of Crime Laboratory Directors. The IU lab does not.

Wagner was the first forensic toxicologist to head the state department in more than a decade—a level of expertise that exceeded that of his predecessors. Wagner said red flags became apparent to him soon after he took over the lab, starting with a methamphetamine case. He recently told The Star the lab "didn't meet minimum industry standards for forensic science" when he arrived. He didn't keep those concerns to himself. "I just saw so much that was wrong that I couldn't allow it to go unreported," Wagner said. "I felt responsible, now, for it."

Then, in the fall of 2008, came what defense attorneys and legal experts say was a critical moment. That was when Wagner met with Johnson and Reasoner from the prosecutors' council. Wagner told them

he planned to launch an audit because of problems at the lab. That
Wagner used the word "audit" is not in dispute. But the main point of
contention between IPAC officials and defense attorneys, as well as
legal experts, is what should have happened next. IPAC chose not to
disclose the information.

"He explained the reason for it in such scientific terms that I'm not
sure I fully understood," Johnson said in an interview with The Star.
"But I felt, well, he's the toxicologist, and he sees problems. That
needs to be done." Johnson, however, said he wasn't alarmed because
Wagner didn't detail his concerns or cite any specific cases. "In terms
of the entire mess he found," Johnson said, "I don't know if he ever
went into much detail."

Wagner, however, recalled that "the gravity of my emotions and
what I said could not have been misleading." Wagner said he was
unaware of any previous audits of the lab and that "it is not standard
procedure to walk in and do an audit." In hindsight, Johnson said, he
should have asked for more details from Wagner about what prompted
the audit and should have had the lab director put that information
in writing. Then, Johnson said, he would have sent a letter out to
prosecutors across the state....

Although Johnson said he didn't think to ask why there was such an
audit, defense attorneys said that if they had heard the state testing
facility responsible for producing critical blood and urine evidence was
undergoing an audit, they most certainly would have asked why.

That wasn't the last time Wagner said he made IPAC or prosecutors
aware of the testing problems. He said he again sounded an alarm
at a training meeting attended by a number of prosecutors on Feb.
12, 2009. He told prosecutors they shouldn't proceed to trial with test
results from 2007 or 2008 without checking with him first. He needed
to examine the paperwork and retest if necessary. "You could see the
air just leave the room," Wagner recalled.

Johnson was not at the meeting, but Reasoner, who was present,
said she did not recall Wagner discussing any problems. IPAC, she
said, would have been responsible for passing the information along
to prosecutors. Wagner's comments to the about 60 prosecutors and
police officers, Reasoner said, were more about giving him time to
review case details before he was called into court to testify.

Tim Sledd, the chief deputy prosecutor in Lawrence County, who
was at the training program, said he did not recall Wagner saying
anything that would raise concerns about widespread problems with
test results. "I would remember," Sledd said, "if I was told the test
result information coming to us was suspect or that we needed to use
caution as we moved forward."

But Summerfield, who also was present, apparently did understand the gravity of Wagner's comments that day. Last July, Summerfield, the deputy prosecutor in Hamilton County, invited Wagner to lunch—and Wagner secretly recorded their three-hour conversation at a Chili's restaurant. At one point during the conversation, almost all of which was about toxicology, they discuss the February 2009 training session. Summerfield, who prosecutes impaired-driving cases involving fatalities, said in the recorded conversation that she went up to Reasoner after the training and told her: "We're screwed. For the next year, we're screwed." Reasoner said she did not recall any such exchange with Summerfield.

But an email provided to The Star, from less than two weeks after the training session, also corroborates Wagner's version. Ed Zych, then a deputy prosecutor in Marion County, wrote to the toxicology lab to say he had heard from Summerfield that prosecutors were supposed to check with Wagner "because there have been some problems with older tests." Zych, now a deputy prosecutor in Shelby County, did not return phone calls from The Star.

The Star also obtained four other emails, involving cases in three different counties, in which prosecutors requested a review of test results or lab workers reported performing reviews for prosecutors. Wagner said other prosecutors, including Summerfield, did indeed check with him on cases headed for trial. But it's unclear how many people pleaded guilty to charges based on a test result that might not have been admissible in court. About 90 percent to 95 percent of impaired-driving cases, attorneys explained, result in plea bargains.

Landis, of the public defenders' council, said positive test results carry enormous weight. Without the knowledge that a positive result could be unreliable, he said, defense attorneys likely would encourage clients to accept a plea in an effort to secure a lesser sentence.

During their lunch conversation, Summerfield also spoke freely—and critically—about IPAC. Some of those comments back up defense attorneys' worst fears about whether IPAC was interested in anything other than hiding the problem. "What amazes me about this," Summerfield said at one point, is the possibility that prosecuting attorneys "don't care" as long as their samples got tested. She also told Wagner that it bothered her that IPAC's attitude about problems at the lab was "just very much close the door and move on." When later contacted by The Star, Summerfield stressed that the conversation with Wagner, including her highly critical comments about IPAC, was in the context of comforting a friend.

...March 19, 2010—is when there appears to be the most telling evidence that IPAC acknowledged there was not only an audit but that there were problems with lab test results. It was then that Johnson shared with the Governor's Council on Impaired & Dangerous Driving his growing and myriad concerns about the lab. One of those complaints was a testing backlog that was so bad some prosecutors were being forced to dismiss cases.

But Johnson also raised another concern. Minutes from that meeting state that Johnson told the council: "When (prosecutors) get the results, there is great concern whether the tests are reliable." That concern, defense attorneys now say, should have been immediately shared with them. But it was not. When asked why, Johnson downplayed his "great concern" comment and said he was referring only to a few cases in which prosecutors received conflicting results. Johnson's other concerns, however, did produce action. The governor's council created an assessment team to examine the performance of the lab, including the growing backlog.

It was in the midst of the assessment team's investigation, on May 12, that Wagner resigned and—on the very next day—his interim replacement, Michael Neerman, sent an email to auditors. "I spoke with my boss, Dr. Michael Vasko, and it is (in the) best interest of ISDT to cease the audit you are performing for the time being," the email said. "Once the dust settles, then perhaps this will resume." IU officials say the audit was stopped merely to focus attention on the backlog. And, they note, it was restarted by Newman.

Newman, who began as a consultant to the Toxicology Department and was hired officially in August as special consultant to the dean of the medical school, appears to have quickly sensed how serious the problems might be. In October, Newman said of what he had seen, "A person who is responsible would not feel comfortable and would feel the need to investigate."

In December, Newman said preliminary results of the audit he restarted were bad enough that he expanded the probe to cover results from 2007 and 2008. Neerman, who succeeded Wagner, also quickly realized the challenges once he took over. When Neerman abruptly resigned in December, he sent Wagner an email that said in part, "I think we both inherited a mess."

The independent audit referred to in the preceding description levied serious findings related to examiner error and misconduct, as reported in Alesia and Evans (2011b):

The first major report from an audit of the Indiana State Department of Toxicology further brings into question the validity of potentially hundreds of drug and alcohol tests performed at the lab in recent years. The findings from the audit, provided to The Indianapolis

Star, showed errors in about 200 of 2,000 marijuana tests reported to law enforcement as having positive results. That includes about 50 described as "a conscious manipulation of results" by lab workers....

Larry Landis, executive director of the Indiana Public Defender Council, called the revelations "shocking" and "inexcusable." "If they're manipulating data, how can you rely on anything they do?" Landis said. "We're talking about people's lives."...

The audit eventually will cover every case from 2007 to 2009 in which the lab reported a positive result—more than 10,000 overall. But [Marion County Prosecutor Scott] Newman said the initial findings are troubling enough that he probably will extend the audit back to 2006. The audit, conducted by outside scientists, is of paper records. "We see a conscious manipulation of results to produce a desired result," Newman said, "and that is the exact opposite of what scientific inquiry should be about."

The most egregious errors, he said, likely were caused by laziness, incompetence, time pressure and a lack of established operating procedures, rather than criminal activity. Newman said lab workers casually used a technique called "manual integration" to "correct" machine readings. The technique, for when the machine has obviously made a mistake, is supposed to be done very sparingly and under strict written procedures.

"Unacceptable, ... especially in a law enforcement situation," said Dwain C. Fuller, a board-certified forensic toxicologist and consultant from Mansfield, Texas, who is not involved in the audit. Fuller said that, as an expert witness for a defense lawyer in such cases, "I can make hay with that."

Steve Johnson, executive director of the Indiana Prosecuting Attorneys Council, said it's too early to predict how many of the errors could have an impact on criminal cases. He said one ray of good news is that in Indiana there is no set level for marijuana intoxication, so any trace is enough for a conviction. But, he said, the scope of problems uncovered by the audit is much worse than he imagined. "This is significant," Johnson said, "but I believe we are on the way to correcting it."

However, in July of 2011, an advisory board in charge of supervising the state Department of Toxicology's transition from Indiana University to a stand-alone state agency, agreed to stop the audit altogether, even though it was only half done. As reported in Alesia and Evans (2011c):

Larry Landis, executive director of the Indiana Public Defender Council, said stopping the audit without an alternative for reviewing the alcohol tests "sounds to me like a cover-up."

> IU hired Colorado-based auditor Forensic Consultants Inc. to examine the paper records for every positive test result from 2007 to 2009. Auditors found errors in 10 percent of marijuana cases and 32 percent of cocaine cases. They were working on the substance involved in the most cases—alcohol—when informed by email to "place a hold" on the audit.
>
> "What they have done," said prominent Indianapolis defense attorney J.J. Paul, "is open Pandora's box, and now they want to close it just as they get to the greatest number of cases that affect the greatest number of people."

In June of 2011, the Indiana State Department of Toxicology (ISDT) was officially removed from Indiana University oversight and re-created as a stand-alone state agency. However, it occupies the same building space. Oversight is currently provided by a three-member panel appointed by, and serving at the pleasure of, the governor's office. This is a necessary first step, but it does not solve the lab's other myriad problems—such as a lack of scientific leadership; lack of knowledge of, and adherence to, scientifically sound protocols; and conformance with transparency in accordance with scientific values and *Brady v. Maryland*. This to say nothing of needing a budget sufficient to the task of hiring, training, and retaining competent forensic scientists.

Because the external audit was halted, the extent of the damage caused by this ongoing scandal may never be fully revealed. It also does not bode well for achieving or maintaining a culture of scientific integrity. Unless new leadership is brought in with the authority, autonomy, and budget to function in a manner that engenders scientific integrity, further error, resignations, and additional misconduct with respect to covering it all up can be expected.

LAB CRISIS #8: PORTLAND METROPOLITAN POLICE CRIME LABORATORY, OREGON

In April of 2012, the Portland Metropolitan Police Crime Laboratory (PMPCL) suspended work in their Handwriting Analysis Unit. This decision was the result of an internal investigation initiated because of the findings in a routine audit back in June of 2011. The audit found problems with the work of two examiners, as reported in Denson (2012):

> The handwriting analysts—Ron Emmons and Christina Kelley—have handled about 80 cases a year, examining magnified images of paper documents, such as wills, suicide notes and bank robbery demands, to determine the likelihood they match a suspect's known writing. Their work has been used in prosecutions of such high-profile cases as the

2008 Woodburn bank bombing that killed two police officers, although the external review found no problems with that case, police said.

The two began work in what is formally known as the Questioned Document Unit in fall 1999. Emmons, 64, had become a handwriting examiner during a 30-year law enforcement career in Alaska. Kelley, 56, spent 17 years in the U.S. Army, where she worked in criminal investigation.

A decade would pass before their troubles trickled into the news.

The audit found that Mr. Emmons and Ms. Kelley were required by lab policy to independently peer review each other's work—to see if they came to the same conclusions. This is a common though less reliable form of internal quality control. The problem is they hadn't been doing it. As reported in Denson (2012):

Kelley told The Oregonian that no one ever told her the confirmation step was required, and she blamed Emmons, as the unit's technical leader, for not making sure they did it. Emmons responded that he wrote the procedures for making confirmations and that he thought he and his partner were following them.

During the audit, Kelley accused Emmons of physically and professionally intimidating her. Lab management forwarded her complaints—including an allegation that Emmons was performing private handwriting exams on state police time—to the state police Office of Professional Standards, which was unable to substantiate her allegations. Emmons, in interviews with The Oregonian, described Kelley's allegations as "totally false."

One Friday last January, Emmons asked Kelley to review his findings in a case he was preparing to forward to the Umatilla County District Attorney's Office. Emmons had examined handwriting samples in the case of George Ardizzone, a state prison inmate serving a 14-year sentence for plotting to get another man to kill his ex-girlfriend near Portland. Ardizzone was now charged with soliciting another prisoner to get a friend on the outside to kill the same ex-girlfriend. Kelley pored through the documents. What happened next remains in dispute.

According to state police, Kelley misled Emmons into believing that she had signed off on his findings in the Umatilla case. This caused Emmons, who believed that one person was behind the writing, to phone the prosecutor with erroneous findings. Kelley had concluded that the writing samples in the Ardizzone case came from two people. But she was afraid to confront Emmons with his error. So instead of telling him his findings were wrong, she simply told him, "It's done."

The following morning, Kelley phoned lab director Barnes to inform him that Emmons had made a false identification in the Ardizzone case. Keith Kerr, a former handwriting examiner who is now director of the state police crime lab in Pendleton, re-examined the case. He spent 16 hours that weekend reviewing the evidence, later telling investigators it took about 20 minutes to corroborate Kelley's finding: Emmons had it wrong.

Emmons, ordered to rework the Ardizzone documents, found that he made an error. The lab did not release any report on the case. Precisely how Emmons made his mistake is unclear. In interviews with The Oregonian, he declined to specify what happened, but said it was the first time he had made a bad finding in a report and that he had relied on his partner of 13 years to catch any errors in his work.

Ardizzone was convicted without the handwriting evidence, said Umatilla County District Attorney Daniel Primus, partly because the inmate he solicited in the murder plot informed to police and wore a body wire in his conversation with Ardizzone. But handwriting evidence, Primus acknowledged, would have made a strong case even stronger.

Emmons' error prompted an internal review of how the mistake happened. State police also opened a criminal investigation, looking into whether Kelley, by allegedly misleading Emmons, had committed the misdemeanor crime of official misconduct.

The criminal probe, which grew to include an investigator from the Clackamas County District Attorney's Office, prompted more allegations. Kelley accused Emmons of being biased toward prosecutors, reaffirmed her belief that her partner might physically or professionally harm her and presented investigators with 14 other cases worked by Emmons—and reviewed by her—that potentially drew inaccurate conclusions.

Kerr, a former handwriting examiner, told investigators that Emmons' blunder raised questions about his competence. He told them, when asked if he had drawn any conclusions about Emmons' statements, "I've got a bad examiner." He also criticized Kelley, telling investigators that she lied and failed to follow procedure, according to a report by an investigator for the Clackamas County DA's office. In interviews for this story, Kelley denied lying.

While both examiners remain on paid suspension, the local DA's office has declined to prosecute either of them for any crimes. However, given the circumstances, ASCLD-LAB has refused to accredit the PMPCL Handwriting Analysis Unit as a result. This means that any new requests for such analysis are being outsourced. Meanwhile, out-of-state examiners are in the process of reviewing 35 of these examiners' cases; and the Washington State Patrol Crime Lab, which has relied on them in the past, is waiting to learn of those external results.

Consequently, as of this writing, the fate and future of the PMPCL Handwriting Analysis Unit are uncertain.

What this scandal reveals is a lab unit suffering from internal animosity, personality issues, and a clear lack of leadership and accountability. It also suggests the need for separation from law enforcement, as at least one of the examiners (Kelley) feels that this is a serious issue while perceiving a lack of internal support for making complaints. This set of problems would be greatly diminished by adequate scientific supervision to ensure that protocols were understood and being followed, combined with effective leadership that is separate from the agenda of police and prosecutions.

LAB CRISIS #9: ST. PAUL POLICE DEPARTMENT CRIME LABORATORY, MINNESOTA

As the result of cross-examination during a court hearing in Dakota County, a well-known secret about the St. Paul Police Department Crime Lab (SPPDCL) became part of the official public record: it lacks adherence to basic or even written scientific protocols, and its personnel are not properly trained. This came with no small amount of help from an expert hired by the defense: forensic scientist Jay Siegel. As reported in Hanners (2012):

> The head of the St. Paul Police Department's beleaguered crime lab had faced hard questioning on the witness stand before, but he'd never had to provide answers that called his unit's scientific integrity into question [see Figure 11-6].
>
> But as a defense attorney peppered him with inquiries at a special court hearing Tuesday, July 17, Sgt. Shay Shackle acknowledged that when it came to the testing of seized drugs, his lab failed to follow even minimum scientific standards.
>
> Shackle was testifying at a court hearing in Dakota County at which 1st District public defenders Lauri Traub and Christine Funk are trying to get suspected drug evidence against their client declared inadmissible.
>
> Their inquiries have disclosed deep and systemic problems within the crime lab that could affect other cases. "How can anyone assess the quality of your lab?" Traub finally asked him.
>
> "I don't know," Shackle replied.
>
> One by one, Traub had read off the 51 standards that a national science group considers the minimum criteria for a crime lab. One by one, Shackle admitted St. Paul's unaccredited lab ignores all but two.
>
> "What makes your lab as good as or better than labs that follow these minimum recommendations?" Traub asked him. A prosecutor

FIGURE 11-6
Sgt. Shay Shackle, then head of the St. Paul Police Department's Crime Lab, photographs the exterior of a homicide crime scene in March of 2012.

objected, but District Judge Kathryn Davis Messerich overruled it, meaning Shackle had to answer.

"I don't think it's as good as or better," he replied. "Could it use improvement? Yes." Phillip Prokopowicz, Dakota County's chief deputy prosecutor, said his office still was assessing the evidence the two public defenders had brought to light.

"This is the first time we've heard a lot of this information," he said. Although he declined to comment on specifics, he said the Dakota County attorney's office needed "an opportunity to digest it a little bit." Aside from processing the suspected drugs seized by St. Paul police, the eight-person crime lab also analyzes substances seized by sheriff's deputies in Ramsey, Dakota and Washington counties, as well as the Minnesota State Patrol.

At the heart of the arguments raised by Traub and Funk is a simple question: If the crime lab fails to abide by minimum scientific standards, how can its findings—often used to send people to prison—be trusted?

A nationally known forensic chemist told the judge the answer was simple: It can't be trusted because it isn't science. "They're doing insufficient, unvalidated testing, being done by untrained analysts who are using equipment that's not being cared for," said Jay Siegel, an analytical chemist, a chemistry professor and a former member of the National Academy of Sciences' Committee on Forensic Science. He said minimum lab standards were needed so that "we don't just have a bunch of cowboys out there throwing drugs at instruments and hoping for results." "This is not high school chemistry. This is sophisticated chemistry," said Siegel, a founding member of the Scientific Working

Group on the Analysis of Seized Drugs, the professional organization that came up with the 51 minimum lab standards that Traub had asked Shackle about.

But after Traub and Funk began questioning criminalists at the St. Paul police crime lab about test results that allegedly showed their client had heroin, they discovered the lab had virtually no written standards or protocols guiding how it performed its work.

They also discovered the three criminalists in the lab who test the suspected drugs lacked any formal training in what they do, and they often misused the lab's gas chromatograph-mass spectrometers, the main tools used to analyze the samples.

They laid out several of their concerns in a motion asking Messerich for a hearing to determine whether the purported evidence had any basis in science. The judge granted their request, and Tuesday was the second day of testimony.

The hearing continues Wednesday, and there may be testimony in August and September as well.

Siegel … said his review of St. Paul's crime lab left him with three major concerns: The criminalists aren't trained for the work they're doing; their lab methods aren't documented; and it appears their misuse of lab instruments could "come up with false positives like crazy." Any of the three is a problem, he said, but together, they mean the results coming out of St. Paul's crime lab, which often wind up in court, aren't reliable. He was particularly critical of the lab's lack of written guidelines or protocols governing how tests are conducted. Two criminalists who testified earlier said the only training they got was on the job, passed on verbally by superiors. "If you don't write it down, it's like passing on oral folklore," Siegel said. "Any scientific laboratory will tell you, 'If it ain't written down, we don't do it.'"

After Siegel finished with his indictment of the lab, Traub called Shackle to the stand. He's been with the St. Paul Police Department since 1982 and was promoted to head the crime lab in 2001. He told Traub he had no scientific background. Shackle testified that once a new criminalist has been trained on the job, there is no further routine review of their work. He also said the crime lab doesn't do proficiency testing to monitor work quality, another shortcoming Siegel had faulted the unit for.

He acknowledged that Jennifer Jannetto, the criminalist who supervises the drug analysts, has more training in latent fingerprint examination than in analyzing drug evidence. He said that although criminalists request to go to training seminars, his superiors often deny the requests for budgetary reasons.

>   Traub asked him question after question about the records that
>   might support the lab's findings. Time and again, Shackle replied,
>   "I have no formal documentation, no" or "I don't know of any formal
>   documentation" or something similar.
>
>   "If the quality can't be reviewed, how can it be trusted?" the public
>   defender asked the cop.
>
>   "It can be reviewed, but it's not being reviewed," he said. "I think it
>   needs to be reviewed."

Additional revelations during the hearing included testimony from one of the
lab's criminalists, also reported in Hanners (2012):

>   During the court hearing, one of the lab's criminalists testified about
>   her test of a sample of suspected heroin. When she analyzed the
>   sample on the department's gas chromatograph-mass spectrometer, it
>   had a peak molecular ion of 405. But heroin (or diacetylmorphine) has a
>   peak molecular ion of 369, so the sample could not have been heroin.
>
>   The criminalist told First Judicial District Public Defender Lauri
>   Traub that she thought the sample was heroin, even though her own
>   analysis showed that chemically, it was something else. Because
>   scientists in the lab don't review each other's work—a feature required
>   in an accredited lab—nobody questioned the criminalist's findings that
>   the sample was heroin.
>
>   The heroin sample was mentioned in a July 17 email that Assistant
>   Dakota County Attorney Chip Grannis wrote to two of his colleagues
>   about his discussion with Jennifer Jannetto, the criminalist who
>   supervises the forensics unit's drug analysts. Grannis had asked
>   Jannetto about the faulty test and she told him it was "some form
>   of contamination," he wrote. "She would need to research further
>   whether that test result can be called heroin," the prosecutor told his
>   colleagues. He also said Jannetto told him the test would be hard to
>   replicate because no records were kept of how the original test was
>   conducted.
>
>   Gas chromatograph-mass spectrometers are run by computer
>   programs that set the device's parameters, operating temperatures and
>   running time. St. Paul's crime lab uses a program known as "DrugsB,"
>   but Shackle and others testified during the hearing that they had no
>   idea where the program came from—or if it produced accurate results.

Officials claimed that Sgt. Shackle's testimony about conditions within the
crime lab, combined with other revelations related to poorly trained examiners giving conflicted and unsupported findings, caught them completely by
surprise; and (likely because of intense media scrutiny) there were immediate
public consequences. First, St. Paul Police Chief Thomas Smith removed Sgt.

Shackle as the head of the SPPDCL, and reassigned him, laterally, to another position within the police department; second, Chief Smith suspended all drug testing in the SPPDCL; and third, "lead prosecutors in Ramsey, Dakota and Washington counties said they asked the Minnesota Bureau of Criminal Apprehension to re-examine all evidence in pending drug cases previously tested at the St. Paul police crime lab" (Gottfried, 2012). Additionally, "the lab's biggest customers—the Minnesota State Patrol and Washington and Dakota counties—said they were taking their business elsewhere because of the problems," meaning they would submit their drugs and other evidence for testing at one of the Minnesota Bureau of Criminal Apprehension's ASCLD-LAB accredited facilities (Gurnon, 2012).

In September of 2012, the St. Paul Police Department hired "Integrated Forensic Laboratories of Euless, Texas, and Schwarz Forensic Enterprises of Ankeny, Iowa, to study the crime lab and figure out how to fix it" with respect to both drug testing and fingerprint examination (Chin and Hanners, 2012). This given additional challenges made against the lab regarding untrained and unqualified fingerprint examiners. As of this writing, past drug and fingerprint cases are being re-examined, and the entire crime lab has been shaken up amidst calls from the defense to shut it down; of the 100 cases retested so far, two have found results conflicting with the SPPDCL's original findings (Baran, 2012). Other cases have been dismissed or been granted generous plea deals. The future of this lab is uncertain (see Figure 11-7), and only time will tell the whole story as further litigation draws out the facts.

What is certain is that the SPPDCL suffered from a lack of scientific knowledge, protocols, and leadership, with their sloppiness and testimony calling into question the fitness of this department to maintain a forensic lab of any kind. This comports with the findings of the present study regarding the

FIGURE 11-7
The St. Paul Police Department Crime Lab.

development and maintenance of scientific culture. However, it should also be noted that this author's research did not connect the SPPDCL to any publicly known instances of forensic fraud from 2000 to 2010.

LAB CRISIS #10: STARK COUNTY CRIME LABORATORY, OHIO

In May of 2012, criminalist Michael Short was fired from the Stark County Crime Laboratory (accredited by ASCLD-LAB) for falsifying reports related to firearms testing. As reported in Balint (2012a):

> Michael Short was dismissed last week by Canton Safety Director Thomas Ream. Disciplinary charges also include improper job performance and insubordination. Short's annual salary was $62,392, according to the mayor's office. Prior to the firing, Short had been placed on paid administrative leave.
>
> Ream said in a report that he fired Short to "ensure the safety and well-being of our community going forward" and "to uphold the professionalism and integrity of the Stark County Crime Laboratory and the city of Canton Police Department."
>
> The falsification violation stems from Short's gunshot-related analysis in January in a felonious assault case…. In paperwork, Short used the term, "using the firearm," which investigators say indicated the gun had been test-fired when it had not.
>
> Short said that the description of "using the firearm" did not mean he test-fired the weapon, according to Ream's report. Short told a police investigator that there was not a code in the computer to specify that he didn't discharge the gun. Short explained that his results —in determining the distance from which the gun was fired—were gained through past experience with firearms and ammunition.
>
> An accreditation program manager told an investigator that basing lab results on experience without conducting the examination is not an acceptable practice when the items that are to be tested are available. In addition, a crime lab employee told an investigator that he returned reports to Short to be done correctly regarding the gun-related analysis and the test-firing of a firearm. The reports, which were not corrected or administratively reviewed, were placed in a bin to be sent back to the submitting law enforcement agency, according to police records.

The severity of the misconduct in this case cannot be understated: supervisors determined that the criminalist wrote a report which suggested testing had been done which hadn't, and when given an opportunity to correct it, he apparently didn't, and even sought to further the deception. Consequently, termination is not only a reasonable response, but is the response that most certainly ensures a culture of scientific integrity within the lab.

However, the Canton Civil Service Commission disagreed. On appeal, Michael Short was reinstated as a criminalist at the Stark County Crime Laboratory. Instead of termination, he was given a 120-day suspension without pay. As reported in Balint (2012b), prosecutors testified to the commission on behalf of Short in favor of reinstatement, and two criminalists from the lab testified on behalf of the city in favor of termination:

> The Civil Service Commission decided that Short had not falsified a report, according to the finding and order it issued in the case. However, according to the document, "Short's failure to follow the administration review process established by the crime lab does constitute insubordination and improper job performance, and is appropriate grounds for disciplinary action by the appointing authority." But "based upon the absence of previous disciplinary violations over the course of his career with the crime lab, termination was not the appropriate remedy," the order said.

Apparently, forensic fraud is either not clearly understood or not taken very seriously by the Canton Civil Service Commission. Their failure to support the decisions of the leadership at the crime lab, based on the facts revealed by their internal investigation, are an affront to good science. It also represents a failure to "uphold the professionalism and integrity" that the laboratory leadership was trying to protect.

This is an isolated instance. Ultimately, however, this decision means that the Stark County Crime Lab currently employs an examiner known by managers and co-workers to have committed evidence-related fraud. This also means that he should no longer be performing casework; if he is ever called to the stand, his supervisors and co-workers can be called as witnesses against him— to repeat their sworn testimony before the Canton Civil Service Commission and destroy his credibility as a witness. In other words, the county is paying him for a job that he can longer perform.

LAB CRISIS #11: U.S. ARMY CRIMINAL INVESTIGATION LABORATORY (USACIL), FT. GILLEM, GEORGIA

Published reports in 2011 and 2012 allege that the U.S. Army Criminal Investigation Laboratory (USACIL) in Ft. Gillem, Georgia (see Figure 11-8), continues to suffer from ongoing management problems and internal allegations of racism, bias, poor leadership, sexual harassment, missing evidence, examiner error,

FIGURE 11-8
The U.S. Army Criminal Investigation Laboratory in Fort Gillem, Georgia

and examiner fraud (Doyle and Taylor, 2011). This includes USACIL handwriting expert Allen Southmayd, who embezzled approximately $68,500 from the American Board of Forensic Document Examiners (where he was treasurer) by writing 19 checks to himself from 2006 to 2007, in order to finance a gambling addiction; he was arrested and convicted for his crimes (Crosby, 2008; Taylor, 2011).[6] It also includes firearms examiner Michael Brooks; as reported in Taylor and Doyle (2011b), his fraud was kept hidden by the USACIL and only made public by the media subsequent to their investigative efforts:[7]

> Brooks had said he'd examined a hat for gunshot residue and concluded that the weapon had been fired at close range. His supervisor, however, later discovered the hat hadn't been tested. The victim allegedly had shot himself in the right temple, but the hole in the hat was on the left side. Brooks, who could not be reached for comment, later destroyed evidence from the case file and lied about his actions, investigators concluded. The lab fired him in 2006.

Brooks was "quietly fired for making a false statement and destroying evidence" (Taylor and Doyle, 2011b). As a consequence of his fraud and misconduct, the USACIL reviewed at least 541 firearms cases to make sure that the forensic examinations had been conducted properly.

USACIL Firearms Branch Chief Donald Mikko, who had been providing information about undisclosed fraud and misconduct at the lab to the media for several years, felt compelled to resign after 21 years of service. He alleges at least

---

[6]Though revealed in 2008, prior to close of data collection efforts, the fraud committed by Allen Southmayd was not discovered by this author until it was reported by the press in 2011. In any case, his fraudulent activity may or may not have been included in the final data set, as it does not appear to be directly related to his evidence-related duties.

[7]Though known to the USACIL, the fraud committed by Michael Brooks was not made public until it was learned of and reported by the press in 2011. Consequently, data from this case of forensic fraud could not have been included in the present study.

two years of harassment and retaliation by supervisors intent on punishing him for being a whistleblower, including lengthy interrogations by his employers. Mikko filed a formal complaint against his supervisors, which has resulted in an investigation of the USACIL, and its leadership, by the Office of Special Counsel. However, the lab is no stranger to such controversy; between 2009 and 2012, there have been eight complaints levied against lab managers and seven internal investigations (Taylor, 2012a and 2012b). Additionally, there is an ongoing Pentagon inspector general inquiry, initiated in 2011, in response to intense media scrutiny of the lab and series of stories that have been published documenting fraud, other misconduct, and error (Taylor, 2012b).

Contemporaneous to the resignation of Donald Mikko, the USACIL lab director Larry Chelko also resigned. He is also the target of numerous active complaints and figures prominently in the internal investigations mentioned. The Army, however, released a statement denying that Chelko's resignation was related to any past or present scandal (Taylor, 2012b).

History of misconduct

The USACIL has an established history of examiner fraud and misconduct (see Figure 11-9). One case in particular is that of Phillip K. Mills, whose data was used in the 2000–2010 study presented in this work. Mills joined the USACIL as a forensic analyst in 1995; in 2002 he failed hair analysis proficiency testing and was pulled from related casework—nine months after the failure; during 2003 and 2004, Mills was found to have cross-contaminated multiple forensic DNA tests and was suspended from DNA casework for almost a year; in April–May of 2005, new "problems" were discovered with Mills' DNA testing methods, including falsified control sample tests, and he was taken off casework entirely (USACIC, 2005). In November of 2005, upon being told that he was going to be fired, Mills resigned. In 2006, retesting of Mills' casework began; in 2008, after three years of investigation and retesting, problems were identified in 25% of Mills' cases at a retesting cost of approximately $1.4 million. Internal investigators ultimately concluded that Mills had routinely dry-labbed DNA cases by entering false control data, which would then be followed up by related sworn testimony in court that failed to acknowledge or admit his underlying falsifications of the tests alleged to have been performed (Taylor and Doyle, 2011a).

The fraud and ineptitude of Phillip Mills had an undeniable impact on casework performed during his active tenure, as reported in Doyle and Taylor (2011):

> Of 465 cases Mills handled from 1995 to 2005, many had problems.
> In a 2002 Navy case, for instance, Mills reported finding semen on a comforter. Four years later, another examiner couldn't find the semen.

FIGURE 11-9

Ironically, the logo for the USACIL actually includes the popular Disney character Mickey Mouse, dressed in the attire of Sherlock Holmes. This is a photo of that logo on the marble floor found at the entrance to the laboratory building.

That same year, Mills found semen on a condom swab in another Navy case. On retesting, no semen could be found. Other times, Mills failed to detect evidence. This raises the possibility that guilty parties escaped justice.

In a 2001 Navy case, for instance, Mills didn't examine a knife presented as evidence. Another lab technician was more thorough several years later, and found the DNA of someone who wasn't the suspect. In 388 cases, there was no evidence left to retest.

Ivor Luke was serving aboard the USS Port Royal in August 1998, when another sailor accused him of sexually assaulting her during a medical exam. Mills conducted the lab exam, reporting that he found bodily fluids on a bed sheet and bra. Luke was convicted in 1999 and sentenced to two years in prison and a bad-conduct discharge. It was only after Luke was released that military officials discovered what Andrew Effron, the chief judge of the U.S. Court of Appeals for the Armed Forces, called "Mills' history of cross-contamination, violation of laboratory protocols, incomplete and incompetent analysis as a DNA examiner and thoroughness issues as a serology examiner."

> Unfortunately for Luke, the Naval Criminal Investigative Service had destroyed the evidence in his case—following military policy at the time—before it could be examined again.
>
> "The government … destroyed the physical evidence at issue, thereby precluding the type of retesting that might have restored some level of confidence in the process," Effron noted. "The evidence of Mills' misconduct undermines the integrity of (Luke's) verdict."
>
> …
>
> Two former Navy lieutenants, Samuel Harris and Roger House, have been luckier, in a manner of speaking. The evidence from an unfounded 2002 sexual assault case involving the two officers was retained, allowing investigators to discover years later that Mills had gotten it wrong. Exonerated by the Navy judge advocate general, Harris and House are pursuing back pay and other remedies through the U.S. Court of Federal Claims.
>
> "I'm disgusted at what he's done to all these people," Harris said of Mills. Other people may have gotten off scot-free because of Mills' errors. Mills didn't find stains or DNA in 49 cases that he analyzed from 1995 to 2005. Because his examinations were "incomplete, rushed and not properly screened," according to a lab review, it's likely that he missed some evidence.

Ultimately, it is impossible to know just how many cases Mills harmed with his fraud; any estimate would be a conservative one. What is known is that the USACIL wanted to keep this scandal as quiet as possible, handling everything internally, and failing to notify attorneys on either side of the results of their investigation (Doyle and Taylor, 2011; Taylor and Doyle, 2011a). This is about as unscientific in nature as it gets, ignoring the fundamental requirements of truth-seeking and transparency.

Laboratory independence

The USACIL is part of the U.S. Army Criminal Investigation Division. As such, it is directly within the chain of command of, and subordinate to, a military law enforcement agency. In terms of its mission and day-to-day functions, and because of its chain of command, it has no clear operational independence from the military or law enforcement. However, because of its military alignment and the subordination of both employees and defendants to the Uniform Code of Military Justice (UCMJ), the USACIL also operates independent of the rest of the forensic science community—with its own set of values and related ethics.

Laboratory accreditation

As reported on the USACIL website (USACIL, 2012): "The USACIL has continuously been an accredited forensic laboratory since 1985, previously under the American Society of Crime Laboratory Directors/Laboratory Accreditation Board (ASCLD/LAB-Legacy Program). In February 2011, the USACIL was accredited by Forensic Quality Services–International (FQS-I), under the internationally recognized standards 'ISO/IEC 17025-2005 General Requirement of the Competence of Testing and Calibration Laboratories.'" This is consistent with the 2000–2010 study, which found a significant relationship between DNA fraud and laboratory accreditation. It also begs the question of how a lab such as this could retain any form of legitimate accreditation, further reinforcing the argument that such accreditations have no actual scientific value.

Isolated or systemic

The leadership of the USACIL has clearly been lacking over the past decade, in that there has been an ongoing failure to prevent, acknowledge, and report examiner misconduct and error; that is, unless compelled by external investigations and public pressure. Such tendencies have created an overall lab culture that is permissive of fraud and incompetence, while also openly hostile toward any effort intent on scientific reform. As with many law enforcement labs, the primary concern of the USACIL is preserving image over providing the substance of good science. Again, the problems at the USACIL are cultural, and a feature of the actions and attitudes of its leadership; they are also therefore systemic.

Potential impact of suggested reforms

This crime lab would enjoy significant benefit from a number of the reforms suggested by our study. First, it could stand to be separated from the military chain of command and its distinctive UCMJ subordinate law enforcement culture. This is a must for the culture of the lab to change; otherwise, the lab itself should be closed and forensic services outsourced to a private concern that would be required to operate with greater accountability and transparency. This because the problems at the lab are not found in the facilities—they are found in the attitudes and beliefs of many of those who work there.

Another suggested reform that would have helped is the transparency requirement. The leadership of this lab seemed to operate as though they were not accountable to anyone outside it. They knew what was happening inside their walls, and that fraud and error were corrupting casework. Where the leadership of the lab failed is in how they handled it: they hid the misconduct, denied it, and punished those who sought to bring it to light. They also destroyed any evidence that might help exonerate convicted defendants, and failed with respect to properly informing attorneys about what was going on.

Transparency is a didactic scientific value and a requirement for overall scientific integrity. Consequently, transparency and accountability to a civilian oversight committee, outside the existing chain of command and not populated by those in the military or law enforcement, would seem prudent—especially with respect to identifying, reporting, and managing misconduct. This kind of accountability would have required the criminal prosecution of all fraudsters and not just their quiet termination; in addition, it would have provided for a more certain place for all employees to levy complaints regarding management, as opposed to being forced to go to the media. This in turn would help to create a more scientific culture, where fraud can be reliably punished and whistleblowers are seen as dutiful stewards of science. As it stands, the opposite is true, reflecting military and law enforcement values, not scientific ones.

LAB CRISIS #12: DEPARTMENT OF PUBLIC HEALTH DRUG LAB, JAMAICA PLAIN, MA

A month before the state police were slated to take over the operation of the Massachusetts Department of Public Health (DPH) drug lab in July of 2012, as part of a new budgetary directive, they were given information about problems and inconsistencies related to the work of criminalist Annie Dookhan. Ms. Dookhan had resigned back in March during an internal DPH investigation of her casework. Once the state police were in charge, they began their own audit of the lab; based on their investigation, assembled by Assistant Attorney General John Vernor, Chief of the Criminal Bureau, on August 17, 2012,[8] Governor Deval Patrick ordered the state police to shut the lab down (see Figure 11-10).

FIGURE 11-10

The William Hinton State Laboratory Institute Building in Jamaica Plain, Massachusetts. This building still houses a number of state-funded research laboratories, and was home to the now-shuttered Department of Public Health drug lab.

---

[8]To be referenced hereafter as Vernor (2012).

Many in the forensic science community voiced their distress regarding this decision early on, claiming that it was too harsh and that problems were limited to a single "bad apple" or "rogue analyst"; that others employed at the lab should not be punished for her misconduct. Some spoke up out of loyalty for those they knew in the lab, unwilling to believe that things were actually that bad, involving professionals that they know and respect. Eventually, as more details became public and the investigative reports from the state police were released, those voices faded. Annie Dookhan was not just an analyst, she was the most productive analyst at the lab; she was in charge of quality control; and supervisors at the lab had known about but ignored her fraud for years.

During her interview with Det. Lt. Robert Irwin of the Massachusetts State Police in late August of 2012, Ms. Dookhan confessed to dry-labbing test results, forging the initials of her co-workers on reports and documentation, and intentionally mixing up drug samples to conceal her fraud (Vernor, 2012): "I messed up bad; it's my fault. I don't want the lab to get in trouble," she told him. What's worse, state police investigators learned that just about everyone in the lab knew what was going on, and that no real action was taken. In mid-October, they arrested Annie Dookhan at her home and charged her with obstruction of justice (see Figure 11-11).

As the result of the state police investigation, it was also eventually revealed that Ms. Dookhan had lied about having a master's degree in chemistry from the University of Massachusetts, as reported in Lavoie and Niedowski (2012):

> A Massachusetts chemist accused of faking drug test results, forging paperwork and mixing samples at a state police lab was arrested Friday in a scandal that has thrown thousands of criminal cases into doubt. Annie Dookhan, 34, was led to a state police cruiser at her

FIGURE 11-11
In mid-October of 2012, Annie Dookhan was arrested at her home in Franklin, Massachusetts.

home in Franklin, about 40 miles southwest of Boston. Dookhan's alleged mishandling of drug samples prompted the shutdown of the Hinton State Laboratory Institute in Boston last month and resulted in the resignation of three officials, including the state's public health commissioner.

State police say Dookhan tested more than 60,000 drug samples involving 34,000 defendants during her nine years at the lab. Defense lawyers and prosecutors are scrambling to figure out how to deal with the fallout. Since the lab closed, more than a dozen drug defendants are back on the street while their attorneys challenge the charges based on Dookhan's misconduct. Many more defendants are expected to be released. Authorities say more than 1,100 inmates are currently serving time in cases in which Dookhan was the primary or secondary chemist.

Dookhan could face more than 20 years in prison if convicted. She is charged with two counts of obstruction of justice, a felony count that carries up to 10 years in prison, and pretending to hold a degree for a college or university, a misdemeanor punishable by as much as a year in jail. She pleaded not guilty Friday afternoon and a judge set bail at $10,000. She was ordered to turn over her passport, submit to GPS monitoring, and not have contact with any former or current employees of the lab.... The two obstruction charges accuse Dookhan of lying about drug samples she analyzed at the lab in March 2011 for a Suffolk County case, and for testifying under oath in August 2010 that she had a master's degree in chemistry from the University of Massachusetts, Attorney General Martha Coakley said at a news conference Friday.

Further detail is provided in Murphy and Lavoie (2012), including the fact that supervisors knew she had been lying about her education since 2010, but did not put a definitive stop to it:[9]

In 2010, supervisors did a paperwork audit of her work but didn't retest any of her samples. They didn't find problems. Dookhan had to send a resume to prosecutors whenever she testified in criminal cases. In 2010, [criminalist supervisor Elizabeth] O'Brien caught

---

[9]It is worth noting that management's attitude of indifference toward phony credentials existed at the lab prior to Ms. Dookhan's hire: in 2003, it was revealed that Ralph Timperi, the Jamaica Plain lab's director for 15 years to that point, had claimed on his resume that he held "a doctorate, when the degree actually was bestowed by an online university that requires no dissertation and that grants diplomas in 72 hours for $499" (Kocian and Smith, 2003). Timperi apologized, and was not disciplined by the Department of Public Health or by the Harvard School of Public Health where he served as adjunct faculty. Mr. Timperi stayed on as the director of the Jamaica Plain lab until 2005. The author was not aware of this instance of forensic fraud until it resurfaced in connection with the current scandal, and therefore data from this examiner was not included in the 2000–2010 study.

Dookhan padding her resume by claiming she had a master's degree in chemistry from the University of Massachusetts. She took it off her resume but later put it back on, O'Brien told police.

In August, another Hinton chemist told investigators her own monthly sample testing volume dropped from about 400 to 200 after Melendez-Diaz, but talk around the lab was that Dookhan was testing 800 a month.

Another colleague wondered in a police interview whether Dookhan had a mental breakdown. Dookhan told investigators she was in the process of a long divorce, but there is no record of any divorce complaint filed at the Norfolk Probate and Family Court. She said she wanted to get her work done and never meant to hurt anyone.

After her March 2012 resignation, while facing an internal department probe, Dookhan told a fellow chemist she used to join for after-work drinks that she didn't want to get her in trouble, too. She told the woman not to call her anymore and to delete all her emails, text messages and records of their phone calls.

The state police investigation also uncovered the fact that Ms. Dookhan was communicating with prosecutors via phone and text messaging, to give them information outside the regular chain of command regarding her findings, and findings on other cases. This inappropriate contact has led to the resignation of at least one prosecutor, Norfolk County Assistant District Attorney George Papachristos, as reported in Estes and Allen (2012):

> The chemist at the center of the state drug lab scandal carried on an unauthorized, sometimes personal, e-mail and phone correspondence with a prosecutor whose drug evidence she analyzed, a violation of office protocol that may give defense attorneys even more ammunition to throw out drug convictions involving Annie Dookhan's work.
>
> Though State Police have concluded that Dookhan was not romantically involved with Norfolk Assistant District Attorney George Papachristos, Dookhan's husband was suspicious. At one point, Dookhan's husband tried repeatedly to contact a startled Papachristos, according to someone involved in the investigation, apparently out of concern that the two were having an affair.
>
> The tone in the dozens of e-mails between the two was sometimes quite familiar, according to the person who has read them. Dookhan opened up about her life, confiding in one e-mail that she was unhappy in her marriage, though it is unclear from a printout of the e-mails whether she sent it. On another occasion, Papachristos reminded her that their relationship was strictly "professional" in response to something Dookhan wrote.

The correspondence, which dates back to 2009, was unusual enough that State Police investigating drug lab misconduct recently interviewed Papachristos about their relationship. Lab protocol calls for prosecutors to communicate through lab supervisors to avoid any question about the integrity of drug evidence, something Dookhan has acknowledged she should have done.

The American Civil Liberties Union has asked Attorney General Martha Coakley and the district attorneys to agree to throw out all drug cases "involving a police officer or prosecutor who, at any time, communicated directly with Annie Dookhan."

"Chemists aren't supposed to be doing favors on a case-by-case basis for a particular police officer or prosecutor," said Matthew R. Segal, legal director of the ACLU Foundation of Massachusetts. "That's a good rule, no matter who the chemist is." Dookhan wrote e-mails and spoke on the phone with other prosecutors, the person involved with the investigation said, but the correspondence with Papachristos stood out.

Papachristos declined to answer questions, but his boss, Norfolk District Attorney Michael W. Morrissey, said Papachristos told him that he and Dookhan had no personal relationship.

"George never socially met her or had a relationship with her," said Morrissey, who took office in 2011. "He met her once in court, and she never testified in any of his cases." However, Morrissey admitted that he has seen only a few e-mails, and he has refused repeated efforts by investigators to provide him with copies of the rest of the correspondence, because they are "the subject of an ongoing investigation" by Coakley and "I don't want to interfere." Several state officials and prosecutors expressed confusion over Morrissey's refusal to accept the e-mails, noting that he should know if one of his subordinates had an inappropriate relationship that could jeopardize cases in his office....

Dookhan analyzed drug evidence for numerous cases in Norfolk Superior Court in Dedham where Papachristos was assigned, including an Oxycodone-dealing conviction obtained by Papachristos that was one of the first to be overturned after allegations against Dookhan became public.

It is unclear exactly how frequently Dookhan analyzed evidence for Papachristos, but Papachristos refers to several different cases in his e-mails.... In the e-mails, Dookhan sent Papachristos chatty messages punctuated by exclamation points, according to the person involved in the investigation who has read the messages. There is no suggestion in the correspondence that he asked her to alter results or provide other favors, but Dookhan had a reputation in the lab for being especially close to Norfolk prosecutors.

Gloria Phillips, an evidence officer, told police that Dookhan "always wanted Norfolk County" cases to analyze. Dookhan appeared to be doing a favor for Norfolk law enforcement officials when she was caught in June 2011 taking evidence from 60 Norfolk drug cases out of a storage area without authorization. Her former supervisor, Elizabeth O'Brien, told State Police Dookhan had taken cases out of order and did not sign them out as required.

Dookhan's co-workers told State Police that she was going through a "long divorce" from her husband, though the two still live together in Franklin. O'Brien added that Dookhan was "going through some personal problems."

In summer 2009, Papachristos told Dookhan with some alarm that her husband had tried to contact him repeatedly, though they did not speak. "I have to tell my bosses," Papachristos told Dookhan. "Tell him not to call again."...

Dookhan and Papachristos continued to correspond for two years after that, including for five months after June 2011 when Dookhan's supervisors say they removed her from doing drug analysis because of questions about her handling of evidence. At one point, Papachristos asks Dookhan how she likes her "promotion," apparently unaware that she has been removed from drug analysis because of questions about her integrity. Later in the year, Dookhan asked Papachristos about his Thanksgiving celebration. Dookhan stressed that she worked alone and that no prosecutors urged her to break the rules.

Nonetheless, Segal said Dookhan's direct contact with prosecutors, without following proper protocol, should be grounds for dismissal of cases, suggesting the prosecutors knew that she would do what they wanted—give them the evidence they needed for drug convictions—without even asking.

The fallout from the scandal is, as of this writing, as follows: Annie Dookhan has been arrested and criminally charged with two counts of obstruction of justice (no trial date set); Linda Han, the Director of Bureau of Lab Sciences, has resigned; Julie Nassif, the Director of the Analytic Chemistry Division, was fired; Department of Public Health Commissioner John Auerbach has resigned; and Norfolk County ADA George Papachristos has resigned. In terms of cases, tens of thousands of Dookhan's results are under review;[10] hundreds have been set aside or overturned; and numerous criminals have been released, at least one of which has already been re-arrested (Randall, 2012).

---

[10]Approximately 60,000 cases, for which Governor Patrick has requested $30 million to cover initial investigative and retesting costs (Salsberg, 2012).

More revelations are sure to come, however, for two reasons: first, Ms. Dookhan's criminal trial is imminent, and unless she pleads out, a host of laboratory personnel will be placed under oath to reveal what they knew and when, which could result in further criminal charges and possibly even arrests; second, the same consequences may arise out of the "independent" investigation into the lab that is to be conducted by Massachusetts Inspector General Glenn Cunha (Ellement, 2012). Until either of these things happens, it will not be possible to completely understand just how systemic and far reaching this scandal is, how many others are involved, and how many cases it will ultimately overturn.

What is known for certain is that the problems in this lab were systemic; they arose from negligent leadership and management; they could have been avoided with a resume check that resulted in termination or a zero tolerance policy toward fraud; and they were exacerbated by an inappropriate relationship between Annie Dookhan, a forensic scientist, and George Papachristos, a prosecutor. These facts and circumstances comport with the findings and recommendations of the present research.

SUMMARY

It is important to bear in mind that the crime lab crises discussed in this chapter have only come to light in the past few years—for the most part. They are therefore only a fraction of the scandals that have occurred since 2000. However, the facts and circumstances from those related to fraud are representative of the data collected in relation to the 100+ forensic examiners, and their many employers, that were analyzed during the 2000–2010 research project.

Additionally, a number of major lab scandals that began during that data collection interval actually spilled over into 2011–2012; this includes continued revelations of forensic fraud, error, and wrongful convictions associated with the closure of the Nassau County crime lab (Det. Lt. James Granelle; see Crowley, 2011); and also with the closure of the North Carolina State Bureau of Investigation crime lab's Bloodstain Unit (SBI Bloodstain Analysts Duane Deaver and Gerald Thomas; see Locke and Neff, 2011). These examiners, and the circumstances of their misconduct, were included in the 2000–2010 data set. However, that data reflected only what was publicly known by the end of 2010; new information about these examiners and their cases is continuously being revealed through litigation (e.g., case impact data), with no end in sight.

In any case, this author observes that the problem of forensic fraud and error, which are clearly joined at numerous points, has actually gotten worse since the closure of data collection efforts in 2010. Not just a function of cultural alignment with law enforcement (though this is a significant issue), these problems are also clearly associated with poor or negligent leadership; decreased budgets;

ignorance of science and scientific integrity; lack of transparency and account-ability; and institutional tendencies toward sweeping things under the rug. The forensic science community has a responsibility to address these issues, and to ensure that good science is being practiced by those who are being properly hired, adequately trained and retained, and fully supported in their objective examination efforts. Unfortunately, the current trend is in the opposite direc-tion, which does not bode well for the quality of future forensic scientists, their work environments, and the integrity of their resultant casework.

References

Adams, D., Pimple, K., 2005. Research Misconduct and Crime Lessons from Criminal Science on Preventing Misconduct and Promoting Integrity. Accountability in Research: Policies and Quality Assurance 12 (3), 225–240.

Aguilera, R., Vadera, A., 2008. The Dark Side of Authority: Antecedents, Mechanisms, and Outcomes of Organizational Corruption. Journal of Business Ethics 77, 431–449.

Aiken, L., West, S., 1991. Multiple Regression: Testing and Interpreting Interactions. Sage Publications, Thousand Oaks, CA.

Ake v. Oklahoma, 1985. United States Supreme Court (470 U.S. 68), February 26.

Akers, R., 2000. Criminological Theories: Introduction, Evaluation, and Application, third ed. Roxbury Publishing Company, Los Angeles.

Akers, R., Matsueda, R., 1989. Donald R. Cressey: An Intellectual Portrait of a Criminologist. Sociological Inquiry 59 (4), 423–438, October.

Albrecht, W.S., Albrecht, C.O., 2003. Fraud Examination and Prevention. South-Western Educational Publishing, Mason, OH.

Albrecht, W.S., Albrecht, C.O., Albrecht, C.C., Zimbelman, M.F., 2011. Fraud Examination, fourth ed. South-Western, Cengage Learning, Mason, OH.

Alesia, M., Evans, T., 2011a. Critics: Potential problems at toxicology lab weren't disclosed. Indystar.com, March 31; http://www.indystar.com/apps/pbcs.dll/article?AID=2011103310394.

Alesia, M., Evans, T., 2011b. Errors found in Indiana state lab toxicology tests. Indystar.com, February 3; http://www.indystar.com/article/20110203/NEWS14/102030409/Errors-found-Indiana-state-lab-toxicology-tests.

Alesia, M., Evans, T., 2011c. Advisory panel halts audit of state toxicology lab. Indystar.com, July 19; http://www.indystar.com/article/20110720/NEWS14/107200325/Advisory-panel-halts-audit-state-toxicology-lab.

American Law Institute, 1965. Restatement of Torts, Second. Vol. 2. American Law Institute, St. Paul, MN.

Anderson, M., Martinson, B., De Vries, R., 2007. Normative Dissonance in Science: Results from a National Survey of U.S. Scientists. Journal of Empirical Research in Human Research Ethics 2 (4), 3–14.

ASCLD, 2011. American Society of Crime Lab Directors. http://www.ascld.org.

ASCLD/LAB, 2011. American Society of Crime Lab Directors/Laboratory Accreditation Board. http://www.ascld-lab.org/.

Aseltine, P., 2011. Captain of human services police charged with falsifying records concerning vacation time & firearms qualification. Press Release, State of New Jersey, Office of the Attorney General, May 17; http://www.nj.gov/oag/newsreleases11/pr20110517b.html.

Babbage, C., 1830. Reflections on the Decline of Science in England, and on Some of Its Causes. B. Fellowes Publisher, London, downloaded March 8, 2010; http://www.gutenberg.org/files/1216/1216.txt.

Balint, E., 2012a. Crime lab worker fired over reports. Canton Republic, May 23; http://www.cantonrep.com/news/x40860394/Crime-lab-worker-fired-over-reports.

Balint, E., 2012b. Crime-lab worker reinstated. Canton Republic, October 24; http://www.cantonrep.com/news/x1757118881/Crime-lab-worker-reinstated.

Baran, M., 2012. Calls for crime lab to shut down amid more evidence doubts. Minnesota Public Radio, September 20.

Barkacs, L., Browne, M., Williamson, C., 2002. The Perspectival Nature of Expert Testimony in the United States, England, Korea, and France. Connecticut Journal of International Law 18, 55–102, Fall.

Barton, G., 2011. Officers' criminal records are tough to track. Milwaukee Journal-Sentinel, October 29.

Batiste, J., 2008. Logan resigns as head of WSP Forensic Laboratory Bureau. Washington State Patrol Media Release, Office of Chief John R. Batiste, February 14.

Begin, B., 2010. Policy on expert witnesses lacking. San Francisco Examiner, April 15; http://www.sfexaminer.com/local/policy-expert-witnesses-lacking.

Benoit, J., Dubra, J., 2004. Why Do Good Cops Defend Bad Cops? International Economic Review 45 (3), 787–809.

Benson, B., 1988. An Institutional Explanation for Corruption of Criminal Justice Officials. Cato Journal 8 (1), 139–163.

Benson, R., 2001. Changing Police Culture: The Sine Qua Non of Reform. Loyola of Los Angeles Law Review 34, 681–690, January.

Berkow, M., 2004. Homeland Security: The Internal Terrorists. Police Chief 71 (6), June; http://www.policechiefmagazine.org/magazine/index.cfm?fuseaction=display_arch&article_id=319&issue_id=62004.

Bernhard, A., 2004. Justice Still Fails: A Review of Recent Efforts to Compensate Individuals Who Have Been Unjustly Convicted and Later Exonerated. Drake Law Review 52, 703–738, Summer.

Black, H.C., 1990. Black's Law Dictionary, sixth ed. West Group, St. Paul, MN.

Bloombaum, M., 1970. Doing Smallest Space Analysis. Journal of Conflict Resolution 14 (3), 409–416.

Bogner, A., Menz, W., 2006. Science Crime: The Korean Cloning Scandal and the Role of Ethics. Science and Public Policy 33 (8), 601–612.

Bohrer, B., 2002. Former crime-lab chief's cases under review: DNA evidence freed a man after 15 years. Philadelphia Inquirer, December 22.

Bolton, R., Hand, J., 2002. Statistical Fraud Detection: A Review. Statistical Science 17 (3), 235–255.

Bopp, W., Schultz, D., 1972. Principles of American Law Enforcement and Criminal Justice. Charles C. Thomas, Springfield, IL.

Bosch, X., Titus, S., 2009. Cultural Challenges and Their Effect on International Research Integrity. Lancet 373 (9664), 610–612.

Botkin, D., 2011. Absolute certainty is not scientific. Wall Street Journal, December 2; http://online.wsj.com/article/SB10001424052970204630904577058111041127168.html.

Botluk, D., 2007. The National Clearinghouse for Science, Technology and the Law: Supporting the Role of Forensic Science in the Administration of Justice. Stetson Law Review 36 (3), 609–620.

Boyd, D., 2011. Fort Worth detective fired, accused of falsifying time sheets. Ft. Worth Star-Telegram, September 30.

Bradford, L., 2007. The Genesis of the CAC [California Association of Criminalists]. CAC News, 3rd Quarter; p. 5 (Originally presented at the 100th Semiannual Seminar of the CAC, Huntington Beach, Fall 2002).

Brady v. Maryland, 1963. U.S. Supreme Court (373 U.S. 83).

Branham, V., Kutash, S., 1949. Encyclopedia of Criminology. Philosophical Library, New York.

Brennan, A., Rostow, C., Davis, R., Hill, B., 2009. An Investigation of Biographical Information as a Predictor of Employment Termination among Law Enforcement Officers. Journal of Police and Criminal Psychology 24, 108–112.

Brookfield, S., 1987. Developing Critical Thinkers. Jossey-Bass, San Francisco.

Brown, A., Hepler, L., 2005. Comparison of Consumer Fraud Statutes Across the Fifty States. Federation of Defense and Corporate Counsel Quarterly 55 (3), 263–308.

Brytting, T., Minogue, R., Morino, V., 2011. The Anatomy of Fraud and Corruption: Organizational Causes and Remedies. Gower, Surrey, UK.

Budowle, B., 2007. Forensic Science: Issues and Direction. Presentation to the National Academy of Sciences, Committee on Identifying the Needs of the Forensic Science Community, June 5; http://sites.nationalacademies.org/PGA/stl/forensic_science/.

Burack, A., 2011. DUI convictions at risk following SFPD revelations. San Francisco Examiner, March 5.

Burack, A., 2012. Former SF crime lab technician Debbie Madden to testify in murder trial. San Francisco Examiner, April 1.

Burns, G., 2012a. Prosecutor Worthy: Testing of 11,303 rape kits rescued from Detroit Crime Lab a long way off. Michigan Live (MLive.com), September 25.

Burns, G., 2012b. Ex-Detroit police homicide leader William Rice in court on criminal enterprise and drug charges. Michigan Live (MLive.com), November 20.

CAC, 2011. Criminalistics Information. California Association of Criminalists; website: http://www.cacnews.org/membership/criminalistics.shtml.

Caldero, M., Crank, J., 2004. Police Ethics: The Corruption of Noble Cause. Anderson, Cincinnati, OH.

Cancino, J., Enriquez, R., 2004. A qualitative analysis of officer peer retaliation. Policing: An International Journal of Police Strategies and Management 27 (3), 320–340.

Capers, B., 2008. Crime, Legitimacy, and Testilying. Indiana Law Journal 83, 835–880, Summer.

Cassidy, J., 2009. Police officer accused of misusing database. Orange County Register, August 14.

Castaneda, R., 2011. Ex-Montgomery officer accused of helping drug ring admits unlawful computer checks. Washington Post, April 27.

Castelle, G., 1999. Lab Fraud: Lessons Learned from the Fred Zain Affair. Champion, 52–57, May; pp. 12–16.

Catano, V., Turk, J., 2007. Fraud and Misconduct in Scientific Research: A Definition and Procedures for Investigation. Medicine and Law 26, 465–476.

CCLRTF, 2009. An Examination of Forensic Science in California. State of California, Office of the Attorney General, California Crime Laboratory Review Task Force, Sacramento, CA, November; http://ag.ca.gov/publications/crime_labs_report.pdf.

Chamberlain v. Mantello, 1997. United States District Court, N.D. New York, No. 95-CV-1050, 954 F. Supp. 499.

Chan, S., 1994. Scores of convictions reviewed as chemist faces perjury accusations forensics. Los Angeles Times, August 21.

Chappell, A., Piquero, A., 2004. Applying Social Learning Theory to Police Misconduct. Deviant Behavior 25, 89–108.

Chemerinsky, E., 2005. An Independent Analysis of the Los Angeles Police Department's Board of Inquiry Report on the Rampart Scandal. Loyola of Los Angeles Law Review 34, 545–657.

Chin, G., Wells, S., 1998. The "Blue Wall of Silence" as Evidence of Bias and Motive to Lie: A New Approach to Police Perjury. University of Pittsburgh Law Review 59, 233–299, Winter.

Chin, R., Hanners, D., 2012. St. Paul: Consultants to review city's police crime lab. Pioneer Press, September 6; http://www.twincities.com/localnews/ci_21484904/st-paul-crime-lab-city-hires-2-consultants.

Chisum, W.J., Turvey, B., 2006. Crime Reconstruction. Elsevier Science, Boston.

Chisum, W.J., Turvey, B., 2011. Crime Reconstruction, second ed. Elsevier Science, San Diego.

CIA, 2011. The World Factbook Online. The Central Intelligence Agency, Langley, VA, ISSN 1553–8133, October 27; https://www.cia.gov/library/publications/the-world-factbook/geos/us.html.

Clarke, R., Felson, M., 2004. Routine Activity and Rational Choice: Vol. 5 (Advances in Criminological Theory). Transaction Publishers, Piscataway, NJ.

Clarke, R., Newman, G., Shoham, S., 1997. Rational Choice and Situational Crime Prevention: Theoretical Foundations. Dartmouth Publishing Co., Boston.

Clayton, M., 2003. Degree duplicity: Fake diplomas are easy to buy online, but colleges are becoming more wary. Christian Science Monitor, June 10.

Cloud, M., 1996. Judges, "Testilying," and The Constitution. Southern California Law Review 69, 1341–1387, May.

Coenen, T., 2008. Essentials of Corporate Fraud. John Wiley & Sons, Hoboken, NJ.

Cohen, J., Cohen, P., West, S.G., Aiken, L.S., 2003. Applied Multiple Regression/Correlation Analysis for the Behavioral Sciences, third ed. Lawrence Erlbaum Associates, Mahwah, NJ.

Cohen, L., Felson, M., 1979. Social Change and Crime Trends: A Routine Activities Approach. American Sociological Review 44 (August), 588–607.

Cole, S., 2005. More than Zero: Accounting for Error in Latent Fingerprint Identification. Journal of Criminal Law and Criminology 95 (3), 985–1078.

Cole, S., 2006. The Prevalence and Potential Causes of Wrongful Conviction by Fingerprint Evidence. Golden Gate University Law Review 37, 39–105, Fall.

Cole, S., 2010. Acculturating Forensic Science: What Is "Scientific Culture," and How Can Forensic Science Adopt It? Fordham Urban Law Journal 38 (2), 435–472.

Collins, J., Jarvis, J., 2007. Blame the judicial system for wrongful convictions, not crime laboratories. Crime Lab Report, June 1; http://www.crimelabreport.com/our_analysis/dontblame.htm.

Colvin, M., Cullen, F., Vander Ven, T., 2002. Coercion, Social Support, and Crime: An Emerging Theoretical Consensus. Criminology 40, 19–42.

Connors, E., Lundregan, T., Miller, N., McEwen, T., 1996. Convicted by Juries, Exonerated by Science: Case Studies in the Use of DNA Evidence to Establish Innocence after Trial. National Institute of Justice, Washington, DC, NCJ 161258, June.

Conway, M., 2003a. 2 lab owners arrested, said to be giving clean results in custody cases. Modesto Bee, August 30; p. A1.

Conway, M., 2003b. Merced CPS Head Reassigned: Social Services Director Takes Over During Drug-Testing Probe. Modesto Bee, September 3; p. B2.

Cooley, C.M., 2004. Reforming the Forensic Community to Avert the Ultimate Injustice. Stanford Law and Policy Review 15, 381–446.

Cooley, C.M., 2006. Reconstructionists in a Post-Daubert and Post-DNA Courtroom. In: Chisum, W.J., Turvey, B. (Eds.), Crime Reconstruction. Elsevier Science, Boston.

Cooley, C.M., 2007a. The CSI Effect: Its Impact and Potential Concerns. New England Law Review 41, 471–501, Spring.

Cooley, C.M., 2007b. Forensic Science and Capital Punishment Reform: An "Intellectually Honest" Assessment. George Mason University Civil Rights Law Journal 17, 300–422, Spring.

Cooley, C.M., 2011. Crime Reconstruction: Expert Testimony and the Law. In: Chisum, W.J., Turvey, B. (Eds.), Crime Reconstruction, second ed. Elsevier Science, San Diego.

Cooley, C.M., Oberfield, G., 2007. Increasing Forensic Evidence's Reliability and Minimizing Wrongful Convictions: Applying Daubert Isn't the Only Problem. Tulsa Law Review 43, 285–380.

Cooley, C.M., Turvey, B.E., 2011. Observer Effects and Examiner Bias: Psychological Influences on the Forensic Examiner. In: Chisum, W.J., Turvey, B. (Eds.), Crime Reconstruction, second ed. Elsevier Science, San Diego.

Cooper, C., 2009a. Yes Virginia, There Is a Police Code of Silence: Prosecuting Police Officers and the Police Subculture. Criminal Law Bulletin 45 (2), 4–20.

Cooper, S., 2009b. Former DA Bob Macy, ex-forensic chemist Joyce Gilchrist settle case. Oklahoma Gazette, June 17; http://truthinjustice.org/gilchrist/macy-gilchrist.htm.

Crank, J., Flaherty, D., Giacomazzi, A., 2007. The noble cause: An empirical assessment. Journal of Criminal Justice 35, 103–116.

Crawford v. Metro, Government of Nashville, et al., 2009. U.S. Supreme Court, 555 U.S. 271, 129 S. Ct 846, 172 L. Ed. 2d 650.

Cressey, D., 1952. Application and Verification of the Differential Association Theory. Journal of Criminal Law, Criminology, and Police Science 43, 43–52.

Cressey, D., 1953/1973. Other People's Money, reprint edition. Wadsworth, Belmont, CA.

Cressey, D., Sutherland, E., Luckenbill, D., 1992. Principles of Criminology, eleventh ed. Altamira Press, Lanham, MD.

Crosby, P., 2008. Army handwriting expert sentenced for embezzlement. Press Release, Department of Justice, January 28; www.usdoj.gov/usao/gan.

Crowley, G., Wilson, P., 2007. Who Killed Leanne Holland? New Holland, Chatswood, NSW.

Crowley, K., 2011. LI Lab Padlocked: Tainted Crime Results. New York Post, February 19.

Curtis, K., Bowman, B., 2007. Memo to the Washington State Forensic Investigations Council. Washington Association of Criminal Defense Lawyers, October 15.

Davidow, J., Teichroeb, R., 2003. Cops who abuse their wives rarely pay the price. Seattle Post-Intelligencer, July 23.

DeForest, P., 2005. Crime Scene Investigation. In: Sullivan, L.E., Rosen, M.S. (Eds.), Encyclopedia of Law Enforcement. Vol. 1. Sage, Thousand Oaks, CA, pp. 111–116.

DeForest, P., Gaennslen, R., Lee, H., 1983. Forensic Science: An Introduction to Criminalistics. McGraw-Hill, New York.

De La Cruz, M., 2003. Narcotic testing results bogus. Merced Sun-Star, August 30.

Denson, B., 2012. Finger-pointing at Oregon Police handwriting unit. Oregonian, November 18.

De Vries, R., Anderson, M., Martinson, B., 2006. Normal Misbehavior: Scientists Talk about the Ethics of Research. Journal of Empirical Research on Human Research Ethics 1 (1), 43–50.

Dewey, J., 1995. Science as Subject-Matter and as Method. Science and Education 4, 391–398, Reprint of Dewey, J. (1909) Science as Subject-Matter and as Method. Science 31 (787), 121–127.

Diehl, C., 2011. Open Meetings and Closed Mouths: Elected Officials' Free Speech Rights after Garcetti v. Ceballos. Case Western Reserve Law Review 61 (2), 551–602.

DHSS, 2005. Public Health Service Policies on Research Misconduct. Federal Register, Department of Health and Human Services 70 (94), 28369–28400.

DiFonzo, J.H., 2005. The Crimes of Crime Labs. Hofstra Law Review 34 (1), 1–11.

DiFonzo, J.H., Stern, R.C., 2007. Devil in a White Coat: The Temptation of Forensic Evidence in the Age of CSI. New England Law Review 41, 504–532, Spring.

Dillon, D., 1972. Foreword. In: O'Hara, C., Osterburg, J. (Ed.), Criminalistics: The Application of Physical Sciences to the Detection of Crime, Second Printing. Indiana University Press, Bloomington, IN.

Donegan, J., Danon, M., 2008. Strain, Differential Association, and Coercion: Insights from the Criminology Literature on Causes of Accountant's Misconduct. Accounting and the Public Interest 8 (1), 1–20.

Dorey, E., 2010. Facing Up to Fraud. Chemistry and Industry 25, 16–17, January.

Dorfman, D., 1999. Proving the Lie: Litigating Police Credibility. American Journal of Criminal Law 26, 455–503.

Dorminey, J., Fleming, A., Kranacher, M., Riley, R., 2010. Enhancing Deterrence of Economic Crimes. CPA Journal, 17–23, July.

Dougherty v. Haag, et al., 2008. Court of Appeals. State of California, Fourth Appellate District, Division Three, G038335 (Super. Ct. No. 05CC06993), filed July 28.

Doyle, M., Taylor, M., 2011. Crime-lab worker's errors cast doubt on military verdicts. McClatchy Newspapers, March 20.

Drake v. Portuondo, 2006. United States District Court. Western District of New York, 99–CV-0681E (Sr), Memorandum and Order, March 16.

Dror, I., Charlton, D., Peron, A., 2006. Contextual Information Renders Experts Vulnerable to Making Erroneous Identifications. Forensic Science International 156, 74–76.

Drumwright, S., 2011. Feds dish out drug charges to former San Francisco crime lab tech. San Francisco Examiner, December 1.

Durose, M., 2008. Census of Publicly Funded Forensic Crime Laboratories, 2005. Office of Justice Programs, Bureau of Justice Statistics, NCJ 222181, July.

Eberly, T., 2008. One-third of Ga. officer recruits have police records. Atlanta Journal-Constitution, October 12.

Edwards, H., Gotsonis, C., 2009. Strengthening Forensic Science in the United States: A Path Forward. National Academies Press, Washington, DC.

Elgin, C., 2011. Science, Ethics and Education. Theory and Research in Education 9 (3), 251–263.

Elias, P., 2012. SF mayor suspends sheriff, seeks removal. San Jose Mercury News, March 21.

Ellement, J., 2012. Governor Deval Patrick taps Inspector General Glenn Cunha to investigate closed drug lab. Boston Globe, November 5.

Elrick, M., 2001. Cops tap database to harass, intimidate: Misuse among police frequent, say some, but punishments rare. Detroit Free Press, July 31.

Emily, J., 2009. Fourth former Dallas officer in fake drug scandal gets one-year probation. Dallas Morning News, March 31.

Eskenazi, J., 2011. Can San Francisco tap into Deborah Madden's pension? San Francisco Weekly, January 4.

Estes, A., Allen, S., 2012. Chemist often called, wrote to prosecutor. Boston Globe, October 17.

Fanelli, D., 2009. How Many Scientists Fabricate or Falsify Research? A Systematic Review and Meta-analysis of Survey Data. Public Library of Science ONE 4 (5), 1–11.

FBI, 2004. Uniform Crime Reporting Handbook. Uniform Crime Reporting Program, Federal Bureau of Investigation, Clarksburg, WV; http://www.fbi.gov/about-us/cjis/ucr/additional-ucr-publications/ucr_handbook.pdf.

FBI, 2006. Crime in the United States–2005. Department of Justice, Federal Bureau of Investigation, Washington, DC, Table 29, September; http://www2.fbi.gov/ucr/05cius/data/table_29.html.

FBI, 2007. Crime in the United States–2006. Department of Justice, Federal Bureau of Investigation, Washington, DC, Table 29, September; http://www2.fbi.gov/ucr/cius2006/data/table_29.html.

FBI, 2008. Crime in the United States–2007. Department of Justice, Federal Bureau of Investigation, Washington, DC, Table 29, September; http://www2.fbi.gov/ucr/cius2007/data/table_29.html.

FBI, 2009a. Crime in the United States–2008. Department of Justice, Federal Bureau of Investigation, Washington, DC, Table 29, September; http://www2.fbi.gov/ucr/cius2008/data/table_29.html.

FBI, 2009b. Uniform Crime Reporting Program Frequently Asked Questions. Department of Justice, Federal Bureau of Investigation, Washington, DC, April; http://www.fbi.gov/about-us/cjis/ucr/frequently-asked-questions/ucr_faqs08.pdf.

FBI, 2010. Crime in the United States–2009. Department of Justice, Federal Bureau of Investigation, Washington, DC, Table 29, September; http://www2.fbi.gov/ucr/cius2009/data/table_29.html.

FBI, 2011. Crime in the United States–2010. Department of Justice, Federal Bureau of Investigation, Washington, DC, Table 29, September; http://www.fbi.gov/about-us/cjis/ucr/crime-in-the-u.s/2010/crime-in-the-u.s.-2010/tables/10tbl29.xls.

FBI, 2012. Laboratory Services, U.S. Department of Justice, Federal Bureau of Investigation; http://www.fbi.gov/about-us/lab.

Feinberg, S., 2007. The Analysis of Cross-Classified Categorical Data, second ed. Springer, New York.

Feynman, R., 2001. The Character of Physical Law. MIT Press, Cambridge, MA.

Findley, K., 2008. Innocents at Risk: Adversary Imbalance, Forensic Science, and the Search for Truth. Seton Hall Law Review 38, 893–973.

Fitch, B., 2011. Focus on Ethics: Rethinking Ethics in Law Enforcement. FBI Law Enforcement Bulletin, October.

Fitzgerald, F., 1998a. Witness faces charges of lying: Officials uncover false credentials. Sun-Sentinel, March 5.

Fitzgerald, F., 1998b. Phony "expert" jailed for 3 years. Sun-Sentinel, December 1.

Flake, N., 2012. Lab errors could affect 1,281 defendants. Your Houston News, May 2; http://www.yourhoustonnews.com/courier/news/lab-errors-could-affect-defendants/article_1daf2822-1a98-5e51-8e92-88c9c7a87c35.html.

Fox, H., 2011. Full Assessment Report, El Paso Police Department, Crime Laboratory El Paso, Texas. ASCLD/LAB-International, June 27; http://www.elpasotexas.gov/police/_documents/FullAssessmentReport.pdf.

Franzen, M., Rödder, S., Weingart, P., 2007. Fraud: Causes and Culprits as Perceived by Science and the Media. Institutional Changes, Rather than Individual Motivation, Encourage Misconduct. EMBO Reports 8 (1), 3–7.

Frye v. United States, 1923. U.S. Supreme Court, 293 F. 1013 (D.C. Cir. 1923).

Garcetti, et al., v. Ceballos, 2006. Supreme Court of the United States. No. 04-473, May 30.

Garcia, V., 2005. Constructing the "Other" within Police Culture: An Analysis of a Deviant Unit within the Police Organization. Police Practice and Research 6 (1), 65–80.

Gardenier, J., 2011. Data Integrity Is Earned, Not Given. Office of Research Integrity Newsletter 19 (3), 3.

Garrett, B., 2008. Judging Innocence. Columbia Law Review 108, 55–142, January.

Garrett, B., Neufeld, P., 2009. Invalid Forensic Science Testimony and Wrongful Convictions. Virginia Law Review 95 (1), 1–97.

Geggie, D., 2001. A Survey of Newly Appointed Consultants' Attitudes Towards Research Fraud. Journal of Medical Ethics 27, 344–346.

George, P., 2012. Panel advises Texas Forensic Science Commission to clear crime lab of misconduct. Austin-American Statesman, July 26; http://www.statesman.com/news/news/local/panel-advises-texas-forensic-science-commission-to/nRqQL/.

Geranios, N., 2003. State Patrol report urges firing of forensic scientist. Associated Press, September 10.

Giannelli, P., 1997. The Abuse of Scientific Evidence in Criminal Cases: The Need for Independent Crime Laboratories. Virginia Journal of Social Policy and Law 4, 439–470.

Giannelli, P., 2001. False Credentials. Criminal Justice 16, 40–64, Fall.

Giannelli, P., 2002. Fabricated Reports. Criminal Justice 16, 49–50, Winter.

Giannelli, P., 2003. The Supreme Court's "Criminal" Daubert Cases. Seton Hall Law Review 33 (4), 1071–1111.

Giannelli, P., 2007. Wrongful Convictions and Forensic Science: The Need to Regulate Crime Labs. North Carolina Law Review 86, 163–236.

Giannelli, P., 2010. Independent Crime Laboratories: The Problem of Motivational and Cognitive Bias. Utah Law Review 2, 247–266.

Giannelli, P., McMunigal, K., 2007. Prosecutors, Ethics, and Expert Witnesses. Fordham Law Review 76, 1493–1537, December.

Gibbens, W., 2010. Investigation Results—Critical Issues within the APD DNA Laboratory. Memorandum from the Manager of the Austin Police Department Crime Laboratory to Sean Mannix, Assistant Chief of Police and Edward Harris, Jr., Chief of Field Operations, March 22.

Giddens, A., 1991. Introduction to Sociology. W.W. Norton and Company, New York.

Gillispie, M., 2004. Experts fault job done by police lab tech, boss. Cleveland Plain Dealer, June 16; p. A1.

Goldman, R.L., 2003. State Revocation of Law Enforcement Officers' Licenses and Federal Criminal Prosecution: An Opportunity for Cooperative Federalism. Saint Louis University Public Law Review, XXII (1), 121–150.

Goldman, R.L., Puro, S., 1987. Decertification of Police: An Alternative to Traditional Remedies for Police Misconduct. Hastings Constitutional Law Quarterly 15, 45–79, Fall.

Goldman, R.L., Puro, S., 2001. Revocation of Police Officer Certification. Saint Louis University Law Journal 45 (2), 541–579.

Gonsowski, R., 2011. Full Assessment Report Connecticut Department of Public Safety Division of Scientific Services Forensic Science Laboratory. ASCLD/LAB-International, October 5; http://www.ct.gov/opm/lib/opm/cjppd/cjabout/crimelabworkinggroup/agendas/20111014_full_assessment_report.pdf.

Goode, W., 1960. A Theory of Role Strain. American Sociological Review 25 (4), 483–496.

Gottfried, M., 2012. St. Paul police crime lab: Sergeant in charge reassigned. Pioneer Press, August 7; http://www.twincities.com/localnews/ci_21254433/sergeant-who-led-troubled-st-paul-police-crime.

Gottschalk, P., 2011. Management Challenges in Law Enforcement: The Case of Police Misconduct and Crime. International Journal of Law and Management 53 (3), 169–181.

Green v. City of Cleveland, et al., 2004. Case No. I: 03CV0906, United States District Court, Northern District of Ohio, Eastern Division, Exhibit A, June 8.

Greiner, J., 2005. Gilchrist's actions spur third trial. Oklahoman, June 15; http://newsok.com/gilchrists-actions-spur-third-trial/article/1526821.

Griffy, L., 2007a. Sex case hinged on phony lab report: S.J. officer's ruse became evidence. San Jose Mercury News, December 16.

Griffy, L., 2007b. Fake lab reports were common: Judge warned cops about using ruses. San Jose Mercury News, December 23.

Grimm, L., Yarnold, P., 1995. Reading and Understanding Multivariate Statistics. American Psychological Association, Washington, DC.

Grolleau, G., Lakhal, T., Mzoughi, N., 2008. An Introduction to the Economics of Fake Degrees. Journal of Economic Issues XLII (3), 673–693.

Gross, H., 1906. Criminal Investigation. G. Ramasawmy Chetty & Co., Madras.

Gross, S., Jacoby, K., Matheson, D., Montgomery, N., Patil, S., 2005. Exonerations in the United States, 1989 through 2003. Journal of Criminal Law and Criminology 95, 523–559, Winter.

Gurnon, E., 2012. St. Paul crime lab: County attorneys will have state lab retest all pending cases. Pioneer Press, August 1; http://www.twincities.com/localnews/ci_21211098/st-paul-crime-lab-county-attorneys-will-have.

Guttman, R., Greenbaum, C., 1998. Facet Theory: Its Development and Current Status. European Psychologist 3 (1), 13–36.

Hanners, D., 2012. Dakota County: Head of St. Paul crime lab put on the spot. Pioneer Press, July 17; http://www.twincities.com/localnews/ci_21096890/st-paul-crime-lab-deficiencies-detailed-dakota-county.

Hansen, D., Culley, T., 1973. The Police Training Officer. Charles C. Thomas, Springfield, IL.

Hardwig, J., 1991. The Role of Trust in Knowledge. Journal of Philosophy 88 (12), 693–708.

Harris, A., 2000. Gender, Violence, Race, and Criminal Justice. Stanford Law Review 52 (4), 777–807.

Harris, G., 2008. Half of doctors routinely prescribe placebos. New York Times, October 22.

Hecht, L., 2001. Role Conflict and Role Overload: Different Concepts, Different Consequences. Sociological Inquiry 71 (1), 111–121.

Heller, K., 2006. The Cognitive Psychology of Circumstantial Evidence. Michigan Law Review 105, 241–305, November.

Hickman, M.J., Piquero, A.R., Lawton, B.A., Greene, J.R., 2001. Applying Tittle's Control Balance Theory to Police Deviance. Policing 24 (4), 497–519.

Holguin, 2007. Top officials hold fake degrees. CBS News, December 5; http://www.cbsnews.com/stories/2004/05/10/eveningnews/main616664.shtml.

Houck, M., Seigal, J., 2010. Fundamentals of Forensic Science, second ed. Elsevier Science, San Diego.

Hsu, S., Jenkins, J., Mellnick, T., 2012. DOJ review of flawed FBI forensics processes lacked transparency. Washington Post, April 17; http://www.washingtonpost.com/local/crime/doj-review-of-flawed-fbi-forensics-processes-lacked-transparency/2012/04/17/gIQAFegIPT_print.html.

Hunt, D., 2012. El Paso City Council hires outside lab to run police department's crime lab. KVIA.com/ ABC 7, August 28; http://www.kvia.com/news/El-Paso-City-Council-hires-outside-lab-to-run-police-department-s-crime-lab/-/391068/16404044/-/2030eb/-/index.html.

Hunter, G., Ferretti, C., 2012. Detroit Police Chief Godbee retires amid alleged sex scandal. Detroit News, October 9; http://www.detroitnews.com/article/20121009/METRO01/210090358/1409/METRO/Detroit-Police-Chief-Godbee-retires-amid-alleged-sex-scandal.

Hutchison, K., 1999. Sitka police chief taken in by diploma scam. Juneau Empire, June 29.

IACP, 2011. What Is the Law Enforcement Oath of Honor? The International Association of Chiefs of Police; http://www.theiacp.org/PoliceServices/ExecutiveServices/ProfessionalAssistance/Ethics/WhatistheLawEnforcementOathofHonor/tabid/150/Default.aspx.

IACP, 2012. Model Policy on Standards of Conduct. The International Association of Chiefs of Police; http://www.theiacp.org/PoliceServices/ProfessionalAssistance/Ethics/ModelPolicyonStandardsofConduct/tabid/196/Default.aspx.

Idaho v. Edward J. Wolfrum, 2007. Court of Appeals. Docket No. 31557, Opinion No. 58, September 6.

Imwinkelried, E., 2003. Flawed Expert Testimony: Striking the Right Balance in Admissibility. Criminal Justice 18, 28–29, 37, Spring.

Inman, K., Rudin, N., 1999. Principle and Practice of Criminalistics: The Profession of Forensic Science. CRC Press, Boca Raton, FL.

Inman, K., Rudin, N., 2006. The Shifty Paradigm, Part II: Errors and Lies and Fraud, Oh My! California Association of Criminalists News, Quarter 1, 16–18.

Interlandi, J., 2006. An unwelcome discovery. New York Times, October 22; http://www.nytimes.com/2006/10/22/magazine/22sciencefraud.html.

IP, 2009. Investigating Forensic Problems in the United States. The Innocence Project, New York; http://www.innocenceproject.org/docs/CoverdellReport.pdf.

Ivkovic, S., 2003. To Serve and Collect: Measuring Police Corruption. Journal of Criminal Law and Criminology 93 (2), 593–649.

James, S., Nordby, J., 2003. Forensic Science: An Introduction to Scientific and Investigative Techniques. CRC Press, Boca Raton, FL.

Jarrett, T., 2011. Judge blasts NYPD, convicts rogue detective. Brooklyn Ink, November 1; http://thebrooklynink.com/2011/11/01/34082–judge-blasts-nypd-convicts-rogue-detective/.

Jeffery, C., 1965. Criminal Behavior and Learning Theory. Journal of Criminal Law, Criminology, and Police Science 56 (3), 294–300.

Jette, A., 2005. Without Scientific Integrity, There Can Be No Evidence Base. Physical Therapy 85 (1), 1122–1123.

Johnson, P., 2012. Letter from the Deputy Assistant Director of the Texas Department of Public Safety Crime Lab to Buddy Meyer, Assistant District Attorney of Travis County, January 6.

Johnson, T., 2008. State crime lab chief resigns after problems raised on DUI evidence. Seattle Post-Intelligencer, February 14.

Johnson, T., Cox, R., 2005. Police Ethics: Organizational Implications. Public Integrity 7 (1), 67–79.

Johnson, T., Lathrop, D., 2007. State lab manager quits after she's accused of signing false statements. Seattle Post Intelligencer, July 31.

Jones, A., 2003. Can Authorship Policies Help Prevent Scientific Misconduct? What Role for Scientific Societies? Science and Engineering Ethics 9 (2), 243–256.

Judson, H., 2004. The Great Betrayal: Fraud in Science. Harcourt, New York.

Kaempffer, W., 2009. Sullied city cop given special probation. New Haven Register, February 3.

Kapardis, A., Krambia-Kapardis, M., 2004. Enhancing fraud prevention and detection by profiling fraud offenders. Criminal Behaviour and Mental Health 14, 189–201.

Kappeler, V., 2006. Critical Issues in Police Civil Liability, fourth ed. Waveland Press, Long Grove, IL.

Karcz, M., Papadakos, P., 2011. The Consequences of Fraud and Deceit in Medical Research. Canadian Journal of Respiratory Therapy 41 (1), 18–27, Spring.

Kassin, S., Drizin, S., Grisso, T., Gudjonsson, G., Leo, R., Redlich, A., 2010. Police-Induced Confessions: Risk Factors and Recommendations. Law and Human Behavior 34, 3–38.

Keaton, R., 2011. Memo from ASCLD-LAB Director Ralph Keaton to Sgt. David Hernandez, El Paso Police Department Crime Laboratory, June 27.

Kelly, J., Wearne, P., 1998. Tainting Evidence: Inside the Scandals at the FBI Crime Lab. Free Press, New York.

Kennedy, D.B., Kennedy, B., 1972. Applied Sociology for Police. Charles C. Thomas, Springfield, IL.

Kidder, D., 2005. Is it "Who I Am", "What I Can Get Away With", or "What You've Done to Me"? A Multi-theory Examination of Employee Misconduct. Journal of Business Ethics 57, 389–398.

Kiertzner, J., 2012. Detroit Police Department commander accused of assaulting mistress. WXYZ Action News 7, October 23; http://www.wxyz.com/dpp/news/region/detroit/detroit-police-department-commander-accused-of-assaulting-mistress#ixzz2DBXimpCG.

King, J., 1999. The Scientific Endeavor is Based on Vigilance, not Trust; Commentary on "Ambiguity, Trust, and the Responsible Conduct of Science" (F. Grinnell). Science and Engineering Ethics 5 (2), 215–217.

Kirk, P., 1974. Crime Investigation, second ed. John Wiley & Sons, New York.

Kirk, P., Bradford, L., 1965. The Crime Laboratory: Organization and Operation. Charles C. Thomas, New York.

Kleinig, J., 1996. The Ethics of Policing. Cambridge University Press, New York.

Kline, S., 1993. Scientific Misconduct: A Form of White Coat Crime. Journal of Pharmacy and Law 2, 15–34.

Klockars, C., 1984. Blue Lies and Police Placebos: The Moralities of Police Lying. American Behavioral Scientist 27 (4), 529–544.

Klockars, C., Ivkovic, S., Haberfeld, M., 2005. Enhancing Police Integrity. U.S. Department of Justice, Office of Justice Programs, National Institute of Justice, NCJ 209269, December.

Klockars, C., Ivkovic, S., Harver, W., Haberfeld, M., 2000. The Measurement of Police Integrity. U.S. Department of Justice, Office of Justice Programs, National Institute of Justice, NCJ 181465, May.

Knapp Commission, 1972. Report of the New York City Commission to Investigate Allegations of Police Corruption and the City's Anti-Corruption Procedures. Bar Press, New York.

Kocian, L., Smith, S., 2003. Lab chief apologizes over online doctorate. Boston Globe, November 13.

Koehler, J., 1993. Error and Exaggeration in the Presentation of DNA Evidence at Trial. Jurimetrics 34, 21–41, Fall.

Koepke, J., 2000. The Failure to Breach the Blue Wall of Silence: The Circling of the Wagons to Protect Police Perjury. Washburn Law Journal 39 (2), 211–241.

Kovner, J., 2012. At embattled state crime lab, limits on evidence set. Hartford Courant, January 9.

Kozarovich, L., 2006. Defense has "very good day" in trial: David Camm's attorneys attack credibility of blood examiner. News and Tribune, January 19; http://newsandtribune.com/davidcamm/x519352896/Defense-has-very-good-day-in-trial/print.

Krambia-Kapardis, M., 2001. Enhancing the Auditor's Fraud Detection Ability: An Interdisciplinary Approach. Peter Lang, Frankfurt.

Kranacher, M., Riley, R., Wells, J., 2010. Forensic Accounting and Fraud Examination. John Wiley & Sons, Hoboken, NJ.

Kreytak, S., 2010. Prosecutor in trouble over 2nd case of withholding evidence. Austin-American Statesman, June 1; http://www.statesman.com/news/news/local/prosecutor-in-trouble-over-2nd-case-of-withholding/nRtJc/.

Krimsky, S., 2007. Defining Scientific Misconduct: When Conflict-of-Interest Is a Factor in Scientific Misconduct. Medicine and Law 26, 447–463.

Krueger, J., Dunning, D., 1999. Unskilled and Unaware of It: How Difficulties in Recognizing One's Own Incompetence Lead to Inflated Self-Assessments. Journal of Personality and Social Psychology 77 (6), 121–134.

Kumar, M., 2010. A Theoretical Comparison of the Models of Prevention of Research Misconduct. Accountability in Research: Policies and Quality Assurance 17 (2), 51–66.

Kumar, V., Ryan, R., 2009. On Measuring Forgiveness: Implications from Smallest Space Analysis of the Forgiveness Likelihood Scale. Current Psychology 28 (1), 32–44.

Kuzma, S., 1992. Criminal Liability for Misconduct in Scientific Research. University of Michigan Journal of Law Reform 25, 357–421, Winter.

Landwehr, S., 2008. Investigation shuts down Hamilton ambulance service. Salem News, September 25; http://www.salemnews.com/local/x1150910441/Investigation-shuts-down-Hamilton-ambulance-service-Lyons-to-serve-town-until-further-notice.

LAPD, 2008. Confidential Consultation with the Latent Print Unit (Report). Los Angeles Police Department, Audit Division Report, June.

Lavoie, D., Niedowski, E., 2012. Mass. chemist in drug test flap is arrested. Associated Press, September 28.

Lee, H., 2009. Four cops fired in drug-warrant case. San Francisco Chronicle, April 25.

Lentini, J., 2009. Forensic Science Standards: Where They Come From and How They Are Used. Forensic Science Policy and Management 1, 10–16.

Leonard, J., Faturechi, R., 2011. Sheriff's department used jail duty to punish deputies. Los Angeles Times, November 12.

Leonard, V., 1969. The Police, the Judiciary, and the Criminal. Charles C. Thomas, Springfield, IL.

Lexchin, J., 2007. The Secret Things Belong unto the Lord Our God: Secrecy in the Pharmaceutical Arena. Medicine and Law 26, 417–430.

Litz, S., 2011. Miami Beach ATV crash probe uncovers lies, false timesheets. NBC-Miami, October 13; http://www.nbcmiami.com/news/Miami-Beach-ATV-Crash-Probe-Uncovers-Lies–131629663.html.

Locke, M., Neff, J., 2011. SBI lab errors might affect 74 more criminal cases. News Observer, March 22.

Locke, M., Neff, J., Curliss, A., 2010. Scathing SBI audit says 230 cases tainted by shoddy investigations. News Observer, August 19; http://www.newsobserver.com/2010/08/19/635632/scathing-sbi-audit-says-230-cases.html.

Longo, A., 2011. Can Oak Ridge science be trusted in Casey Anthony case? Bay News 9, March 23; http://www.baynews9.com/article/news/2011/march/221903/.

Lord, A., 2010. The Prevalence of Fraud: What Should We, as Academics, Be Doing to Address the Problem? Accounting and Management Information Systems 9 (1), 4–21.

Luiggi, C., 2010. Postdoc fudged epigenetic data. Scientist, September 22; http://classic.the-scientist.com/blog/display/57696/.

Maahs, J., Pratt, T., 2001. Uncovering the Predictors of Correctional Officers' Attitudes and Behaviors: A Meta-Analysis. Corrections Management Quarterly 5 (2), 13–19.

Magid, L., 2001. Deceptive Police Interrogation Practices: How Far Is Too Far? Michigan Law Review 99, 1168–1210, March.

Maier, T., 2003. Inside the DNA Labs. UPI Insight Magazine, June 23, vol. 19, issue 13.

Malgwi, C., Rakovski, C., 2009. Combating Academic Fraud: Are Students Reticent about Uncovering the Covert? Journal of Academic Ethics 7, 207–221.

Mallory, D., 2012. Guy Vallero Appointed Director of State Crime Lab. State of Connecticut, Office of the Governor, Press Release, November 19.

Marche, G., 2009. Integrity, Culture, and Scale: An Empirical Test of the Big Bad Police Agency. Crime, Law and Social Change 51 (5), 463–486.

Marshall, E., 2000. How Prevalent Is Fraud? That's a Million-Dollar Question. Science 290 (5497), 1662–1663.

Martinelli, T., 2006. Unconstitutional Policing: The Ethical Challenges in Dealing with Noble Cause Corruption. Police Chief 73 (10), 148, 150, 152–154, 156.

Martinson, B., Anderson, M., de Vries, R., 2005. Scientists Behaving Badly. Nature 435 (9), 737–738.

Marusic, A., Katavic, V., Marusic, M., 2007. Role of Editors and Journals in Detecting and Preventing Scientific Misconduct: Strengths, Weaknesses, Opportunities, and Threats. Medicine and Law 26, 545–566.

Matsueda, R., 2006. Differential Social Organization, Collective Action, and Crime. Crime, Law and Social Change 46 (1–2), 3–33.

May, L.D., 2005. The Backfiring of the Domestic Violence Firearms Bans. Columbia Journal of Gender and the Law 14 (1), 1–35.

May, L.S., 1936. Crime's Nemesis. MacMillan, New York.

McClam, E., 2004. Stewart trial's ink expert cleared. Washington Post, October 6; p. E01.

McClurg, A., 1999. Good Cop, Bad Cop: Using Cognitive Dissonance Theory to Reduce Police Lying. U.C. Davis Law Review 32, 389–453, Winter.

McConkey, T., 2005. State of Minnesota, Ramsey County, District Court, Felony Warrant and Order No. K1-05-818, filed on March 7, 2005.

McCormack, R.J., 1996. Police Perceptions and the Norming of Institutional Corruption. Policing and Society 6, 239–246.

McDowell, R., 2010. Fat Finger, Falsification, or Fraud? Spectroscopy 25 (12), 15–18.

McEachran, D., 2008. Forensic Investigations Council Report on the Washington State Toxicology Laboratory and the Washington State Crime Laboratory. Washington State Forensic Investigations Council, April 17; http://www.governor.wa.gov/boards/profiles/1000219.asp.

McMunigal, K., 2007. Prosecutors and Corrupt Science. Hofstra Law Review 36 (2), 437–450.

McQuaid, H., 2011. Crime lab problems put some trials on hold. CT News Junkie, December 29; http://www.ctnewsjunkie.com/ctnj.php/archives/entry/crime_lab_problems_put_some_trials_on_hold/.

Melendez-Diaz v. Massachusetts, 2009. U.S. Supreme Court, Case No. 07-591, June 25.

Merced County, 2011. Merced County Organization Chart, updated June 2011; http://www.co.merced.ca.us/documents/CountyExecutive Office/org_chart_2011_june.PDF.

Metzger, P., 2006. Cheating the Constitution. Vanderbilt Law Review 59 (2), 475–538.

Midkiff, C.R., 2004. More Mountebanks. In: Saferstein, R. (Ed.), Forensic Science Handbook, second ed. Vol. 2. Prentice Hall, Upper Saddle River, NJ.

Milicia, J., 2007. Lab audit: Cleveland juries not misled. Associated Press, February 17.

Mitroff, I., 1974. Norms and Counter-Norms in a Select Group of the Apollo Moon Scientists: A Case Study of the Ambivalence of Scientists. American Sociological Review 39 (4), 579–595.

Mnookin, J., Cole, S., Dror, I., Fisher, B., Houck, M., Inman, K., Kaye, D., Koehler, J., Langenburg, G., Risinger, D., Rudin, N., Siegel, J., Stoney, D., 2011. The Need for a Research Culture in the Forensic Sciences. UCLA Law Review 58 (3), 725–779.

Moenssens, A., 1993. Novel Scientific Evidence in Criminal Cases: Some Words of Caution. Journal of Criminal Law and Criminology 84, 1–21, Spring.

Moles, R., 2004. A State of Injustice. Lothian Books, Melbourne.

Mollen, M., 1994. Commission Report, The City of New York. Commission to Investigate Allegations of Police Corruption and the Anti-Corruption Procedures of the Police Department, published July 7.

Moore, J., 2008. Channel 2 finds nearly 1,400 certified officers with criminal records. Action News 2, December 8; http://www.wsbtv.com/videos/news/channel-2–finds-nearly-1400–certified-officers/vCLXw/.

Moore, S., 2009. Science found wanting in nation's crime labs. New York Times, February 4; http://www.nytimes.com/2009/02/05/us/05forensics.html.

Moran, G., 2006. Criminalist who testified on DUIs falsified résumé. San Diego Union Tribune, March 22; http://www.utsandiego.com/uniontrib/20060322/news_7m22duiguy.html.

Moreno, J. 2004. What Happens When Dirty Harry Becomes an (Expert) Witness for the Prosecution? Tulane Law Review, 79 (1), 1–54.

Morlin, B. 2008. Diploma mill ringleader pleads guilty. Spokesman Review, March 27; http://www.spokesmanreview.com/breaking/story.asp?ID=14288.

Morn, F., 1995. Academic Politics and the History of Criminal Justice Education. Greenwood Press, Westport, CT.

Morrin, B., 2011. 1,100 drug cases could be challenged after lab investigation. KBOI2.com, June 30; http://www.kboi2.com/news/local/124777384.html.

Moxley, S., 2008a. CSI games: If DNA evidence doesn't fit in Orange County, alter it? Orange County Register, March 12, http://www.ocweekly.com/2008-03-13/news/csi-games/.

Moxley, S., 2008b. Wrongly imprisoned OC man wins state payment. Orange County Register, April 22; http://blogs.ocweekly.com/navelgazing/2008/04/wrongly_imprisoned_oc_man_wins.php.

MSP, 2008. Detroit Police Department Firearms Unit Preliminary Audit Findings as of September 23, 2008. Audit Report by the Michigan State Police Forensic Science Division.

Murdoch, G., 2009. Faking the Results: Scientists Consider New Ways to Prevent and Spot Research Misconduct. Popular Science, October, 29–31.

Murphy, B., Lavoie, D., 2012. A closer look at the accused rogue chemist Annie Dookhan. Associated Press, October 14.

Murphy, E., 2007. The New Forensics: Criminal Justice, False Certainty, and the Second Generation of Scientific Evidence. California Law Review 95, 721–797, June.

NAS, 2002. Integrity in Scientific Research: Creating an Environment that Promotes Responsible Conduct, National Academy of Sciences Committee on Assessing Integrity in Research Environments. National Academies Press, Washington, DC.

NAS, 2004. Forensic Analysis Weighing Bullet Lead Evidence, National Academy of Sciences Committee on Scientific Assessment of Bullet Lead Elemental Composition Comparison. National Academies Press, Washington, DC.

NAS, 2009. On Being a Scientist: A Guide to Responsible Conduct in Research, third ed. National Academy of Sciences Committee on Science, Engineering, and Public Policy. National Academies Press, Washington, DC.

Neavling, S., Ashenfelter, D., Damron, G., 2011. Dangerous debris, evidence left in closed Detroit Police crime lab. Detroit Free Press, May 27.

Newsome, R., 1995. Fraud Investigation. In: Bailey, W. (Ed.), The Encyclopedia of Police Science, second ed. Garland, New York.

News Release, 2011. Maryland police officer charged with drug trafficking conspiracy and computer fraud: She allegedly used her police powers to access law enforcement databases to obtain information concerning a co-conspirator and his drug associates. U.S. Immigration and Customs Enforcement, March 16; http://www.ice.gov/news/releases/.

O'Brien, G., 2007. King county prosecutors shockingly decline to prosecute resigned crime lab manager Anne Marie Gordon. Washington State DUI Blog, November 10; http://www.seattle-duiattorney.com/blog/king-county-prosecutors-shockingly-decline-to-prosecute-resigned-crime-lab-manager-anne-marie-gordon/.

O'Hara, C., Osterburg, J., 1972. An Introduction to Criminalistics: The Application of Physical Sciences to the Detection of Crime, Second Printing. Indiana University Press, Bloomington, IN.

OIG, 2004. The FBI DNA Laboratory: A Review of Protocol and Practice Vulnerabilities. U.S. Department of Justice, Office of the Inspector General, May, Washington, DC.

O'Leary, M., 2012. Connecticut crime lab's accreditation restored. New Haven Register, February 7.

Olsen, L., 2002. Reopened rape case dogs crime lab worker. Seattle Post-Intelligencer, October 10; http://www.seattlepi.com/news/article/Reopened-rape-case-dogs-crime-lab-worker-1098198.php.

Olsen, L., 2003. Crime lab worker failed to qualify to test hair samples. Seattle Post-Intelligencer, January 1; http://www.seattlepi.com/news/article/Crime-lab-worker-failed-to-qualify-to-test-hair-1104439.php.

ORI, 1995. ORI Guidelines for Institutions and Whistleblowers: Responding to Possible Retaliation against Whistleblowers in Extramural Research. Office of Research Integrity, U.S. Department of Health and Human Services, Washington, DC; http://ori.hhs.gov/documents/guidelines_whistle.pdf, November 20.

ORI, 2000. Managing Allegations of Scientific Misconduct: A Guidance Document for Editors. Office of Research Integrity, U.S. Department of Health and Human Services, Washington, DC; http://ori.hhs.gov/documents/masm_2000.pdf.

ORI, 2005. Press Release—Dr. Eric T. Poehlman. Office of Research Integrity, U.S. Department of Health and Human Services, Washington, DC, March 17; http://ori.hhs.gov/misconduct/cases/press_release_poehlman.shtml.

ORI, 2009a. Handling Misconduct—Inquiry Issues. Office of Research Integrity, U.S. Department of Health and Human Services, Washington, DC; http://ori.hhs.gov/misconduct/inquiry_issues.shtml, updated December 6.

ORI, 2009b. The Office of Research Integrity Annual Report 2009. Office of Research Integrity, U.S. Department of Health and Human Services, Washington, DC; http://ori.hhs.gov/documents/annual_reports/ori_annual_report_2009.pdf.

ORI, 2010. Case Summaries. Office of Research Integrity Newsletter 19 (1), 6–8.

ORI, 2011a. Case Summaries. Office of Research Integrity Newsletter 19 (2), 6–7.

ORI, 2011b. Case Summaries. Office of Research Integrity Newsletter 19 (3), 6–8.

Osborne, J., 2001. Perry to decide if DPS lab must face legislative inquiry. Austin-American Statesman, January 4; p. B7.

Ostas, D., 2007. When Fraud Pays: Executive Self-Dealing and the Failure of Self-Restraint. American Business Law Journal 44 (4), 571–601.

Paoline, E., 2004. Shedding Light on Police Culture: An Examination of Officers' Occupational Attitudes. Police Quarterly 7 (2), 205–236.

Papandrea, M., 2010. The Free Speech Rights of Off-Duty Government Employees. Brigham Young University Law Review 6, 2117–2174.

Parrish, D., 1996. The Scientific Misconduct Definition and Falsification of Credentials. Professional Ethics Report IX (4), 1–5.

Patrick, R., 2009. Corrupt city cop pleads to drug, evidence charges. St. Louis Today, August 29.

Patton, N., 2008. Worthy: Findings about Detroit crime lab appalling. Detroit Free Press, October 30.

Peterson, J., Hickman, M., 2005. Census of Publicly Funded Forensic Crime Laboratories, 2002. U.S. Department of Justice, Office of Justice Programs, Bureau of Justice Statistics Bulletin, Washington, DC, NCJ 207205, February.

Peterson, J., Leggett, A., 2007. The Evolution of Forensic Science: Progress Amid the Pitfalls. Stetson Law Review 36, 621–660, Spring.

Pettigrew, A., 1968. Inter-Group Conflict and Role Strain. Journal of Management Studies 5 (2), 205–218.

Popper, K., 1963. Conjectures and Refutations. Routledge and Keagan Paul, London.

Popper, K., 2002. The Logic of Scientific Discovery. Routledge, New York.

Porter, L.E., Warrender, C., 2009. A Multivariate Model of Police Deviance: Examining the Nature of Corruption, Crime and Misconduct. Policing and Society 19 (1), 79–99.

Prather, S., 2005. Minnesota crime lab supervisor charged with cocaine possession. Twin Cities Pioneer Press, March 7.

Puente, M., 2009. Murder convict Thomas Siller gets new trial due to shoddy scientific work. Cleveland Plain Dealer, June 20.

Pyrek, K., 2007. Forensic Science Under Siege. Academic Press, Boston.

Quail, M.T., 2010. Actual or Potential Fraud: A Closer Look at Emergency Medical Services (EMS) Training. Journal of Legal Nurse Consulting 21 (4), 3–9.

Quaintance, Z., 2008. McAllen crime lab hires DNA supervisor despite cheating accusations. Monitor, January 30; http://www.themonitor.com/news/nelson-8562-lab-dna.html.

Raeder, M., 2007. See No Evil: Wrongful Convictions and the Prosecutorial Ethics of Offering Testimony by Jailhouse Informants and Dishonest Experts. Fordham Law Review 76 (3), 1413–1452.

Ragland v. Commonwealth of Kentucky, 2006. Supreme Court of Kentucky. No. 2002-SC-0388-MR, 2003-SC-0084-TG, 191 S.W.3d 569, March 23.

Randall, E., 2012. Man released from prison thanks to Dookhan re-arrested thanks to cocaine. Boston Daily, November 13; http://blogs.bostonmagazine.com/boston_daily/2012/11/13/police-watching-prisoners-released-dookhan/.

Raven, P., Johnson, G., 1986. Biology. Times Mirror/Mosby College Publishing, St. Louis, MO.

Redman, B., Kaplan, A., 2005. Off with their Heads: The Need to Criminalize Some Forms of Scientific Misconduct. Journal of Law, Medicine and Ethics 33 (2), 345–348.

Redman, B., Mertz, J., 2005. Evaluating the Oversight of Scientific Misconduct. Accountability in Research: Policies and Quality Assurance 12 (3), 157–162.

Reid, S., 2003. Crime and Criminology, tenth ed. McGraw-Hill, Boston.

Reider, B., 2010. Fabrication, Falsification et al. American Journal of Sports Medicine 38 (3), 445–447.

Resnick, D., 2003. From Baltimore to Bell Labs: Reflections on Two Decades of Debate about Scientific Misconduct. Accountability in Research 10 (2), 123–135.

Reynolds, S., 2004. ORI Findings of Scientific Misconduct in Clinical Trials and Publicly Funded Research, 1992–2002. Clinical Trials 1 (6), 509–516.

Richardson, A., 2004. Robert K. Merton and Philosophy of Science. Social Studies of Science 34 (6), 855–858.

Rider, R., 2010. United States v. Hayes: Retroactive removal of your ability to be a police officer. Officer.com; http://www.officer.com/article/10232309/united-states-v-hayes.

Ridolphi, K., Possley, M., 2010. Preventable Error: A Report on Prosecutorial Misconduct in California 1997–2009. Northern California Innocence Project at Santa Clara University School of Law, Santa Clara, CA.

Risinger, D.M., Saks, M.J., Rosenthal, R., Thompson, W.C., 2002. The Daubert/Kumho Implications of Observer Effects in Forensic Science: Hidden Problems of Expectation and Suggestion. California Law Review 90 (1), 1–56.

Risinger, D.M., Saks, M.J., Rosenthal, R., Thompson, W.C., 2003. Context Effects in Forensic Science: A Review and Application of the Science of Science to Crime Laboratory Practice in the United States. Science and Justice 43 (2), 77–90.

Rodriguez, J., 2006. Ray Cole, Former Criminalist, San Diego County Sheriff's Crime Laboratory. Memo from the Office of the District Attorney, County of San Diego to the Office of the Public Defender, Office of the Alternate Public Defender, and the Office of Private Conflict Counsel, March 15.

Rodriquez, R., 1997. Some police say domestic violence law a threat to their jobs. CNN, January 6; http://www.cnn.com/US/9701/06/domestic.abuse.cops/.

Rogers, B., 2008. DPS crime lab tech gets 45 years for stealing cocaine. Houston Chronicle, February 8.

Ronald, K., 2007. Garcetti v. Ceballos: The Battle Over What It Means Has Just Begun. Urban Lawyer 39 (4), 983–1015.

Ross, S., 1964. Scientist: The Story of a Word. Annals of Science 18 (2), 65–85.

Rothwell, G., Baldwin, J., 2007. Whistle-Blowing and the Code of Silence in Police Agencies: Policy and Structural Predictors. Crime and Delinquency 53 (4), 605–632.

RTTN, 2010. 2010 Report to the Nations on Occupational Fraud and Abuse. Association of Certified Fraud Examiners, downloaded August 15, 2011; http://www.acfe.com/rtn.aspx.

Rubin, J., Winton, R., 2008. LAPD finds faulty fingerprint work: Report cites two cases of false accusations but the total isn't known. Los Angeles Times, October 17; http://articles.latimes.com/2008/oct/17/local/me-fingerprints17.

Rubin, J., Winton, R., 2009. LAPD fingerprint expert charged with assault. Los Angeles Times, January 24; http://www.latimes.com/news/printedition/california/la-me-finger-print24-2009jan24,0, 362282.story.

Rudewicz, F., 2011. The Fraud Diamond: Use of Investigative Due Diligence to Identify the Capability Element of Fraud. Connecticut Turnaround Association Management Newsletter 4 (1), 1–3, February.

Ruiz-Palomino, P., Martinez-Canas, R., 2011. Supervisor Role Modeling, Ethics-Related Organizational Policies, and Employee Ethical Intention: The Moderating Impact of Moral Ideology. Journal of Business Ethics 102, 653–668.

Saferstein, R., 2010. Criminalistics: An Introduction to Forensic Science, tenth ed. Prentice Hall, Upper Saddle River, NJ.

Saks, M., 2001. Scientific Evidence and the Ethical Obligations of Attorneys. Cleveland State Law Review 49 (3), 421–438.

Saks, M., 2003. Ethics in Forensic Science: Professional Standards for the Practice of Criminalistics. Jurimetrics: Journal of Law, Science and Technology 43, 359–363.

Saks, M., 2010. Forensic Identification: From a Faith-Based "Science" to a Scientific Science. Forensic Science International 201, 14–17.

Saks, M., Koehler, J., 2005. The Coming Paradigm Shift in Forensic Identification Science. Science 309 (5736), 892–895.

Saks, M.J., Lanyon, R.I., Costanzo, M., 2007. Pitfalls and Ethics of Expert Testimony: Expert Psychological Testimony for the Courts. Lawrence Erlbaum Associates, Mahwah, NJ.

Saks, M.J., Risinger, D.M., Rosenthal, R., Thompson, W.C., 2003. Context Effects in Forensic Science: A Review and Application of the Science of Science to Crime Laboratory Practice in the United States. Science Justice 43 (2), 77–90.

Salsberg, B., 2012. Gov. Patrick seeks $30m for costs of Mass. drug lab scandal. Associated Press, October 31.

Salzberg, A., 2007. DNA Proves a Notorious Analyst Engaged in Fraud and Misconduct Leading to Two More Wrongful Convictions, Innocence Project Says. Press Release. The Innocence Project, New York.

Samuel, A., 1994. Forensic Science and Miscarriages of Justice. Medicine, Science, and the Law 34, 148–150.

San Diego County, 2011. Online Employment Application Guide. County of San Diego, Department of Human Resources; http://www.sdcounty.ca.gov/hr/jobs/Online_Employment_Application_Guide.pdf.

Sangha, B., Roach, K., Moles, R., 2010. Forensic Investigations and Miscarriages of Justice. Irwin Law Press, Toronto.

Sasse, S., 2005. Motivation and Routine Activities Theory. Deviant Behavior 26 (6), 547–570.

SATF, 2009. False Reports and Case Unfounding. Attorney General's Sexual Assault Task Force, State of Oregon, Position Paper, January 22.

Savino, J., Turvey, B., 2011. Rape Investigation Handbook, second ed. Elsevier Science, San Diego.

Scamahorn, L., 2002. Letter to F. Joseph Vetter, First Sergeant, Manager, Evansville Regional Laboratory, Subject "Floyd County Prosecutor," dated February 11.

Scheck, B., Neufeld, P., Dwyer, J., 2000. Actual Innocence: Five Days to Execution, and Other Dispatches from the Wrongly Convicted. Doubleday, New York.

Schemo, D., 2008. Diploma Mill Concerns Extend Beyond Fraud. New York Times, June 29; http://www.nytimes.com/2008/06/29/us/29diploma.html.

Schladen, M., 2011. El Paso City Council considers closing crime lab. El Paso Times, July 15.

Schmitt, B., 2009. Detroit cop's story varies in crime lab case. Detroit Free Press, April 2.

Scott, J., 2000. Rational Choice Theory. In: Browning, G., Halcli, A., Webster, F. (Eds.), Understanding Contemporary Society: Theories of the Present. Sage, Thousand Oaks, CA.

Seigel, J., Saukko, P., Knupfer, G., 2000. The Encyclopedia of Forensic Science. Vols. 1–3. Academic Press, London.

Seitz, V., 2008. Washington v. Ashanti Q. Coats, King County District Court, Case No. C00689836, Findings and Order on Defense Motion, January 7.

Seron, C., Pereira, J., Kovath, J., 2004. Judging Police Misconduct: "Street-Level" versus Professional Policing. Law and Society Review 38 (4), 665–710.

Serrano, R., 2011. Kenneth Melson, who oversaw ATF's Fast and Furious, steps down. Los Angeles Times, August 30.

Shane, J., 2010. Performance Management in Police Agencies: A Conceptual Framework. Policing: An International Journal of Police Strategies and Management 33 (1), 6–29.

Shockley-Eckles, M., 2011. Police Culture and the Perpetuation of the Officer Shuffle: The Paradox of Life behind "The Blue Wall." Humanity & Society 35, 290–309, August.

Singer, R., 2004. Memo to Ms. Patricia S. Lough, San Diego Police Department, re: Ethics complaint filed with AAFS Ethics Committee against Rod Englert, November 10 (Memo on file with the author).

Skolnick, J.H., 2002. Corruption and the Blue Code of Silence. Police Practice and Research 3, 7–19.

Skolnick, J.H., 2005. Corruption and the Blue Code of Silence. In: Sarre, R., Das, D.K., Albrecht, H.J. (Eds.), Police Corruption: An International Perspective. Lexington Books, Oxford.

Slobogin, 1997. Deceit, Pretext, and Trickery: Investigative Lies by the Police. Oregon Law Review 76, 775–816, Winter.

Smilon, M., Hadad, H., Gaffney, M., 2004. Secret Service Laboratory Director Charged with Committing Perjury at Martha Stewart–Peter Bacanovic Trial. Press Release, Public Information Office, U.S. Attorney's Office, Southern District of New York, May 21.

Smith, R., 2003. Serious Fraud in Australia and New Zealand. Series No. 48. Australian Institute of Criminology, Canberra.

Smith, T., 2008. Police provided false testimony in rape case: Judge considers dismissal of indictment against Marsalis. Idaho Mountain Express, December 3.

Solomon, J., 2003. New allegations target two FBI crime-lab scientists. Seattle Times, April 16; http://community.seattletimes.nwsource.com/archive/?date=20030416&slug=fbilab16.

Sovacool, B., 2008. Exploring Scientific Misconduct: Isolated Individuals, Impure Institutions, or an Inevitable Idiom of Modern Science? Bioethical Inquiry 5 (4), 271–282.

SPD, 2012. Policy and Procedure Manual. Seattle Police Department, February 1; http://www.seattle.gov/police/publications/policy/spd_manual.pdf.

Spector, E., 2008. Should Police Officers Who Lie Be Terminated as a Matter of Public Policy? Police Chief 75 (4), 10 April.

Staff, 2011. State forensic lab loses accreditation. Hartford Courant, August 17; http://articles.courant.com/2011-08-17/community/hc-forensic-lab-0818-20110817_1_crime-laboratory-directors-techniques-for-dna-test-tests-in-criminal-cases.

Stanbrook, M., MacDonald, N., Flegel, K., Hébert, P., 2011. The Need for New Mechanisms to Ensure Research Integrity. Canadian Medical Association Journal 183 (12), E766.

Starrs, J.E., 1993. The Seamy Side of Forensic Science: The Mephitic Stain of Fred Salem Zain. Scientific Sleuthing Review 17, 1–8.

Starrs, J.E., 2004. Mountebanks among Forensic Scientists. In: Saferstein, R. (Ed.), Forensic Science Handbook, second ed. Vol. 2. Pearson/Prentice Hall, Upper Saddle River, NJ.

Steiner, D., 2008. Washington v. Ahmach, Sanafim, et al. King County District Court, Case No. C00627921, et al., Order Granting Defendant's Motion to Suppress, January 30.

Stelloh, T., 2011. Detective is found guilty of planting drugs. New York Times, November 2; http://www.nytimes.com/2011/11/02/nyregion/brooklyn-detective-convicted-of-planting-drugs-on-innocent-people.html.

Steneck, N., 2007a. Assessing the Integrity of Publicly Funded Research. In: Steneck, N., Scheetz, M. (Eds.), Investigating Research Integrity Proceedings of the First ORI Research Conference on Research Integrity: Proceedings of the First ORI Research Conference on Research Integrity. Office of Research Integrity, Washington, DC, pp. 1–16.

Steneck, N., 2007b. Introduction to the Responsible Conduct of Research, rev. ed. Office of Research Integrity, Washington, DC , August.

Stepankowski, A., 2009. Troopers with fake diplomas suspended, not fired. Daily News Online, October 31; http://www.tdn.com.

Stephens, D., 2011. Letter to Rosemary Lehmberg, Travis County District Attorney, December 27.

Stout, B., 2011. Ethics and Academic Integrity in Police Education. Policing 5 (4), 300–309.

Strumpf, D., 2006. False witness: An expert's problematic résumé and court testimony could jeopardize hundreds. San Diego City Beat, March 15.

Sullivan, J., 1977. Introduction to Police Science, third ed. McGraw-Hill, New York.

Sullivan, J., 2007. State Patrol probes work of firearms examiner. Seattle Times, April 27; http://seattletimes.nwsource.com/html/localnews/2003683329_thompson27m.html.

Sullivan, J., 2008. 9 troopers on leave while state checks their degrees. Seattle Times, October 21; http://seattletimes.nwsource.com/html/localnews/2008290900_diplomas21m.html.

Sunhara, D.F., 2004. A Social–Psychological Model of Unethical and Unprofessional Police Behaviour. Canadian Review of Policing Research, 1, December 16; http://crpr.icaap.org/index.php/crpr/issue/view/1.

Sunstein, C., 2005. Group Judgments: Statistical Means, Deliberation, and Information Markets. New York University Law Review 80, 962–1049 June.

Sutherland, E., 1947. Criminology, fourth ed. Lippincott, Philadelphia, PA.

Sutherland, E., Cressey, D., 1966. Principles of Criminology, seventh ed. Lippincott, New York.

Taylor, M., 2011. Beyond missteps, military crime lab roils with discontent. McClatchy Newspapers, June 26; http://www.mcclatchydc.com/2011/06/26/116410/beyond-missteps-military-crime.html.

Taylor, M., 2012a. Crime lab whistle-blower targeted. McClatchy Newspapers, March 20; http://www.sacbee.com/2012/03/20/4351021/crime-lab-whistle-blower-facing.html.

Taylor, M., 2012b. Office of Special Counsel investigating Army Criminal Investigation Lab. McClatchy Newspapers, May 4.

Taylor, M., Doyle, M., 2011a. Army slow to act as crime-lab worker falsified, botched tests. McClatchy Newspapers, March 20.

Taylor, M., Doyle, M., 2011b. More errors surface at military crime labs as Senate seeks inquiry. McClatchy Newspapers, May 15; http://www.mcclatchydc.com/2011/05/15/114221/more-errors-surface-at-military.html.

Teichroeb, R., 2004a. Forensic scientist in crime lab tied to wrongful convictions in Oregon. Seattle Post-Intelligencer, December 27; p. A1.

Teichroeb, R., 2004b. Oversight of crime-lab staff has often been lax. Seattle Post-Intelligencer, July 23.

Terrill, W., Paoline, A., Manning, P., 2003. Police Culture and Coercion. Criminology 41 (4), 1003–1034.

TFSC, 2011. Regarding Austin Police Department Forensic Science Division Crime Laboratory Investigation. Memorandum of the Texas Forensic Science Commission, September 8; http://www.fsc.state.tx.us/documents/M_APD090811FINALexecuted092811.pdf.

TFSC, 2012. Austin Police Department Crime Laboratory Controlled Substances Investigation. Report of the Texas Forensic Science Commission, October 5; http://www.fsc.state.tx.us/documents/APDFinalReport102312.pdf.

Thomas, G., 2007. Regulating Police Deception during Interrogation. Texas Tech Law Review 39, 1293–1319, Summer.

Thompson, W., 2006. Tarnish on the "Gold Standard": Understanding Recent Problems in Forensic DNA Testing. Champion, January/February, 10–12.

Thompson, W., 2009. Beyond Bad Apples: Analyzing the Role of Forensic Science in Wrongful Convictions. Southwestern University Law Review 37, 1027–1050.

Thornton, J., Peterson, J., 2007. The General Assumptions and Rationale of Forensic Identification. In: Faigman, D., Kaye, D., Saks, M., Sanders, J. (Eds.), Modern Scientific Evidence: The Law and Science of Expert Testimony. Vol. 1. West Publishing Group, St. Paul, MN.

Tilbert, J., Emanuel, E., Kaptchuk, T., Curlin, F., 2008. Prescribing "Placebo Treatments": Results of National Survey of U.S. Internists and Rheumatologists. British Medical Journal (BMJ) 337, a1938.

Titus, S., Wells, J., Rhoades, L., 2008. Repairing Research Integrity. Nature 453 (19), 980–982.

Turner, R., 1995. Forensic Science. In: Bailey, W. (Ed.), The Encyclopedia of Police Science, second ed. Garland, New York.

Turvey, B., 2003. Forensic Frauds: A Study of 42 Cases. Journal of Behavioral Profiling 4 (1).

Turvey, B., 2011. Criminal Profiling: An Introduction to Behavioral Evidence Analysis, fourth ed. Elsevier Science, San Diego.

Turvey, B., Petherick, W., 2010. An Introduction to Forensic Criminology. In: Turvey, B., Petherick, W., Ferguson, C. (Eds.), Forensic Criminology. Elsevier Science, San Diego.

Underwood, G., 1997. Freedom nears for Erdmann as judge clears way for parole. Lubbock Avalanche-Journal, April 27.

Ungvarsky, E., 2007. Remarks on the Use and Misuse of Forensic Science to Lead to False Convictions. New England Law Review 41, 609–622, Spring.

U.S. v. Ellingford, 2011. U.S. District Court, District of Idaho, Case No. CR-10-24-E-BLW, September 6.

U.S. v. Hayes, 2009. Supreme Court of the United States. No. 07-608, February 24.

USACIC, 2005. DNA Examiner Suspended at Army's Criminal Investigation Laboratory; CID Commander Orders Independent Reviews. U.S. Army Criminal Investigation Command, CID Public Affairs Office Memo, August 26.

USACIL, 2012. U.S. Army Criminal Investigation Laboratory. Website: http://www.cid. army.mil/usacil.html.

Van Der Beken, J., 2010. Problems of S.F. toxicologist not disclosed. San Francisco Chronicle, May 26.

Vaughn, M., Cooper, T., del Carmen, R., 2001. Assessing Legal Liabilities in Law Enforcement: Police Chief's Views. Crime and Delinquency 47 (1), 3–27.

Vernor, J., 2012. Memo and State Police interviews compiled by Assistant Attorney General John Vernor, Chief of the Criminal Bureau, to District Attorney C. Samuel Sutter, Bristol County District Attorney's Office, September 17.

Verstraete, A., 2011. President's Message. The International Association of Forensic Toxicologists, October 21; http://www.tiaft.org/president_message.

Vold, G., Bernard, T., 1986. Theoretical Criminology, third ed. Oxford University Press, New York.

Vollmer, A., 1971. The Police and Modern Society. Patterson Smith, Montclair, NJ.

Waddington, P., 1999. Police (Canteen) Sub-culture: An Appreciation. British Journal of Criminology 39 (2), 287–309.

Washington v. Amach, et al., 2008. District Court of King County. Case No. C00627921 et al., Decided January 30.

Weed, D., 1998. Preventing Scientific Misconduct. American Journal of Public Health 88 (1), 125–129.

Wells, J., 2010. Principles of Fraud Examination, third ed. John Wiley & Sons, Hoboken, NJ.

Westmarland, L., 2005. Police Ethics and Integrity: Breaking the Blue Code of Silence. Policing and Society 15 (2), 145–165.

White, E., 2012. Detroit chief steps down amid sex probe. Associated Press, October 8; http:// www.policeone.com/chiefs-sheriffs/articles/6005947-Detroit-chief-steps-down-amid-sex-probe/.

Wilson, P., 1992. Justice and Nightmares: Success and Failures of Forensic Science in Australia and New Zealand. New South Wales University Press, Sydney.

Winton, R., 2009. Errors trigger reviews of LAPD fingerprint files. Los Angeles Times, January 15; http://articles.latimes.com/2009/jan/15/local/me-fingerprint15.

Wolfe, D., Hermanson, D., 2004. The Fraud Diamond: Considering the Four Elements of Fraud. CPA Journal, 38–42, December.

Wolfe, S., Picquero, A., 2011. Organizational Justice and Police Misconduct. Criminal Justice and Behavior 38 (4), 332–353.

Wooten, B., 2007. Milwaukee police, city won't tell public how many officers have criminal convictions. Front Page Milwaukee, February 12.

Wright, R.G., 2011. Retaliation and the Rule of Law in Today's Workplace. Creighton Law Review 44 (3), 749–768.

Wrigley, D., 2012. Fallout from DPS crime lab testing problems continues. KTRK-TV, ABC13, September 27; http://abclocal.go.com/ktrk/story?section=news/local&id=8827578.

Wyckoff, D., 2005. An Open Letter from ASCLD/LAB to Forensic Science Organizations. CAC News, 39, 1st Quarter.

Yaniv, O., 2011. Judge shocked by "cowboy culture" of cops. New York Daily News, November 1; http://articles.nydailynews.com/2011-11-01/news/30348008_1_narcotics-cops-plant-drugs-cowboy-culture.

Young, D., 1996. Unnecessary Evil: Police Lying in Interrogations. Connecticut Law Review 28, 425–477, Winter.

Zion-Hershberg, B., 2006. Analyst felt pressured in Camm's first trial. Evansville Courier-Journal, Wednesday, February 1.

Index

Note: Page numbers followed by "f" denote figures; "t" tables and "b" boxes.

277